AF569561

SHOCK OF THE NEWS

JUDITH BRODIE with Sarah Boxer, Janine Mileaf, Christine Poggi, and Matthew Witkovsky

SHOCK OF

THE NEWS

National Gallery of Art, Washington, in association with Lund Humphries

The exhibition is organized by the National Gallery of Art, Washington

The exhibition is supported by The Leonard and Evelyn Lauder Foundation

It is also supported by an indemnity from the Federal Council on the Arts and the Humanities

The catalogue has been made possible, in part, by the Corinne H. Buck Charitable Lead Trust

Exhibition dates

National Gallery of Art, Washington, September 23, 2012–January 27, 2013

10 9 8 7 6 5 4 3 2 1

Library of Congress Cataloging-in-Publication Data

Brodie, Judith.
Shock of the news / Judith Brodie ; with Sarah Boxer, Janine Mileaf, Christine Poggi, and Matthew Witkovsky.
pages cm
The exhibition is organized by the National Gallery of Art, Washington.
Includes bibliographical references and index.
ISBN 978-1-84822-121-5 (alk. paper)
1. Newspapers in art–Exhibitions. 2. Art, Modern–Themes, motives–Exhibitions. I. National Gallery of Art (U.S.) II. Title.
N8233.N48B76 2012
709.040074'753–dc23
2012020226

British Library Cataloging-in-Publication Data

A catalogue record for this book is available from the British Library

Produced by the Publishing Office, National Gallery of Art, Washington
www.nga.gov

Judy Metro, *editor in chief*
Chris Vogel, *deputy publisher and production manager*

Designed by Wendy Schleicher, *design manager*

Edited by Laura Jones Dooley, Chesterfield, Virginia

With Tam Curry Bryfogle, *senior editor*; Sara Sanders-Buell, *photography rights coordinator*; John Long, *assistant production manager*; and Mariah Shay, *production assistant*

Typeset in Scala Pro and Scala Sans Pro by the National Gallery of Art, Washington, Publishing Office

Printed on 115# Garda Silk by Capital Offset Company Inc., Concord, New Hampshire

---

Published in association with Lund Humphries

Lund Humphries
Wey Court East, Union Road
Farnham, Surrey
GU9 7PT, UK

Lund Humphries
101 Cherry Street
Burlington, VT
05401-4405, USA

www.lundhumphries.com

Note to the Reader

Dimensions are given in inches, with centimeters following. Height precedes width, which precedes depth.

Works in the exhibition are presented on full pages in the catalogue, with numerous plates positioned near detailed discussions in the introductory essay, followed by a sequence of plates in generally chronological order.

All works in the exhibition are identified by plate number, artist, title, date, medium, dimensions, and credit line. In addition, a number of plates—primarily of works not discussed in the essays—include supplemental commentaries.

Details at section openings

p. vi: Edward Burra, *Composition Collage*, 1929 (pl. 41)

p. xiv: Kurt Schwitters, *Untitled (The Hitler Gang)*, 1944 (pl. 12)

p. 90: John Heartfield, *Wer Bürgerblätter liest wird blind und taub...*, February 9, 1930 (pl. 8)

p. 102: Jean Dubuffet, *Message: La clef est sous le volet*, 1944 (pl. 47)

p. 114: Laurie Anderson, *New York Times, Horizontal/China Times, Vertical*, 1976 (pl. 50)

p. 128: Jorge Macchi, *Monoblock (3)*, 1999 (pl. 27)

CONTENTS

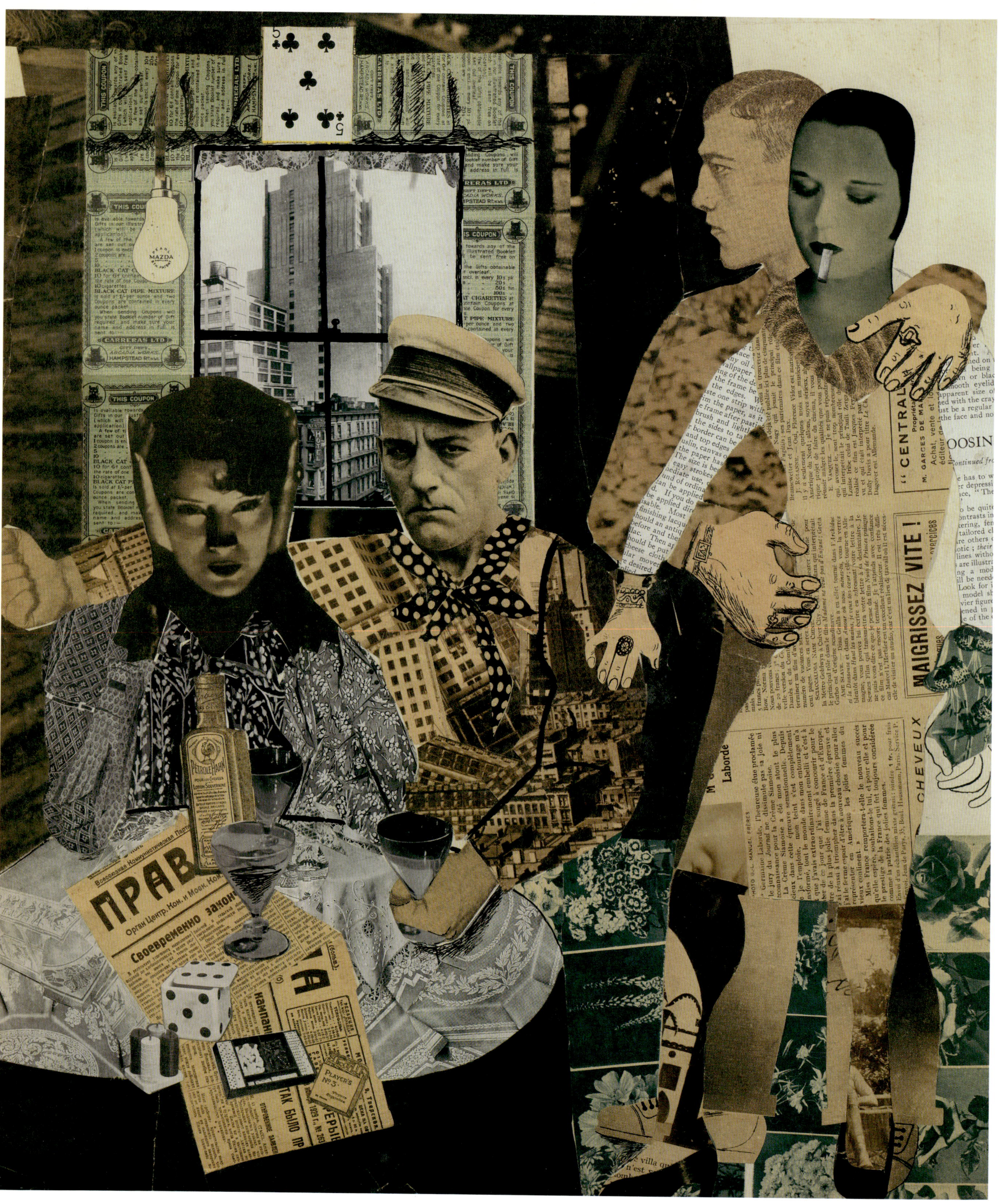
THIS COUPON
CARRERAS LTD
MAZDA
BLACK CAT PIPE MIXTURE
ПРАВ
Своевременно
кампани
PLAYER'S
No3
« CENTRAL
MAIGRISSEZ VITE !
CHEVEUX
Laborde

DIRECTOR'S FOREWORD

A painting below by Lyonel Feininger from 1909 shows pedestrians striding along the streets of Weimar, Germany, so absorbed in their newspapers that they are oblivious to their surroundings. Even the looming presence of the Church of Saints Peter and Paul does not divert their attention. If Feininger, who died in 1956, were alive today and inclined to depict the same scene, the figures would likely have their eyes glued to smartphones.

In its own time Feininger's *Newspaper Readers* signaled a condition of modern mass-media culture: not only did people from all walks of life have equal access to the newspaper, but most had the requisite skills to read one. The situation was relatively new. The mechanically printed newspaper, in existence since the early seventeenth century, had never before been so widely available to an increasingly literate public. Paris around 1909, the place and time that our *Shock of the News* exhibition takes as its beginning, was home to an estimated fifty daily papers with some six million copies circulating every twenty-four hours.

Filippo Tommaso Marinetti, the founder of futurism, and Pablo Picasso, the co-inventor of cubism, were quick to register the newspaper's ubiquity and intensified influence. Marinetti co-opted the front page of *Le Figaro* in 1909, maneuvering his impassioned account of the birth of futurism and the movement's first manifesto into the most widely circulated newspaper in Europe. Picasso incorporated actual newspaper into works of art starting in 1912, thereby prompting a novel approach to representation. Instead of relying on illusionistic rendering, an artist could simply introduce the real thing.

Though their strategies differed, these two figures were pivotal in the extended history of the newspaper's impact on modern art. Artists over the next century turned to the paper as the basis for verbal and visual puns, as a source of found language, and as a means to mark time and place. They deployed headlines and articles as agents of political critique and adopted the newspaper's layout as a graphic armature. Some depended on its rows of small text to suggest atmosphere, while others were drawn to its lowly status and impermanence. By snipping and overdrawing pages, transferring fragments to canvas, embalming full sheets in encaustic, excising texts—even gilding whole editions of a newspaper—a spectrum of artists pursuing various agendas have transformed the familiar daily into an artwork of protean identity and compelling interest.

The title of this catalogue and accompanying exhibition plays on that of Robert Hughes' popular BBC television series (1980) and related book, *The Shock of the New: Art and the Century of Change* (London, 1980). Given Picasso's penchant

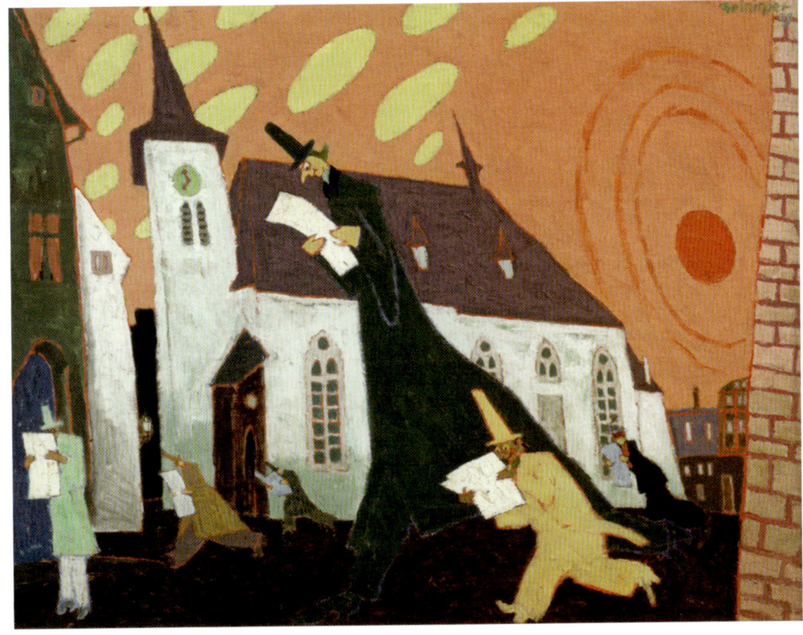

RIGHT Lyonel Feininger, *Newspaper Readers*, 1909, oil on canvas, Collection of Judy and John M. Angelo

for using the newspaper to create puns, the wordplay seems apt. Our exhibition opens with Marinetti, Picasso, Georges Braque, and Juan Gris at the beginning of the twentieth century and closes with Mario Merz, Marine Hugonnier, and Kim Rugg at the beginning of the twenty-first century. In between, it considers works by artists such as John Heartfield and Paul Klee in the 1930s, Kurt Schwitters and Hans Richter in the 1940s, Robert Rauschenberg and Jasper Johns in the 1950s, Robert Morris and Joseph Beuys in the 1960s, Sarah Charlesworth and Laurie Anderson in the 1970s, John Cage and Adrian Piper in the 1980s, and Robert Gober and Jorge Macchi in the 1990s. In fact, most art movements of the twentieth century took account of the newspaper phenomenon, starting with cubism and extending through conceptualism and beyond. Even today, with online newspapers eclipsing "hard copy" versions, artists show no lack of interest in printed newspapers.

Conceived by Judith Brodie, curator and head of the department of modern prints and drawings at the National Gallery of Art, this exhibition should shape our understanding of modern artists and the newspaper and inspire further investigation. Although a handful of recent exhibitions in Europe and the United States have explored this topic, *Shock of the News* is the first to offer a systematic examination of the subject over the course of a century. It is also the first to propose a conceptual model — based on Marinetti's and Picasso's seminal roles — through which to view this history.

Exhibitions, especially those dependent on loans of works of art from abroad, require considerable resources; thus, we are enormously grateful to the Leonard and Evelyn Lauder Foundation for its generous sponsorship. Profound thanks go as well to the public and private lenders who made possible the realization of *Shock of the News* by temporarily parting with cherished works from their collections. We are deeply appreciative of the broad support this project has received from near and far.

Earl A. Powell III

LENDERS TO THE EXHIBITION

Bauhaus-Archiv, Berlin

Beinecke Rare Book and Manuscript Library, Yale University

Merrill C. Berman

James Castle Collection and Archive

Collection Ohnesorge Martin-Malburet

Collezione Merz, Torino

The Dalí Museum, Saint Petersburg

Des Moines Art Center

EG Collection, Milan

Eric and Elizabeth Feder

Gagosian Gallery, New York

Gail and Tony Ganz, Los Angeles

Glenstone

Robert Gober and Matthew Marks Gallery

Peggy Guggenheim Collection, Venice

Hirshhorn Museum and Sculpture Garden, Washington

Christine and Mark Husser

Ellsworth Kelly

Alden and Mary Kimbrough

Kunstsammlung Nordrhein-Westfalen, Düsseldorf

Kurt und Ernst Schwitters Stiftung, Hannover

Los Angeles County Museum of Art

The McNay Art Museum, San Antonio

The Metropolitan Museum of Art, New York

Moderna Museet, Stockholm

Robert Morris and Leo Castelli Gallery

The Museum of Modern Art, New York

Museum Schloss Moyland, Bedburg-Hau

National Gallery of Art, Washington

National Gallery of Art Library, Washington

Private collections

Madeline and Bruce Ramer

Ryerson and Burnham Libraries, The Art Institute of Chicago

Ryo Toyonaga and Alvin Friedman-Kien

Dean Valentine and Amy Adelson, Los Angeles

Walker Art Center, Minneapolis

Whitney Museum of American Art, New York

Barbara Wien, Berlin

Zentrum Paul Klee, Bern

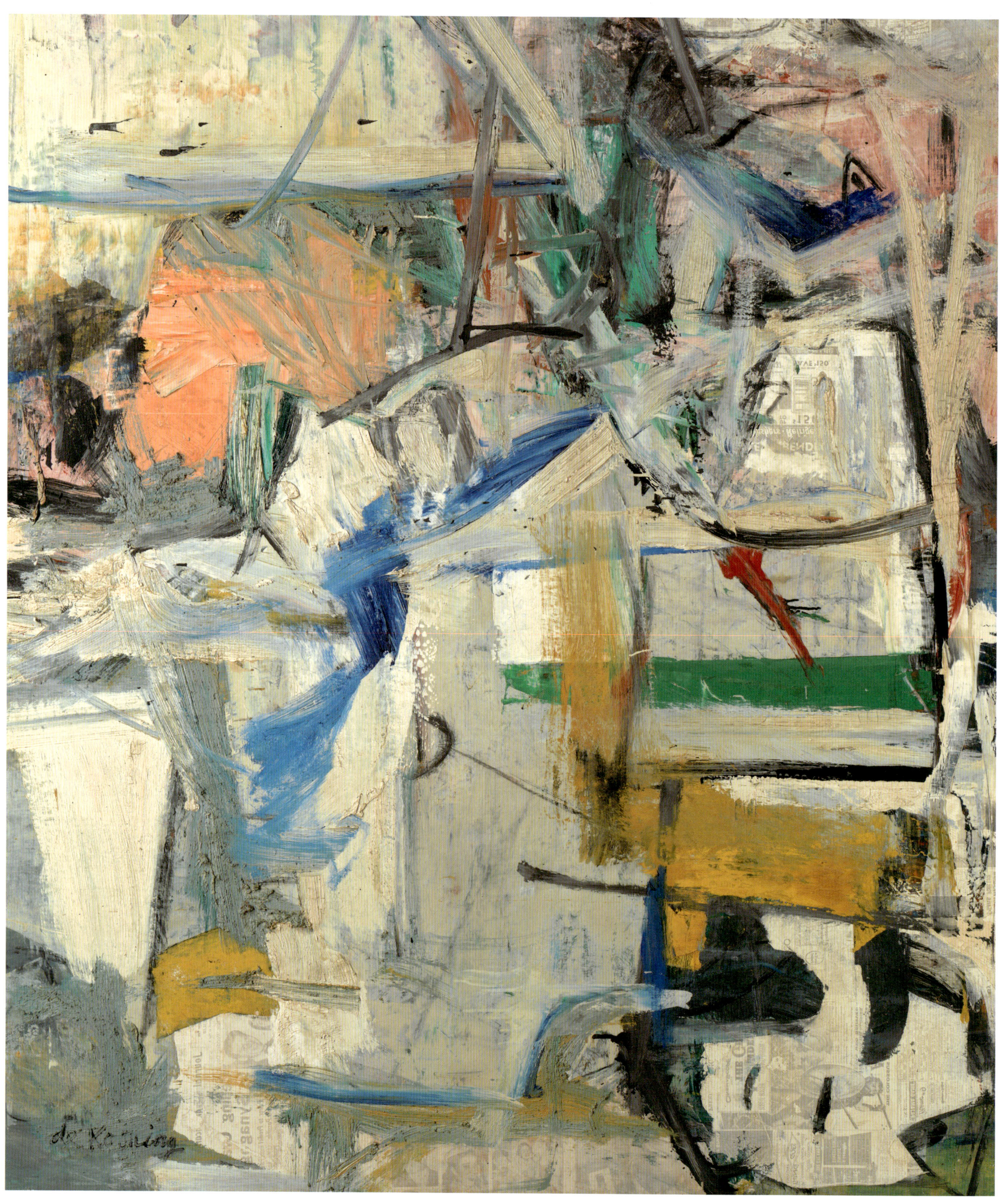

INTRODUCTION

Judith Brodie

Shock of the News looks at a phenomenon that has engaged artists from 1909 to the present. Here dubbed the "newspaper phenomenon," it traces back to Filippo Tommaso Marinetti's publication of the first futurist manifesto on the front page of *Le Figaro* in 1909 and Pablo Picasso's incorporation of a fragment of real newspaper into a *papier collé* almost four years later, in 1912. The trend spread quickly—indeed at breakneck speed—across Continental Europe and to the United States.

Marinetti and Picasso pursued agendas that were poles apart. Nonetheless, their closely sequenced actions prompted visual artists to think about the newspaper more broadly—as a means of political critique, as a collection of ready-made news to appropriate or manipulate, as a source of language and images, as a typographical grab bag, and more.

Many of the works discussed in the following essays and displayed in the accompanying exhibition are well known. Some, such as Picasso's *Guitar, Sheet Music, and Glass* (1912), have been exhaustively studied, its small section of newsprint pored over for meaning (pl. 2). But few works of art that incorporate, comment on, or model themselves on the newspaper have received comparable study. My coauthors and I hope to level the playing field on that count and call attention to a history that has never received systematic or focused consideration.

The majority of artists are represented by one exemplary work. Given the overwhelming number who contributed to the newspaper phenomenon and the constraints of the exhibition and catalogue, only a selection of artists could be included, with such regrettable exclusions as Conrad Atkinson, Alighiero Boetti, Marianne Brandt, Sophie Calle, Nancy Chunn, Guy de Cointet, Felix Droese, Hans Haacke, William H. Johnson, Joseph Kosuth, Adam McEwen, Joan Miró, Victor Pasmore, Michelangelo Pistoletto, Shozo Shimamoto, Daniel Spoerri, Antoni Tàpies, Franz West, and others. The exhibition's compass also, admittedly, gravitates toward Europe and the United States, areas of my expertise.

Most twentieth-century art movements took account of the newspaper phenomenon, with the notable exceptions of surrealism and abstract expressionism. The surrealists' interest in the individual subconscious was, it would seem, an unlikely fit for the publically minded newspaper. And given abstract expressionism's roots in surrealism, as well as its self-reflexive focus, chances were doubled that the extrospective newspaper would rarely make its presence known in works by the likes of Jackson Pollock, Barnett Newman, or Mark Rothko. The telephone pages on which Franz Kline made action paintings approximate newsprint, and three paintings by Willem de Kooning that feature newspaper transfer stand as exceptions to the rule. De Kooning would press pages of the newspaper onto his still-wet paint surfaces to retard drying, and when the newsprint offset onto the paint, as it inevitably did, he had the option of either rubbing it out with brushwork or preserving it intact. In *Attic* (1949) he retained only the transfer of a seated bather, but in *Gotham News* (1955) and *Easter Monday* (1955–1956) (facing page), he elevated the transfers from subtext to motif. (Unfortunately, none of these paintings was able to travel to our exhibition.) In the 1960s and 1970s, de Kooning would revive this scheme in works painted or imprinted directly onto newspaper (pl. 52).

More surprising, pop art has a smaller presence in the history than one might anticipate. With the exception of Andy Warhol, most pop art-

Willem de Kooning, *Easter Monday* (detail), 1955–1956, oil and newspaper transfer on canvas, The Metropolitan Museum of Art, Rogers Fund, 1956

ists were as likely to appropriate images from glossy magazines, mail order catalogues, and comic books as they were from the newspaper. They did not generally discriminate. And when they turned to the newspaper as a source—typically for an ad—they rarely made it explicit by including a vestige of a headline or a trace of text from an adjoining article. A distinct departure (aside from Warhol) is Richard Hamilton's *Swingeing London 67* (1968), which features news articles published in the wake of Mick Jagger's arrest on February 12, 1967. The print not only cries out newspaper but captures the interdependency between pop culture and the tabloid press (fig. 1).

The opening essay looks at the history of the newspaper phenomenon through the lens of Marinetti's front-page maneuver in *Le Figaro* and Picasso's use of real newspaper in his *papiers collés*. It covers a full century, 1909–2009, and its methodology is that of the case study, comparing and contrasting works to determine their underlying meanings or strategies. The prevailing message is that we must "read" these newspapers in the broadest sense of the term.

Sarah Boxer, who was a reporter and critic at the *New York Times* from 1989 to 2006, gives a passionate and personal account of artists' love-hate relationship with the newspaper, beginning with Stéphane Mallarmé. She argues that Mallarmé, the "supposed archenemy of newspapers," was not above pilfering from the papers' attributes. She sees Picasso, James Joyce, and others in the same boat, covetous of the paper and sometimes acting against it in spite.

Janine Mileaf and Matthew Witkovsky view the newspaper as a consummate temporal marker, "yellowing almost before one's eyes" and dispensing news that is current one day and obsolete the next: "a quickly spent commodity." They draw on the writings of Walter Benjamin, Karl Kraus, and Mallarmé, and they lead us—with an eye to "news time, the temporal pace that structures all modernity"—through a survey that begins with Marinetti and Picasso and concludes with Hans-Peter Feldmann and his historic *9/12 Front Page*, a roomful of newspapers published the day after the terrorist attacks of September 11, 2001.

In the final essay, Christine Poggi describes the daily paper as a complex and complicated offering of diverse voices and styles—a "montage of elements," as it were. Rather than representing a unified present, she points to the paper as encompassing the past and the future as well. The newspaper, after all, covers events from previous days and offers forecasts of those to come. Poggi makes the case that artists since World War II have taken account of the newspaper's multidimensionality by treating it "as a physical substance whose thick, stratified structure yields similarly thick, stratified works." Her postwar analysis begins with a newspaper cutout by Ellsworth Kelly and concludes with Mario Merz's neon-topped stacks of bound newspaper, *À Mallarmé* (2003).

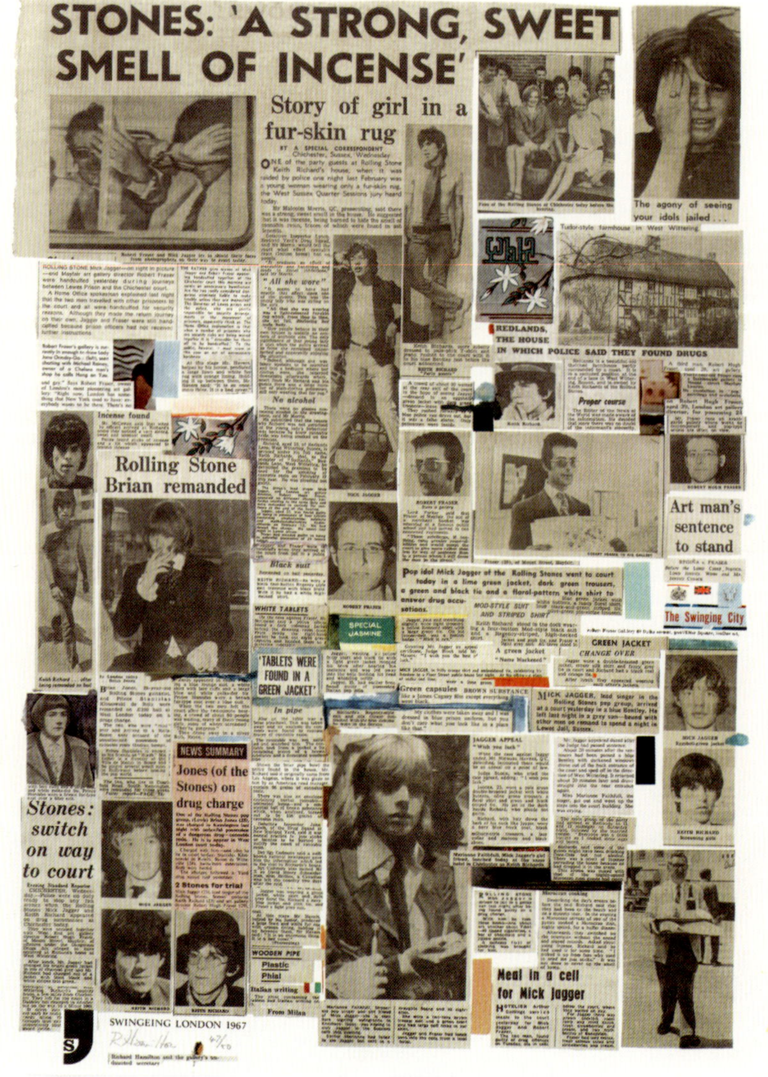

1

FIG. 1 Richard Hamilton, *Swingeing London 67*, 1968, photolithograph

The works of art in this exhibition were selected with care, each chosen with the knowledge that it had a significant contribution to make. The essayists, however, were given free rein to discuss those that best pertained to their topic or argument. Inevitably, not every work in the exhibition found a place in an essay. And because all of them have a story to tell (and a few begged for further coverage), close to half are discussed in individual commentaries.

My reading of the newspaper phenomenon favors Marinetti and Picasso. Marinetti extended the story of modernism from the "shock of the new" to the "shock of the news," and Picasso created the first self-consciously modern work of art to incorporate real newspaper. But the study of modern artists and the newspaper is a relatively new one, and others may frame the discussion differently or dispute my conclusions. If the exhibition and catalogue serve to open the field and encourage original thinking on the subject, they will have more than fulfilled my expectations.

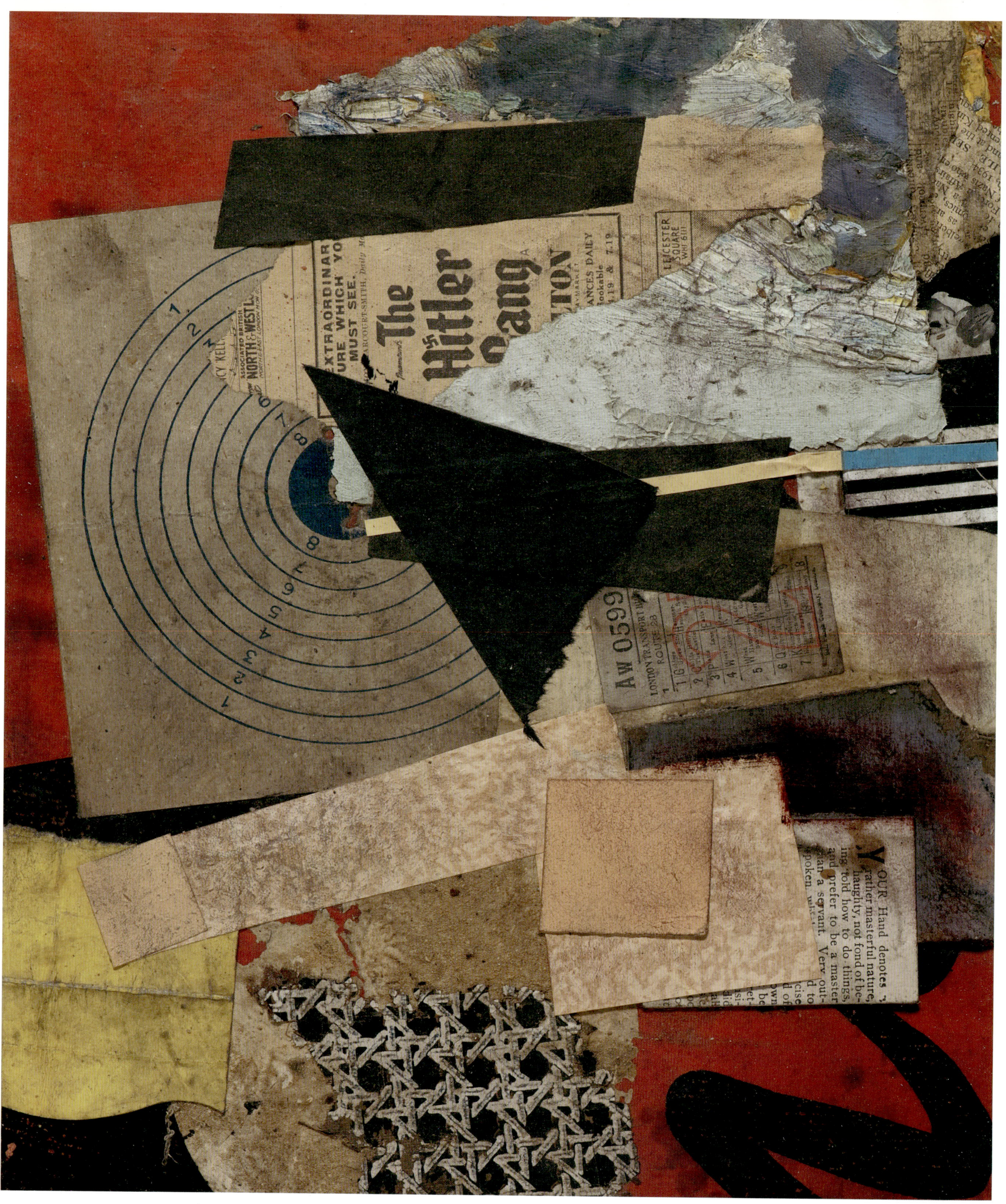

The Hitler Gang
Aw 0599
LONDON TRANSPORT
YOUR Hand denotes

READING THE NEWSPAPERS, 1909 – 2009

Judith Brodie

"Sufficient for the day is the newspaper thereof."
James Joyce, 1922

A first glance at the front page of *Le Figaro* on February 20, 1909, must have been a shock for readers (pl. 1). The day's lead story, the *premier-Paris,* signed by the Italian poet and playwright Filippo Tommaso Marinetti, was a wildly impassioned account of the birth of futurism and an inflammatory eleven-point manifesto calling for people to "glorify war" and to "destroy museums, libraries, academies." An adjoining statement by the editor denied all responsibility for Marinetti's "singularly audacious ideas."[1] Indeed, initial reactions were mainly dismissive. Yet word of the futurist movement traveled quickly. Newspapers and journals all across Europe picked up the story, and within weeks translations appeared as far away as Moscow.

Marinetti's call to arms shared front-page coverage with a report about a lavish event at the Élysée Palace and miscellaneous items featured in the paper's *Échos* section, ranging from weather conditions across Europe to an announcement of a new couturier salon on the boulevard Malesherbes. In short, the context was decidedly mainstream, bourgeois, and consumer-oriented, a setting that only heightened the shock value of Marinetti's message. The page is now an icon in the history of European modernism. Although other newspapers had published the manifesto weeks before, *Le Figaro* was the first to issue it in conjunction with Marinetti's narrative, called "the Founding."[2] Curiously, scholars have either missed or ignored the fact that the Founding was not published in *Le Figaro* as Marinetti presumably submitted it. More than ten paragraphs were removed before publication.[3] One scholar suggests "editorial intervention" at work. Granted, these passages mention corpses, a coffin, a guillotine blade, death, and the black breast of a Sudanese nurse, but it would be hard to argue that they were more outrageous than those that were printed in the newspaper.[4] The decision probably came down to space. Instead of trimming the lengthy report about a swanky event at the Élysée Palace, the editor went after Marinetti's rant.

Given that the manifesto was already in circulation and that *Le Figaro* issued a botched version of the Founding, the iconicity of that front page may have less to do with the content of its lead story and more with the fact that Marinetti had managed to proclaim his audacious notions on page 1 of the most widely circulated newspaper in Europe. By maneuvering his proclamation into the spotlight, he engineered the first avant-garde co-option of the newspaper, extending the story of modernism from the "shock of the new" to the "shock of the news."[5]

No artistic manifesto had yet achieved such prominence, although a significant precedent of

1

FILIPPO TOMMASO MARINETTI

Le Futurisme *("Founding and Manifesto of Futurism")*, *in* Le Figaro

February 20, 1909, newspaper, 24 ½ × 17 ½ (62.2 × 44.5), Collection Ohnesorge Martin-Malburet

On the bottom of the last column of *Le Figaro*'s front page, peripheral to Marinetti's call to arms, there is an article headlined "Le complot Caillaux" (the Caillaux plot). It tells of a scheme by the French finance minister, Joseph Caillaux, to institute an income tax. Years later Caillaux would be named prime minister and undergo severe attack in the pages of *Le Figaro*. The newspaper's editor, Gaston Calmette (whose name we see at the top left of the page), not only published damaging material about the prime minister but threatened to print compromising love letters, from years earlier, from Caillaux to his mistress at the time. In response to this threat, that mistress—now the prime minister's wife—walked into the offices of *Le Figaro* on March 16, 1914, and shot and killed Calmette.

55e Année — 3e Série — N° 51 | Samedi 20 Février 1909

Gaston CALMETTE

LE FIGARO

H. DE VILLEMESSANT

SOMMAIRE

Le Futurisme

Manifeste du Futurisme

LA VIE DE PARIS

"Le Roi" à l'Élysée... Palace

Les Courses

A Travers Paris

Échos

Nouvelles à la Main

Le complot Caillaux

FIG. 1 Émile Zola, "J'Accuse . . . !" in *L'Aurore*, January 13, 1898, Bibliothèque nationale de France

another sort, Émile Zola's famous "J'Accuse . . . !" declaring his position on the Dreyfus case, had monopolized the front page of *L'Aurore* on January 13, 1898 (fig. 1). Marinetti, who revered Zola and had an exceptionally good nose for publicity, would have followed the extraordinary public debate sparked by that front page and grasped the newspaper's incendiary role. He clearly recognized its potential for disseminating a message with unmatched speed and understood what futurism, with its iconoclastic ideals, had to gain from the imprimatur of an establishment newspaper. Despite *Le Figaro*'s conservative political leanings, it had long served as a platform for progressive writers (George Sand, Guy de Maupassant, and Marcel Proust, among others) and a launching pad for such literary manifestos as Jean Moréas' symbolist manifesto, published in the paper's literary supplement on September 18, 1886.[6] But coverage in the literary supplement was a far cry from coverage on the front page.

As radical as his co-option of the newspaper was, Marinetti made no claim to the February 20, 1909, *Le Figaro*'s being a work of art. He saw the incursion as one more weapon in an arsenal aimed at scandalizing *Le Figaro*'s readers and spreading his radical program. Propagating a subversive agenda was a means to *make* news. But by planting what even he referred to as "delirious writings" on the pages of a respectable daily, he advanced a tactic that had far-reaching implications and prompted visual artists to think about the newspaper more broadly: as a means of political critique, as a collection of ready-made news to appropriate or manipulate, as a model on which to base newspapers of their own making. Marinetti thus led the way for media-savvy artists to find in the pressroom a new mode of artistic production outside the hermetic confines of the studio and beyond the walls of art galleries and museums.

Nearly four years after Marinetti's manifesto was published, Pablo Picasso cut a small section from the front page of the November 18, 1912, edition of *Le Journal* and incorporated it into a work known today as *Guitar, Sheet Music, and Glass* (pl. 2). The procedure required little manual effort or technical skill. But it did amount to a radically new way of thinking about representation. Instead of depicting the likeness of a newspaper, Picasso used the real thing. Here he took his cue from Georges Braque, who earlier that fall had incorporated three pieces of commercially made, imitation wood-grain wallpaper into a composition, considered the first cubist pasted-paper collage, or *papier collé*. Braque gets top billing in this contest, but in terms of the history of artists' engagement with the newspaper, Picasso takes the spotlight. His *Guitar, Sheet Music, and Glass* is widely considered the first self-consciously modern work of art to incorporate real newsprint.[7]

To be clear, this was not the first time that actual newspaper made its way into an artistic production. One art historian cites a *découpage* folding screen, signed and dated A. G. Schumann (1797), which incorporates playing cards, bank notes, and a Leipzig newspaper. And Hans Christian Andersen, the Danish children's storywriter, made a newspaper cutout of a figure in 1830. There are also examples of newspaper fragments in Victorian era albums. Even Picasso made

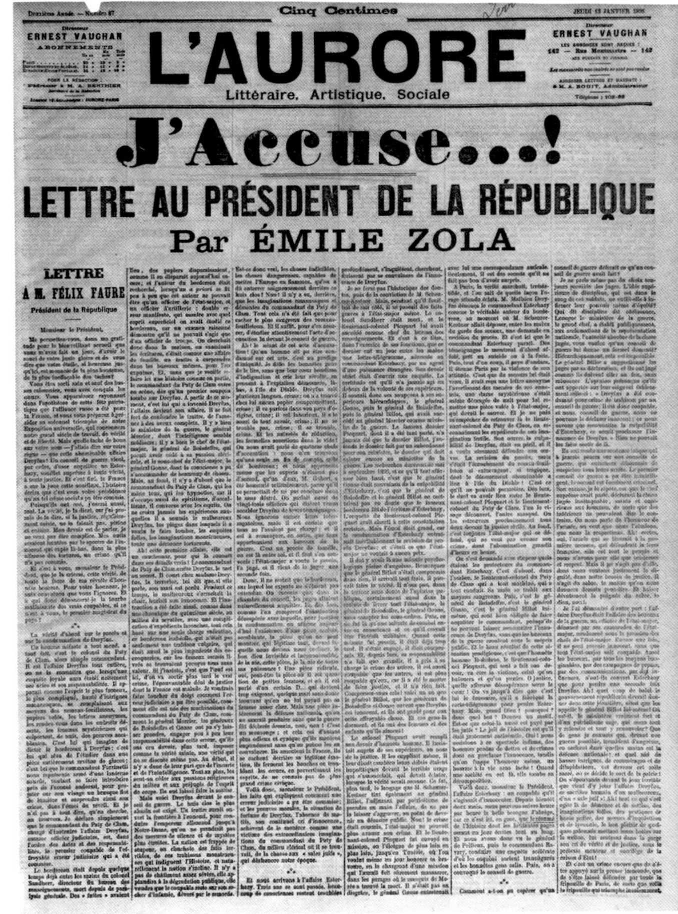
Cinq Centimes

ERNEST VAUGHAN

L'AURORE

Littéraire. Artistique. Sociale

J'Accuse...!

LETTRE AU PRÉSIDENT DE LA RÉPUBLIQUE

Par ÉMILE ZOLA

LETTRE

À M. FÉLIX FAURE

Président de la République

1

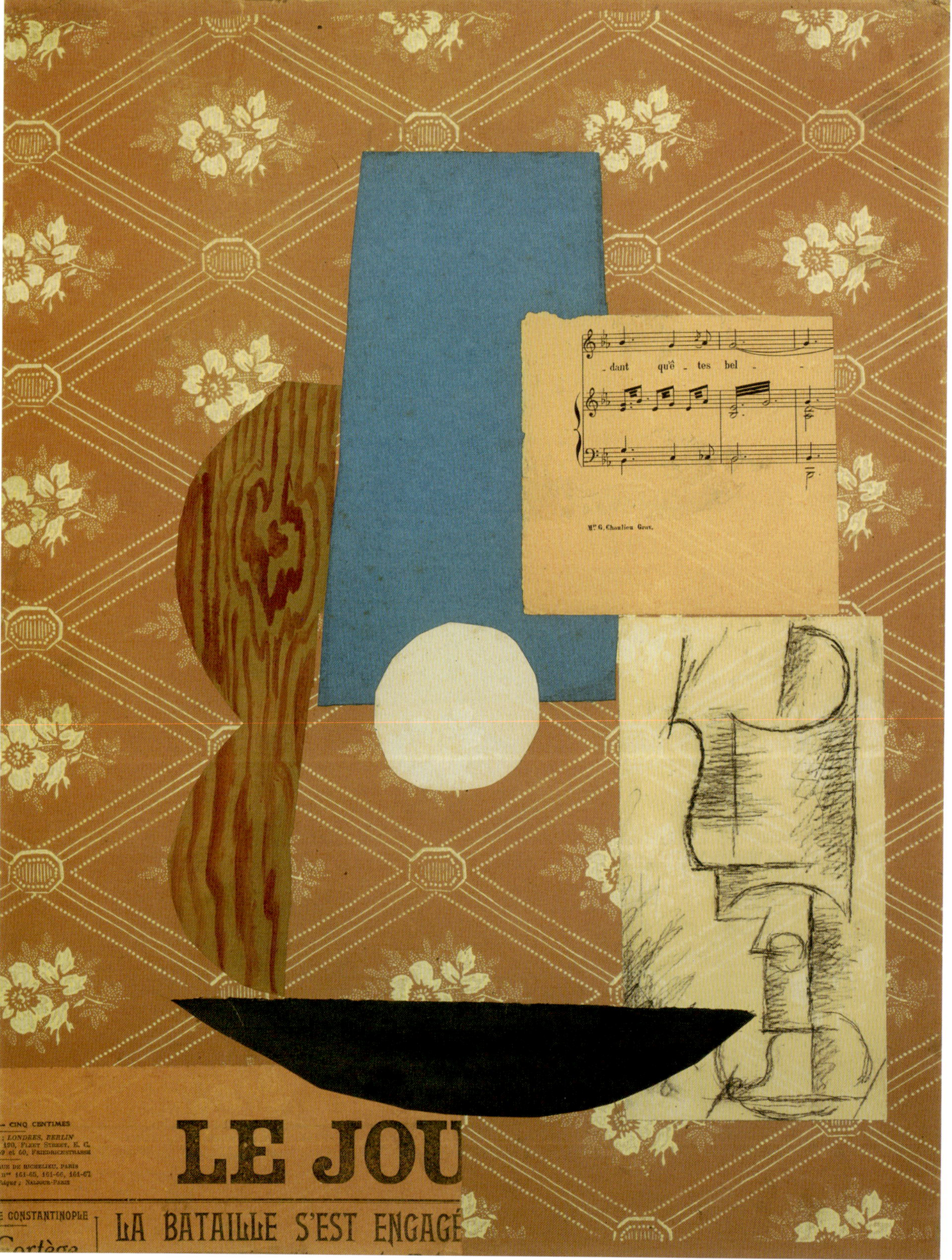

2

PABLO PICASSO

Guitar, Sheet Music, and Glass

1912, sheet music, newspaper, colored and white paper, charcoal, and hand-painted faux bois paper on wallpaper, 18 7/8 × 14 3/8 (47.9 × 36.5), Collection of the McNay Art Museum, Bequest of Marion Koogler McNay

sketches on newspaper before 1912. None of these, however, was meant to be self-consciously modern or was aimed at elevating collage to an independent art form.[8]

The historical significance of the *papiers collés* was slow to be recognized. When critics and art historians turned their attention to them around the middle of the twentieth century, they were viewed through a formalist lens. The critic Clement Greenberg was so focused on cubism's "shuffling and shuttling between surface and depth" that he deemed the incorporation of lettering (including newsprint) "extraneous" to the motif and chiefly an optical device meant to affirm the flatness of the picture plane.[9] And before Greenberg, none other than Christian Zervos, compiler of the canonical Picasso catalogue raisonné, paid little attention to the newspapers' texts, at times assigning dates to works without regard for the documentation provided by the newspapers themselves.[10]

Astonishingly, the texts to be found in cubist works went mainly uninvestigated until 1973, when Robert Rosenblum published his landmark essay, "Picasso and the Typography of Cubism."[11] There he dealt with Picasso's (as well as Braque's) most favored masthead, *Le Journal,* the title of a Paris daily as well as the generic French word for newspaper. Picasso had trimmed it to "LE JOU" in *Guitar, Sheet Music, and Glass,* which Rosenblum associated with *le jour* ("the day"), *jouer* ("to play"), and the risqué *jouir* ("to enjoy" or, in sexual slang, "to come").[12] The wordplay may seem simple, even puerile, but Picasso's understanding of French was rudimentary at the time.[13]

Beneath "LE JOU" are the words "LA BATAILLE S'EST ENGAGÉ," truncating a longer headline: "LA BATAILLE S'EST ENGAGÉE FURIEUSE sur les Lignes de Tchataldja" (The battle is furiously joined at the Tchataldja front), which strikes a more sober note. But Picasso was averse to fixing any one meaning to the newspaper fragments he introduced into his works. Thus we might presume that he was telegraphing his antimilitarist views or anxieties about the war in the Balkans.[14] Or we might deduce that he was addressing the subject of collage itself, pitting it against the high art of painting or, more specifically, the prevailing conventions of representation.[15] Or Picasso may simply have been issuing a private communiqué, alerting Braque, with whom he was engaged in a friendly rivalry, that their personal artistic battle had begun.[16] In fact, all of these associations may be "in play."

Picasso was just as reluctant to favor a single mode of representation. *Guitar, Sheet Music, and Glass* displays a number of representational modes, two plainly contradictory ones being the patched-together guitar and the more traditional (albeit cubist-style) charcoal-hatched wine glass. The *papier collé* also carries multiple signs: the square segment of sheet music features notes that are meant to be read, as are the words in the newspaper fragment. Jeffrey Weiss suggests music as a conceptual model for Picasso's newspaper *papiers collés.* "Sheet music and newsprint implicate two forms of reading," he observes, "which is a measured temporal operation. This condition is amplified by the fact that music is a time-based art form and that newsprint signifies the fleeting present of today's news."[17] The work likewise invites several visual interpretations: the wallpaper that serves as the composition's backing could be seen as representing a wall behind the still-life objects, as a horizontal covering on which the objects rest, or even as a wall on which the *papier collé* itself might hang. There is no single correct reading of these paper elements, any more than there is one correct reading of the newspaper fragment.

Indeed the fragment from the front page of *Le Journal* carries various meanings and fulfills numerous roles. It represents a newspaper as a whole; embodies topicality in its reference to the Balkans; registers temporality in its propensity to discolor; denies craft in its rejection of virtuoso skill; parodies the trompe-l'oeil tradition in its dismissal of illusionistic rendering; airs an allegiance to that which is workaday, prosaic, and accessible; capitalizes on the newspaper as a typographical grab bag; and formally anchors the other visual elements in the composition. Above all, its presentation of words and language invites reading. The newsprint fragment affixed to *Guitar, Sheet Music, and Glass* is nothing less than a model of modern multitasking, a single entity in service to multiple strategies.[18]

In the wake of Marinetti's coup on the front page of *Le Figaro* and Picasso's introduction of real newspaper in *Guitar, Sheet Music, and Glass,* a host of other artists took up the newspaper. Between 1913 and 1919 alone, these included: Johannes Baader, Georges Braque, Umberto Boccioni, Josef Čapek, Carlo Carrà, Alexandra Exter, Emil Filla, Juan Gris, George Grosz, Otto Gutfreund, Raoul Hausmann, Hannah Höch, Paul Klee, Kazimir Malevich, Lyubov Popova, Enrico Prampolini, Man Ray, Diego Rivera, Ottone Rosai, Kurt Schwitters, Gino Severini, Mario Sironi, Ardengo Soffici, Joseph Stella, Varvara Stepanova, and Max Weber. Countless more followed suit, with the result that most art movements of the twentieth century took account of the newspaper phenomenon. Even today, with so many newspapers in jeopardy, the phenomenon shows no signs of abating.

What follows are focused readings of works made by some of the artists cited above plus artists whose works came after 1919. The approach is roughly chronological, although a *papier collé* by Picasso is featured in a discussion of a much later cutout by Ellsworth Kelly. The comparison of a painting from around 1952 by Robert Rauschenberg and a print from 1986 by John Cage also departs from the chronological progression, but the pairing is based on the two artists' close relationship as colleagues and collaborators.

The newspaper strategies developed by Marinetti and Picasso provide anchors for fifteen sections that cover topics ranging from the predictable (major historical events, such as World War II) to the unexpected (encryption). The dual aim is to reveal the deep richness of this history by approaching the works of art from various vantage points, teasing out motivations and underlying messages, and opening up new interpretations by literally "reading the newspapers," a method that has been afforded to Picasso but only haphazardly applied to others.

Épater le bourgeois

The central newsprint fragment in Braque's *Bottle, Glass, and Newspaper* (late 1913 or 1914) includes a prominent advertisement for a women's comportment manual, *L'amour obligatoire* (Mandatory love), written by the Comtesse de Tramar, a popular turn-of-the-century antifeminist author (pl. 3).[19] Tramar opposed equal rights for women and believed that fantasizing about such liberties would lead to a woman's discontent.[20] Braque may have been familiar with Tramar's views, or possibly he was attracted to the book's provocative title. Either way, his decision to use this fragment could not have been arbitrary. It is juxtaposed with another newspaper ad for Motobloc automobiles, above the charcoal-drawn letters "JOU AL" (shorthand for *Journal*).[21] These two ads overtly demarcate gendered spaces in the *papier collé*—the male domain indicated by the modern automobile and the female domain indicated by love and the constraints of etiquette. If one accepts this reading, it is hard not to see an image of a vulva in the imitation wood-grain paper, which literally underlies the ad for *L'amour obligatoire.* Similarly, one might see a phallic reference in the straight verticals of the wood-grain paper on the left and, for that matter, the bottle rim to its immediate right. Braque is usually characterized as being more circumspect than Picasso, as both an artist and an individual. But here he holds a mirror up to society in a surprisingly audacious and graphic manner.

Braque's contemporary Juan Gris pointed a direct finger at societal norms in *Glasses, Teacup, Bottle, and Pipe on a Table* (1914) (pl. 4).The cubist still life, which is dominated by an exotic pattern of stepped rectangular cuboids that signify a tabletop, incorporates a rather large portion of the April 26, 1914, front page of *Le Matin,* featuring before-and-after photographs of a marble lion in the place de la Concorde. The "before" photograph, taken in 1889, shows the base of the statue plastered with electoral postings. The "after" photograph, from 1914, shows it clean and bare. A caption above reads: "Une des consequences de loi restreignant l'affichage électoral" (A consequence of the act restricting electoral billposting), referring to a law passed in 1910. The proliferation of postings around the turn of the century, electoral and otherwise, provoked considerable debate among French citizens—some thinking it picturesque and others deeming it unsightly.[22] Gris' inclusion of a news item addressing France's

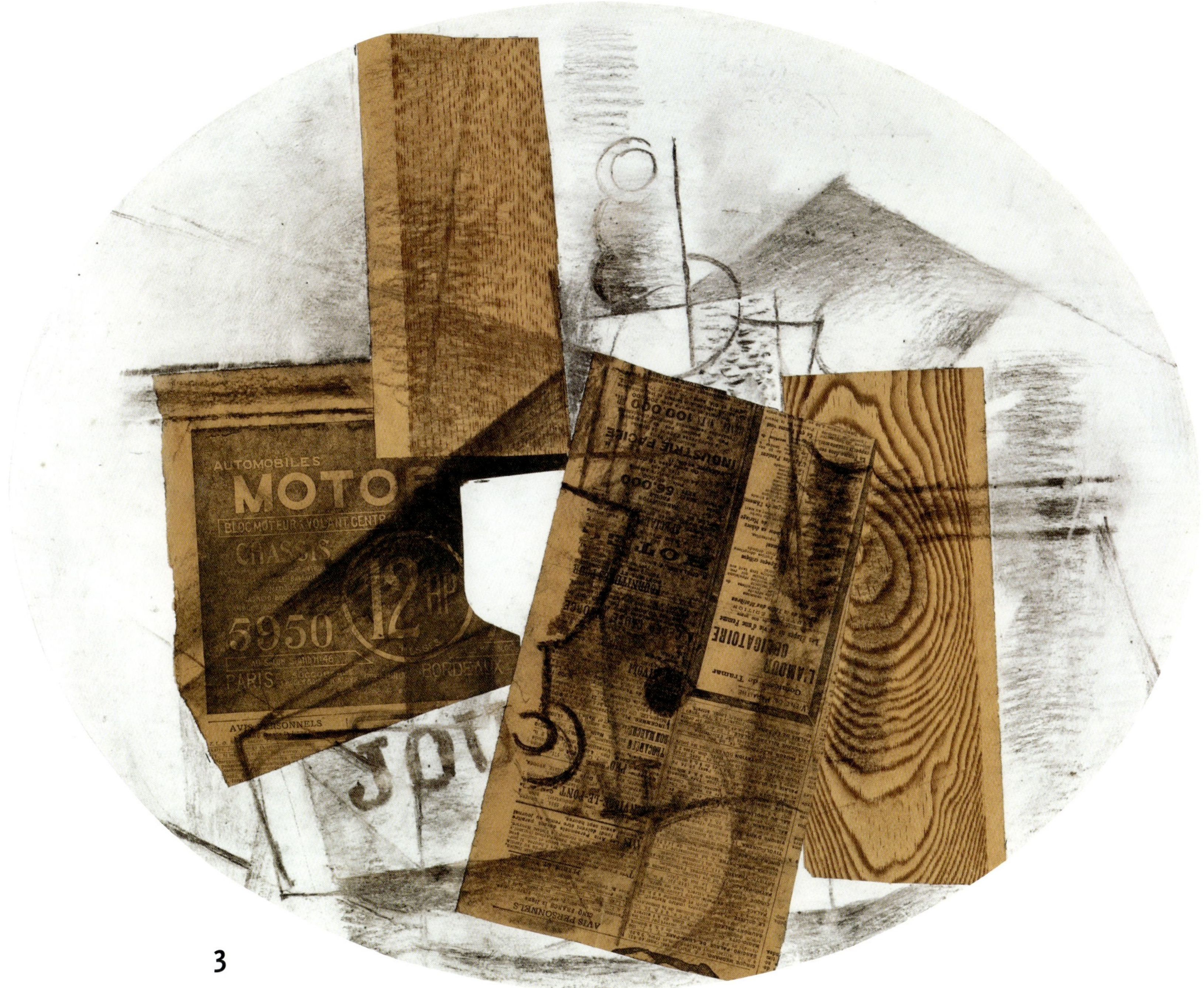

3

GEORGES BRAQUE

Bottle, Glass, and Newspaper

late 1913 or 1914, charcoal, faux bois paper, and newspaper on painted board, 19 ⅞ × 24 ¼ (50.5 × 61.6)

Private collection

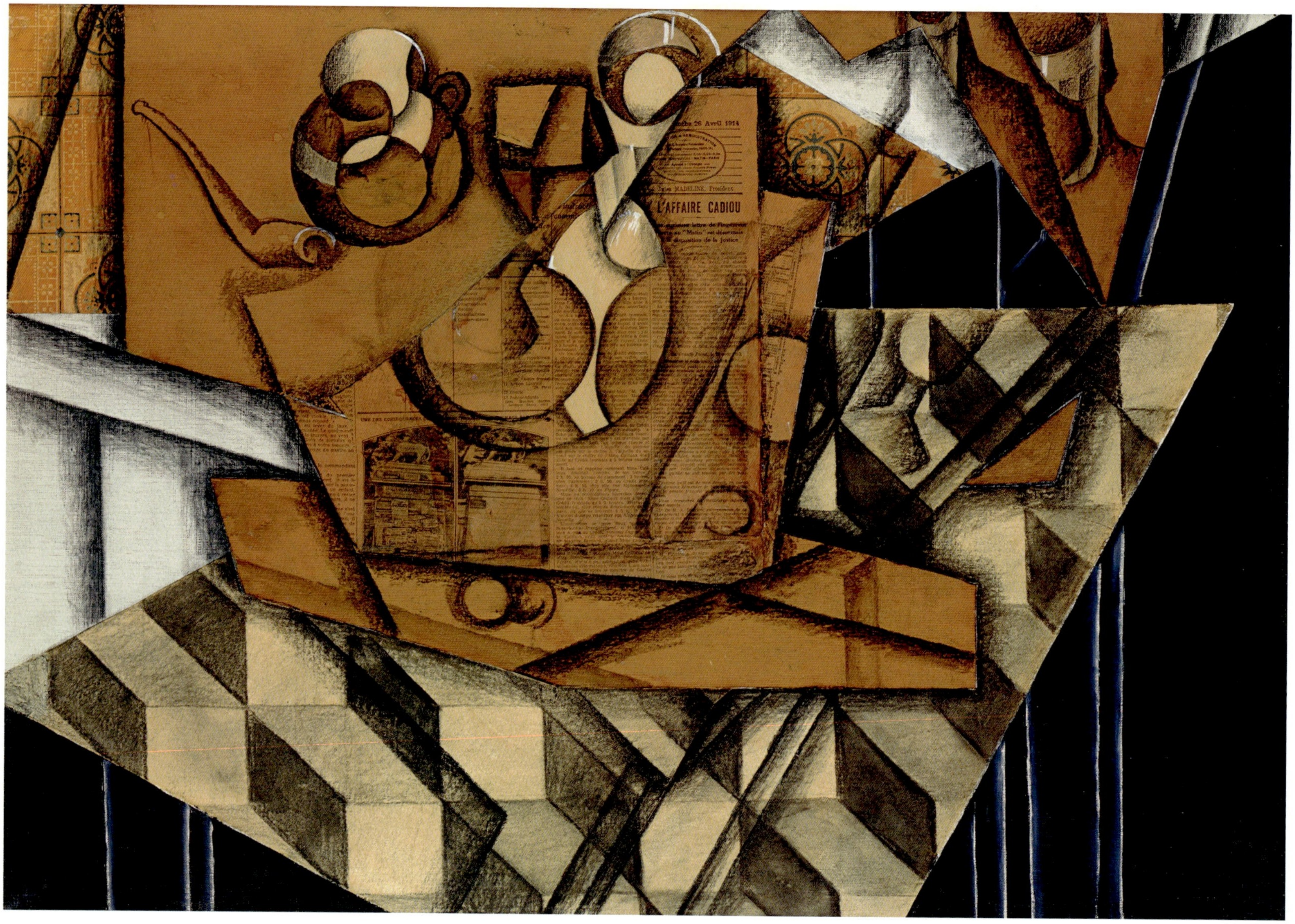

4

JUAN GRIS

Glasses, Teacup, Bottle, and Pipe on a Table

1914, oil, pasted paper, and charcoal on canvas, 25 ⅝ × 36 ¼ (65.1 × 92), Kunstsammlung Nordrhein-Westfalen, Düsseldorf

FIG. 2 Richard Caton Woodville, *War News from Mexico*, 1848, oil on canvas, Crystal Bridges Museum of American Art, Bentonville, Arkansas

FIG. 3 Gino Severini, *Still Life: Bottle + Vase + Journal + Table*, 1914–1915, charcoal, gouache, and newspaper on paper, The Metropolitan Museum of Art, Alfred Stieglitz Colletion, 1949

clean-up campaign, in a painting that itself incorporates pasted-paper elements, was clearly a message laced with irony and aimed at mocking the tidy aesthetics of the bourgeois.[23]

News from the Battlefield

The idea that artists could use the newspaper to convey a message was hardly a new one. The American artist Richard Caton Woodville had done exactly that in *War News from Mexico* in 1848 (fig. 2). Additional examples could be cited, but the point to be made is that a painting such as Woodville's required complicated staging and considerable time and mastery. The more novel option of simply incorporating real newspaper not only streamlined the process but had the added benefit of distinguishing an artist's work as vanguard.

Futurist artists powered their messages with news from the battlefield. In *Still Life: Bottle + Vase + Journal + Table* (1914–1915), Gino Severini incorporated two fragments clipped from the front page of the September 3, 1914, edition of the French newspaper *La Presse* (fig. 3). One addresses Italy's potential role in the newly declared war, and the other highlights images of French soldiers in the trenches. The implication was that Italy should get off the sidelines and into the fighting. But the packaging of that message in a still life (granted, an exceptionally dynamic one) weakened its impact. Although the futurists pushed hard for

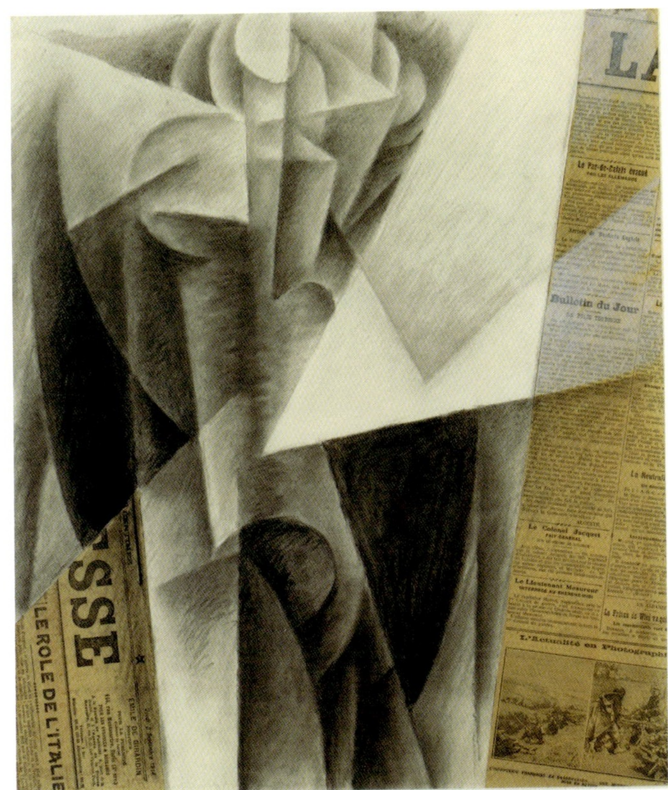

3

Italy's intervention in the war, their delivery rarely matched the wallop of Marinetti's in *Le Figaro*.

In distinction, Carlo Carrà mustered up impressive message-power in his dynamo of a collage, *Manifestazione interventista* (Interventionist demonstration) of 1914 (p. 97, fig. 5), but his *Pursuit* (*Inseguimento*) (1915) falls short in that regard (pl. 5). If the rider on horseback was meant to be a cavalry officer, the result is more sporting than bellicose, as if Carrà were promoting a pastime rather than a war.[24] The name "Joffre," that of the French general who defeated the Germans at the Battle of the Marne, appears in stenciled letters on the left. But the various clippings, primarily from French and Italian newspapers, mostly emphasize nonmilitary topics ranging from sports events to music-hall entertainments to leisure motoring (the triangular segment at the bottom). Only two clippings plainly reference the war: one reading "a COSC / NUOVA," taken from a pro-intervention pamphlet, *Per la coscienza della Nuova Italia* (Consciousness of a new Italy), and the other, a very small clipping citing the Balkans that forms

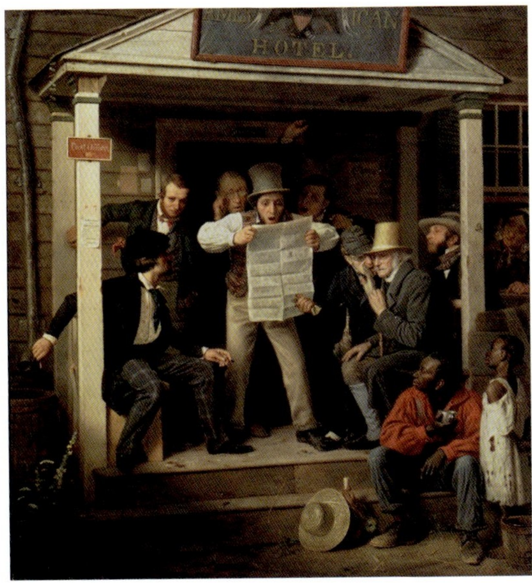

2

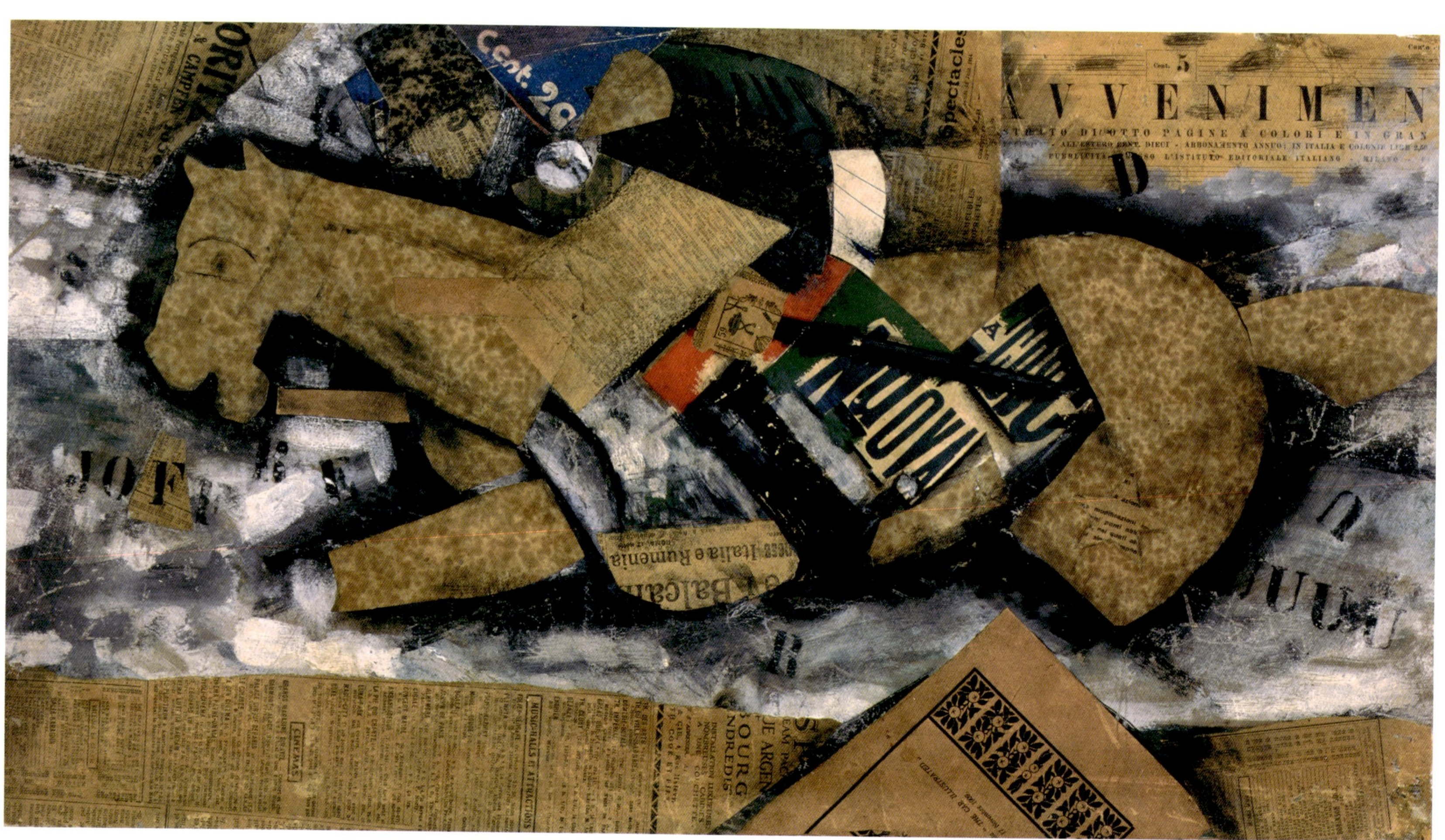

5

CARLO CARRÀ

Pursuit (Inseguimento)

1915, tempera, charcoal, and collage on cardboard, 15⅜ × 26¾ (39 × 68), Gianni Mattioli Collection. Long-term loan to the Peggy Guggenheim Collection, Venice

FIG. 4 Man Ray, *Presse-papier à priape* (Priapus paperweight), 1920, marble, Private collection

the contour of the horse's breast. (Given the proximity of the one that begins "a COSC" to the horse's haunch, Carrà was also likely punning on *coscia,* the Italian word for thigh.) The Balkans clipping came from the January 13, 1915, edition of *Il Popolo d'Italia,* whose editor-in-chief, Benito Mussolini, lobbied hard for Italy's intervention in the fighting; the Italians would not enter the conflict for another four and a half months. By the end of the war, sentiments and artistic interests would change. Carrà transitioned to *pittura metafisica,* or metaphysical painting—already evident in *Pursuit*—and Severini began to explore classicism.

Encrypted Newspapers

Picasso culled information from newspapers that escaped most readers' notice. Some of the drawn contour lines, for example, in his *Head of a Man with a Moustache* of 1913 (pl. 6) seem inspired by individual letters spotted on the inverted news page and used as visual cues. Thus, the two double-arched contours (shaped like loose 3s) near the drawing's center mirror the reversed *B*s in the word "SCRUBB'S." The extended V-shapes that rise from the man's moustache parallel the upside-down *A*s that bookend "AMMONIA." And the sweeping spherical contour of the man's head echoes the reversed *C* in "SCRUBB'S."

Man Ray delved deeper (pl. 7). If you were to turn his *Transmutation* (1916) ninety degrees clockwise, so that the newspaper page was vertical and the text upside down, two circles, with the collage letters *B* and *H* (now sideways), would rest at the bottom right of the page. These circles overlap a rectangle that frames a picture of a woman (now inverted), her hands neatly folded. The rectangle is topped by another circle, with the letter *R* superimposed.

Compare a later work by Man Ray, *Presse-papier à priape* (Priapus paperweight) (1920), made up of a cylinder and three spheres that mimic an erect phallus and scrotum (fig. 4). The evidence is suggestive: Man Ray anticipated the Priapus paperweight in *Transmutation.* This is not to claim that he traced the form's outline or even knowingly recalled *Transmutation* when he made the paperweight four years later. But it is to say that Man Ray first unearthed this unintended witticism on a page of the *New York Sun.*

Many of the collage elements (*R, H, 3, B,* and the smaller *B* and *8* in red) are either symmetrical or near-symmetrical shapes and are positioned over the eyes of faces on the page, as if they (all women save one) were peering out through spectacles.[25] Viewed retrospectively by way of the Priapus paperweight, it takes little imagination to see what the group is staring at.

Man Ray also truncated the spelling of the word "theater" to create "THEATR," which spans much of the work's upper register. In an article titled "Cryptography and the Arensberg Circle," Francis Naumann explains that Duchamp and Man Ray, members of Walter Arensberg's circle, were influenced by the art collector's passion for cryptography, including anagrams.[26] Naumann points out that *priape* is an anagram of *papier,* both appearing in the title *Presse-papier à priape.* Could the word "THEATR" in *Transmutation* be rearranged to read "THE ART"? Or more intriguingly given the now uncovered Priapus, "THREAT"?[27]

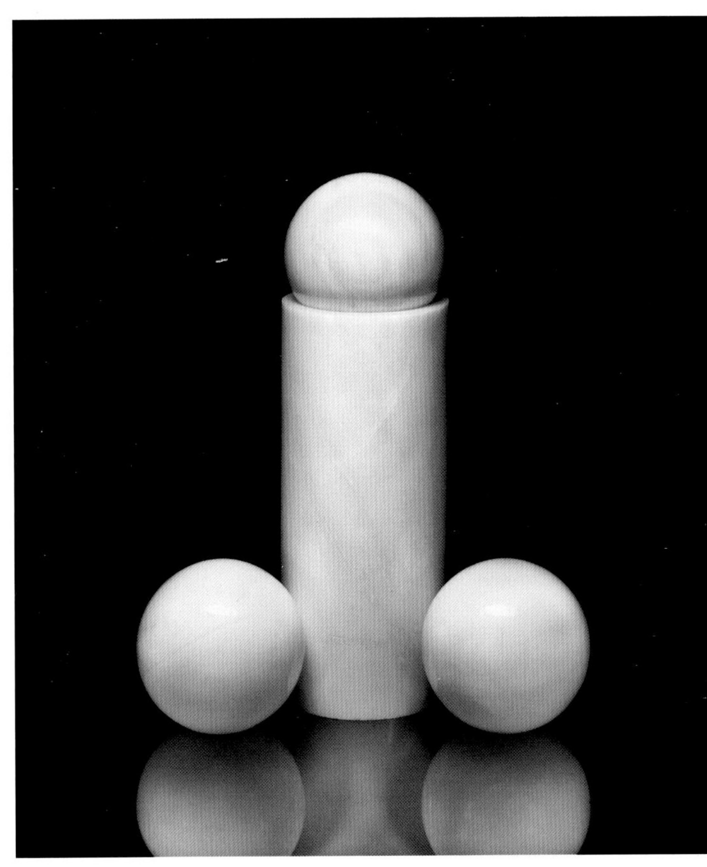

4

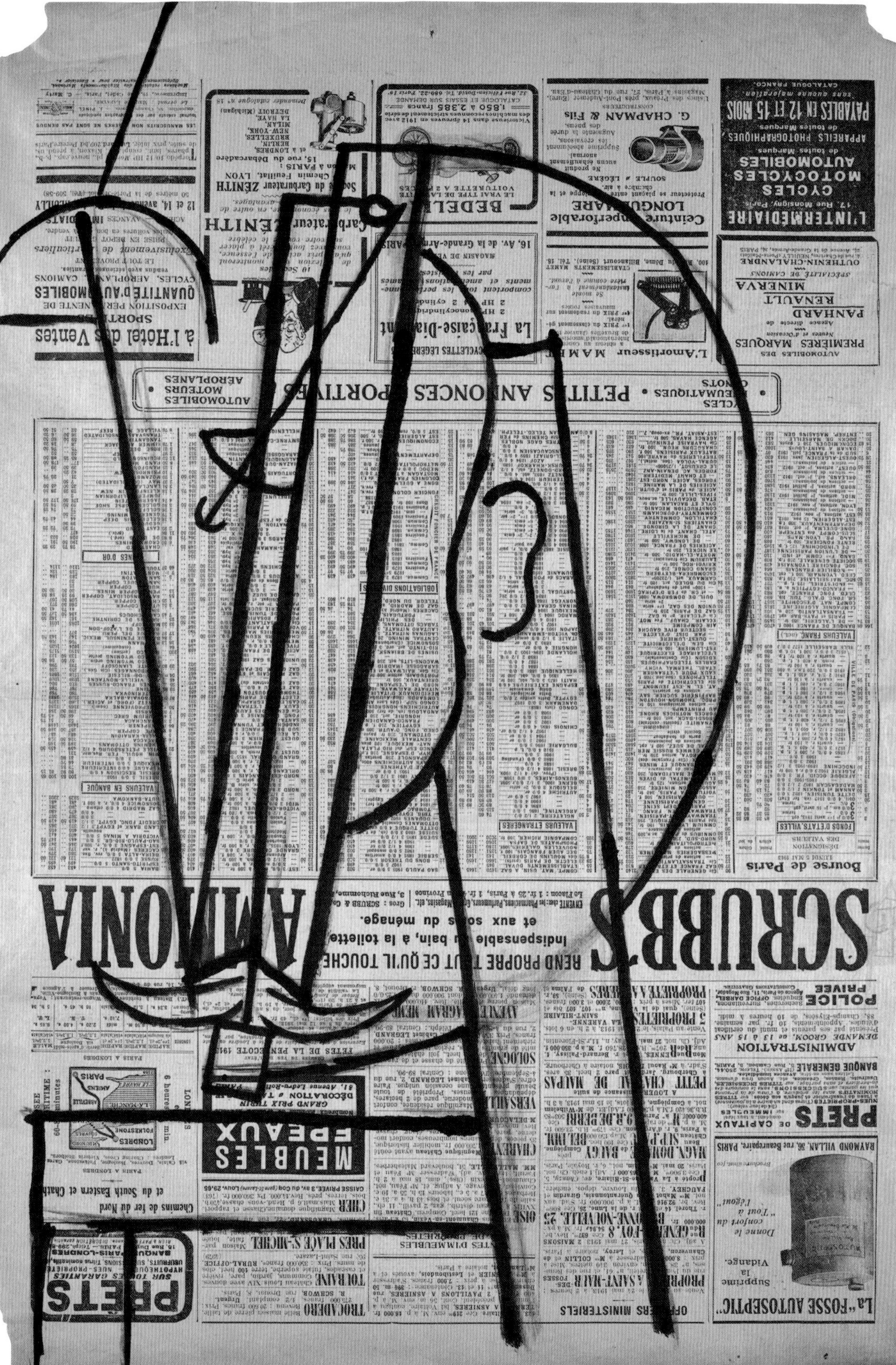

6

PABLO PICASSO

Head of a Man with a Moustache

1913, ink, charcoal, and graphite on newspaper, 21 ⅞ × 14 ¾ (55.5 × 37.4), Private collection

The oversized advertisement for Scrubb's Ammonia and its claim to be as "*indispensable*" to one's personal grooming habits as to the maintenance of one's home must have struck Picasso, as it does us today, as oddly comic. No less striking is the towering appearance of an English product name in a French newspaper. Indeed, it is hard to imagine a word less French than Scrubb's. The escalating number of foreign products advertised in early twentieth-century French newspapers brought anomalies such as this one into sharp relief.

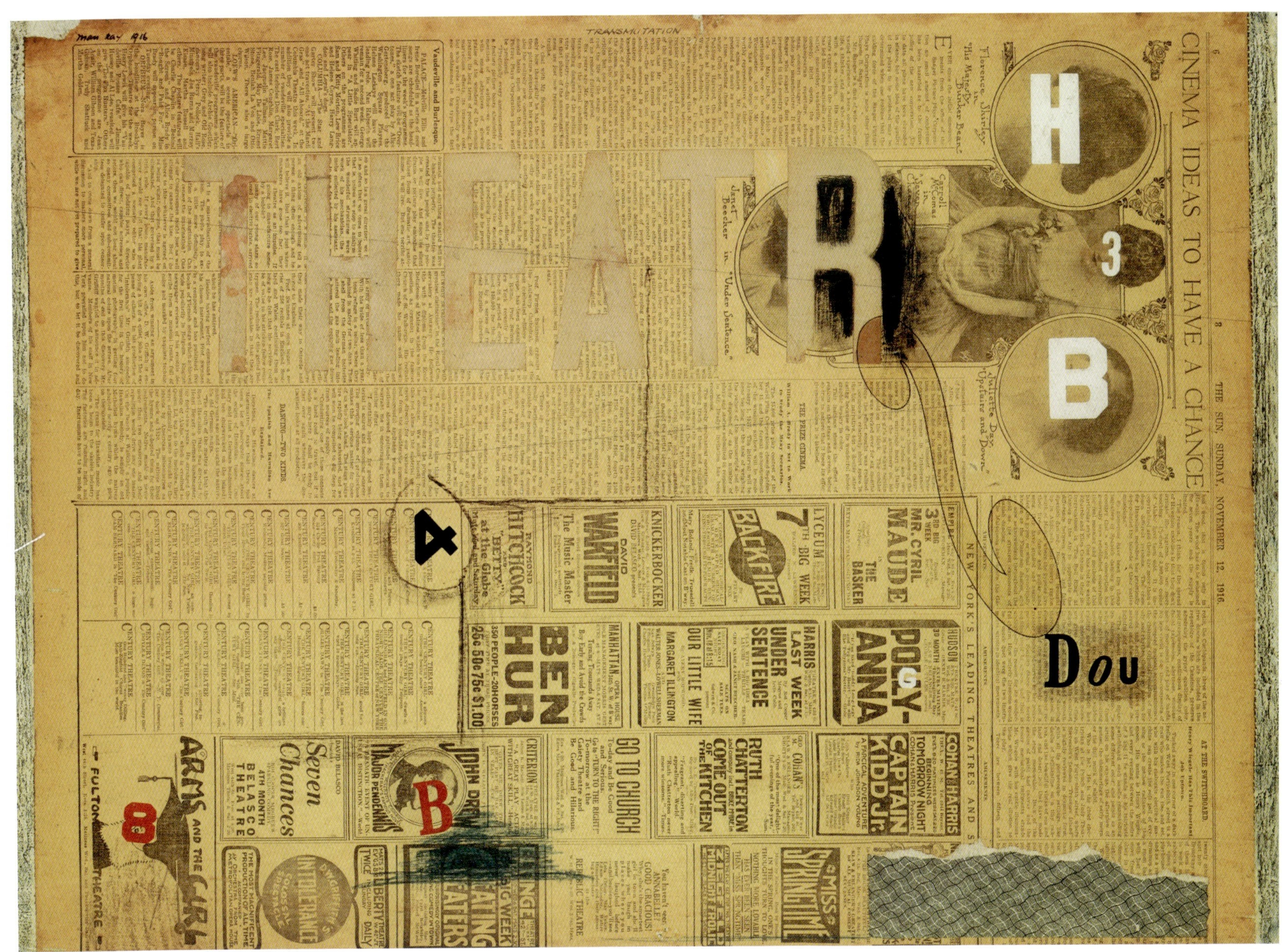

7

MAN RAY

Transmutation

1916, watercolor, ink, crayon, charcoal, graphite, and collage on newspaper, 17½ × 23⅞ (44.5 × 60.5), Moderna Museet, Stockholm

Political Pundits

Dada artists did not weigh in on the war until 1916, and their derisive response was unlike that of the futurists' rallying cry. Similarly, their picture-based collages shared little in common visually with those of the cubists or futurists. The change in aspect is exemplified in the postwar photomontages (collages made from photographs) of Hannah Höch, the only woman active in Berlin Dada. Höch occasionally used text and images scissored from standard newspapers but typically relied on imagery published in Germany's new illustrated newspapers, crossbreeds of the dailies and the weekly magazines. For example, the source for most of the clippings in *Dada-Rundschau* (Dada panorama) (1919) was the *Berliner Illustrirte Zeitung* [sic], or *BIZ*, the country's most widely circulated illustrated paper (fig. 5).

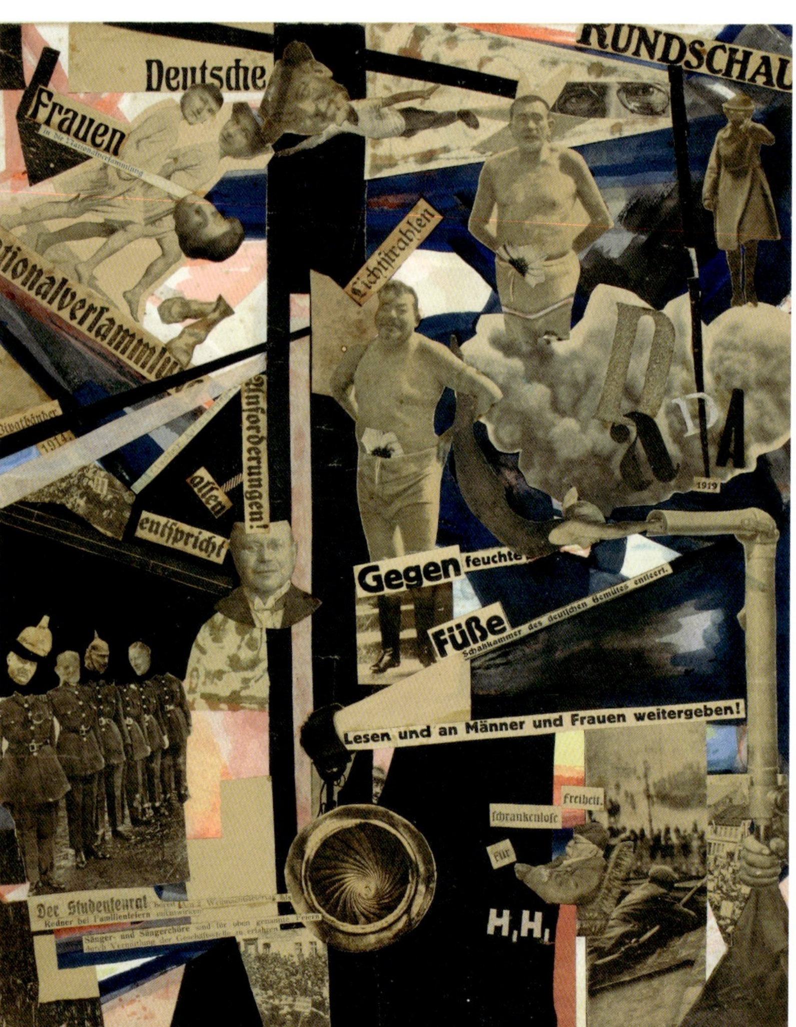

5

FIG. 5 Hannah Höch, *Dada-Rundschau* (Dada panorama), 1919, photomontage and collage with gouache and watercolor on board, Berlinische Galerie, Landesmuseum für Moderne Kunst, Photographie und Architektur

While applauding the role of Germany's recently empowered women, Höch took a swipe at Weimar president Friedrich Ebert and his defense minister, Gustav Noske, adorning them with flowers and exposing them in bathing suits, flabby bellies and all.[28] Nor did she show much in the way of deference for American president Woodrow Wilson, attaching his head to the diminutive body of a female acrobat turned sideways (upper center). Meanwhile, the lithe figure of another female acrobat is pictured in a daring midair dive (center right), and toga-clad women (upper left) are staged prancing forward near text that reads "Deutsche / Frauen / in die Nationalversammlung" (German women into the National Assembly). Thirty-six women had won assembly seats in the first German election in which women were granted the right to vote. Höch signed the composition (lower right) "Schrankenlose Freiheit für H.H." (Unrestrained freedom for H[annah] H[öch]).

The historian Jochen Hung comments that these "weekly illustrated papers with their (mainly) unpolitical entertainment and objective reportages should be seen as a new product, not just a newspaper with more images." The approach was in marked contrast to the customary pedagogical tone adopted by German journalists, who saw themselves as "educators whose job it was to state their opinions and convince the reader." Indeed many dismissed the illustrated papers "as an 'Americanization' of the press," having in mind the populist-based newspapers of Joseph Pulitzer and William Randolph Hearst.[29]

John Heartfield (who helped organize the First International Dada Fair in 1920, in which Höch's *Dada-Rundschau* was exhibited) was among the most politically motivated of the Berlin Dadaists. He went on to publicize his views in photomontages created for the popular communist paper *Arbeiter Illustrierte Zeitung*, or *AIZ*, for which he worked from 1929 to 1938.[30] Heartfield's cover for the February 9, 1930, issue of *AIZ* shows a lumpish man in a leather shoulder harness, the sort used to carry heavy loads (pl. 8). His head is wrapped in pages from two newspapers: *Vorwärts*, the Social Democratic Party's official organ, and *Tempo*, a mass-market tabloid. Heartfield's

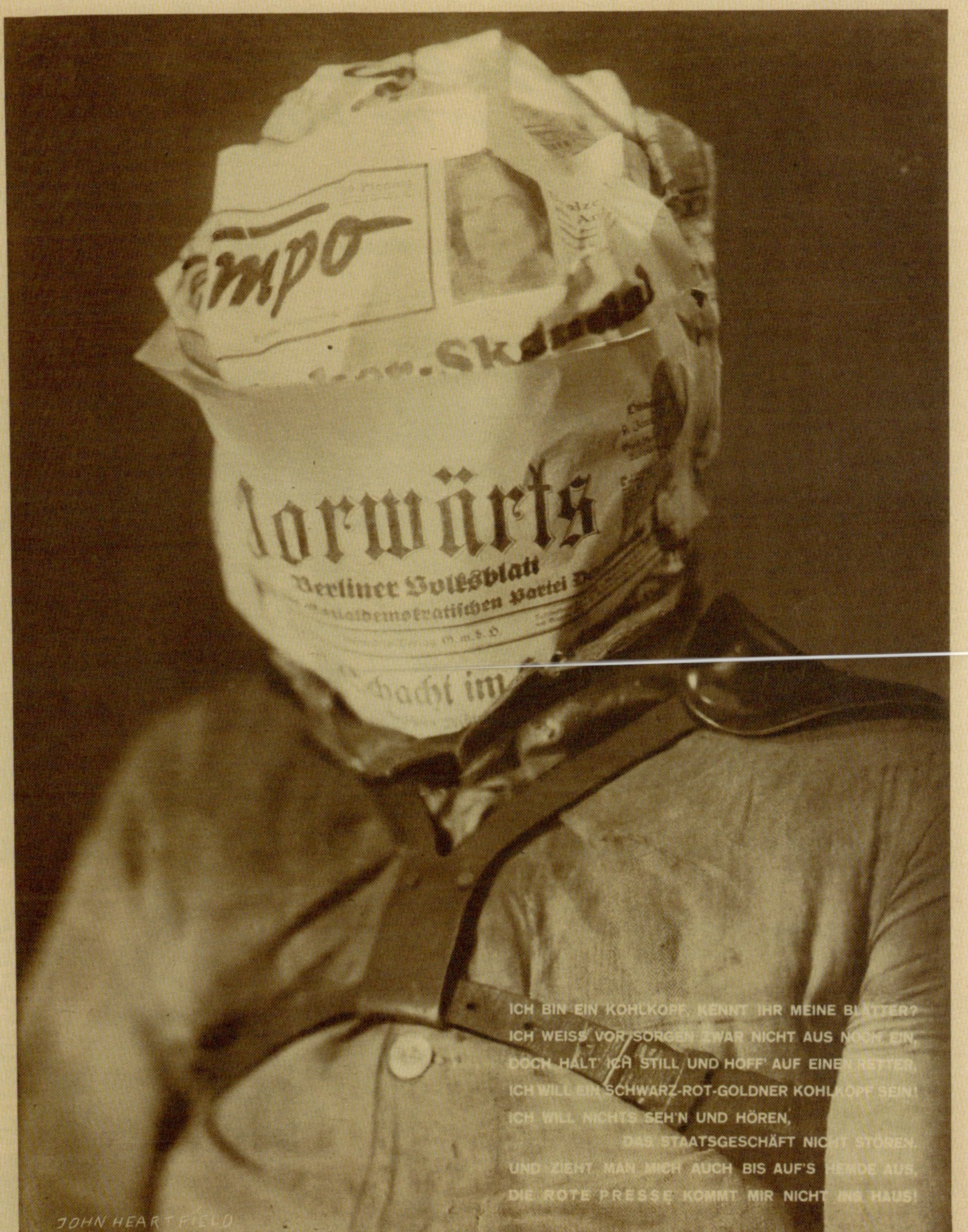

8

JOHN HEARTFIELD
Wer Bürgerblätter liest wird blind und taub. Weg mit den verdummungsbandagen! *(Whoever reads bourgeois newspapers goes blind and deaf. Away with bandages that make you dimwitted!), in* Arbeiter Illustrierte Zeitung *9, no. 6,* February 9, 1930, copperplate photogravure, 15 × 10 ½ (38.1 × 26.7), The Metropolitan Museum of Art, Ford Motor Company Collection, Gift of Ford Motor Company and John C. Waddell, 1987

criticism was targeted at both the party and the bourgeois press. His message to *AIZ*'s readers—spelled out in the work's boldface caption—could not have been more explicit: "Whoever reads bourgeois newspapers goes blind and deaf."

The papers that shroud the man's head render him mute and blind and simulate the overlapping leaves of a head of cabbage, an association reinforced in the accompanying text's introductory line: "Ich bin ein Kohlkopf. Kennt ihr meine Blätter?" (I am a cabbage head. Do you know my leaves?). The passage sets up a pun on *Blätter*—a word that can mean either the "leaves" of a cabbage plant or a newspaper's "pages" or "leaves."[31] It additionally plays on the opening lyrics of the early nineteenth-century national anthem of Prussia: *Ich bin ein Preusse, kennt ihr meine Farben?* (I am a Prussian, do you know my colors?).[32] The shortened singular form *Blatt* (leaf or sheet) also appears in *Vorwärts*' subtitle, *Berliner Volksblatt* (Berlin people's paper).

Given Heartfield's opposition to the Social Democratic Party, it is not surprising that he would target *Vorwärts,* its official newspaper. A small portion of the paper's headline—*Schacht im*—is legible and refers to the president of the Reichsbank, Hjalmar Schacht, who would resign a month later over the terms of war reparations imposed on Germany. The placement of the headline—"Schacht" is situated precisely at the Cabbagehead's collar—not only implicates the Reichsbank president but references Schacht's habit of wearing high starched collars.[33] (Heartfield would later lampoon Schacht in two *AIZ* photomontages.)[34]

Heartfield's additional target was *Tempo,* a relatively new paper whose design and program were unlike those of the staid and established *Vorwärts. Tempo* featured bold headlines and abundant photographs and was among a recent outcrop of Berlin newspapers published in tabloid format.[35] It was also distinguished by its decidedly modern look, as evidenced by the cursive typestyle of its truncated masthead, which stands in marked contrast to *Vorwärts*' traditional black-letter type. The articles on *Tempo*'s pages were heavily skewed to sensational reporting and, in the eyes of some, represented a dangerous incursion of American values. Heartfield may have played that view out by letting the paper's partial and crumpled headline, *Skandal,* slip into the composition.

Höch's compromising photographs of Ebert and Noske were scandalous, and Heartfield's photomontage for *AIZ* rivaled the shock value of Marinetti's writing in *Le Figaro*. And while Heartfield's message may not have been shocking to *AIZ*'s left-wing readers, his tactic for visualizing that message made waves. The image became widely known—"What German worker does not know the 'cabbage head'?" asked one contemporary—and set a standard of biting political critique that artists have aspired to ever since.[36] More, by specifically partnering with *AIZ,* Heartfield can be counted among those media-savvy artists for whom Marinetti laid the groundwork.

Figures in the News

Raoul Hausmann was deeply invested in the expressive use of typography, as indicated by his *Salomo Friedländer (Mynona)* of 1919, which is a typographic portrait of sorts (pl. 9). Friedländer was a German philosopher and writer, active in Dada circles, who went by the pen name Mynona ("anonym" backwards). His egg-shaped head, protruding ear, and tuft of hair were made from newspaper clippings and fragments of woodcuts and poems snipped from Dada publications.[37] The most prominent of the pasted-on elements are the letters *e Pe,* clipped from the nameplate of the French newspaper *Le Petit Journal* and used to represent the subject's eyes, much as Picasso used an inverted *T* to describe the figure's nose in *Head of a Man* (see p. 117, fig. 2).[38]

A portrait of a very different sort is Arthur Dove's *The Critic* (1925): a damning assessment of the conservative American art critic Royal Cortissoz, who wrote for the *New York Tribune* (pl. 10). Cortissoz never hid his disdain for modernism, which he dubbed "Ellis Island art" and described in terms that were outrageous.[39] Dove cut a paper-doll figure from a review by Cortissoz of paintings by Thomas Eakins, George Luks, and John Singer Sargent. The review extols the work of these artists, reserving special praise for Eakins, whose painting, he writes, is like a rock that "stands up against all the fluctuations of fashion

9

RAOUL HAUSMANN

Salomo Friedländer (Mynona)

1919, newspaper, woodcut, and journal clippings on silver Japanese paper, 10 × 8⅜ (25.5 × 21.2), Collection Merrill C. Berman

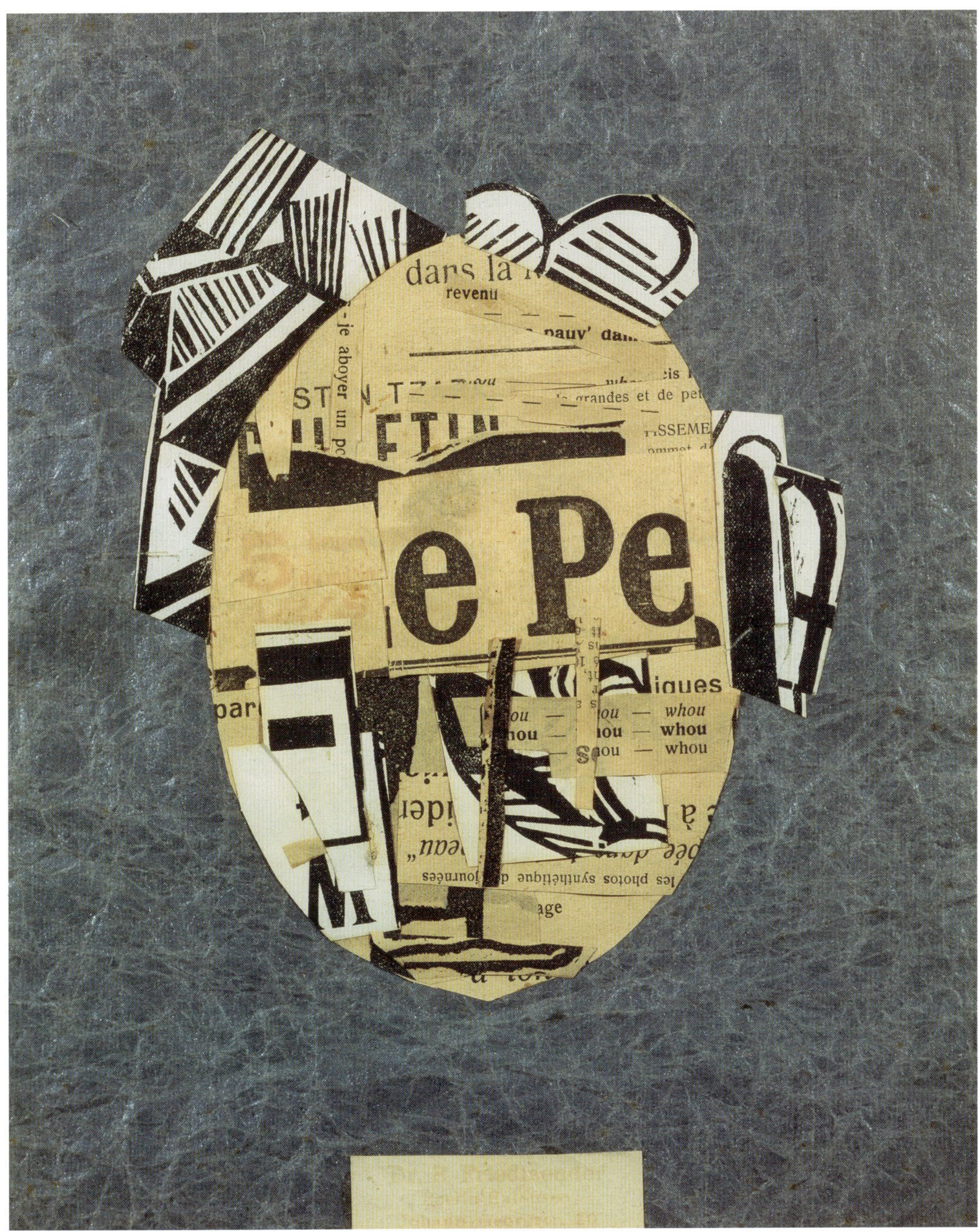

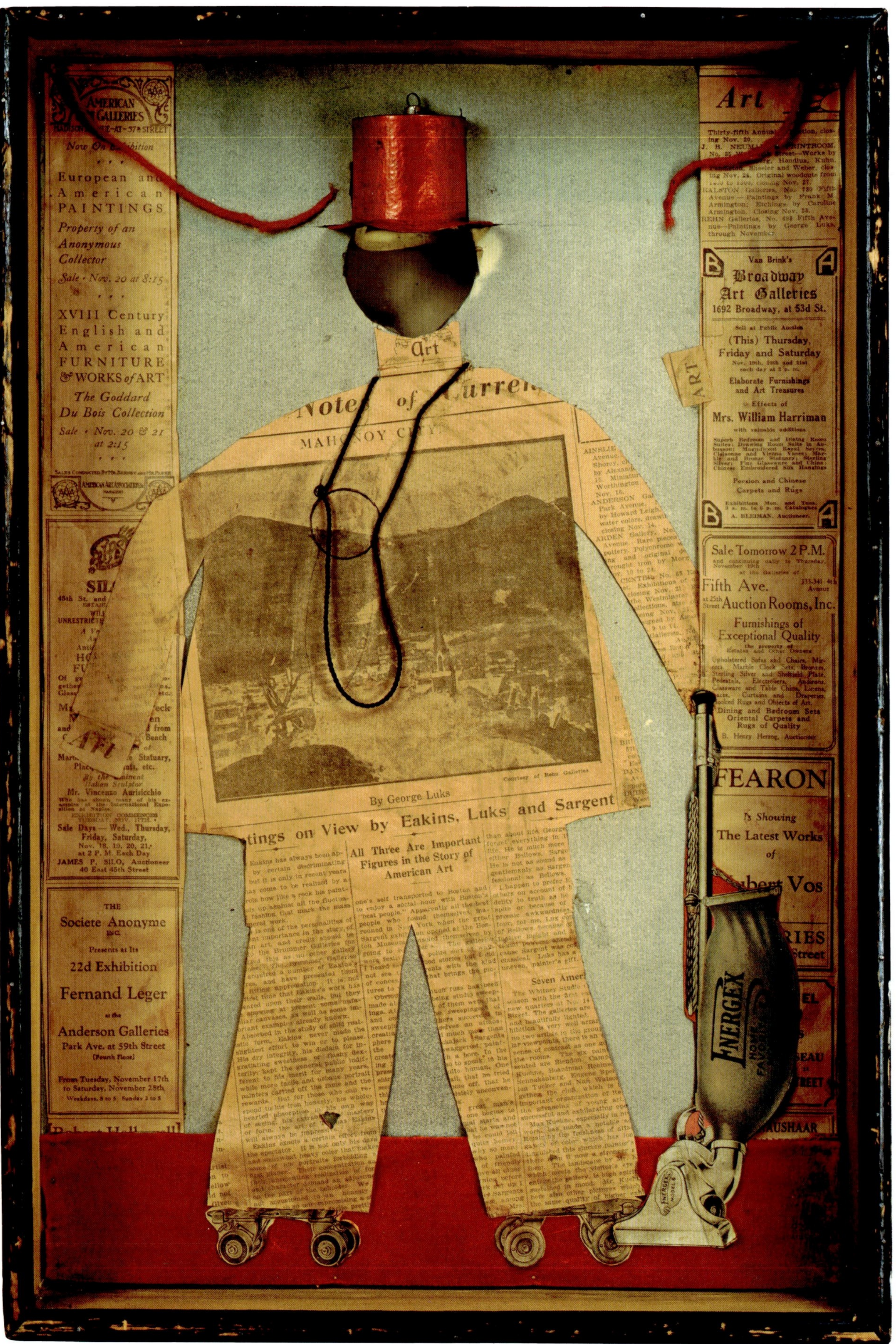

10

ARTHUR DOVE

The Critic

1925, newspaper, paper, commercial ornament, fabric, cord, yarn, watercolor, and graphite on board; artist's frame: 19 ½ × 13 × 2 ¼ (49.5 × 33 × 5.7), Whitney Museum of American Art, New York, Purchase, with funds from the Historic Art Association of the Whitney Museum of American Art, Mr. and Mrs. Morton L. Janklow, the Howard and Jean Lipman Foundation, Inc., and Hannelore Schulhof

FIG. 6 Raoul Hausmann, *Der Kunstkritiker* (The art critic), 1919/1920, photomontage and collage, Tate Collection, Purchased 1974

FIG. 7 Detail from Norman Rockwell, *Freedom from Fear*, 1943, oil on canvas, Norman Rockwell Museum Collections

that mark the mass of ephemeral work." In much the way that Gris drew irony from the article about electoral postering, Dove drew irony from Cortissoz's rebuke of "ephemeral work," making it the centerpiece of a collage composed largely of ephemeral newspaper. He portrays an empty-headed critic, vacuum at hand and wearing roller skates, speeding from gallery to auction house in his campaign to rid the world of modernist waste.

Debra Bricker Balken dissociates Dove from the "anarchy of mainstream Dadaist art," but cites *The Critic* as an exception, noting that it "draws on Dada's ironical and frequently sardonic critiques of contemporary culture."[40] There is an intriguing Dada forerunner to Dove's portrait: Hausmann's photomontage-collage from 1919/1920, *Der Kunstkritiker* (The art critic) (fig. 6). Like Hannah Höch (with whom he was romantically involved in 1915–1922), Hausmann used images snipped from the pages of Berlin's illustrated newspapers. His art critic has an oversized head pasted to an undersized body and holds a suggestively placed pencil in his hand, ready to puncture the reputations of hardworking artists. Could Dove have seen the work? It is unlikely. Could he have felt a stronger tie to Dada than has generally been acknowledged? Quite possibly, yes.

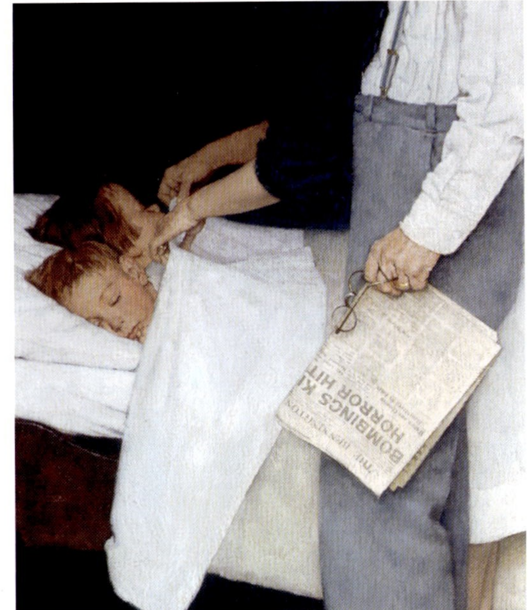

7

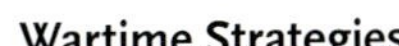

Wartime Strategies

Though one would have expected a global conflict on the magnitude of World War II to generate a flood of newspaper-related art, such was not the case. Newspapers continued to be used as traditional narrative props, as in Norman Rockwell's *Freedom from Fear* of 1943 (fig. 7), but most vanguard artists temporarily abandoned the newspaper as subject and object. Two important exceptions were Hans Richter and Kurt Schwitters. As Germans living in exile, they both had sober responses to the war. Richter took it on like a reporter: asking the questions who, what, when, where, and why, and answering them in the form of a sequence of newspaper articles. Schwitters put himself in the place of a newspaper reader, stunned by what caught his eye and driven to call it to our attention. Their approaches reflect a larger shift that occurred at the time. Faced with the cataclysmic circumstances of the war, most artists adhered to the news and stayed clear of satire.

Hans Richter gave the newspaper a primary role in his nearly sixteen-foot-long scroll-like *Stalingrad (Victory in the East)* (1943–1944), offering

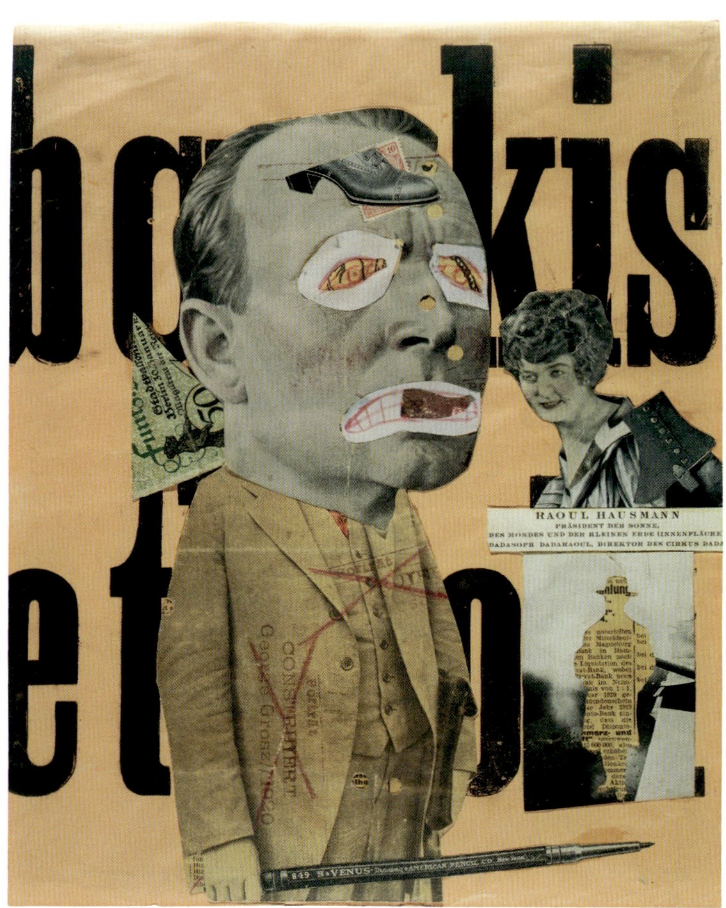

6

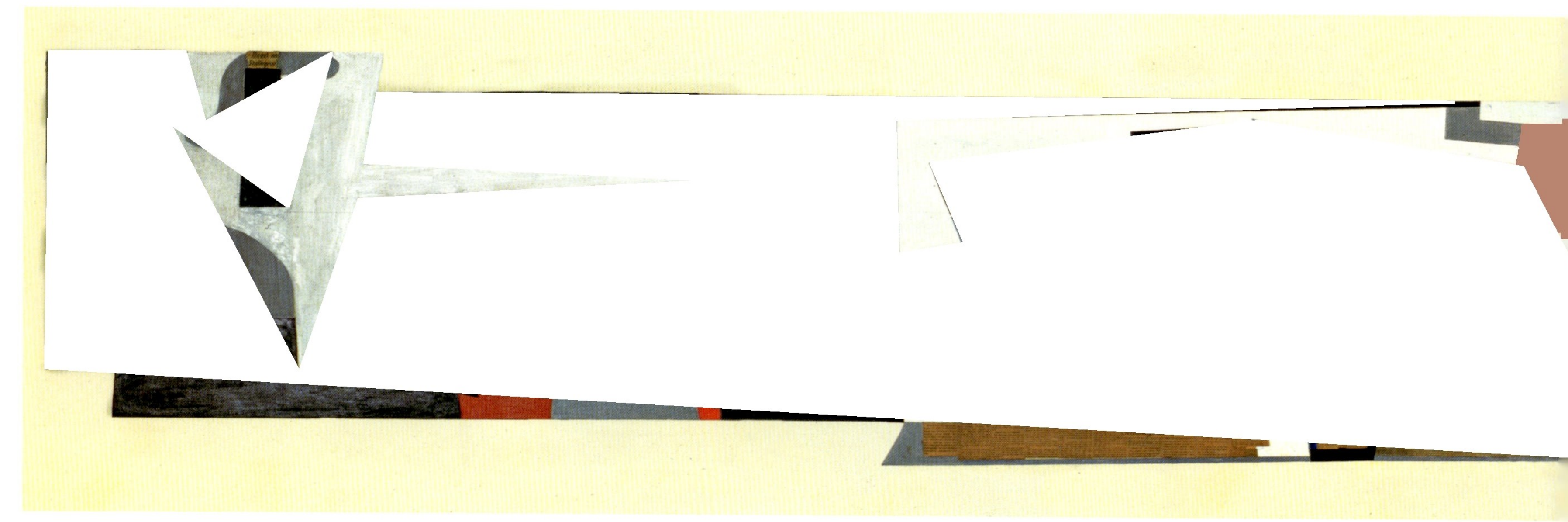

11

HANS RICHTER

Stalingrad (Victory in the East)

1943–1944, oil and newspaper on cloth, 35 ¼ × 188 ⅞ (89.5 × 479.7), Hirshhorn Museum and Sculpture Garden, Smithsonian Institution, Gift of Mrs. Hans Richter, 1976

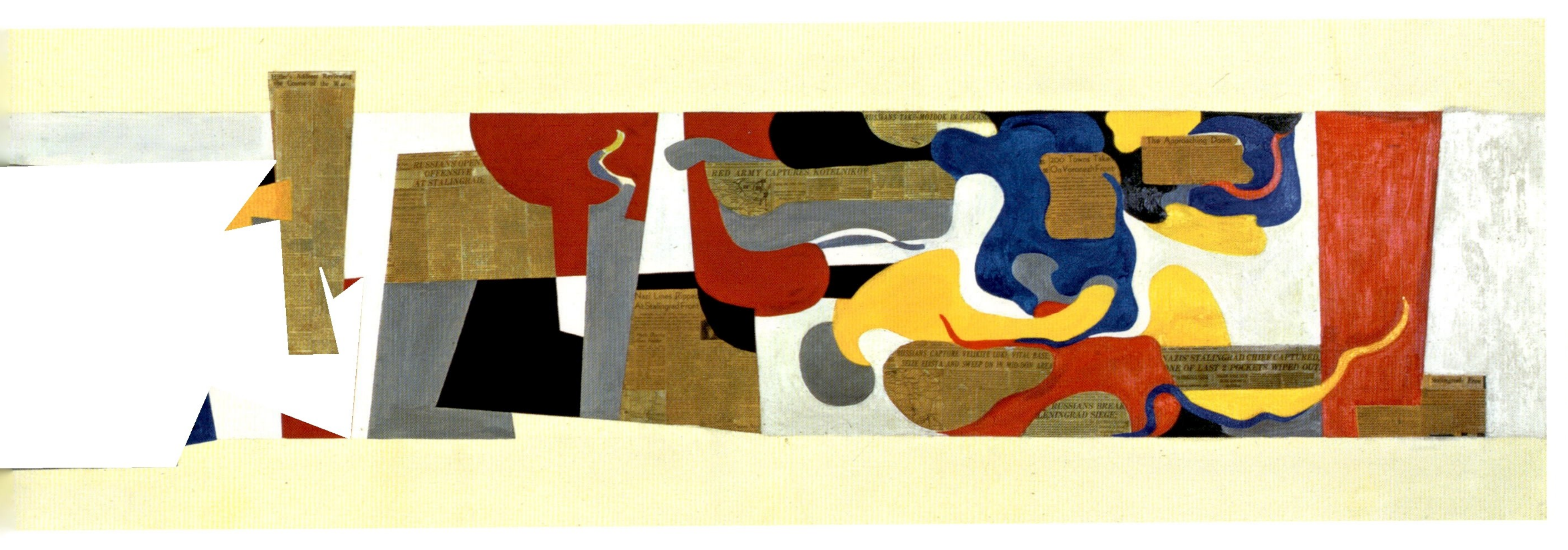
RED ARMY CAPTURES KOTELNIKOV
The Approaching Doom
LENINGRAD SIEGE

viewers a chronological span reading left to right of newspaper articles that trace the Battle of Stalingrad from onset to conclusion (pl. 11).[41] The first article, published on August 26, 1942, bears the headline "Reich Plans Talks to Re-Map Europe" and reports on Germany's plans for "fixing the map of the new Europe." The last article, with the dateline February 3, [1943], bears the headline "Stalingrad Free" and announces that "the Battle of Stalingrad, one of the greatest of the war, ended dramatically yesterday when the Red Army crushed the last desperate German resistance amidst the ruins of the proud Russian bastion on the Volga." Germany's plans for a New Order in the Soviet Union had failed, and as a nearby article suggests ("The Approaching Doom"), the "beginning of the end" of the German Reich was nearing.

The irregular white form at the far left of the composition replicates the map of Europe, but with Germany's territory covered by the "Re-Map Europe" article, which Richter cut into a trapezoid. He positioned a similarly shaped black trapezoid (a stand-in for Germany) on the Russian front. Angular forms that dominate the work's first two-thirds represent the Nazi war machinery, while the last third is taken up with organic forms and exuberant color. In Richter's words: "the straight line of invincible successful 'generals' is swallowed by the people of all colors, by the joy of victory, by the dance of organic curves."[42] So determined was Richter to have people read *Stalingrad*'s newspaper texts that he restructured their layouts, with the result that sentences read continuously rather than being broken at the site of a cut (fig. 8, detail of pl. 11). Nothing was to impede Richter's presentation of the facts. Picasso sometimes preserved a text's readability by cutting along a newsprint column, but Richter's dynamic shapes required painstaking retailoring.

Best known today for his groundbreaking abstract films made with Viking Eggeling, Richter immigrated to the United States in 1941 and became director of the Film Institute of City College in New York. His interest in politically minded art and the universal language of abstraction were joined in *Stalingrad.* So, too, was his experience of living in both Germany and the United States, for the work is a curious merging of Bauhaus aesthetics and American modernism (think Jazz Age Stuart Davis).

Having had his works confiscated and shown in *Entartete Kunst* (the Nazis' "Degenerate Art" exhibition), Kurt Schwitters fled Germany for Norway in 1937, and when that country was invaded in 1940, he immigrated to England, where he remained until his death. Contrary to expectations, Schwitters was not especially engaged with the newspaper. This avid accumulator of ephemera usually favored printed items that evoked the past rather than the insistent "now" of the daily paper. But in a collage from 1944, *Untitled* (*The Hitler Gang*), he used the newspaper to powerful effect (pl. 12). The work includes an advertisement torn from a London newspaper, promoting a Paramount Pictures film, *The Hitler Gang,* then playing at a Leicester Square theater. Amid an assortment of weathered papers, geometric forms, and

FIG. 8 Detail from Hans Richter, *Stalingrad (Victory in the East)*, 1943–1944. See also pl. 11

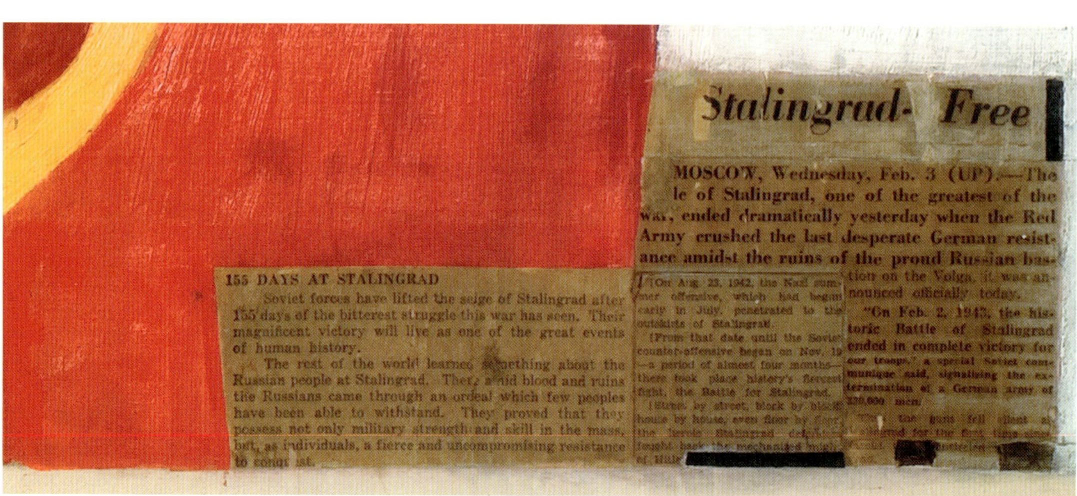

8

12

KURT SCHWITTERS

Untitled (The Hitler Gang)

1944, collage, oil, canvas, cardboard, and pasteboard on paper, 13¾ × 9⅝ (34.8 × 24.6), Kurt and Ernst Schwitters Stiftung, Hannover / The Kurt und Ernst Schwitters Stiftung was founded by the Schwitters family with the support of NORD / LB Norddeutsche Landesbank, the Niedersächsische Sparkassenstiftung (Savings Bank Foundation of Lower Saxony), The Niedersächsische Lottostiftung (The Lottery Foundation of Lower Saxony), the Cultural Foundation of the Federal States, the State Minister at the Federal Chancellery for Media and Cultural Affairs, the Ministry for Science and Culture of the Land of Lower Saxony, and the City of Hannover

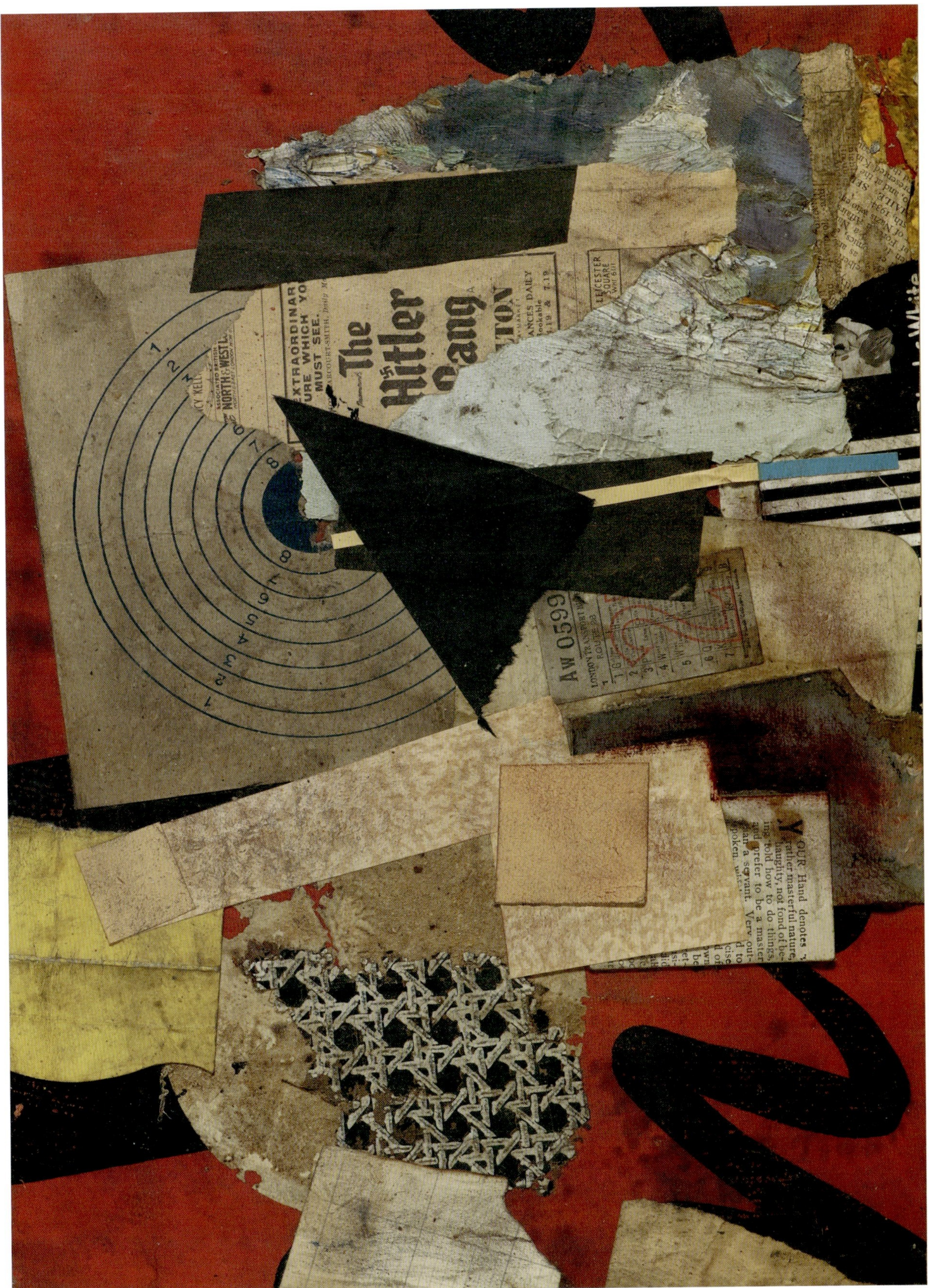

a fragment of imitation chair caning (presumably a nod to Picasso's seminal painting with collage, *Still Life with Chair Caning,* 1912), the word "Hitler," in black-letter type, adds a decisive charge, reinforced by a small swastika that serves as the dot over the *i* in "Hitler." To have the swastika almost normalized—used as a decorative typographical element—heightens the work's chill, as does the sense of how quickly the modern world absorbs history and repackages it as bourgeois entertainment.

Shaded Meanings

Apparently to Picasso's way of thinking, newsprint could double as shading, atmosphere, or even wood grain. Prominent words in the inverted newsprint fragment in *Head of a Man* (1912) register the war in the Balkans (*Armistice, Sofia*), but the lines of type are essentially drained of content value and recast as chalky gray lines (pl. 13).[43] More in play is a three-part variation on a theme, in which rows of mechanically printed type echo a cluster of drawn charcoal lines above and, still higher above, a pattern of painted watercolor lines. The charcoal lines suggest shading or atmosphere while the watercolor lines represent wood grain. Thus words can shift from being read as language to being understood as purely visual signs. Again, there is no fixed interpretation.

The rows of type that run diagonally across Ellsworth Kelly's cutout from 1949, *Head with Beard*, similarly read as chalky gray lines (pl. 14). Intriguingly, Kelly also adopted the almond-shaped eye and mouth used by Picasso in *Head of a Man*. Asked if his use of newspaper at the time had anything to do with the older artist, Kelly stated: "I was deconstructing Picasso, trying to get [him] off my shoulder."[44] More than thirty-five years after Picasso had introduced newspaper into his compositions, even after the shattering effects of World War II, artists were still wrestling with his legacy. Kelly learned from Picasso but went on to create a work of a distinctly different type.

Picasso inverted the newsprint fragment in his *papier collé* whereas Kelly rotated the newspaper more than ninety degrees for his cutout. Surely neither artist wanted viewers to read the papers with their heads strained at a tilt. Why then did they misalign the texts? Presumably to underscore the idea that conventional reading was not the point. One bit of text in Kelly's work, however, does stand out and begs to be read: the headline "H.C. Lytton, 102, Chicago Merchant, Dies."[45] Kelly was a young man when he made the cutout, and for years it has gone by the title *Head with Beard*. But he has recently acknowledged that it was made as a self-portrait, which suggests that his inclusion of an article about the death of a centenarian was meant as a meditation on youth and old age.

Black and Ashen Newspapers

Robert Rauschenberg enrolled at Black Mountain College in North Carolina in 1948, with the express ambition of studying with former Bauhaus instructor Josef Albers. How Rauschenberg was influenced by Albers is hard to gauge. Albers was a demanding teacher, and Rauschenberg was not his favorite student. But it is worth considering whether Rauschenberg's adoption of newspaper as an artistic material was partly owing to his instructor. At the Bauhaus, and later at Black Mountain, Albers regularly assigned projects that required either using newspaper or depicting newsprint. An example is *Contrast Study* (1929/1930) by Eugen Batz, made while Batz was a student at the Bauhaus in Dessau (pl. 15).

At Black Mountain in 1951, Rauschenberg began a series of so-called black paintings that typically incorporate newspaper. The visibility of the newspapers in the black paintings ranges from total obscurity to legibility. Those in *Asheville Citizen* (c. 1952) are legible, although their sideways orientation is not especially conducive to reading (pl. 16). Rauschenberg wanted to demonstrate that a painting "could have the dignity of not calling attention to itself, that it could only be seen if you really looked at it."[46] Accordingly, *Asheville Citizen* demands close looking.

Two full sheets of newspaper occupy nearly half the painting's surface: the August 3, 1951, and March 29, 1952, editions of the *Asheville Citizen*. Their spreads include an article about a high-stakes dice game involving Senator Joseph

13

PABLO PICASSO

Head of a Man

1912, charcoal, newspaper, colored paper, and hand-painted faux bois paper on paper, 24⅝ × 18½ (62.5 × 47), Private collection

In this *papier collé*, Picasso was more focused on the newspaper's formal qualities than its reading potential; otherwise, he would not have turned the newsprint fragment upside down. He evidently adhered the fragment before adding lines and shading in charcoal, using the newsprint's format as a kind of blueprint for the composition as a whole. The newsprint's blank lines (the thin horizontal and vertical spaces devoid of text) are loosely echoed in the charcoal-drawn, scaffoldlike pattern at lower right and reverberate elsewhere in the artwork.

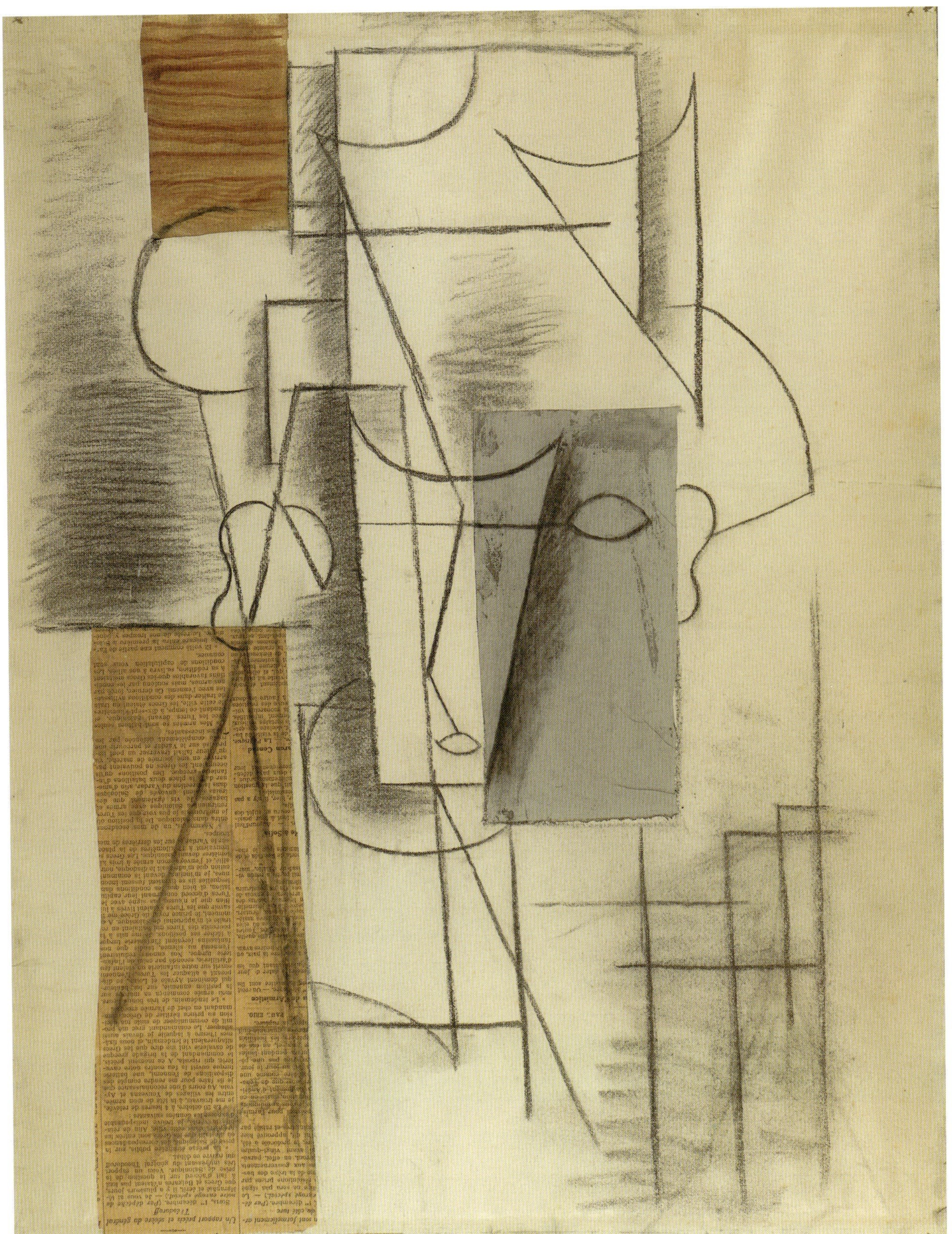

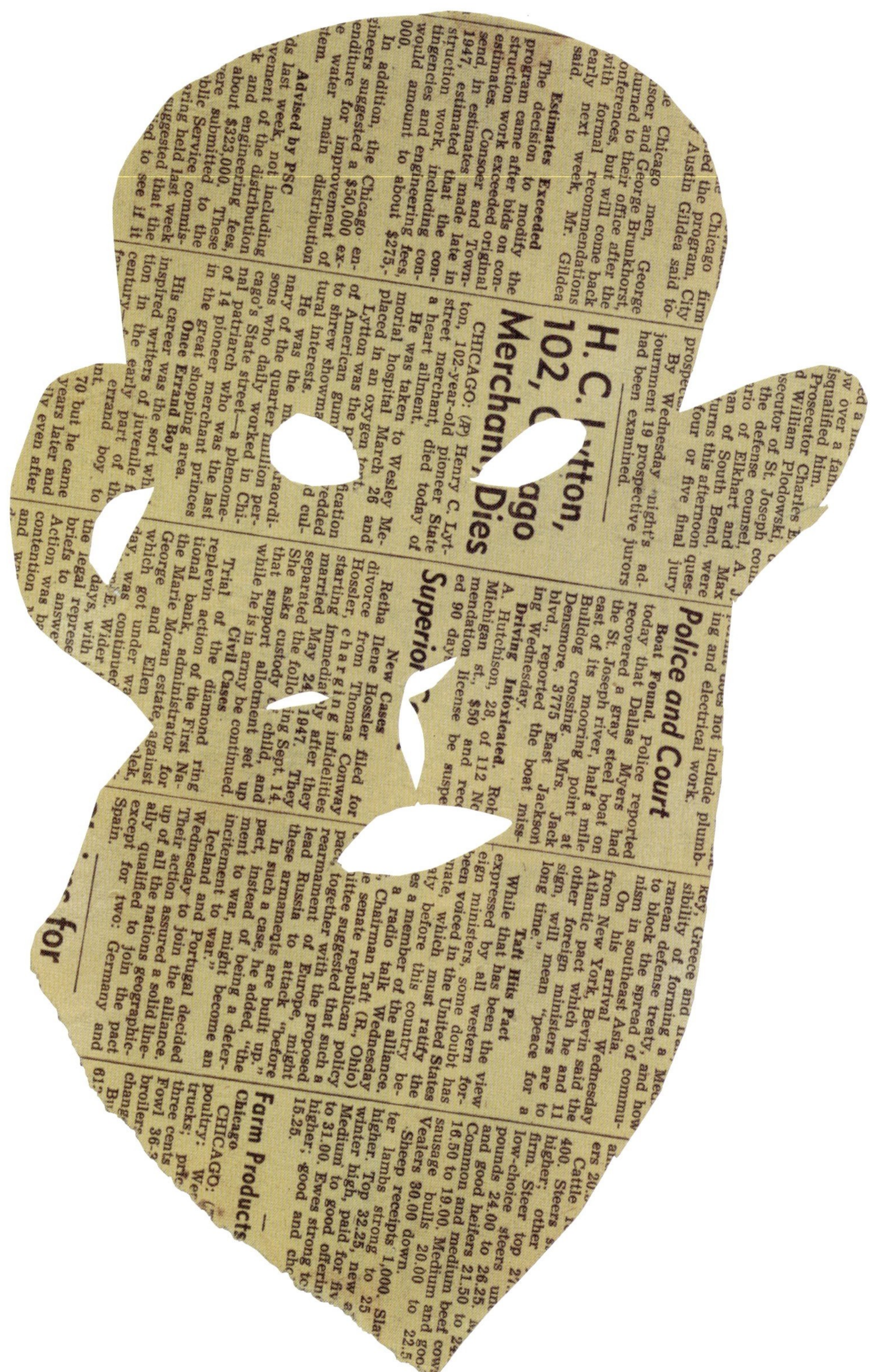

14

ELLSWORTH KELLY

Head with Beard

1949, newspaper cutout, 10 ¼ × 6 ¼ (26 × 15.9), Collection of the artist

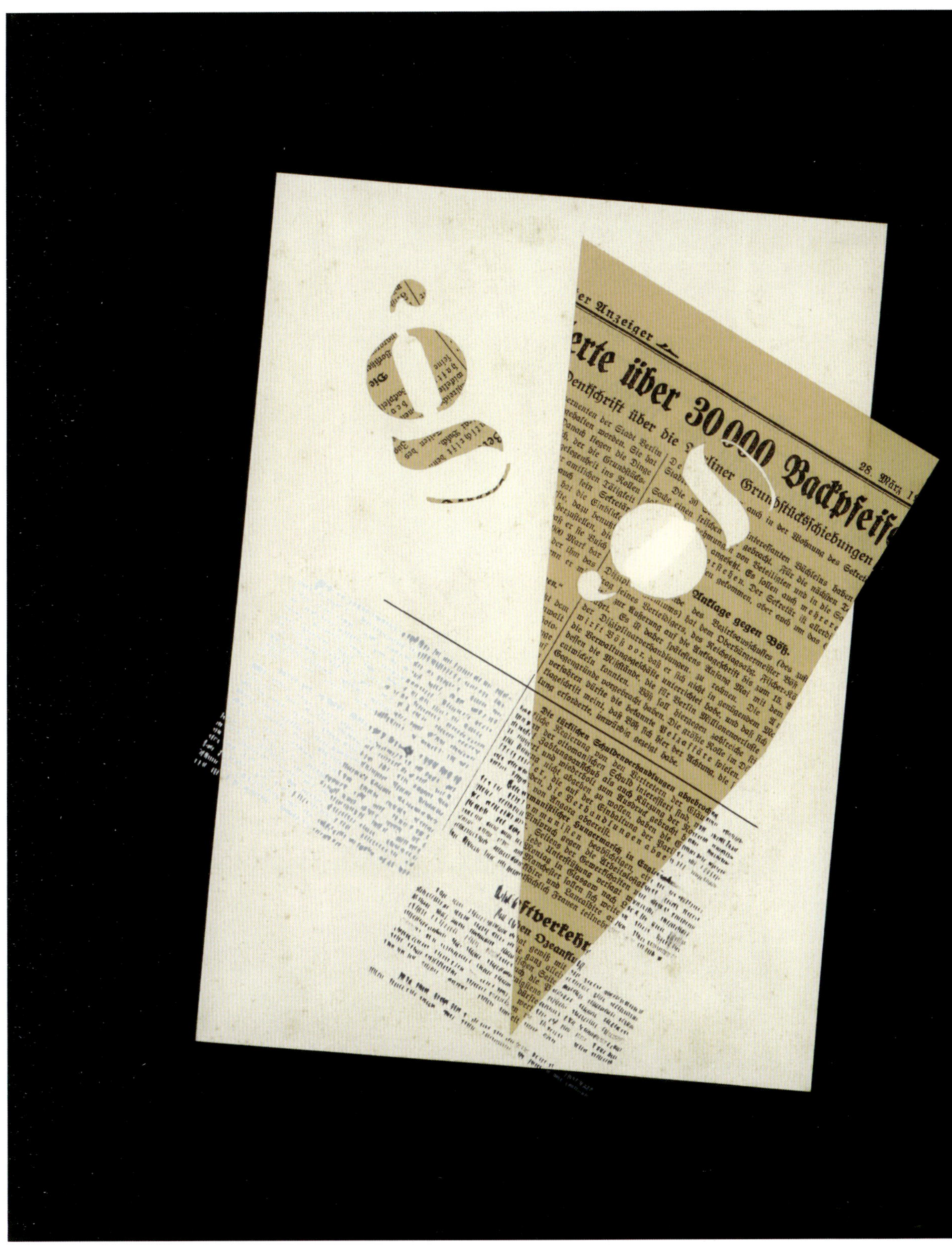

15

EUGEN BATZ

Contrast Study

1929/1930, newspaper, gouache, and white paper on black paper, 16¾ × 13 (42.5 × 32.9), Bauhaus-Archiv Berlin

---

Made for Josef Albers' *Vorkurs* (preliminary course) at the Bauhaus, Batz's *Contrast Study* not only incorporated newspaper but simulated newsprint text by making tiny dash marks in black and gray ink. His choice of the letter *g* (excised from the newspaper and adhered to its left) may not have been arbitrary but may allude to the first name of Gustav Böss, mayor of Berlin, who resigned amid scandal in 1929. The triangular segment of newspaper in *Contrast Study* features an article about Böss and his dealings with the Sklarek brothers, Jewish clothing merchants who bribed city officials by offering them bargains such as fur coats sold for a fraction of the actual cost—a bargain that cost the mayor his political career.

16

ROBERT RAUSCHENBERG

Asheville Citizen

c. 1952, oil and newspaper on canvas (two panels), 74 × 28 ½ (188 × 72.4), The Museum of Modern Art, New York, Purchase, 1999

17

JOHN CAGE

Eninka 22

1986, burned, smoked, and branded Japanese Gampi paper mounted on paper (unique impression), 25 ¼ × 18 ⅞ (64.1 × 47.9), Collection of Ryo Toyonaga and Alvin Friedman-Kien

McCarthy; a report on a local citizen being drafted into the Marine Corps; announcements of wrestling matches and gospel singing; a picture of the Whittier Elementary School basketball team; and the daily crossword, which establishes a uniform grid within the newspaper's overall gridlike format.[47] A real estate listing "For Colored" ("JUST what you've been waiting for" reads the promotion) might draw our attention today, but few would have batted an eye in 1952, particularly in the South.

Spanning the two panels' divide at the far right, "WANT SOMETHING GOOD?" stands out in black type. Even placed at a ninety-degree angle, the phrase is clearly visible. It must have caught Rauschenberg's eye and appealed to his sense of humor, as if the abstruse painting, in need of explanation or Madison Avenue hype, was promoting itself—not only as something we should want but as an example of "good" art.

An interviewer once asked Rauschenberg's mentor, John Cage, if there was a connection between the younger artist's black paintings and his own use of burned newsprint in a 1986 series. To the interviewer's eyes, the black paintings had an "oily smoked effect" as if they were "burnt." Cage warmly praised them ("I love those works"), but as to whether the black paintings were an influence, his response was: "not consciously."[48]

Eninka 22 from the 1986 series (pl. 17) was made by placing a number of crumpled newspaper pages (a number determined by chance operations) on top of a press bed, igniting the newspaper, and next laying a dampened sheet of Japanese Gampi paper over the burning pages. The burning newspaper and Gampi were then run through the press. The flames were extinguished in the process and traces from the newspaper offset onto the Gampi. Subsequently, the Gampi was mounted to a sheet of handmade paper and branded with an iron ring, its placement and temperature also determined by chance operations.

The procedure was repeated, resulting in an edition of fifty unique prints. Some sustained burn holes and scorch marks; others remained intact. Some were receptive to the newspaper's ink; others less so. *Eninka 22* (*eninka* has been translated as circle/stamp/fire in Japanese) remained largely intact, toned by smoke, and crisply marked by newsprint.[49] We can make out a few letters and even a few words, but for all practical purposes—and by chance—the newspaper's reporting function was invalidated.

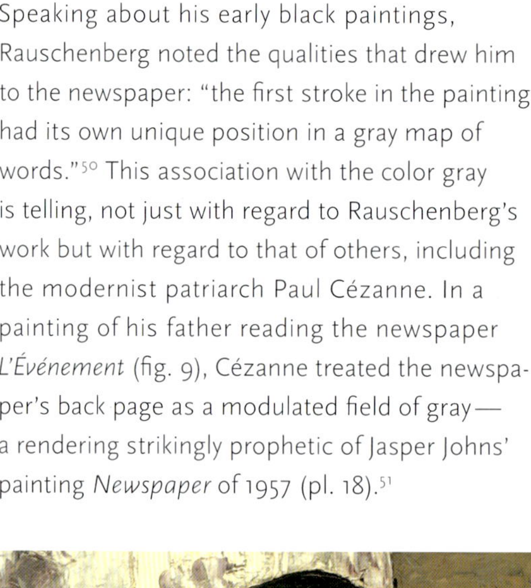

Gray Newspapers

Speaking about his early black paintings, Rauschenberg noted the qualities that drew him to the newspaper: "the first stroke in the painting had its own unique position in a gray map of words."[50] This association with the color gray is telling, not just with regard to Rauschenberg's work but with regard to that of others, including the modernist patriarch Paul Cézanne. In a painting of his father reading the newspaper *L'Événement* (fig. 9), Cézanne treated the newspaper's back page as a modulated field of gray—a rendering strikingly prophetic of Jasper Johns' painting *Newspaper* of 1957 (pl. 18).[51]

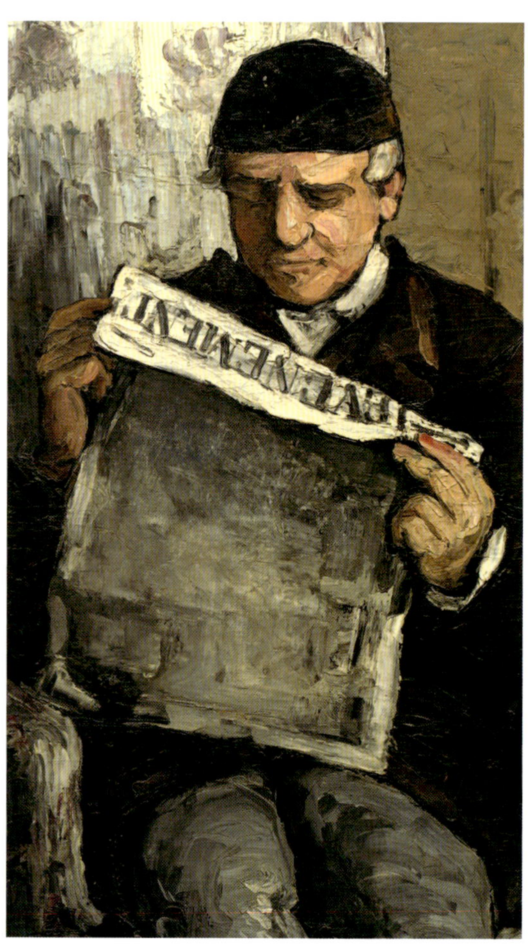

9

FIG. 9 Detail from Paul Cézanne, *The Artist's Father, Reading* L'Événement, 1866, oil on canvas, National Gallery of Art, Washington, Collection of Mr. and Mrs. Paul Mellon, 1970

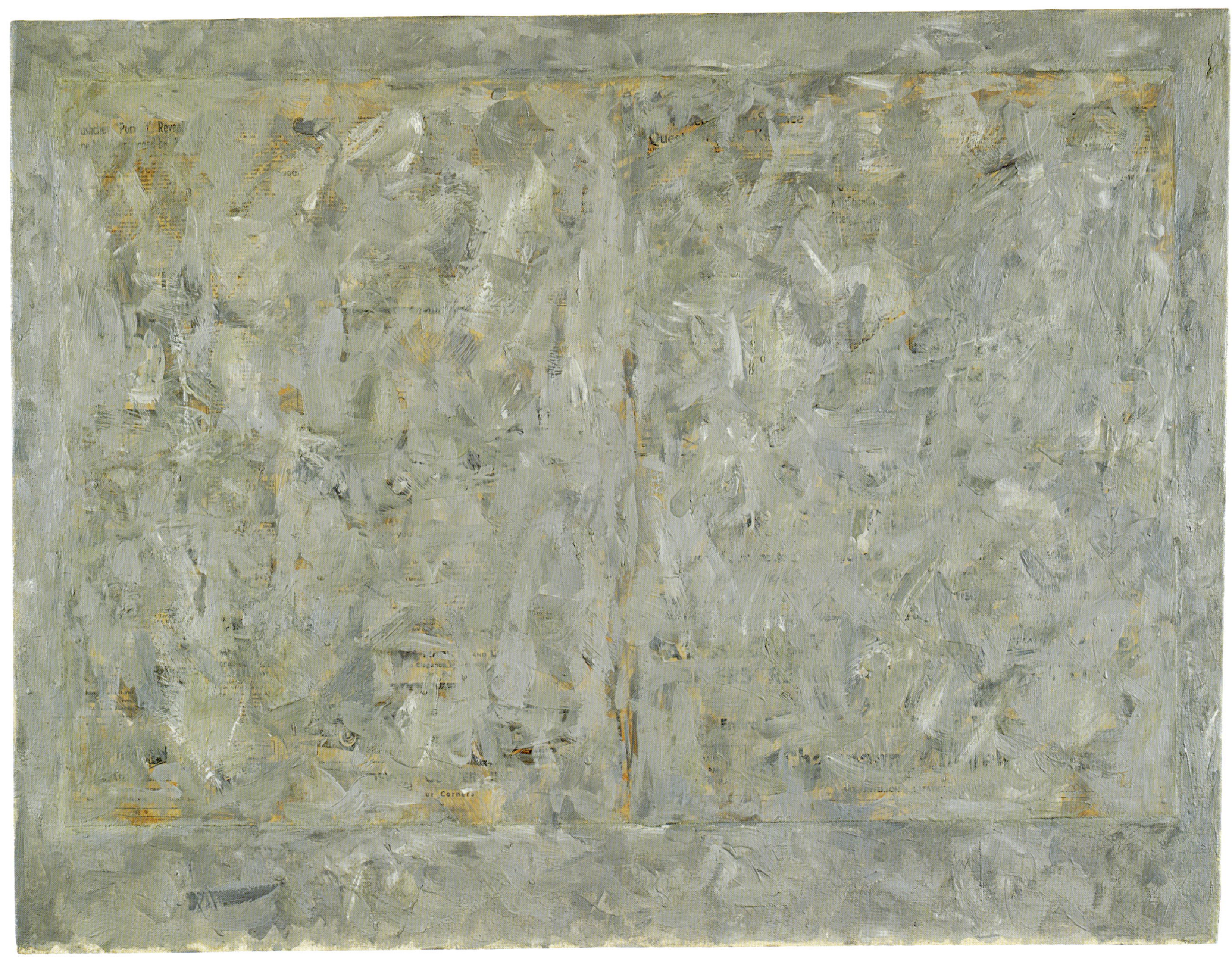

18

JASPER JOHNS

Newspaper

1957, encaustic and newspaper on canvas, 27 × 36 (68.6 × 91.4), Private collection

Johns embedded a double-page spread in *Newspaper,* deliberately emphasizing its central fold—the axis of the two pages, if you will—by applying vertical brushstrokes that run counter to the painting's dominant multi-directional strokes.[52] Johns has a penchant for things that are hinged and can pivot: for example, the wooden flaps that conceal or expose the nine anatomical fragments in his *Target with Plaster Casts* (1955).[53] He also has a penchant for dividing works down the center, either with a device, such as a wooden slat or broom, or through the use of two adjacent or conjoined panels. A line down the center can suggest a crease or a fold—and with the idea of the fold comes the notion of one side impressing itself onto the other, a doubling of sorts and a very Johnsian strategy.

The idea of pressing or touching is reified in many of Johns' works—his Skin drawings, for example, made by impressing (and imprinting) his face and the palms of his hands onto paper. The reference to touch in *Newspaper* is more discreet. Touch is indicated in the paint strokes that sensuously press up against the newspaper's ragged bottom edge, as if fingering it—intriguingly bringing us back to the painting by Cézanne—his father fingering the edges of *L'Événement* as he holds the paper upright. Johns was receptive to the tactile aspect of the newspaper, apparently as was Cézanne.

James Meyer writes that "gray was more appropriate for a 'conceptual' art; it stimulated vision the least. Perceptually inert, it did not occlude the presentation of ideas."[54] Cézanne's and Johns' gray newspapers are far from perceptually inert. But the gray in Robert Morris' *Crisis* (*Act of War: Cuba*) of 1962 operates as Meyer describes (pl. 19). Morris nearly obliterated a double-page spread of the *New York Mirror* with swathes of watery gray paint, exercising about as much artistry as a subpar housepainter. For Morris, artistry was not the point. And what seems to be a gray picture lacking in painterly quality and devoid of content turns out to be more than that. At the upper right, a headline dimly emerges: "WE BLOCKADE CUBA WITH 40 WARSHIPS." The newspaper was published at the height of the Cuban Missile Crisis, on October 23, 1962. Was Morris' defacement of the paper meant as a rejection of Cold War politics? Was the looming threat of mutually assured destruction simply too hideous to confront? Or was he alerting us to a credibility gap—that the information being fed to the press by the administration was untrustworthy? By the close of the decade, Morris would state that his "first principle for political action, as well as art action, is denial and negation."[55] In fact, Morris called a one-man strike in 1970, closing down his solo exhibition at the Whitney Museum of American Art weeks ahead of schedule, roused by profoundly troubling events following the exhibition's opening on April 9: the United States' bombing of Cambodia on April 29; the National Guard's killing of four students at Kent State University on May 4; and, on a local level, New York construction workers' attack on antiwar protesters (the so-called Hard Hat Riot) on May 8.[56]

Despite their shared grayness, reliance on newspaper, and superficial visual likeness, these works by Johns and Morris are radically different. Whereas Johns embalmed the newspaper in waxy encaustic, as if to seal and preserve its high-art status, Morris nearly drowned it in gray paint, as if to repudiate it and any potential for "artistic" beauty.

It is hard to imagine either Johns or Morris taking up the newspaper as a challenge to artistic norms. Some fifty years after Picasso's use of newspaper as a material in his *papiers collés,* far from being a transgressive choice, it was historically grounded, perhaps not with the pedigree of ancient encaustic but well beyond the point of causing a fuss.

Newsmakers

Zola's monopolization of the front page of *L'Aurore* and Marinetti's commandeering of the *premier-Paris* in *Le Figaro* opened the way for visual artists to get into the act—not in the form of traditional illustration but in launching papers of their own. Man Ray's *The Ridgefield Gazook,* a four-page newspaper issued once, on March 31, 1915, exemplifies the humor that underlies many artists' newspapers (fig. 10). It features a zany assortment of puns and drawings aimed both at the art world and at newspapers in general. Its front page spotlights two insects copulating,

19

ROBERT MORRIS

Crisis (Act of War: Cuba)

1962, paint on newspaper,
15 ¼ × 21 ½ (38.7 × 55),
Collection of the artist,
courtesy Leo Castelli Gallery

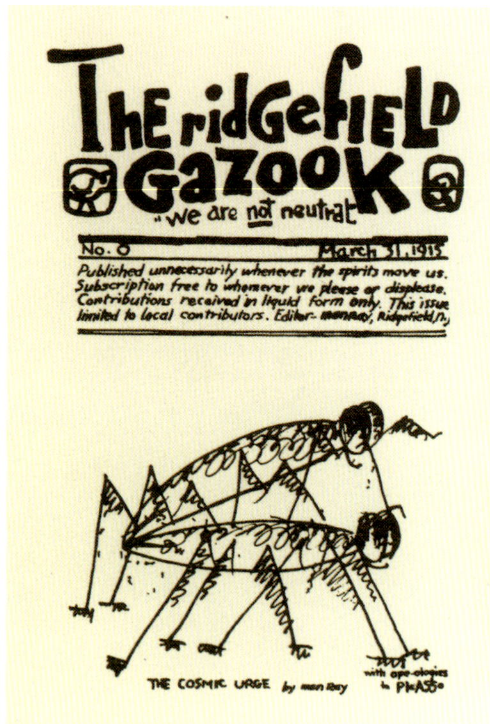
THE RIDGEFIELD GAZOOK
"We are not neutral"
No. 0 March 31, 1915
Published unnecessarily whenever the spirits move us. Subscription free to whomever we please or displease. Contributions received in liquid form only. This issue limited to local contributors. Editor- manray, Ridgefield, N.
THE COSMIC URGE by man Ray
with ape-ologies to PICASSo

10

FIG. 10 Man Ray, *The Ridgefield Gazook*, March 31, 1915

inscribed: "with ape-ologies to PICASSo."[57] Beneath the masthead, Man Ray outlined the paper's program and expectations: "Published unnecessarily whenever the spirits move us. Subscription free to whomever we please or displease. Contributions received in liquid form only."

Bloom-Zeitung (Bloom newspaper) (1963) exhibits a similar zaniness (pl. 20). Conceived by the German artists Bazon Brock, Bernhard Jäger, and Thomas Bayerle, *Bloom-Zeitung* is best characterized as a newspaper intervention. It is an after-the-fact reworking of the April 8, 1963, edition of Germany's popular tabloid *Bild-Zeitung*. The artists substituted the name "Bloom"—the everyman of James Joyce's *Ulysses*—in place of many hundreds, if not thousands, of words in the tabloid's pages. The doctored newspaper ends up being so Bloom-centric that most items surrender their original meaning and become nonsensical. *Bloom-Zeitung* was distributed in Frankfurt, free of charge, on the eve of June 16, the day (in 1904) chronicled in Joyce's *Ulysses* and celebrated annually as Bloomsday.[58]

The *Gazook*'s nod to Picasso was more like a disclaimer, letting it be known that anything like the high art of Picasso would not be found on its pages. *Bloom-Zeitung*'s tribute to Joyce approximated an acknowledgment of the futility of equaling his brilliant wordplay. Throwing up their hands, the artists who conceived *Bloom-Zeitung* staged an antitribute predicated on wordplay taken to the absurd. The scheme did not sit well with the victimized newspaper. Frankfurt police hauled Bazon Brock's dealer in for questioning after staff at *Bild-Zeitung* alerted authorities to the production of knockoffs of the "original" tabloid.[59]

Bloom-Zeitung was one of a spate of newspapers produced in the 1960s, which fall into the category of "faux" or "mock" papers. A precursor was the four-page *Dali News* (1945), the brainchild of Salvador Dalí, who issued two editions of the paper: one in November 1945 and the other in November 1947 (pl. 21). Unlike Man Ray's *Gazook*, which would never be mistaken for a standard newspaper, the *Dali News* could pass for one, at least momentarily. No stranger to self-promotion, Dalí more than matched Marinetti's flair for publicity, as demonstrated in the oversized headline, "EXTRA! Dali Triumphs in Apotheose of Homerus," a reference to his painting *The Apotheosis of Homer*, pictured on an inside page.[60] The subject of that painting—the poet Homer's elevation to divine status—was an apt theme for the egomaniacal Dalí, who filled the paper with items devoted to himself. Even the page 1 article, "Richard Wagner Reported Killed," was self-serving. In a review of "Mad Tristan," a ballet inspired by Wagner's *Tristan und Isolde*, for which Dalí designed the sets and costumes, the dance critic for the *New York Times* had referred to the painter's "deliberate attempt at iconoclasm."[61] Dalí was outraged, avowing in the article that he was not an iconoclast ("I am all for images and not against them") and, furthermore, that the report of Wagner's "killing" was both exaggerated and false.

The self-promotion that fueled Dalí's paper is likewise apparent in Yves Klein's *Dimanche—Le journal d'un seul jour* (Sunday—The newspaper for a single day) of 1960 (pl. 22). Modeled on the Sunday edition of *France-Soir*, Klein's four-page paper was devoted to such widely diverse topics as the theater, the void, color, and judo. The common denominator was that all of the

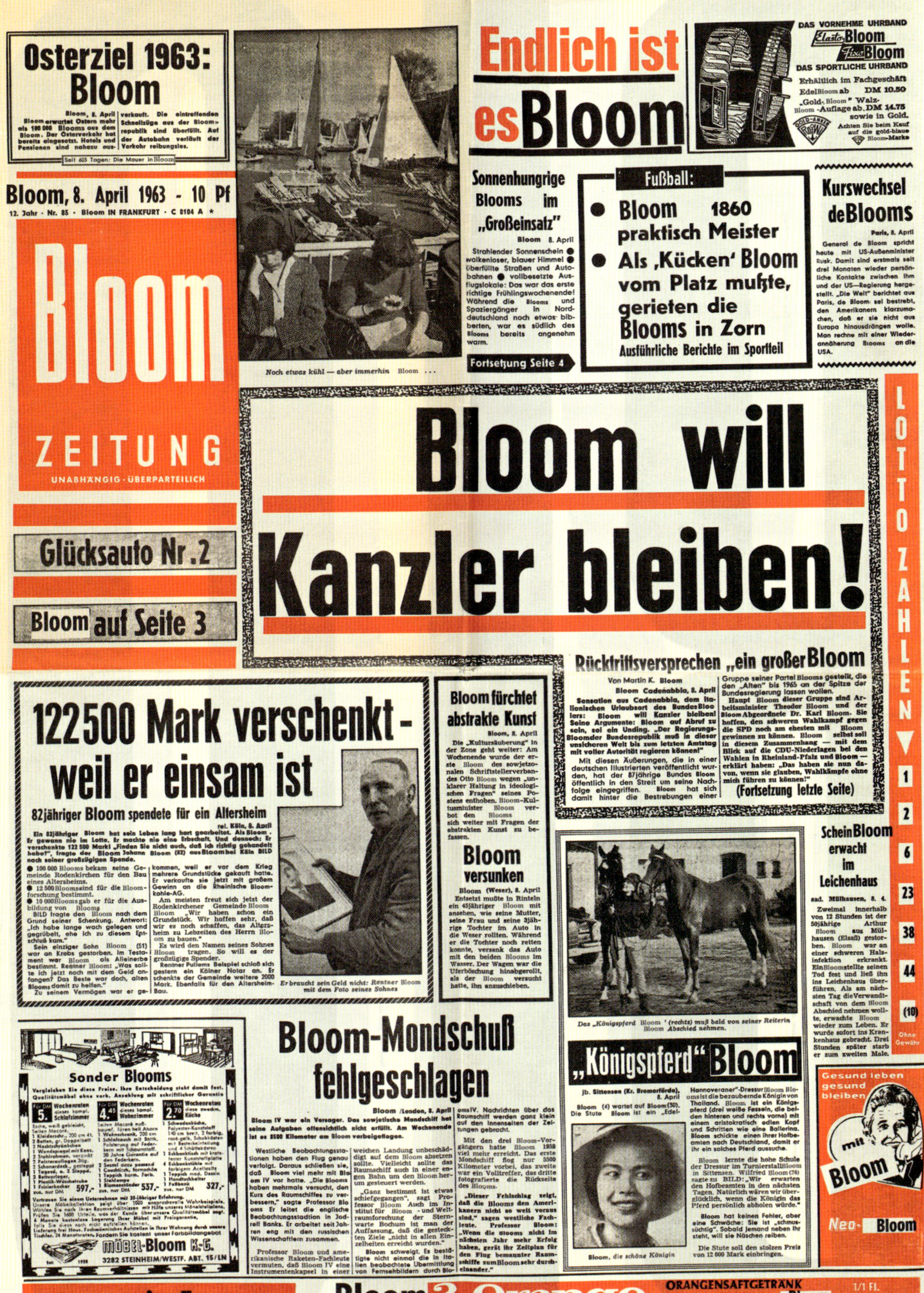

Osterziel 1963: Bloom

Seit 605 Tagen: Die Mauer in Bloom

Bloom, 8. April 1963 - 10 Pf

12. Jahr - Nr. 85 - Bloom IN FRANKFURT - C 8184 A

Bloom ZEITUNG

UNABHÄNGIG · ÜBERPARTEILICH

Glücksauto Nr. 2

Bloom auf Seite 3

Noch etwas kühl — aber immerhin Bloom ...

Endlich ist es Bloom

DAS VORNEHME UHRBAND Elasta-Bloom Flex-Bloom DAS SPORTLICHE UHRBAND

Erhältlich im Fachgeschäft Edelbloom ab DM 10.50

„Gold-Bloom" Walz-Bloom-Auflage ab DM 14.75 sowie in Gold.

Achten Sie beim Kauf auf die gold-blaue Bloom-Marke

Sonnenhungrige Blooms im „Großeinsatz"

Bloom 8. April

Strahlender Sonnenschein ● wolkenloser, blauer Himmel ● überfüllte Straßen und Autobahnen ● vollbesetzte Ausflugslokale: Das war das erste richtige Frühlingswochenende! Während die Blooms und Spaziergänger in Norddeutschland noch etwas bibberten, war es südlich des Blooms bereits angenehm warm.

Fortsetzung Seite 4

Fußball:

● Bloom 1860 praktisch Meister

● Als „Kücken" Bloom vom Platz mußte, gerieten die Blooms in Zorn

Ausführliche Berichte im Sportteil

Kurswechsel de Blooms

Paris, 8. April

Bloom will Kanzler bleiben!

LOTTOZAHLEN 1 2 6 23 38 44 (10) Ohne Gewähr

Rücktrittsversprechen „ein großer Bloom"

Von Martin K. Bloom

(Fortsetzung letzte Seite)

122500 Mark verschenkt - weil er einsam ist

82jähriger Bloom spendete für ein Altersheim

Er braucht sein Geld nicht: Rentner Bloom mit dem Foto seines Sohnes

Bloom fürchtet abstrakte Kunst

Bloom versunken

Schein Bloom erwacht im Leichenhaus

Das „Königspferd" Bloom (rechts) muß bald von seiner Reiterin Bloom Abschied nehmen.

„Königspferd" Bloom

Bloom, die schöne Königin

Sonder Blooms

MÖBEL-Bloom K.G. 3282 STEINHEIM/WESTF. ABT. 15/LN

Bloom-Mondschuß fehlgeschlagen

Gesund leben gesund bleiben mit Bloom

Neo-Bloom

Besser in Form mit Bloom 3-Orange ORANGENSAFTGETRÄNK MIT NATÜRLICHEM Bloom 1/1 Fl. DM 1.30

20

BAZON BROCK, BERNHARD JÄGER, AND THOMAS BAYERLE

Bloom-Zeitung *(Bloom newspaper)*

1963, offset lithograph, 22 ½ × 29 ½ (57.2 × 75), National Gallery of Art, Washington

21

SALVADOR DALÍ

Dali News

November 20, 1945, offset lithograph, 24 × 18 (61 × 45.7), The Dalí Museum, Saint Petersburg, Florida

See on page 4 an article censored by Salvador Dali

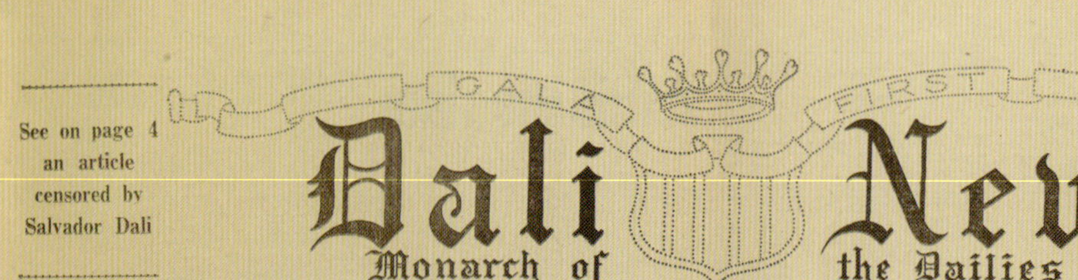

PRICE 25 Cts.

VOL. I. NO. 1. NEW YORK, TUESDAY, NOVEMBER 20, 1945.

EXTRA!

BULLETIN

DALI LAUNCHES HIS WINTER OFFENSIVE

New York, November 20. – Salvador Dali opens his Exhibition this afternoon at 4:00 at the Bignou Galleries – 32 East 57th Street.

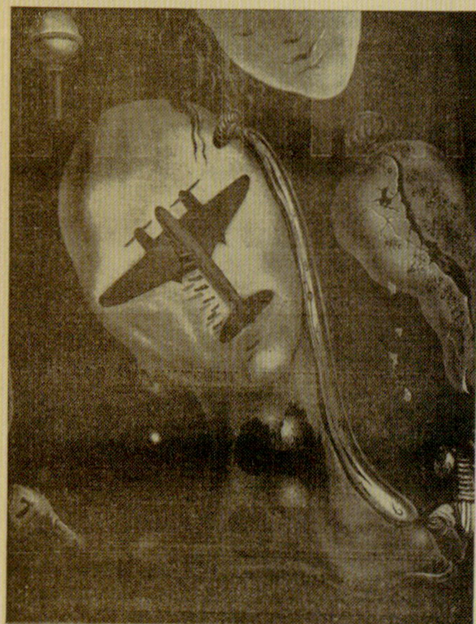

ATOMICA MELANCHOLICA
Recent painting by Salvador Dali.

DALI TRIUMPHS IN APOTHEOSE OF HOMERUS

RICHARD WAGNER REPORTED KILLED

Mad Tristan — Butchered or glorified Wagner?

I have never found in my life anything heavier and more difficult to stir than a choreograph. Nevertheless, I have already supported the weight of five ballets. "Bacchanale", with Wagner's music, Apotheosis of the Crutches, Siren with the Head of a Fish, Louis II of Bavaria falling dead in the center of four lugubrious umbrellas planted in the earth, and which, opening all four at a time synchronized to the collapse of the body, provoked the enthusiasm of the public. It was one of my quite good theatrical ideas. John Martin, critic of the New York Times liked "Bacchanale". I also, even though being in Paris at that time, I never saw it. My ballet, "Labyrinth", with Schumann's music, too confused and improvised, notwithstanding the sensational costume of a cock. John Martin did not like it. Neither did I. "Cafe de Chinitas" with music by Garcia Lorca. Triumph of the patron of the theatre, Marquis de Cuevas; the most brilliant moment of the lamented Argentinita. A gigantic guitar-woman bleeding, crucified against the eternal Spanish wall of the "Fusilamiento de Torrijos". Around the sides of the stage, 1,000 saffron-colored guitars. Everyone adored "Café de Chinitas", John Martin included. The "Coloque Sentimental" arrived, and New Yorkers regaled themselves with a backdrop representing 6,000 bearded cyclists balancing heavy stones on their heads and drawing along majestically, some death shrouds, others wedding veils... I don't remember what John Martin said about it, but the critic of **Sunday issue of "The New** York Times", Nov. 5, said:

The week's sensational backdrop was provided by Salvador Dali, and New York had its first glimpse of this rara avis on Monday night when Ballet International opened in Columbus Circle with all the glamour that attaches to gala events of this kind. It was a lavish and scintillan occasion.

Writing about ballet itself

(Continued on page 3.)

YVES KLEIN PRÉSENTE :
LE DIMANCHE 27 NOVEMBRE
1960

NUMÉRO UNIQUE

FESTIVAL D'ART D'AVANT-GARDE
NOVEMBRE - DÉCEMBRE 1960

La Révolution bleue continue

SEANCE DE 0 HEURE A 24 HEURES

Dimanche

27 NOVEMBRE

Le journal d'un seul jour

0,35 NF (35 fr.) Algérie : 0,30 NF (30 fr.) - Tunisie : 27 mil. Maroc : 32 f m. - Italie : 50 lires - Espagne : 3 pes. 5

THEATRE DU VIDE

Le théâtre se cherche depuis toujours ; il se cherche depuis le début perdu.

Le grand théâtre, c'est l'Eden en fait ; l'important est d'établir une bonne fois nos positions statiques, chacun d'une manière individuelle et non plus personnelle dans l'univers. Depuis longtemps déjà j'annonce partout que je suis le peintre... Je n'en connais pas d'autre aujourd'hui ! Je tiens à dire aussi : « Je suis l'acteur, je suis le compositeur, l'architecte, le sculpteur. » Je tiens à dire : « Je suis. » L'on m'objectera sans doute que cela a déjà été hurlé de toutes sortes de manières variées ; c'est certainement juste. Par conséquent, je répète peut-être cela, mais conscient, bien conscient d'avoir atteint le droit de le dire : et voilà que, pour moi comme pour tous, il n'y a plus rien à faire ; le théâtre officiel, aujourd'hui, c'est « être » et je « suis » bien effectivement tout ce que l'on veut bien que je « sois » et même tout ce que l'on ne veut pas que je « sois » ! J'atteindrai même à ne plus « être » du tout un jour !... Mais, que l'on ne s'y trompe pas : il ne s'agit pas de moi quand je dis je, moi, mon, etc.

C'est parce que l'esprit dans lequel je vis est un esprit d'émerveillement, stabilisé et continu, un esprit classique, que je n'ai aucun caractère d'avant-garde, de cette avant-garde qui, elle, vieillit si vite, de génération en génération.

Mon art n'appartiendra pas à l'époque, pas plus que l'art de tous les grands classiques n'a appartenu aux époques où ils ont vécu, parce que je cherche avant tout, comme eux, à créer dans mes réalisations cette « transparence », ce « vide » incommensurable dans lequel vit l'esprit permanent et absolu délivré de toutes dimensions !

Non, je ne me laisse pas prendre à mon propre jeu en parlant aujourd'hui d'un théâtre du vide avec un tel avant-propos orgueilleux, égocentrique et même vaniteux sans doute en apparence : mon théâtre prendra une valeur universelle dans la mesure même où mes compagnons connaîtront mieux ma pensée que moi-même je ne la connais, car s'ils sont des milliers, ils la refléteront des milliers de fois alors que moi je suis seul.

★

Je me rends très bien compte que je me présente, tout seul, en écrivant ces lignes avec ce qui semblerait une sorte de complexe du plus fort. Je signale à ceux qui seraient assez aveugles et maladroits pour me donner l'avantage d'attaquer mon exaspération du moi qu'il est bien facile de m'entraîner à la défaite mais à cette sorte de défaite que sont les veilles des grandes victoires définitives pour ceux qui entrent dans le grand jeu et savent s'exposer.

J'ai lutté contre ma vocation de « peintre », en parlant au Japon pour y vivre l'aventure Judo et Arts martiaux anciens : de même j'ai lutté contre ma vocation « d'homme de théâtre » ; mais précisément, le Judo par la pratique physique et spirituelle des Katas, s'est constitué malgré moi, ma formation dans cette discipline de l'art qu'est le théâtre, d'une manière imprévisible, mais tout aussi profitable et profonde, sinon peut-être plus encore, que n'importe quelle autre. En présentant ce qui suit, j'obéis à une nécessité profonde, j'agis en réaliste plein de gros bon sens. J'aime Molière et Shakespeare parce que, dans leur œuvre, se trouve cette transparence du vide qui me fascine.

Pour moi « théâtre » n'est pas du tout synonyme de « Représentation » ou de « Spectacle ».

D'importants chercheurs qui, eux, ont été d'avant-garde, comme Tafroff, par exemple, voulaient théâtraliser le théâtre.

Evreinoff rêvait du monodrame, de la théâtralité dans la vie quotidienne, pensée — geste — parole.

Stanislavsky, réaliste extrémiste, aurait souhaité la mort effective et définitive de l'acteur qui doit jouer sa mort en scène. Le précurseur Dada Vakhtangof enferma le public dans une salle de théâtre pendant deux heures dans le seul but cynique de les enfermer tout simplement. Cet événement faisait partie, d'ailleurs, de son « théâtre de la révolte » et s'intitulait « La Soirée insolite ».

Le Tchécoslovaque Burian créa un théâtre synthétique ; les personnages de sa pièce, « Roméo et Juliette », étaient des machines fantastiques et infernales qui évoluaient sur la scène pendant que les acteurs en coulisse disaient le texte. Amphithéâtroff montait des pièces laconiques de dix minutes, coupées de discussions ; les discussions faisaient partie évidemment du programme. Ce qui l'amènera à déclarer souvent à son public, qui lui commandait d'avance ses représentations, qu'il était prêt à supporter les tomates, les œufs pourris, mais en aucune manière, les pavés.

Les phonographes, dans « Les Mariés de la Tour Eiffel », de Jean Cocteau, sont aussi de très beaux phénomènes.

★

Il serait trop long de citer ici toutes les tentatives qui ont été faites pour sortir de la convention, de l'optique apprise, de l'académisme, dans le domaine du spectacle de la représentation théâtrale depuis le début du siècle. Je crois que presque tout a été fait, jusqu'à Jacques Polieri dans sa mise en scène de la pièce de Tardieu ces temps derniers, qui fait entendre des voix sur la scène où trois panneaux-écrans sont là pour tout décor et toute présence ! (Son idée d'ailleurs est de faire vivre et parler les décors.)

Bravo ! — Quel bonheur que tout cela ait existé, mais attention ; j'avertis bien le lecteur, mon œuvre théâtrale n'a rien, absolument rien à voir avec l'une quelconque de ces directions ou recherches sauf, peut-être, avec celles d'Antonin Artaud, qui sentait venir ce que je propose aujourd'hui ici. Cependant Artaud, comme bien d'autres « Grands » du vrai théâtre, se perdait dans cette fausse conception artificielle et intellectuelle du Verbe qui en a dérouté tant si longtemps. Pour ma part, je ne sais qu'une chose, c'est « qu'au commencement était le Verbe, et le Verbe était Dieu » ; deux fois « être » pour deux fois « Verbe » plus « Dieu », en tout cinq points qui, si on les médite un peu, disent bien ce qu'ils veulent dire : le « Verbe » dans cette aforme n'est pas « Parole » articulée ni même désarticulée.

★

Ce que je désire : Plus de rythme, surtout plus jamais de rythme !

Et puis mon œuvre n'est pas une « recherche », elle est mon sillage. Elle est la matière même de la vitesse statique vertigineuse, à laquelle je me propulse sur place dans l'immatériel ! Attention encore, je tiens à bien préciser que je ne dis pas, en parlant de mon œuvre : « C'est bien plus beau parce que c'est inutile » ! Non, je dis : « C'est ainsi ce sera ainsi, et personne ne pourra jamais rien faire pour que ce ne soit pas ainsi » ! Pourquoi ? Parce que, précisément c'est « classique » !

★

...Ainsi, très vite, on en arrive au théâtre sans acteur, sans décor, sans scène, sans spectateur... plus rien que le créateur seul qui n'est vu par personne, excepté la présence de personne et le théâtre-aspectacle commence !

L'auteur vit sa création : il

● SUITE EN PAGE 2

ACTUALITÉ

DANS le cadre des représentations théâtrales du Festival d'Art d'Avant-Garde de novembre-décembre 1960, j'ai décidé de présenter une ultime forme de théâtre collectif qu'est un dimanche pour tout le monde.

Je n'ai pas voulu me limiter à une matinée ou à une soirée.

En présentant le dimanche 27 novembre 1960, de 0 heure à 24 heures, je présente donc une journée de fête, un véritable spectacle du vide, au point culminant de mes théories. Cependant, n'importe quel autre jour de la semaine aurait pu être aussi utilisé.

Je souhaite qu'en ce jour la joie et le merveilleux règnent, que personne n'ait le trac et que tous, acteurs-spectateurs, conscients comme inconscients aussi de cette gigantesque manifestation, passent une bonne journée.

Que chacun aille dedans comme dehors, circule, bouge, remue ou reste tranquille.

Tout ce que je publie aujourd'hui dans ce journal est antérieur à la présentation de ce jour historique pour le théâtre.

Le théâtre doit être ou doit tout au moins tenter de devenir rapidement le plaisir d'être, de vivre, de passer de merveilleux moments, et de comprendre chaque jour mieux le bel aujourd'hui.

Tout ce que je publie dans ce journal ont été mes étapes jusqu'à ce jour glorieux de réalisme et de vérité : le théâtre des opérations de cette conception du théâtre que je propose n'est pas seulement la ville, Paris, mais aussi la campagne, le désert, la montagne, le ciel même, et tout l'univers même, pourquoi pas ?

Je sais que tout va fonctionner très bien inévitablement pour tous, spectateurs, acteurs, machinistes, directeurs et autres.

Je tiens à remercier ici M. Jacques Polieri, directeur du Festival d'Art d'Avant-Garde, pour son enthousiasme, en me proposant de présenter cette manifestation « le dimanche 27 novembre ».

Yves KLEIN.

L'ESPACE, LUI-MEME.

UN HOMME DANS L'ESPACE !

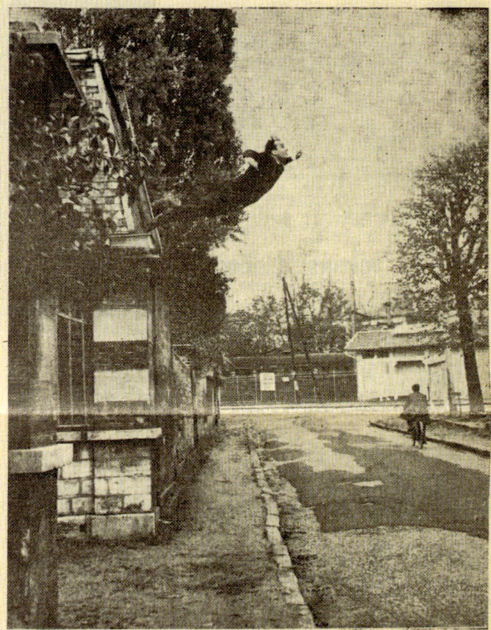

(Photo Shunk-Kender)

Le peintre de l'espace se jette dans le vide !

Le monochrome qui est aussi champion de judo, ceinture noire 4e dan, s'entraine régulièrement à la lévitation dynamique ! (avec ou sans filet, au risque de sa vie).

Il prétend être en mesure d'aller rejoindre bientôt dans l'espace son œuvre préférée : une sculpture aérostatique composée de Mille et un Ballons bleus, qui, en 1957, s'enfuit de son exposition dans le ciel de Saint-Germain-des-Prés pour ne plus jamais revenir !

Libérer la sculpture du socle a été longtemps sa préoccupation. « Aujourd'hui le peintre de l'espace doit aller effectivement dans l'espace pour peindre, mais il doit y aller sans trucs, ni supercheries, ni non plus en avion, ni en parachute ou en fusée : il doit y aller par lui-même, avec une force individuelle autonome, en un mot, il doit être capable de léviter. »

Yves :

« Je suis le peintre de l'espace. Je ne suis pas un peintre abstrait, mais au contraire un figuratif, et un réaliste. Soyons honnêtes, pour peindre l'espace, je me dois de me rendre sur place, dans cet espace même »

Sensibilité pure

Une petite salle.

Les spectateurs, après avoir dûment payé chacun leur entrée, assez chère... pénètrent dans la salle et prennent place.

Le rideau est baissé. La salle illuminée.

Dès que la salle est pleine, un homme se présente sur la scène, devant le rideau toujours baissé et déclare :

« Mesdames, Messieurs en raison des circonstances, ce soir nous allons être contraints de vous enchainer chacun à vos sièges (et, de plus, vous bâillonner) pour la durée de la représentation.

» Cette mesure de sécurité est nécessaire, afin de vous protéger contre vous-même, en présence de ce spectacle particulièrement dangereux, d'un point de vue affectif pur !

» Nous exprimons d'avance nos regrets au personnes qui ne pourraient supporter d'être ainsi enchainées et bâillonnées avant le lever du rideau et nous les prions aimablement de bien vouloir quitter la salle pour se faire rembourser à la sortie. Aucune personne non enchainée solidement à son siège ne sera tolérée dans la salle pendant le spectacle. Merci »

...Aussitôt un groupe d'enchaineurs-bâillonneurs pénètrent dans la salle et, systématiquement, rang après rang, paralysent rapidement tous les spectateurs.

● SUITE EN PAGE 2

22

YVES KLEIN

Dimanche—Le journal d'un seul jour *(Sunday—The newspaper for a single day)*

November 27, 1960, offset lithograph, 22 × 15 (55.9 × 38.1), National Gallery of Art, Washington, Donald and Nancy de Laski Fund, 2010

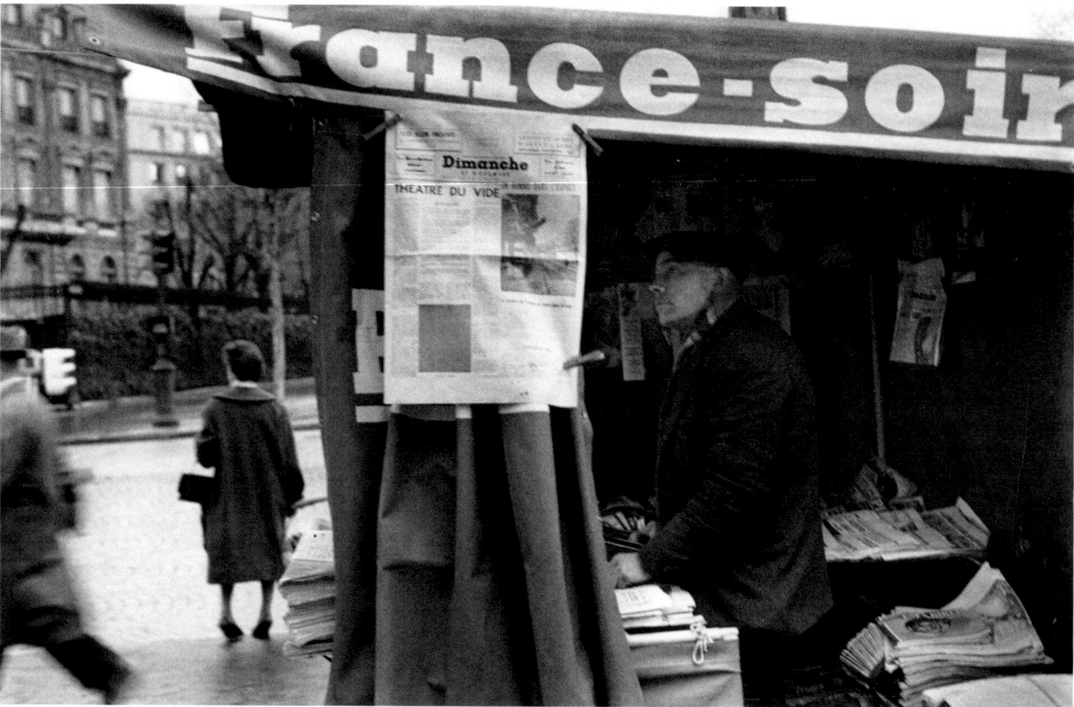

11

topics were of interest to Klein. It was on the front page of *Dimanche* that Harry Shunk's now famous photograph, *Leap into the Void,* was first published. The photo shows Klein leaping from a building's second-story window, his arms outstretched like the wings of a bird. Was he prepared to risk life and limb by flinging himself into space? Hardly. Klein landed on a safety net that was doctored out of the image. Such manipulation of photographs—in short, playing with the truth—is endemic to faux newspapers.

On *Dimanche*'s last page, in a brief article titled "La Statue," Klein wrote of his dream to "go out into the crowd" and "become a journalist/reporter."[62] The remark points up his desire to work beyond the confines of the artist's studio and in the public sphere. And *Dimanche* migrated into that sphere when Klein arranged for the paper's sale (thirty-five francs per copy) at Paris newsstands for a single day, on November 27, 1960 (fig. 11). Browsers and passersby, most presumably with little awareness of or interest in contemporary art, were enlisted as unwitting participants in his newspaper publication-turned-event.

Dalí, the surrealist, and Klein, the cofounder (with Pierre Restany) of *nouveau réalisme* (new realism), are odd bedfellows. But their pairing indicates a shared tendency for works that are self-promotional. Readers of the *Dali News* surely recognized that they could not take Dalí's reporting seriously. But if they browsed the articles and emitted a knowing sigh, the paper would have served its purpose, which was to keep Dalí's name in the news. By staging *Dimanche*'s release as an event, Klein actually surpassed Dalí, producing not just a house organ but a happening of sorts that drew additional coverage on the street.

Newspapers in Flux

Artists and historians disagree as to whether the international and interdisciplinary collective known as Fluxus endures to the present, but all acknowledge that the group was most active in the 1960s and 1970s. The Fluxus manifesto, written by George Maciunas in 1963, declared its aim to "purge the world of bourgeois sickness" and "promote a revolutionary flood and tide in art."[63] If this all sounds a bit familiar, it is because every art manifesto written after 1909 owes a debt to Marinetti.

The strategies that dominated the newspaper phenomenon's first fifty years were mainly derived from Picasso. Even the futurists adopted his cut-

FIG. 11 Paris newsstand, November 27, 1960, with Yves Klein's *Dimanche–Le journal d'un seul jour* on display, Yves Klein Archives, Paris

FIG. 12 Fluxus, *a V TRE EXTRA*, March 24, 1979, offset lithograph, Collection Walker Art Center, Minneapolis, Walker Special Purchase Fund, 1989

and-paste methods. But the balance shifted in the 1960s when Marinetti's strategies edged their way to the fore, due in part to a general departure from modernism to postmodernism, the emergence of conceptual and performance art, and the highly charged politics of the decade. Marinetti's tactics were well suited to these conditions. And while most postmodern artists working with the newspaper would not cite Marinetti as an influence, his strategies inform their work.

It is hard to imagine anyone mistaking the first Fluxus newspaper, *cc V TRE* (January 1964), for a conventional one (pl. 23). Although its design was not credited, the paper betrays the graphic style of the group's principal organizer, Maciunas, both in its use of his signature typewritten text (upper right column) and in its reliance on well-defined text blocks that set off such baffling Dada-like headlines as "ALL TELEPHONE NUMBERS HAVE BEEN CHANGED" and "Floor Wears Out After 192 Years."

Fluxus issued eleven newspapers between 1964 and 1979, the last being *a V TRE EXTRA* (March 24, 1979), a tribute to Maciunas, who had died the previous year (fig. 12).[64] Although the first Fluxus newspaper would never be mistaken for a conventional one, the later *a V TRE EXTRA* could pass for the real thing. It is a calculated fake

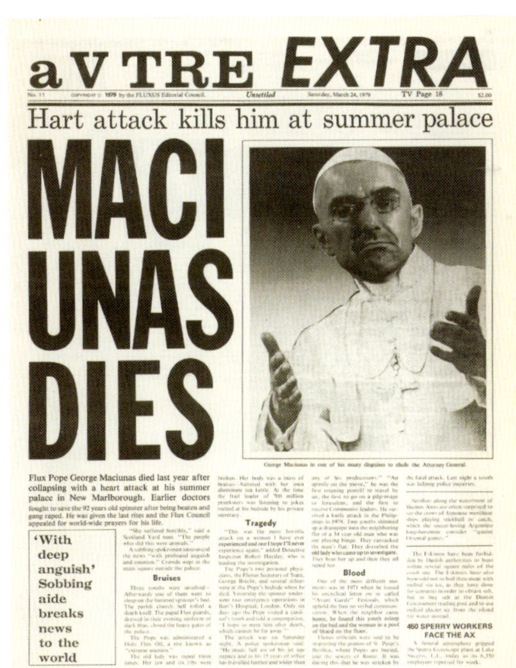

aV TRE EXTRA

No. 11 copyright © 1979 by the FLUXUS Editorial Council. Unsettled Saturday, March 24, 1979 TV Page 18 $2.00

Hart attack kills him at summer palace

MACIUNAS DIES

George Maciunas in one of his many disguises to elude the Attorney General.

Flux Pope George Maciunas died last year after collapsing with a heart attack at his summer palace in New Marlborough. Earlier doctors fought to save the 92 years old spinster after being beaten and gang raped. He was given the last rites and the Flux Council appealed for world-wide prayers for his life.

'With deep anguish' Sobbing aide breaks news to the world

Bruises

Tragedy

Blood

450 SPERRY WORKERS FACE THE AX

12

invested with irony—its wit aimed at the "world of bourgeois sickness" and the establishment press. Indeed, the paper parodied what many in the early post-Vietnam era viewed as standard newsroom practices: falsifying news or inventing it out of whole cloth. This strategy became the stock-in-trade of artists' newspapers in the last quarter of the twentieth century.

In highly dramatic terms, the headline article describes how doctors were unable to save Flux Pope George Maciunas after he had been beaten and raped. In fact, the real Pope Paul VI *had* died seven months earlier, and Maciunas *had* been brutally beaten by men brandishing metal pipes a few years earlier (in the article the attackers are said to have wielded a "battered aluminum tea kettle").

Under a doctored photograph showing Maciunas as Pope Paul VI, the caption reads: "George Maciunas in one of his many disguises to elude the Attorney General." (In the fraudulent world of faux newspapers, masquerading runs rampant.) As incredible as it may seem, the caption is more true than not. While involved in organizing cooperative artist-owned buildings in Soho between 1966 and 1975, Maciunas infuriated New York authorities by refusing to submit required documents. The attorney general's office retaliated by issuing so many warrants for his arrest that Maciunas took to wearing elaborate disguises in public.

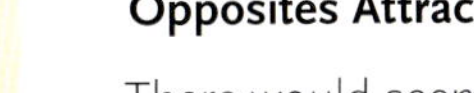

Opposites Attract

There would seem to be no commonality between Warhol's study for *Flash—November 22, 1963* (1968), and Douglas Huebler's *Location Piece #6—National* (1970) (pls. 24, 25). Though made only two years apart and both photography-based, Warhol's pop image and Huebler's conceptual project seem worlds apart.

Warhol chose the front page of the *New York World-Telegram*, published on November 22, 1963, the day of President John F. Kennedy's assassination. The headline was among the bluntest and most graphically compelling of any that day. In unprecedented four-inch type, it read: "President Shot Dead." An article on the same front page stated that "news of President Kennedy's shooting was heard in stunned disbelief." It continued:

FLUXUSFLUXUSFLUXUSFLUXUSFLUXUSFLUXUS

cc V TRE

FLUXUSFLUXUSFLUXUSFLUXUSFLUXUSFLUXUS

EDITED BY GEORGE BRECHT AND FLUXUS EDITORIAL COUNCIL FOR FLUXUS JANUARY 1964 SINGLE ISSUE 80 CENTS, $6 PER YEAR

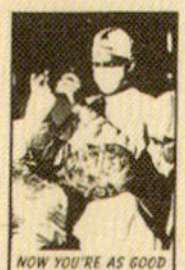

A LINE 1088 MILES LONG

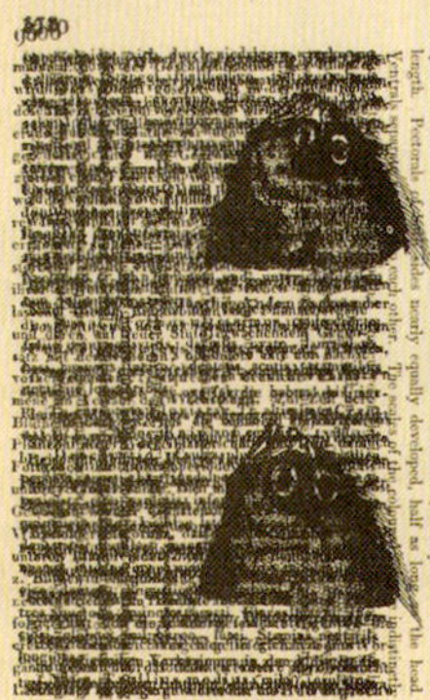

NEW FLUXUS EDITORIAL COUNCIL

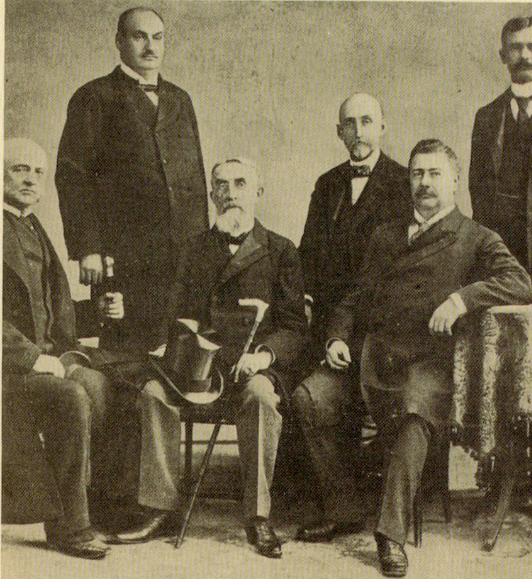

FLUXUS 1963 EDITIONS, AVAILABLE NOW FROM FLUXUS P.O. Box 180, New York 10013, N.Y. or FLUXUS 359 Canal St. New York. CO 7-9198

FLUXUS a Monthly Review of the University of Avant-Garde Hinduism. edited by Nam June Paik $10 per year.
FLUXUS b L'OPTIQUE MODERNE Collection de presente par DANIEL SPOERRI, avec, en regard, D'INUTILES NOTULES par François Dufrêne, $5 (20 copies left)
FLUXUS c WATER YAM, arranged by George Brecht in wood box, $5 in "special box" $10 works from 1963 - $ 1 per year
FLUXUS cc V TRE, monthly newspaper, edited by George Brecht, $6 per year, 80c per issue
FLUXUS d CHIEKO SHIOMI: "Endless box" $20
FLUXUS dd CHIEKO SHIOMI: events in wood box $2
FLUXUS h LA MONTE YOUNG: Compositions 1961 bound in linen: $3, in paper cover: $1
FLUXUS hh LA MONTE YOUNG: Trio for strings, bound in linen: $3, in paper cover: $1
FLUXUS k ROBERT WATTS: events in wood box $3
FLUXUS n BEN VAUTIER: "Mystery box" $2
FLUXUS q AYO: "Tactile box" (100 variants) ea. $20
FLUXUS r TAKEHISA KOSUGI: events in wd. box $2

FLUXUS 1964 EDITIONS:
FLUXUS e EMMETT WILLIAMS: complete works $8 works from 1964 - by subscription
FLUXUS f ROBERT FILLIOU: complete works, $6
FLUXUS g NAM JUNE PAIK: list of publications by special request
FLUXUS i BEN PATTERSON: complete works, $6 works from 1964 - by subscription
FLUXUS j DICK HIGGINS: Jefferson's Birthday, $6 (works from April 1962 to April 1963)
FLUXUS kk Robert Watts: OBJECTS (list by request)
FLUXUS kkk ROBERT WATTS: "Suitcase" $40
FLUXUS nn BEN VAUTIER: complete works $8
FLUXUS p ALISON KNOWLES: canned bean roll $6
FLUXUS m HENRY FLYNT: essays

Most materials originally intended for Fluxus yearboxes will be included in the FLUXUSccV TRE newspaper or in individual boxes.

ALL TELEPHONE NUMBERS HAVE BEEN CHANGED

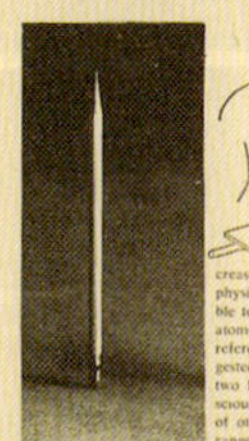

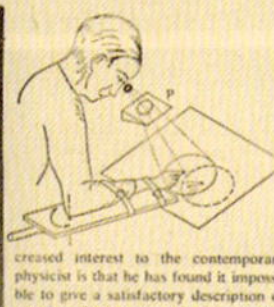

creased interest to the contemporary physicist is that he has found it impossible to give a satisfactory description of atomic phenomena without explicit reference to consciousness. It was suggested by one physicist that there are two kinds of reality: that of my consciousness, which is absolute, and that of other objects, which is relative and ranges over a wide spectrum.

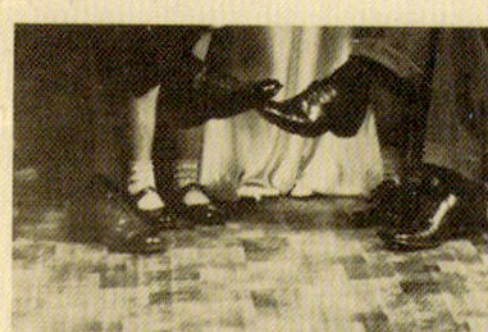

Floor Wears Out After 192 Years

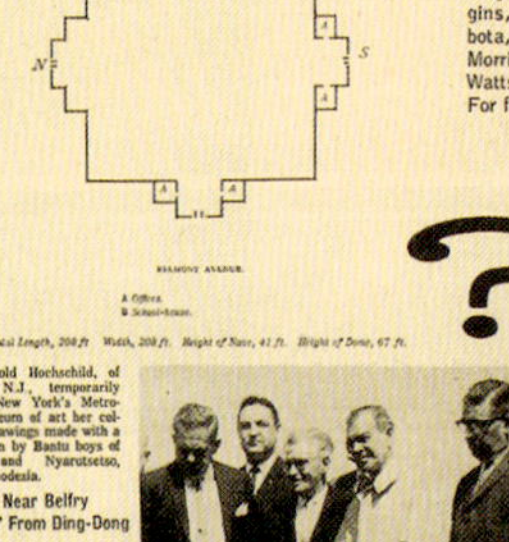

FLUXUSFESTIVAL IN NY MARCH-MAY

Street events, demonstrations, concert hall events, film, music, wrvr radio program, exhibit tour, environments, bazaar, auction, feast, lectures etc.etc.etc.etc.etc.etc. Akiyama, Brecht, Cale, Corner, De Ridder, Filliou, Higgins, Ichiyanagi, Jones, Kaprow, Knowles, Kosugi, Kubota, Koepcke, Mac Low, Maciunas, de Maria, Mekas Morris, Paik, Patterson, Shiomi, Schmit, Tone, Vautier, Watts, Williams, Young will participate in this festival. For further information write PO BOX 180 NY 10013

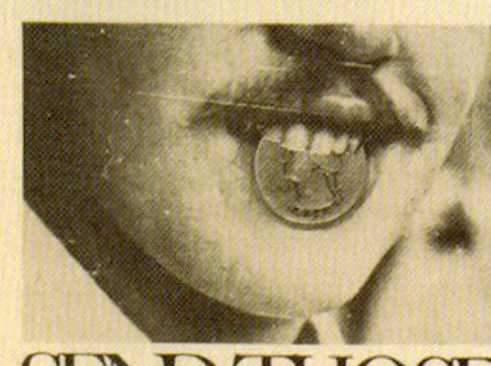

SEND THOSE $ TO FLuXuS

$60 Million Offering

Limited Time! Limited Quantities!

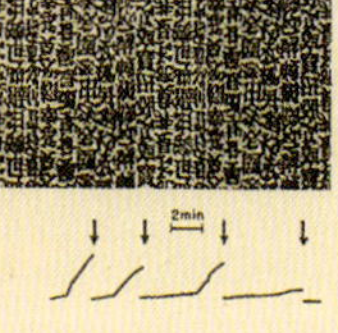

Mrs. Harold Hochschild, of Princeton, N.J., temporarily loaned to New York's Metropolitan Museum of art her collection of drawings made with a ballpoint pen by Bantu boys of Chirodzo and Nyarutsetso, Southern Rhodesia.

Residents Near Belfry 'Batty' From Ding-Dong

DOYLESTOWN, Pa.—Twenty residents claim the ding-dong from the belfry in the courthouse is driving them to distraction.

They petitioned the county commissioners for a little less noise.

The carillon atop the county's new courthouse rings every quarter hour, thirteen hours a day, seven days a week.

"It becomes highly distracting and even nerve-racking," said the petitioners, referring to themselves as a captive audience. Ring it less frequently, they demanded.

The commissioners said they would consider the matter. They cannot hear the bells inside the courthouse.

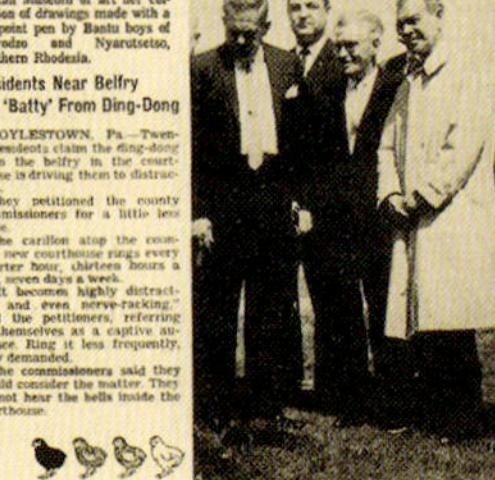

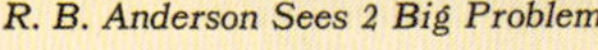

R. B. Anderson Sees 2 Big Problems

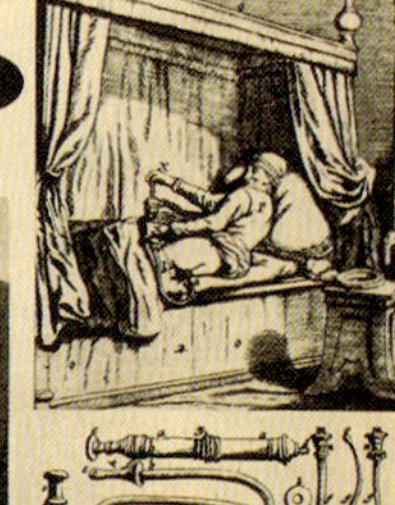

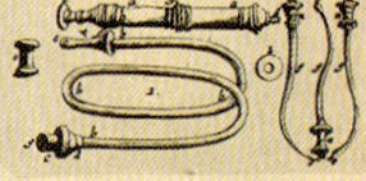

Fluxus Machine No. 44

S2E7

Battle fatigue

Teacher: How many wars has this country had, Petey?
Petey: Seven.
Teacher: Enumerate them, please.
Petey: One, two, three, four, five, six, seven!
Mary Nelson, Carlisle, Pennsylvania

23

FLUXUS

cc V TRE

January 1964, offset lithograph, 22 ¾ × 17 (57.8 × 43.2), Collection Walker Art Center, Minneapolis, Acquired with Walker Art Center library funds; transfer to Walker Art Center permanent collection, 1990

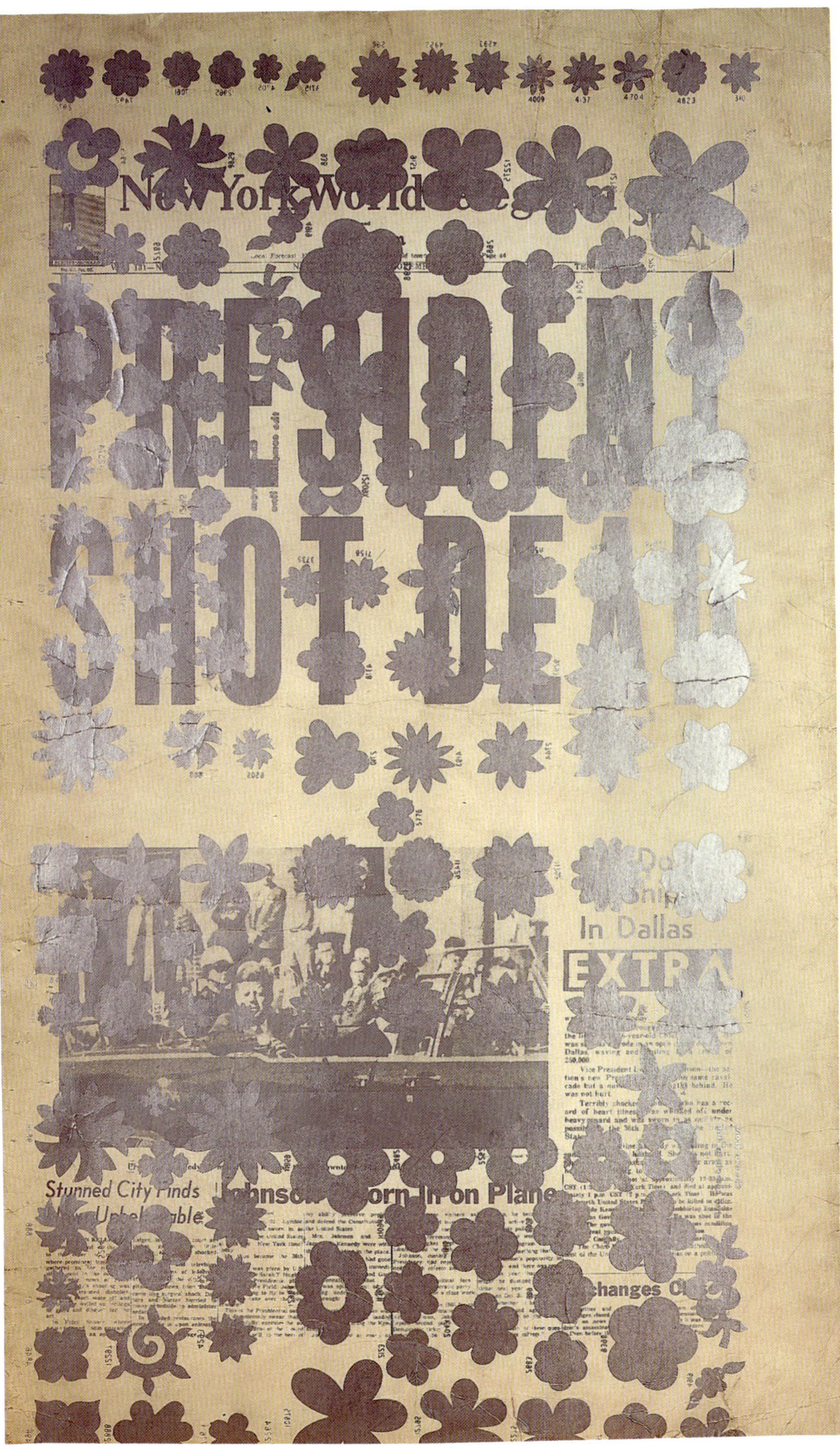

24

ANDY WARHOL

Study for* Flash — November 22, 1963, *portfolio cover

1968, silkscreen ink on paperboard

41 × 23 ⅞ (104.1 × 60.6), Courtesy Gagosian Gallery

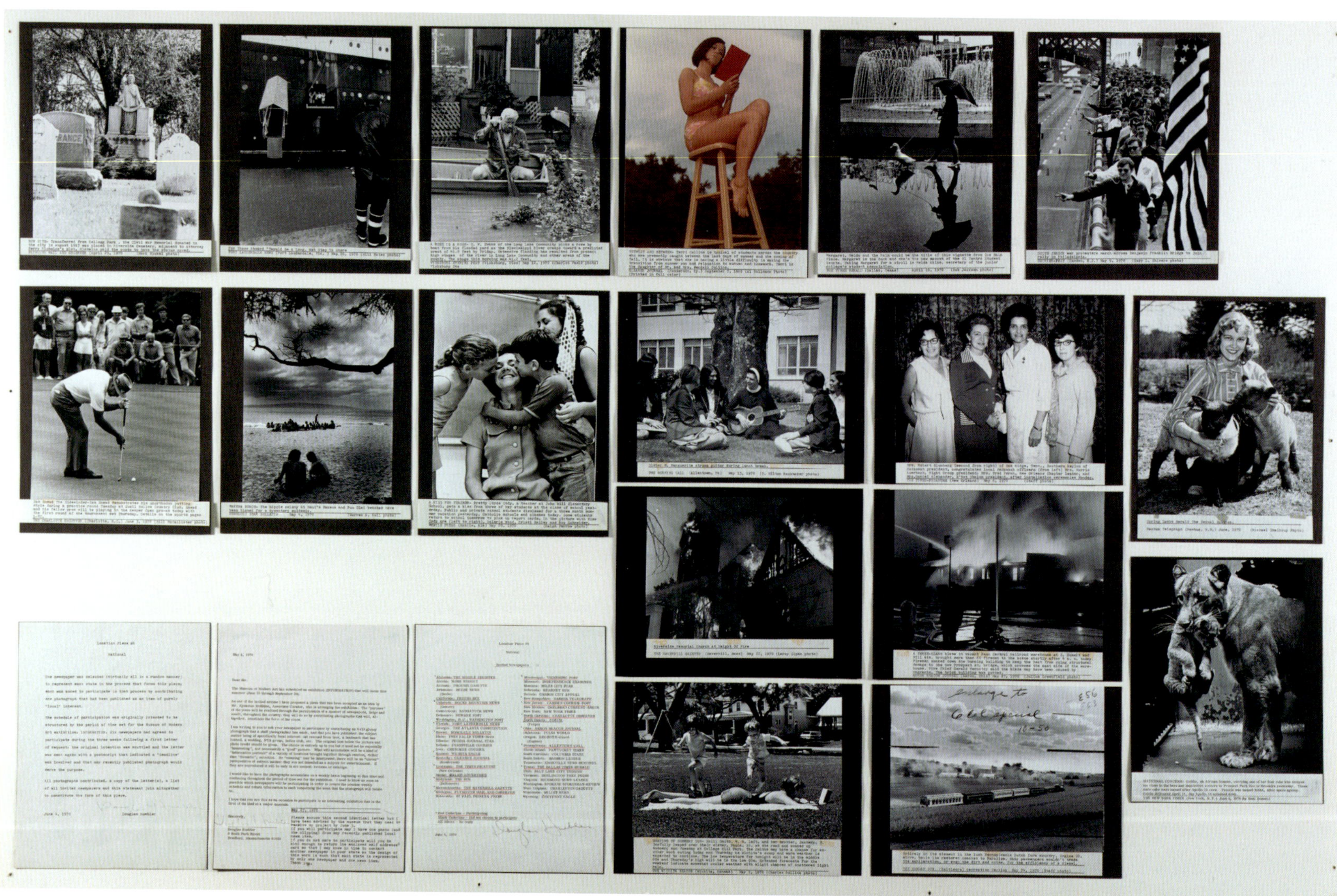

25

DOUGLAS HUEBLER

Location Piece #6 — National

1970, seventeen photographs with typewritten captions and text, dimensions vary, The Museum of Modern Art, New York, Larry Aldrich Foundation Fund

"Over radio and television into the rooms of hundreds of patients in the city's hospitals, the news from Dallas came like surgical shock. Doctors and nurses hurried to many a bedside to administer sedatives." Warhol blanketed the *New York World-Telegram* page with a template of cheery flowers—a juxtaposition that seems not only anomalous but irreverent.

Warhol claimed to have had almost no reaction to the news of President Kennedy's death.[65] Hal Foster describes such a response as a "strategy of mimetic defense"—the taking on of a shocking event to guard against it.[66] This would account for Warhol's fixation on the assassination and his indifferent treatment of a newspaper page that shocked and devastated most others. Warhol's anesthetizing defense against shocking events was, in Foster's words, to "drain them of affect."[67] Warhol strived for numbness.

Huebler's *Location Piece #6—National* is almost an exercise in neutrality. The artist mailed a form letter to newspapers across the United States, explaining that he had been asked to participate in an exhibition at New York's Museum of Modern Art and that the piece he planned to exhibit would be realized "through the participation of a number of newspapers, large and small, throughout the country." The letter asked each newspaper to contribute "an 8 × 10 glossy photograph that a staff photographer [had] made" and that had been published in their paper. The subject matter, Huebler explained, should be "of specifically local interest: cat rescued from tree, a landmark that has burned, a wedding, PTA group, ladies club, etc." He went on: "The choice is entirely up to you but it need not be especially 'interesting,' nor necessarily a 'good' picture."

Seventeen newspapers ranging from Alabama's *Mobile Register* to Texas' *Dallas Times-Herald* submitted photographs. They include the golfer Sam Snead making a putt (*Charlotte Observer*); South Jersey war protestors en route to a rally (Camden's *Courier-Post*); and a color photo of a young woman, dressed in a two-piece bathing suit, absorbed (or so we are meant to believe) in a book (the *Gleaner Journal* of Henderson, Kentucky).

Huebler submitted the piece to Kynaston McShine, the exhibition's curator, with an accompanying letter: "Enclosed is the 'Newspaper piece' (Location Piece #6–1970) as it exists right now.... The subject matter of this work, as with all my work, is intended to be contentless.... I set the work in process with neutral intentions and stand neutral afterwards. That I settled for what I got is important rather than any cause for frustration." He added, "It is important that all enclosed documents be displayed.... There are any number of ways that they can be stuck to the wall and any arrangement at all: strung out, blocked out, anything."[68]

Warhol employed neutrality in an attempt to defuse an event that no amount of flowers could be expected to achieve. Huebler used neutrality to debunk the notion of the original work of art or the artist as expressive genius. He positioned himself as a passive medium, content to supply a setting or context for the artistic choices of others. Though Huebler's *Location Piece* looks nothing like Warhol's, they share a strategy of neutrality. One artist used neutrality to fend off feelings of trauma and grief, the other to deny expectations about "interesting" art.

Heavy Editing

Both Sarah Charlesworth and Jorge Macchi have at times practiced heavy editing. Charlesworth removed the newspaper's text to focus on its images, knowing that a picture is worth a thousand words. Macchi removed the text to create a delicately minimalist work that carries a lingering sense of absence.

Inspired by an important conceptual photography exhibition organized by Seth Siegelaub in 1969 (one that included works by Douglas Huebler), Charlesworth took up photography.[69] Her *Modern History* includes series and individual photographs made between 1977 and 2003—all newspaper-based and all notable for their heavy editing. Charlesworth looks at the medium of photography with a critical eye, examining how mass-media photographs construct different "pictures" of the same event. *April 21, 1978* (1978) from *Modern History* traces a single photograph's appearance on the front page of forty-five different

26

SARAH CHARLESWORTH

Modern History: April 21, 1978

1978, seventeen from the complete set of forty-five gelatin silver prints, same dimensions as the original newspapers, Collection Walker Art Center, Minneapolis, Justin Smith Purchase Fund, 2003

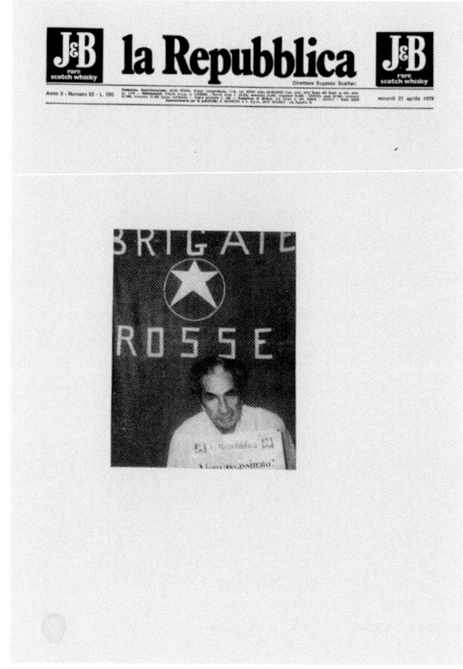

J&B la Repubblica J&B

BRIGATE ROSSE

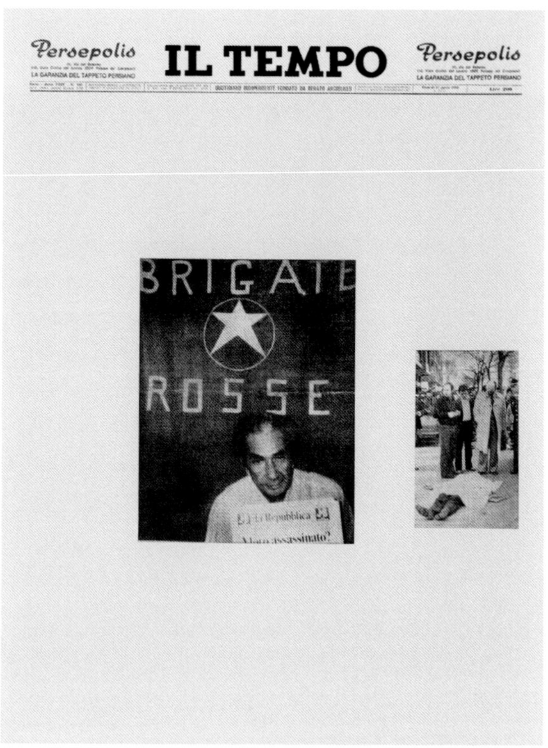

Persepolis IL TEMPO Persepolis

BRIGATE ROSSE

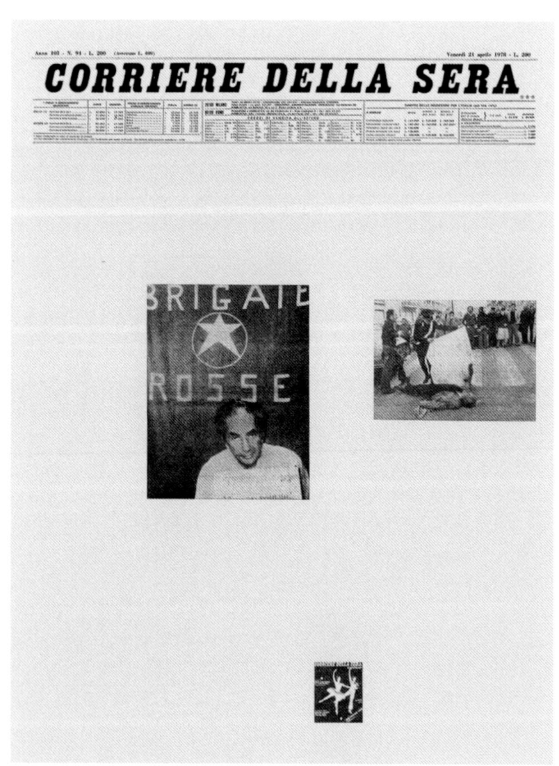

CORRIERE DELLA SERA

BRIGATE ROSSE

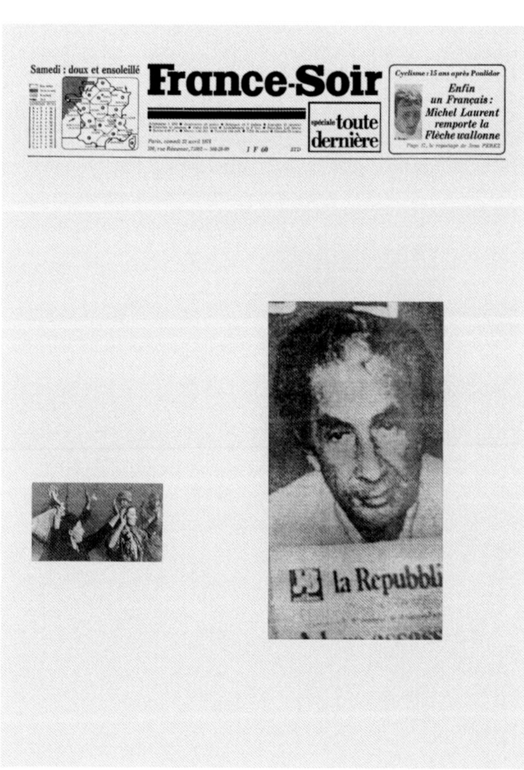

Samedi : doux et ensoleillé

France-Soir

spéciale toute dernière

Cyclisme : 15 ans après Poulidor

Enfin un Français : Michel Laurent remporte la Flèche wallonne

la Repubbli

Neue Zürcher Zeitung

und schweizerisches Handelsblatt

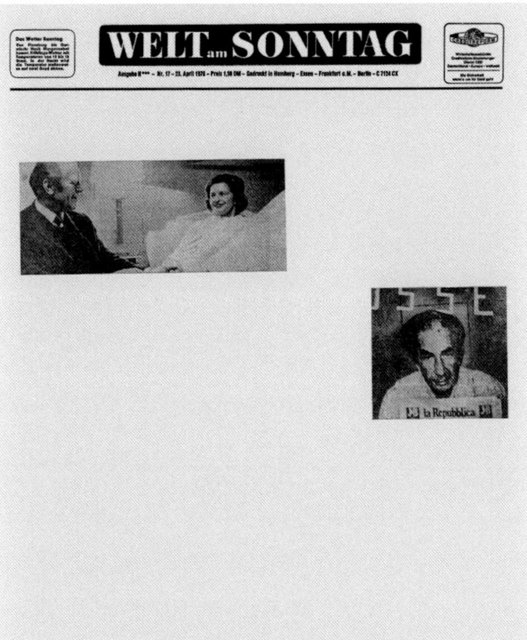
WELT am SONNTAG

la Repubblica

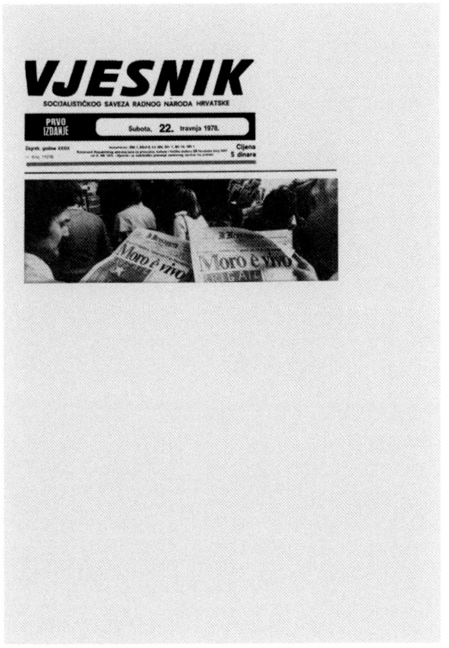
VJESNIK

SOCIJALISTIČKOG SAVEZA RADNOG NARODA HRVATSKE

PRVO IZDANJE

Subota, 22. travnja 1978.

Cijena 5 dinara

Moro è vivo

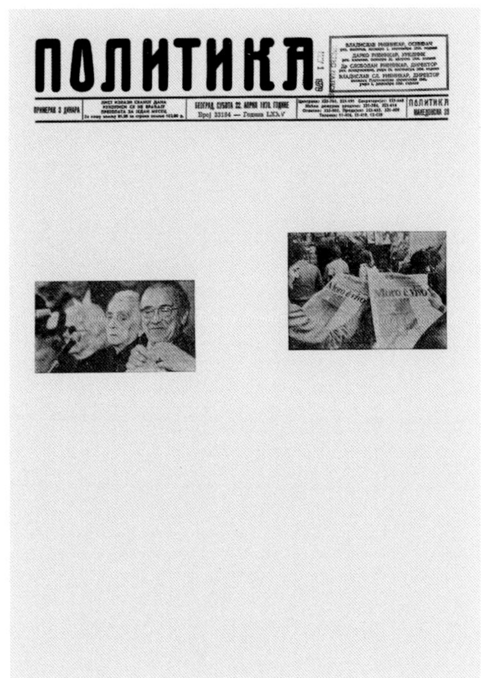
ПОЛИТИКА

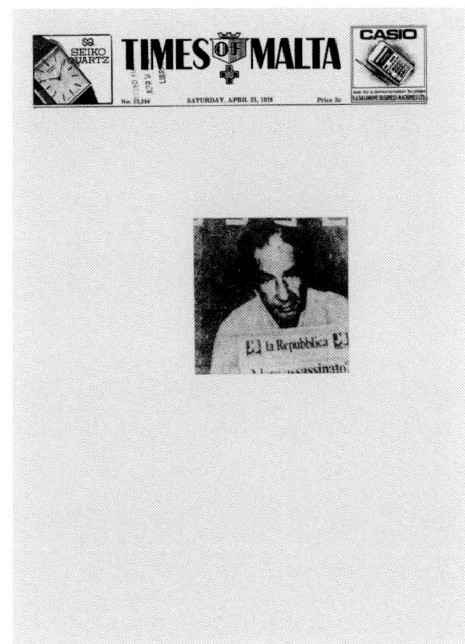
SEIKO QUARTZ

TIMES OF MALTA

CASIO

SATURDAY, APRIL 22, 1978

la Repubblica

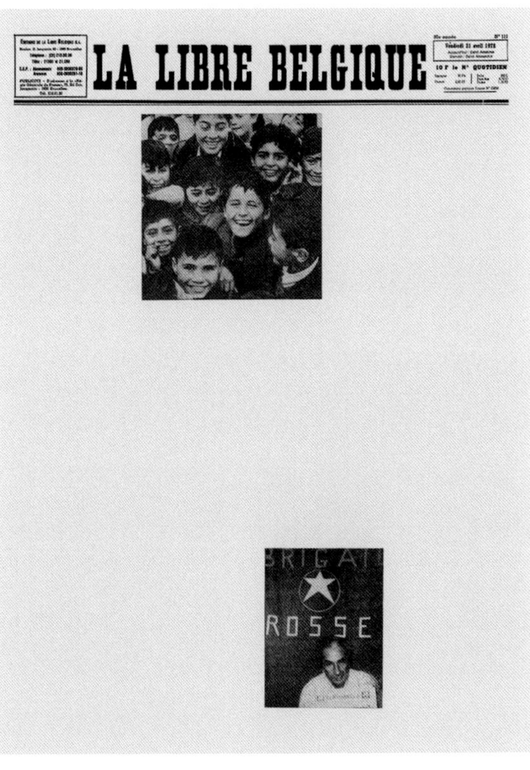
LA LIBRE BELGIQUE

BRIGATE ROSSE

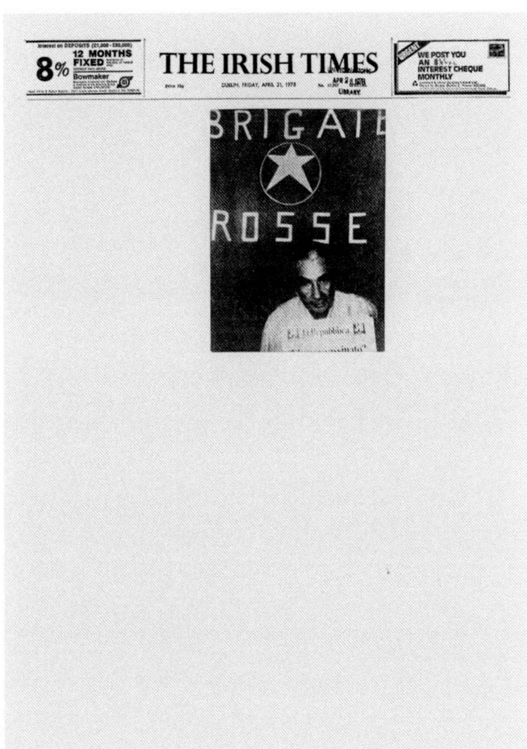
8% 12 MONTHS FIXED

THE IRISH TIMES

WE POST YOU AN INTEREST CHEQUE MONTHLY

BRIGATE ROSSE

la Repubblica

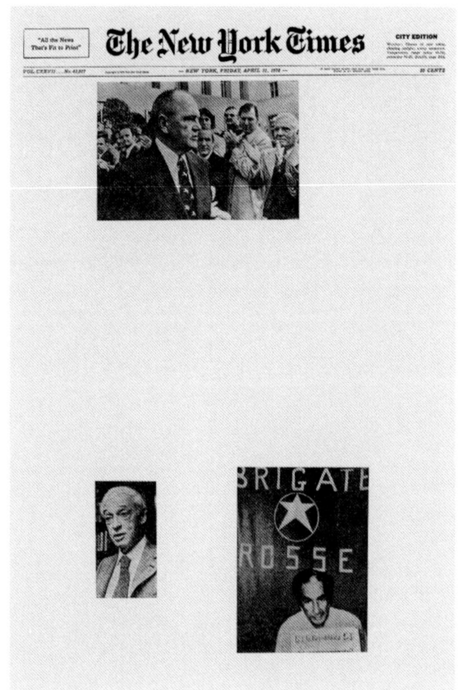
"All the News That's Fit to Print"

The New York Times

CITY EDITION

NEW YORK, FRIDAY, APRIL 21, 1978

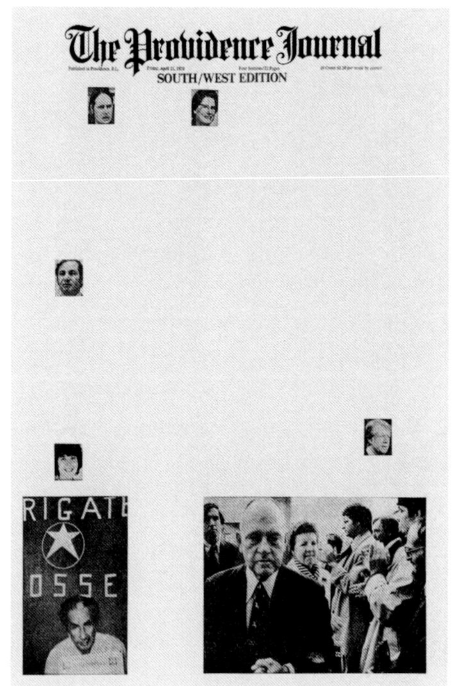
The Providence Journal

SOUTH/WEST EDITION

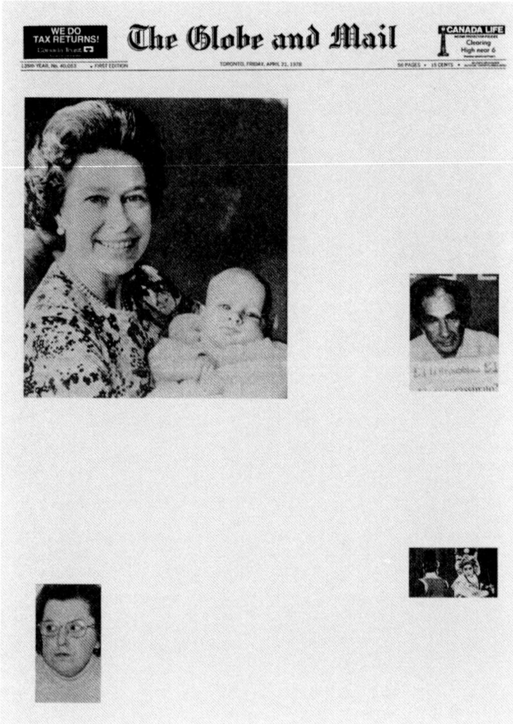
WE DO TAX RETURNS!

The Globe and Mail

CANADA LIFE

Clearing
High near 6

TORONTO, FRIDAY, APRIL 21, 1978

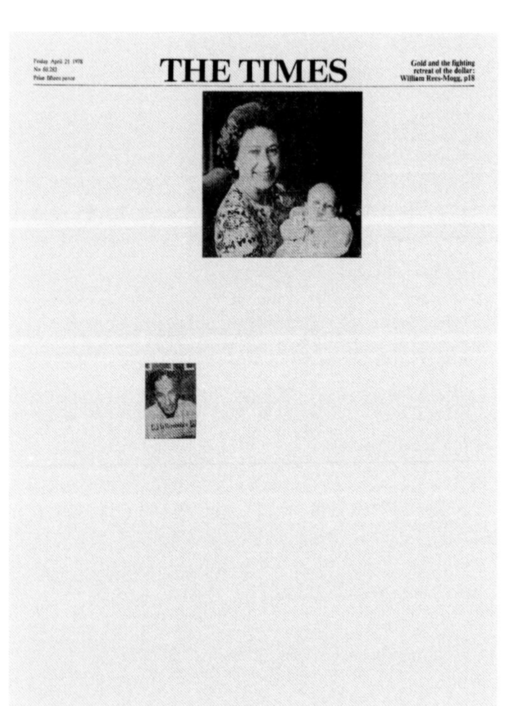
THE TIMES

Gold and the fighting retreat of the dollar: William Rees-Mogg, p18

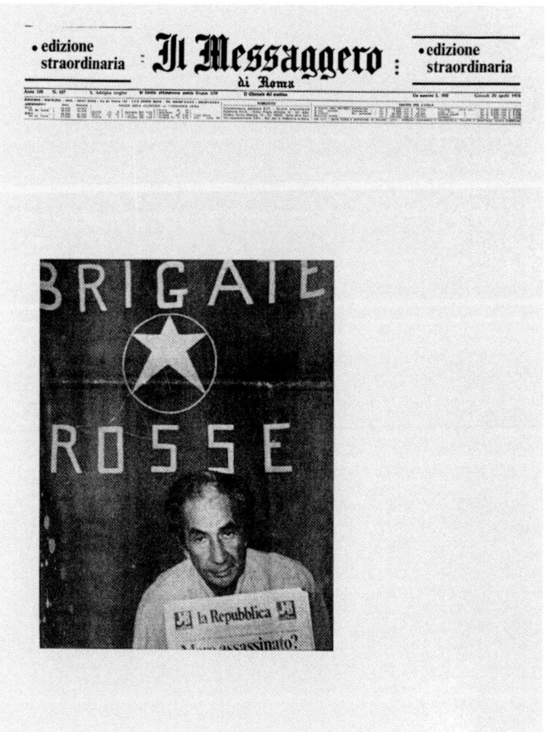
• edizione straordinaria

Il Messaggero di Roma

• edizione straordinaria

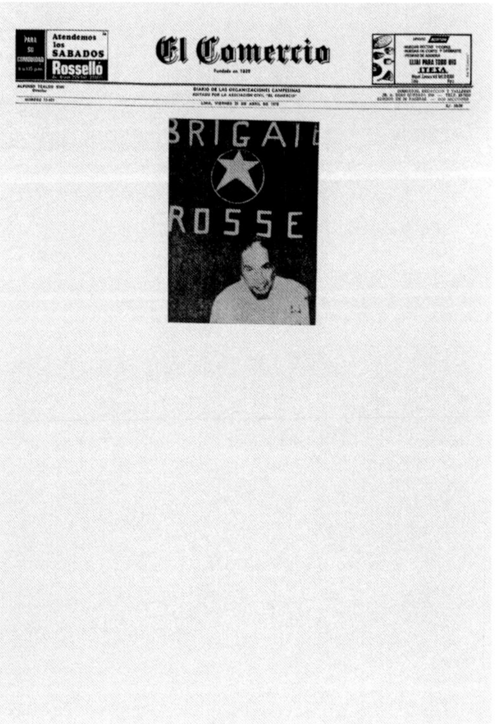
Atendemos los SABADOS
Rosselló

El Comercio

FIG. 13 Detail of *La Nacíon* from Sarah Charlesworth, *Modern History: April 21, 1978*. See also pl. 26

newspapers (pl. 26). Charlesworth remained true to the originals — photos, mastheads, and dimensions are all accurately maintained — but the texts were deleted.

The photograph that Charlesworth tracked shows a sunken and weary Aldo Moro, positioned in front of a Brigate Rosse (Red Brigade) banner, holding a copy of the April 19 edition of *la Repubblica*. The former prime minister of Italy had been kidnapped by Red Brigade militants on March 16, 1978. Thirty-six days later, Moro's captors released this photograph confirming that he was still alive. Nineteen days hence, after failed negotiations and manhunts by the Italian government, the Red Brigade brutally shot and killed Moro.

Charlesworth re-presents forty-five newspapers that published the captors' photo on the front page of their April 21 edition. They tell different stories and underscore how "objective" images can skew our understanding of history. Fourteen newspapers granted the picture sole prominence on the page. Thirty-one ran additional pictures ranging from an upbeat Betty Ford recovering from breast cancer surgery to a beaming Queen Elizabeth holding her first grandchild. In London and Toronto, the queen's picture dominated the front page of the *Times* and *Globe and Mail* that day, greatly overshadowing the captors' photograph.

Moro's photograph was variously sized and cropped — and further mediated in the case of several newspapers, which used photographs of *other* newspapers' front pages. Thus readers of the Argentine daily newspaper *La Nación,* not only received news of the event but news of its reception in Italy, demonstrating that we do not all get the same picture of the news (fig. 13).

Jorge Macchi's work similarly involves heavy editing but with a light result.[70] For his *Monoblock (3)* (1999), the Buenos Aires artist excised the obituary texts from five pages of *La Nación,* leaving behind Christian crosses, Stars of David, and a solitary crescent moon and star like individual grave markers (pl. 27). One page was laid on top of another, evoking a graveyard such as the Old Jewish Cemetery in Prague, where graves are layered ten or more deep. The work also inversely

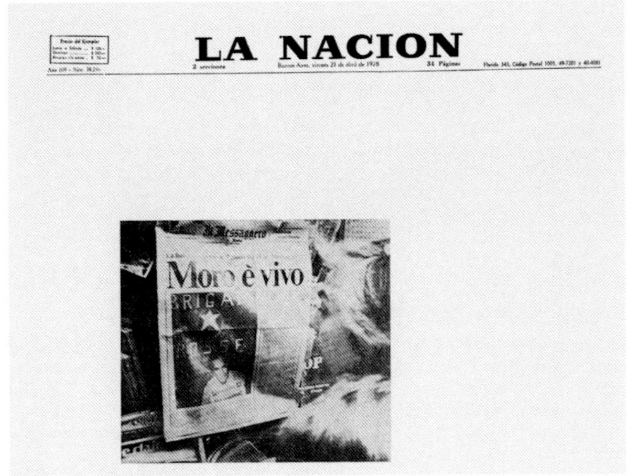

13

calls to mind the cubists' cut-and-paste practice. Whereas Picasso and Braque incorporated individual newspaper cuttings into their *papiers collés,* Macchi salvaged what remained after the newspaper cuttings were excised.

Thinking back to Charlesworth's *April 21, 1978,* it is notable that two of the newspapers that published the photograph of Moro on their front page were from Argentina: *La Nación* and *Clarín.* Both also gave the image sole prominence. (Amazingly, only two Italian newspapers did the same: *Il Messaggero* and *la Repubblica*.) This was not a matter of happenstance. More than 50 percent of Argentines have some Italian ancestry, and many hold dual citizenship. Kidnappings motivated by politics or ransom were also endemic in Argentina in the 1970s. Additionally, the country was in the throes of what is known as the Dirty War (1976–1983), when ten to thirty thousand citizens (sources disagree on the number) were abducted and "disappeared." By publicizing the kidnapping of Moro — a Christian Democrat who, when he was abducted, was on his way to enact a historic compromise with the Italian Communist Party — the newspaper was sending a message to its readers that communists could not be trusted and that Marxist-Leninist offshoots such as the Red Brigade supported crimes of violence. This message was of course duplicitous: the right-wing military regime that ruled Argentina was engaged in a campaign of widespread violence.

The suggestion is not that Macchi, whose adulthood coincided with Argentina's transition

27

JORGE MACCHI

Monoblock (3)

1999, cut newspaper pages,
22 × 14⅞ (55.9 × 37.8),
Christine and Mark Husser

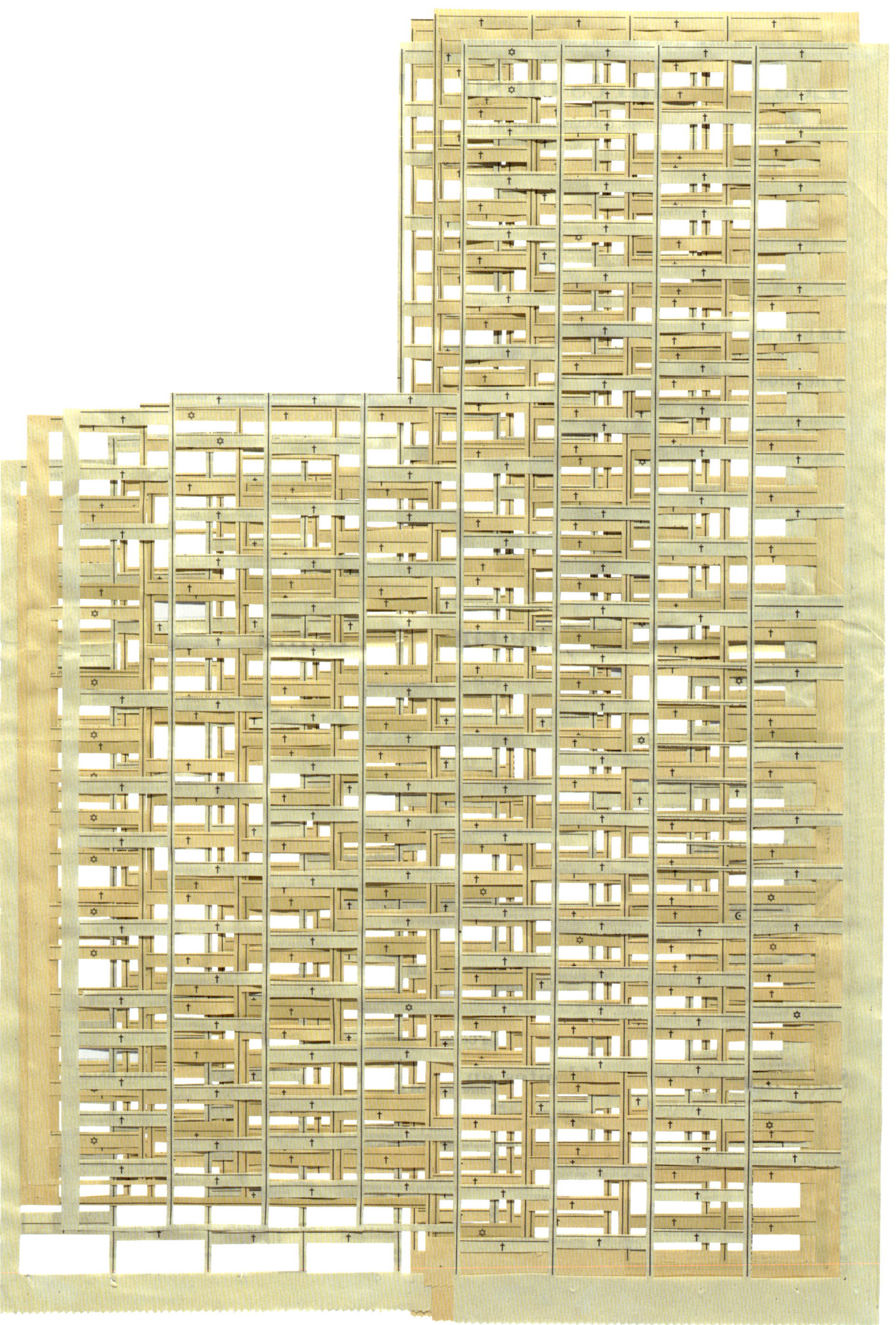

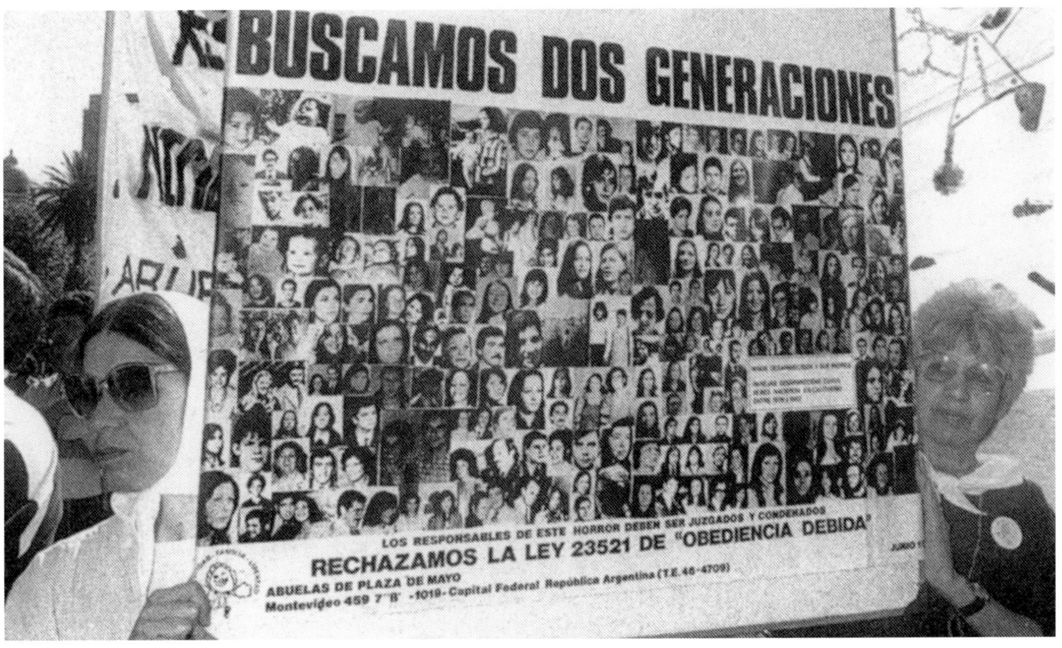

14

FIG. 14 Grandmothers of the Plaza de Mayo with pictures of *los desaparecidos*, those who disappeared in Argentina's "Dirty War" of 1976–1983. Photograph taken from Enrique Rosito et al., *Abuelas de Plaza de Mayo: fotografía de 30 años de lucha* (Buenos Aires, 2007)

to democracy, set out to recall those events in *Monoblock (3)* but that those events haunt the country's collective psyche. Generally speaking, Macchi is not a politically motivated artist. But each hollowed-out space on the newspaper obituary pages evokes a person's absence and cannot help but bring to mind the faces of Argentina's *desaparecidos* (the disappeared) (fig. 14).

The Scrupulous Fabricator

If modern art is a hoax—a charge that has dogged it since its beginnings—Robert Gober does nothing to refute the charge.[71] At the top of a stack of newspapers made by Gober in 1992 is a page with a photograph of a bride gazing dreamily into the distance (pl. 28). Even without visible text, we recognize the photo as an advertisement for bridal wear. Above the image, an article carries the headline "Vatican Condones Discrimination Against Homosexuals." And to its right: "Youth Worker Held In Death of Son, 9." Everything seems plausible, and there appears no reason to doubt the genuineness of this newspaper, which looks so true to life. But something is vaguely amiss. The model in the picture seems a little too full-figured; her shoulders look a bit too beefy; her facial features are unlike those of a model. Once this anomaly comes to light, other items on the page become suspect. Was that really the wording of the Vatican headline in the *Times*? Was the nine-year-old boy actually beaten to death by his mother with a ten-inch piece of "broomstick"? And is it purely coincidental that abutting the article is the Fresh Air Fund's promotional filler "Summer Is for Children"?

The facts are as follows: The bride is none other than the artist himself, disguised in a wig and a wedding gown.[72] And the Vatican article was published by the *Times* but with a differently worded headline: "Vatican Condones Gay-Rights Limits." Gober's subversive intervention not only points up the *Times'* euphemistic wording of the headline but the larger truth that putting limits on gay rights *is* discrimination against homosexuals. Gober's *Newspaper* drew the ire of the Catholic League when it was exhibited at the San Francisco Museum of Modern Art in 2000. In a press release, the league's president—apparently without irony—called the work fraudulent and a hoax. "By altering the headline," he stated, "Gober shows that he is not only a bigot, but a dishonest one at that."[73] Not only is fraudulence the subject of Gober's work, but he is attacked for employing it himself.

Another of Gober's newspapers, from 1991, is presented as a page from the October 4, 1960, edition of the *New York Times* (pl. 29). Again, it

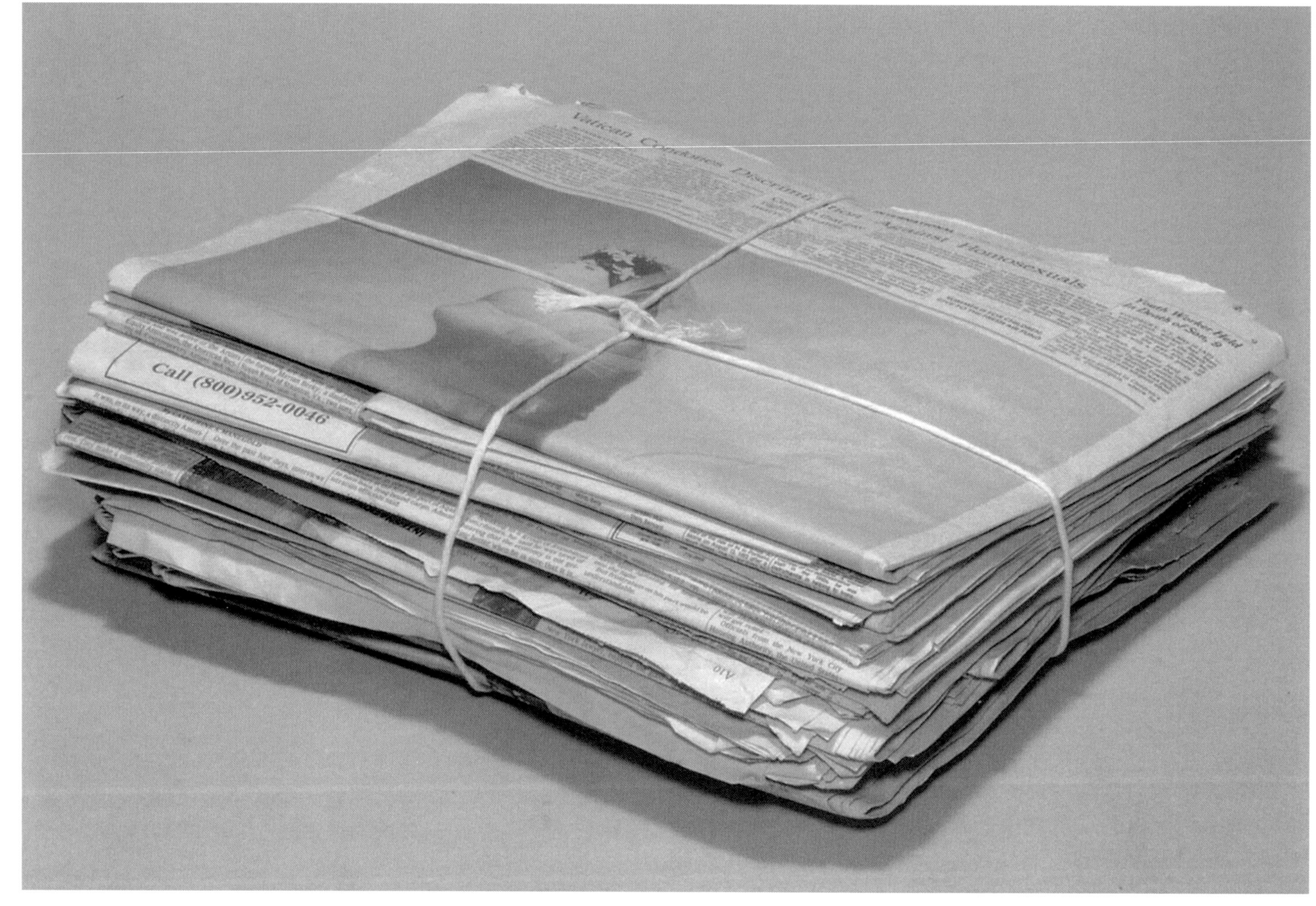

28

ROBERT GOBER

Newspaper

1992, photolithographs on archival paper, twine, 6 × 16 ¼ × 13 ¼ (15.2 × 41.3 × 33.7), Courtesy of the artist and Matthew Marks Gallery

29

ROBERT GOBER

Untitled

1991, photolithograph, hand-colored with coffee, 22⅛ × 13⅞ (56.2 × 35.2), National Gallery of Art, Washington, Gift of the Collectors Committee, 2010

B10 THE NEW YORK TIMES **METROPOLITAN** THURSDAY, OCTOBER 4, 1960

Girl Lived in a Closet, California Police Say

SAN BERNARDINO, Calif., Oct. 25 (AP) — A 12-year-old girl has been found locked in a filthy closet, where, the police say, her parents kept her confined for much of her life.

The girl was found Monday night in the reeking, cockroach-infested closet, which was kept closed by a bent nail, said Sgt. Jenifer Kauffman of the San Bernardino police.

Her parents, Joseph and Sandra Sauceda, were charged Wednesday with felony child endangerment, and the father also was charged with felony child abuse, Ms. Kauffman said.

The police were tipped by a relative. When they asked the Saucedas to show them the girl, they took officers to the closet, Ms. Kauffman said.

Officers said the girl was lying in her own feces and wore a urine-stained sweatsuit.

Investigators say the child rarely left the closet and had probably been kept locked up at other homes where the family lived during the past decade, Ms. Kauffman said.

"Obviously, it's a terrible, traumatic condition," said Sgt. Bob Evans. "It will probably take years to recover from."

The couple was held in this city 60 miles east of Los Angeles in lieu of $50,000 bail each.

The girl, whose name was not disclosed, and her six brothers and sisters, ages 2 months to 15 years, were turned over to the county Child Protective Services. There was no evidence that the other children were abused, Ms. Kauffman said.

Joseph Sauceda, 33, denied that he and his 31-year-old wife abused their daughter. He said the closet was not a cell and that his family was a loving one.

Miss Rubinson, A Buyer, Marries

Heather Linn Rubinson, a daughter of Dr. Kalman Rubinson of New York and the late Irene Rowe Rubinson, was married yesterday to Michael Warren Schechter, the son of Ruth Canaan of Great Neck, L.I., and Marvin L. Schechter of Old Westbury, L.I. Rabbi Lawrence M. Colton performed the ceremony at the Tower Suite in New York.

Mrs. Schechter has a bachelor's degree in fine arts and an M.B.A. from New York University. She is an assistant buyer at Tiffany's in New York. Her father is an associate professor of physiology and biophysics at N.Y.U. Her grandfather, the late Dr. Irving Rowe, was a physicist and the chief scientist at the United States Office of Naval Research in New York.

The bridegroom, a magna cum laude graduate of N.Y.U., is an associate at Mentor Partners, an investment firm in New York. His mother is the vice president of corporate communications at U.S. Tele-Comm Inc., a private pay phone company in Great Neck. His father is the senior partner in the New York law firm of Tunstead, Schechter and Torre.

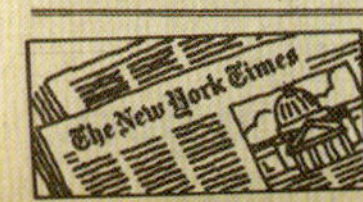

Randy A. Gilman, Gemologist, Weds

Randy Allyn Gilman, a daughter of Mrs. Herbert Gilman of West Hartford, Conn., and the late Mr. Gilman, was married yesterday at the Pierre in New York to Henri Zvi Bolimovsky, the son of Mr. and Mrs. Moisha Bolimovsky of Tel Aviv. Rabbi Sol Roth and Cantor Joseph Malovany performed the ceremony.

Mrs. Bolimovsky, a graduate of Union College, is a gemologist in New York for Best Products, a retail holding company in Richmond. Her father was the founder and chairman of Ames Department Stores in Rocky Hill, Conn. Her mother, Evelyn Gilman, is a retired teacher.

The bridegroom, a graduate of the University of Toronto, is an architect and commercial planner in New York. His father, who is retired, was a jeweler in Tel Aviv.

Theater, anyone?

Check the Theater Directory for Broadway & Off-Broadway shows . . . every day in The New York Times.

Lottery Numbers

Oct. 5, 1960

New York Numbers — 061
New York Win 4 — 3441
New Jersey Pick-It — 199
New Jersey Pick 4 — 6607
Connecticut Daily — 827
Connecticut Play 4 — 2022
Connecticut Lotto — 9, 10, 14, 17, 24, 43

Oct. 4, 1990

New York Pick 10 — 2, 3, 4, 6, 9, 11, 14, 17, 19, 21, 28, 43, 45, 49, 50, 58, 59, 62, 68, 71

Your Money: Saturday, in Business Day

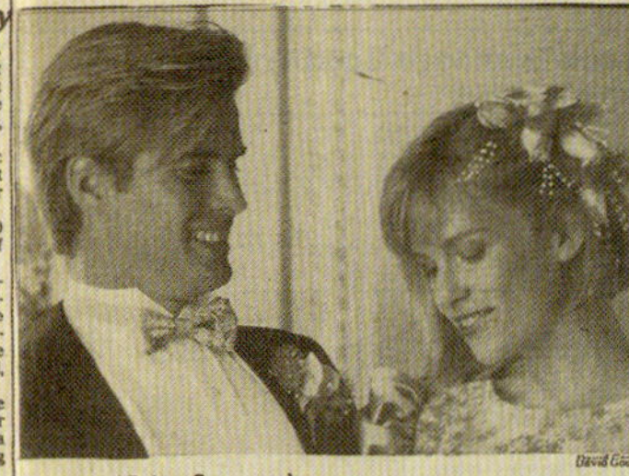

Susan and Robert Greenwood

Susan Fisher Weds R. A. Greenwood

Susan Grossman Fisher, the daughter of Mr. and Mrs. Bernard Grossman of Scarsdale, N.Y., was married yesterday at her home in New York to Robert Arthur Greenwood, a son of William Greenwood of Bradenton, Fla., and the late Mildred Greenwood. Rabbi Richard S. Chapin performed the ceremony.

Mrs. Greenwood and her husband, both 44 years old, are principals in the Berkshire Bank, a private commercial bank in New York. The bride graduated cum laude from the University of Wisconsin and has a master's degree in personnel administration and an M.B.A. from Columbia University. Her first marriage ended in divorce, as did her husband's. Her father, who is retired, was the president of Laurel Printing in New York.

Mrs. Greenwood is the president of the New York Women's Forum and is a member of the National Advisory Council of the United States Small Business Administration.

The bridegroom is a graduate of the University of Oklahoma with an M.B.A. from Bucknell University. His father retired as a vice president of the Chase Manhattan Bank in New York.

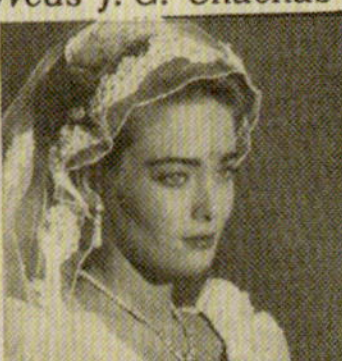

Diane Dougherty Weds J. G. Chachas

Diane Young Dougherty, a television sales executive, and John Gregory Chachas, an associate at the First Boston Corporation, both of New York, were married in Washington yesterday afternoon at St. Sophia's Greek Orthodox Cathedral by the Rev. John Tavlarides. The ceremony was followed by another marriage service last evening at the Metropolitan Memorial United Methodist Church in Washington, conducted by the Rev. William Holmes.

Mrs. Chachas is a daughter of Mr. and Mrs. Thomas J. Dougherty of Bethesda, Md. The bridegroom is the son of Mr. and Mrs. Gregory Chachas of Salt Lake City.

The bride, 27 years old, is a national account sales executive with Capital Cities/ABC. She is a graduate of Barnard College. Her father is a senior vice president of the Metromedia Company. Her mother, Anne D. Dougherty, recently completed two terms as the president of Hospice Care of the District of Columbia.

The bridegroom, 25, is an associate in mergers and acquisitions at First Boston. He is a graduate of Columbia University and has an M.B.A. degree from Harvard University. His mother, Mary P. Chachas, is a community relations associate at the University of Utah Medical Center in Salt Lake City. His father is a lawyer and manages family mineral and other business interests in Salt Lake City.

Diane Chachas

Teen Watches as Dog Is Killed With Wrong Injection by Vet

FORT WORTH, Sept. 29 (AP) — A teen-age boy who took his dog to a veterinarian for a rabies vaccination watched as his pet was mistakenly put to sleep.

"It was a real tragedy, very serious," said Dr. Keith Sultemeier, the veterinarian who operates the clinic in Azle, northwest of Fort Worth.

Tony McCarty, 15 years old, and his mother took their 2½-year-old dog, a pit bull and chow mix named Runt, to the clinic on Thursday, about the same time another similar dog, a female mix of pit bull and chow, was taken in for euthanasia, Dr. Sultemeier said.

The boy was with Runt when the dog got the lethal injection instead of the rabies shot. "The lady and her son came in with a dog for a fairly straightforward vaccination and walked out without the dog," Dr. Sultmeier said. "We are at fault."

The veterinarian bought the boy a full-blooded chow puppy. The mother, Pam Peyton, said she would not sue.

Ms. Froom Weds A Fellow Student

Mignon Froom and Brian Jeffrey Benjamin, both third-year medical students at the University of Rochester, were married yesterday at the Country House, a restaurant in Stony Brook, L.I. Rabbi Joseph Topek officiated. The bride, who is 29 years old, is the daughter of Dr. and Mrs. Jack Froom of Stony Brook. Her husband, who is 24, is a son of Mr. and Mrs. Harvey P. Benjamin of Voorhees, N.J.

Mrs. Benjamin, who is known as Mimi, is a magna cum laude graduate of Brandeis University.

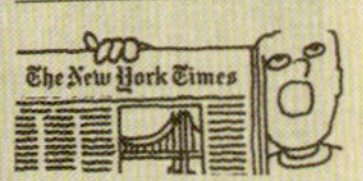

Boy Drowns in Pool

WALLINGFORD, CT Oct.3 (AP)- State officials are questioning a report by local authorities that the drowning of a small boy in a near-empty backyard pool was accidental. According to the initial police report the child's mother, Leah Gober, found her six year old son Robert late Monday evening face down in about three inches of water. State officials have refused to release details but are holding the child's mother for questioning. The family was draining the pool for winter.

Weather Report

Meteorology: Pennsylvania State University

Metropolitan Forecast

High pressure over the South will direct unseasonably warm air into the region this weekend. Aside from a few high clouds, skies will be clear and temperatures will average more than 15 degrees above normal. A cold front will reach northern New York state tomorrow and may cross the region early next week.

New York City: Today, sunny, breezy, warmer. High 83. Tonight, clear, quite mild. Low 64. Tomorrow, mostly sunny, very warm. High 85.

Long Island: Today, sunny, breezy, warmer. High 81. Tonight, clear, quite mild. Low 61. Tomorrow, mostly sunny, very warm. High 83.

Westchester and Rockland: Today, sunny, breezy, warmer. High 79. Tonight, clear, quite mild. Low 58. Tomorrow, mostly sunny, very warm. High 81.

New Jersey: Today, sunny, breezy, warmer. High 84. Tonight, clear, quite mild. Low 62. Tomorrow, mostly sunny, very warm. High 87.

Connecticut: Today, sunny, breezy, warmer. High 80. Tonight, clear, quite mild. Low 59. Tomorrow, mostly sunny, very warm. High 83.

Extended Forecast: Monday and Tuesday will continue to be unseasonably warm, though cloudier. Showers are possible later Tuesday as a cold front nears the region.

National Forecast

Powerful winds coursing through the northern Rockies gusted to 87 miles an hour at Choteau, Mont., on Thursday, a precursor to a strong cold front coming ashore in the Pacific Northwest. Today, the upper-level reflection of the front, marked by a southwest sag in the jet stream from Montana to northern California, will stall through tomorrow morning. In response, high-level winds will blow from the central Rockies to the Great Lakes, impeding the eastward advance of the cold front.

The delay of the front will allow an area of high pressure off the Middle Atlantic Seaboard to act like a heat pump, fostering sunny, unseasonably warm weather in the Northeast this weekend. Humidity will not significantly rise across the region before Monday, owing to the fact that moist air will have to take a circuitous route, slowly spreading north from the western Gulf Coast and then northeast from the lower Mississippi Valley.

The only snag in the weather pattern in the Northeast is the arrival of clouds and showers in northern New England. The cause of the showers there is the collision of cool air that is moving across eastern Canada and warm air from the heat pump high off the Middle Atlantic Coast.

In the wake of the sluggish front, cold air will continue to gather in the northern Rockies. Snow, caused by winds from the east being forced up the mountains, will fall in the Tetons of Wyoming, the Bitterroots of Montana and in Yellowstone Valley, where two large forest fires, fanned by gale-force winds, were out of control on Friday.

Meanwhile, a disturbance from Mexico will spread showers into parts of Texas, Oklahoma and Kansas. In the Tropics, Hurricane Klaus will continue to drift northwestward in the Caribbean.

Today's High Temperatures and Precipitation

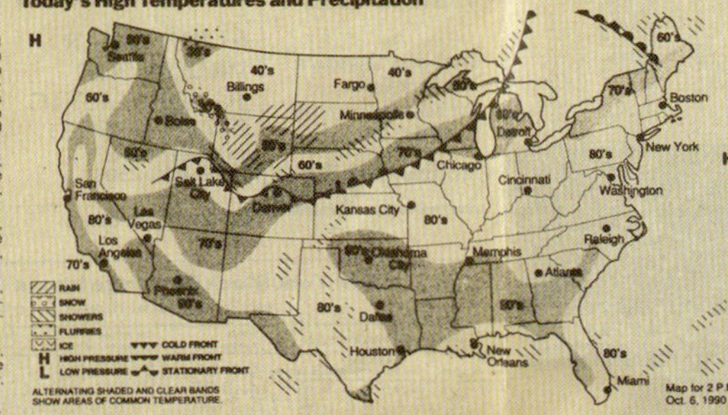

Today's Sunshine and Clouds

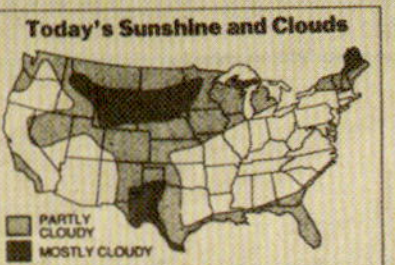

Weather Highlight

Record warmth will cover the southern half of the nation this weekend as very warm air reaches the Northeast today. The upper Plains will be much colder.

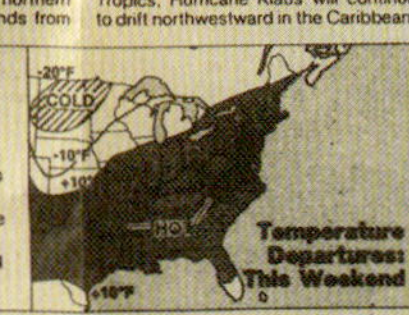

United States and Foreign Cities

Metropolitan Almanac

Regional Recreation

R. Gober '91

all seems rather plausible until a simple Internet search brings everything into question. The most dubious stories — "Girl Lived in a Closet, California Police Say," and "Teen Watches as Dog Is Killed with Wrong Injection by Vet" — turn out to be true (at least they show up in other newspapers), whereas the wedding announcements that seem above suspicion do not match up. The photographs are of people whose marriages occurred in the 1960s, and the texts describe couples married in the 1990s — a strange case of mismatched lovers. Located in the rightmost column, a brief feature bearing the headline "Boy Drowns in Pool" (see p. 98, fig. 6) relates events surrounding the drowning of a young boy in a near-empty backyard pool: "According to the initial police report the child's mother, Leah Gober, found her six year old son Robert late Monday evening face down in about three inches of water." This is a fabricated tale about the artist's own death-by-drowning at the age of six. And we learn, as we read on, that the boy's mother is being held for questioning: not a comforting domestic scenario. Gober brands the paper with the aura of home by carefully hand-painting two coffee rings onto the page (now faded, lower right of the page, midway down the column "United States and Foreign Cities"). Coffee rings are the inevitable domestic mishap, perhaps evoking images of an adult, conceivably a neighbor, seated at a kitchen table reading with horror about the accidental death of little Bobby Gober. By bringing the human-interest story close to home and implying the permeable divide between the public's consumption of news and private experience, Gober likewise brings home the frightening prospect that this tragedy could be our own.

The urge to fiddle with the news puts Gober in good company. No less a figure than Edgar Allan Poe published an invented account of a seventy-five-hour ocean crossing in a lighter-than-air balloon for the *New York Sun,* on April 13, 1844, which left readers scrambling for copies. And Guillaume Apollinaire apparently fabricated entire dispatches from London and New York while working as a translator for a Paris newspaper during World War I.[74] According to his biographer, Apollinaire had come to believe that there was "no better way to influence events."[75]

Gober is a fabricator on two scores: both an inventor of tales and a creator of meticulously produced faux newspapers, so true to life that they could pass as the real thing. Gober's drive to simulate reality borders on obsession, and his newspapers reflect that in such maniacal details as their hand-torn top and bottom edges made ragged to simulate those of a real newspaper. His passion for mimesis and striving for technical brilliance curiously reverses the usual dynamics of an artist's newspaper. In contrast to the norm, Gober's papers are printed with photolithography, a process now familiar more in the fine arts than in mass-production technology. They are also designed to endure, printed on archival-grade papers rather than ephemeral newsprint. Gober's use of fine-art processes and upgraded materials raises questions about his intentions.

Gober's newspapers are not available at newsstands and are pitched to knowing audiences at art galleries and museums. Unlike most faux newspapers, which are, in the main, relatively inexpensive, Gober's carry a hefty price. They bear his handwritten signature and are issued in small editions and identified according to fine arts' terminology: "edition of ten plus two artist's proofs," and "hand-colored with coffee by the artist, 75 unique pieces."

In large measure, these circumstances reflect the current high-powered art market and its sophisticated workings. (One hardly ever hears Gober's works described as artist's newspapers, as if they bear no relation to the genre.) But this circumstance also speaks to a broader shift in perception. Those artists who engaged with newspapers in the first postwar decades, Claes Oldenburg for example, were generally drawn to them because of their debased status (not to say their cheap availability). Unquestionably Oldenburg's newspaper works have accrued substantial monetary value in the past half-century, but they were originally exhibited and marketed under very different conditions than Gober's or, for that matter, those that served most artists engaged with the newspaper in recent decades. As the financial status of the newspaper industry is cast in doubt, paradoxically, the value of the newspaper as a motif has risen in the art world.

Relics

If the twenty-first-century newspaper is headed toward extinction, one conscientious artist/historian will have left us a meticulous record. A first glance at Paul Sietsema's *Modernist Struggle* (2008) may give the impression that the artist used real newspaper, but these images were hand-rendered in ink (pl. 30). The larger depiction is of a half-page from the April 26, 2005, arts section of the *New York Times;* the smaller one is of a fragment from the October 7, 2004, edition of the *Los Angeles Times.* Sietsema transcribed the text from the papers word for word. Unlike Gober, he does not tamper with the news. His strategy is to juxtapose items so as to point out their common (or contradictory) themes.

Most prominent on the *Times* page is a review of an exhibition of artifacts at the Grand Palais in Paris ("France's New Look at Brazil's Indians"), illustrated with pictures of a mummified head and a feathered headdress. According to the review, the exhibition's centerpiece is a collection of works assembled by the French structural anthropologist Claude Lévi-Strauss. To the right is a review of "Luminescence Dating," a play about two archaeologists who become romantically involved. And farthest to the right is an article ("Modernists Struggle with Traditionalists Over Guns") that tells of an Eskimo village in Hooper Bay, Alaska, which allows Eskimos to use hunting rifles but bars police from carrying guns. "The [gun] debate ebbs and flows in town meetings and wherever else it happens to come up," writes the reporter. "It is a passionate, disjointed conflict that signals the larger phenomenon of a traditional people facing the pressures of the modern world." The modern world and its bourgeois culture is manifest in the *Times* ad that reads "Madison Avenue / Where Fashion Meets Art."

There is hardly an aspect of Sietsema's work that does not suggest metaphor or call attention to overlapping themes. The struggle between modernists and traditionalists in the Eskimo village alludes to a similar struggle within the art world. Fleeting news comes up against preserved artifacts. Ephemeral entertainments share coverage with ancient traditions. There is mention of a real social scientist and two actors who play social scientists. Madison Avenue culture rubs shoulders with two endangered cultures. Trompe-l'oeil precision is pitted against a splotch of white paint that has all the signs of a mishap, evoking the opposition of realism and abstraction.

Nearly a century after Picasso parodied illusionistic rendering by incorporating real newspaper into his *papiers collés,* why would Sietsema revive the age-old tradition of trompe-l'oeil rendering, determinedly going against the grain of the modernist program? No doubt he viewed the newspaper differently from Picasso. The once vital and ubiquitous newspaper, which signaled modern culture in 1912, has by now acquired a patina. Sietsema approached the newspaper as a cultural relic, similar to the mummified head.

There is something contradictory, even absurd, about Jim Hodges' twenty-first-century campaign to gild newspapers (pl. 31). The newspaper, after all, is infamous for its cheap materials and ephemerality, while gold aligns with preciousness and durability. Hodges enters into a dialogue that began over a century ago. Mallarmé railed against the newspaper's prose, deeming it valueless compared to the gold of poetry. And in the words of David Cottington, Picasso aimed to turn "the dross of the vernacular . . . into the gold of art."[76]

While Hodges' campaign falls at the high end of the spectrum, it is evidence of a general rise in the number of contemporary artists engaged with the newspaper and their changed perception of its worth. Gober, Sietsema, and Hodges all supplant its cheap makeup by introducing archival-grade papers, even 24K gold. The artist Fred Tomaselli, a professed newspaper junkie, selects items from the *New York Times* and digitally scans them onto watercolor paper, subsequently coloring them by hand. Tomaselli explains that he prefers the watercolor paper's

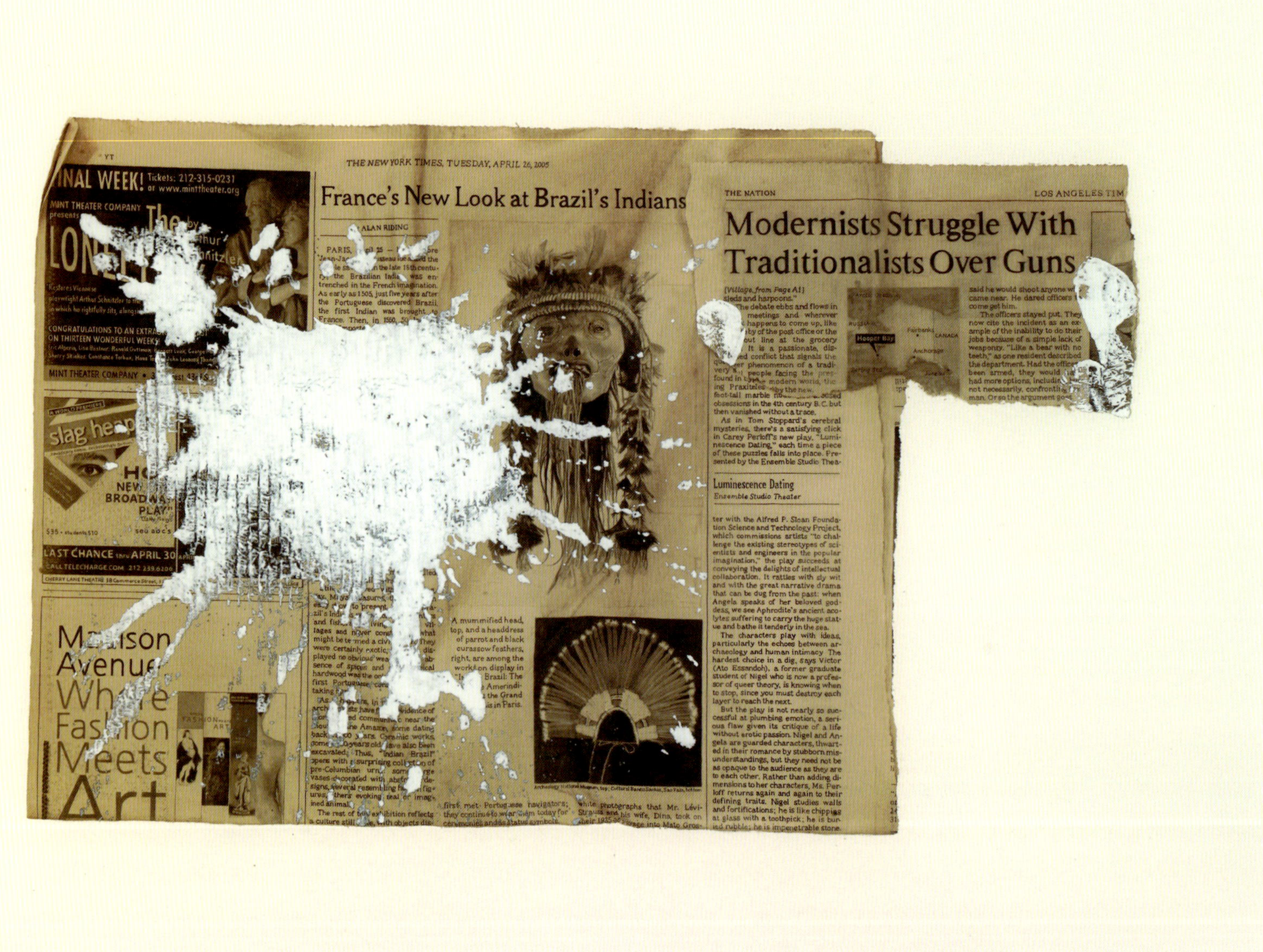

30

PAUL SIETSEMA

Modernist Struggle

2008, ink and enamel on paper, 29 ¼ × 39 ¾ (74.3 × 101), Collection of Dean Valentine and Amy Adelson, Los Angeles

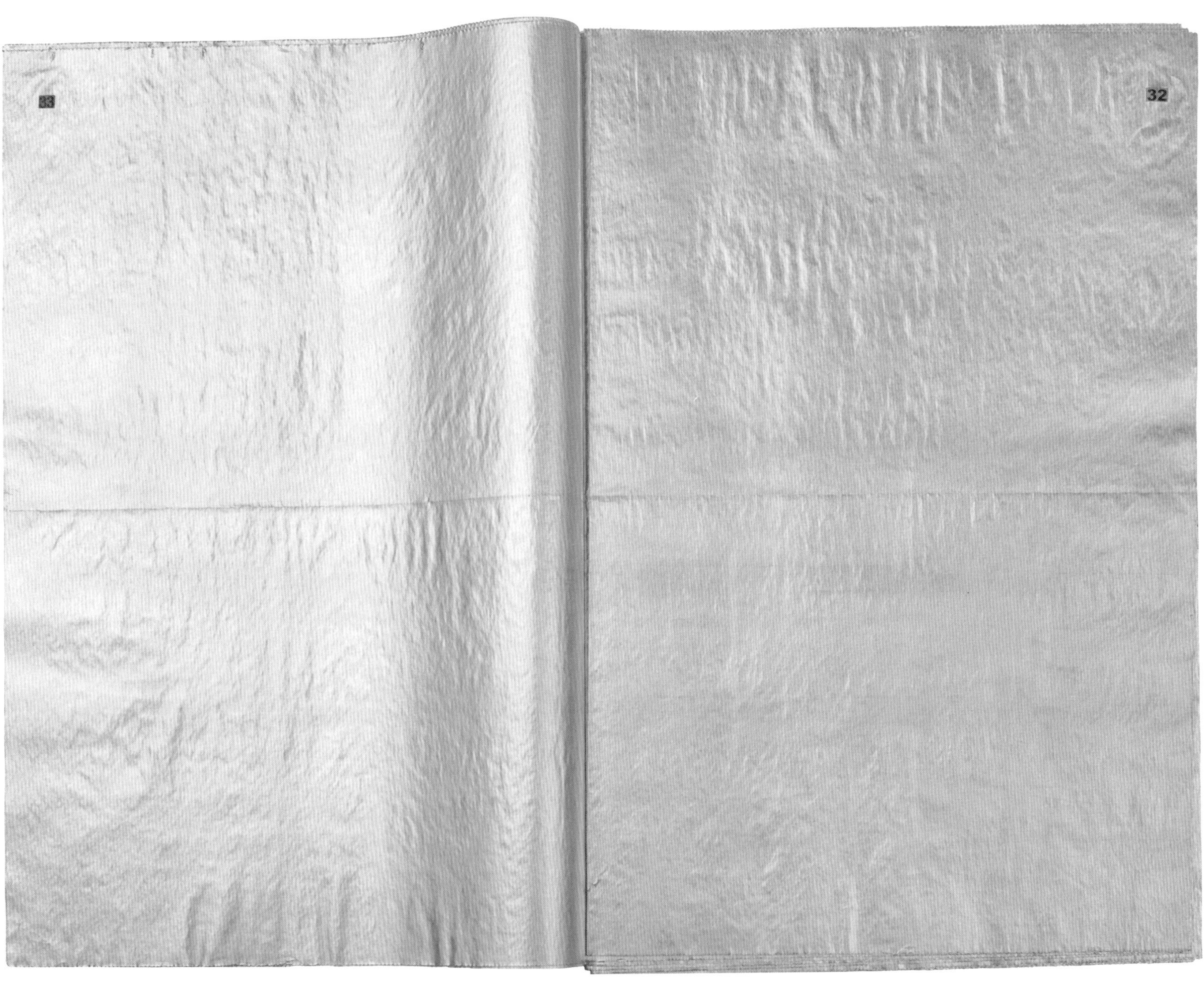

31

JIM HODGES

The Good News / Al Arab Al Yawm, 8/6/2008 (Amman, Jordan)

2008–2009, 24K gold on newspaper, open: 22 ¾ × 30 (57.8 × 76.2), Collection of Eric and Elizabeth Feder

surface but is quick to add that he also strives to ensure the work's longevity.[77] The artist Aleksandra Mir and her assistants spent months copying ten thousand front pages from New York's *Daily News* and the *New York Post,* ritualistically re-presenting hundreds of them in the form of handmade drawings. Peruvian artist Fernando Bryce shares the same compulsion but focuses on faithful transcriptions of historic newspapers. One detects a memorializing tendency at work.

"Just chimney soot on chopped up trees" is how an insider sums up the newspaper.[78] Reduced to its elemental basics, the newspaper hardly seems worth the flood of attention it has received from artists. But the evidence speaks otherwise. A montage by a lesser-known photographer, Semen Fridliand, may provide the most revealing lens through which to appraise our wide-ranging history.

Fridliand's work shows a young woman peering out through a dizzying haze of French newspapers (pl. 32). The Russian photojournalist published it in 1927 in the Soviet illustrated magazine *Ogonëk* (The flame) and again in 1929, in *Foto-Auge* (Photo eye), a book of montages edited by Franz Roh and Jan Tschichold.[79] In *Ogonëk,* the work was titled *The Face of the Bourgeois Press;* in *Foto-Auge,* it was called *Die käufliche Presse* (The venal press).[80] Either designation leaves little doubt about the message being touted, specifically that bourgeois newspapers may very well cloud your vision. According to John Heartfield, bourgeois newspapers could also leave you blind and dimwitted.

Artists of various persuasions have responded to the newspaper in modes that seem utterly dizzying. Marinetti led the way by carrying out a raid on the pages of an establishment daily, enlisting it as a propaganda tool. Picasso recognized the newspaper's ability to multitask. Arthur Dove demonstrated that what critics publish in the newspaper can come back to bite them. Hans Richter created a history painting in newspaper and oils that rivaled the scale and impact of the grand tradition. Ellsworth Kelly used newspaper to "deconstruct" Picasso. Robert Morris repudiated what he read in the newspaper by drowning it in gray. Sarah Charlesworth gave us visual proof that newspapers construct different "pictures" of the same event, and Robert Gober used the paper to test our ability to discern fact from fiction. Even those who would have us believe that they remained numb to disturbing headlines understood that the newspaper could still deliver a shock.

The newspaper scrim that shades the young woman's face in Fridliand's montage also suggests a kaleidoscopic view. Every turn of the instrument generates a new configuration, and there is no way to predict what the next view will be. This sense of continual shift evokes a phrase made famous in *The Original Amateur Hour,* a popular radio and television show that aired in the United States from 1934 to 1970. Every program would begin with the spinning of a wheel and the host's voice intoning the words "round and round she goes, and where she stops nobody knows." Although the history of modern artists' engagement with the newspaper may be anchored in the strategies mapped out by Marinetti and Picasso, the newspaper phenomenon has also shown a remarkable ability to adapt to and shift with the times. With the influence of the Internet impinging on the newspaper's vigor, and even its existence, it is natural to feel that we are at a crossroads. But as with the proverbial wheel going round and round, it is impossible to know how things will spin out.

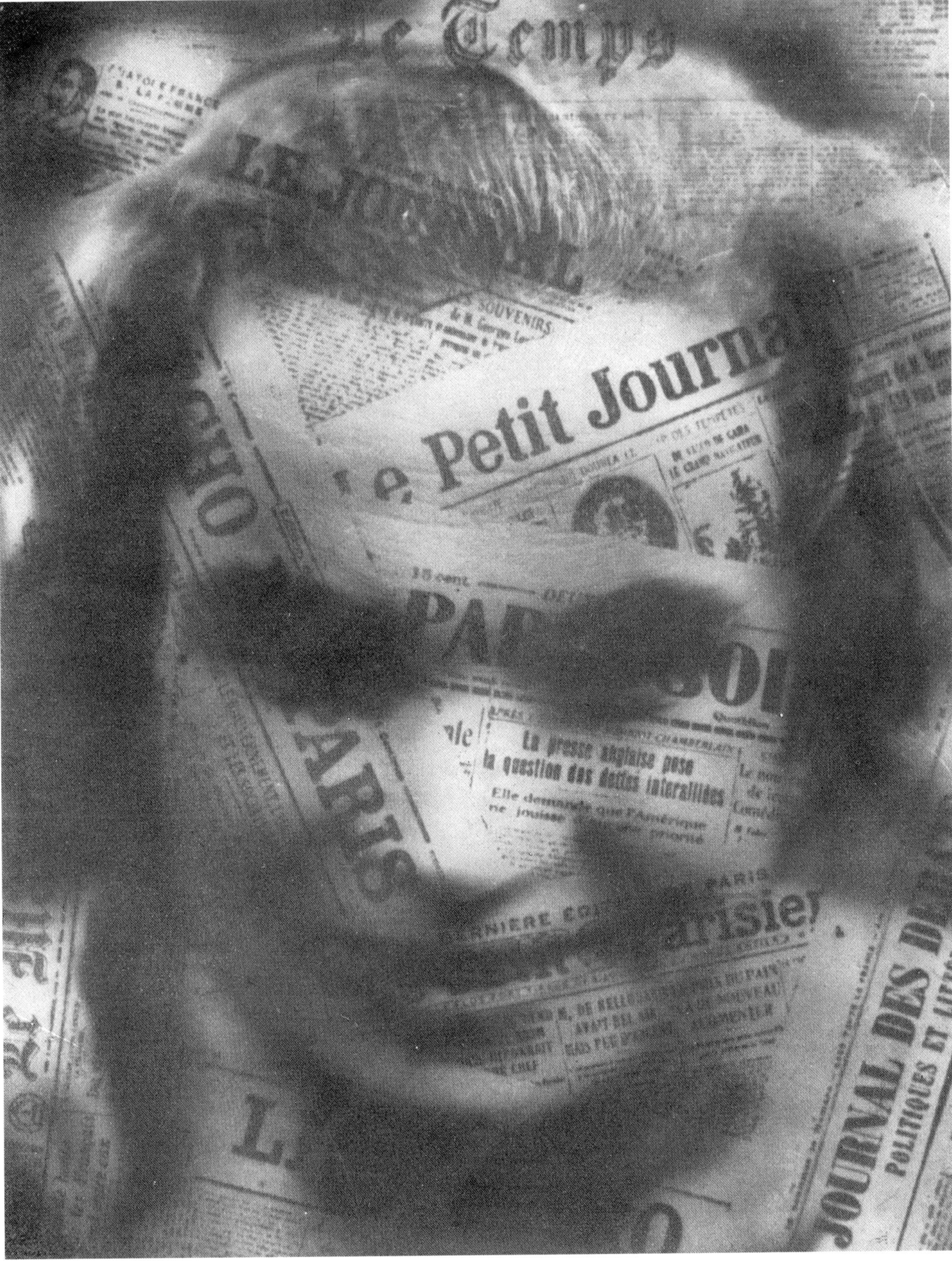

32

SEMEN FRIDLIAND

Die käufliche Presse

(The venal press), in **Foto-Auge**

1929, halftone reproduction, 6 ¼ × 8 ¼ (16 × 21), National Gallery of Art Library, David K. E. Bruce Fund

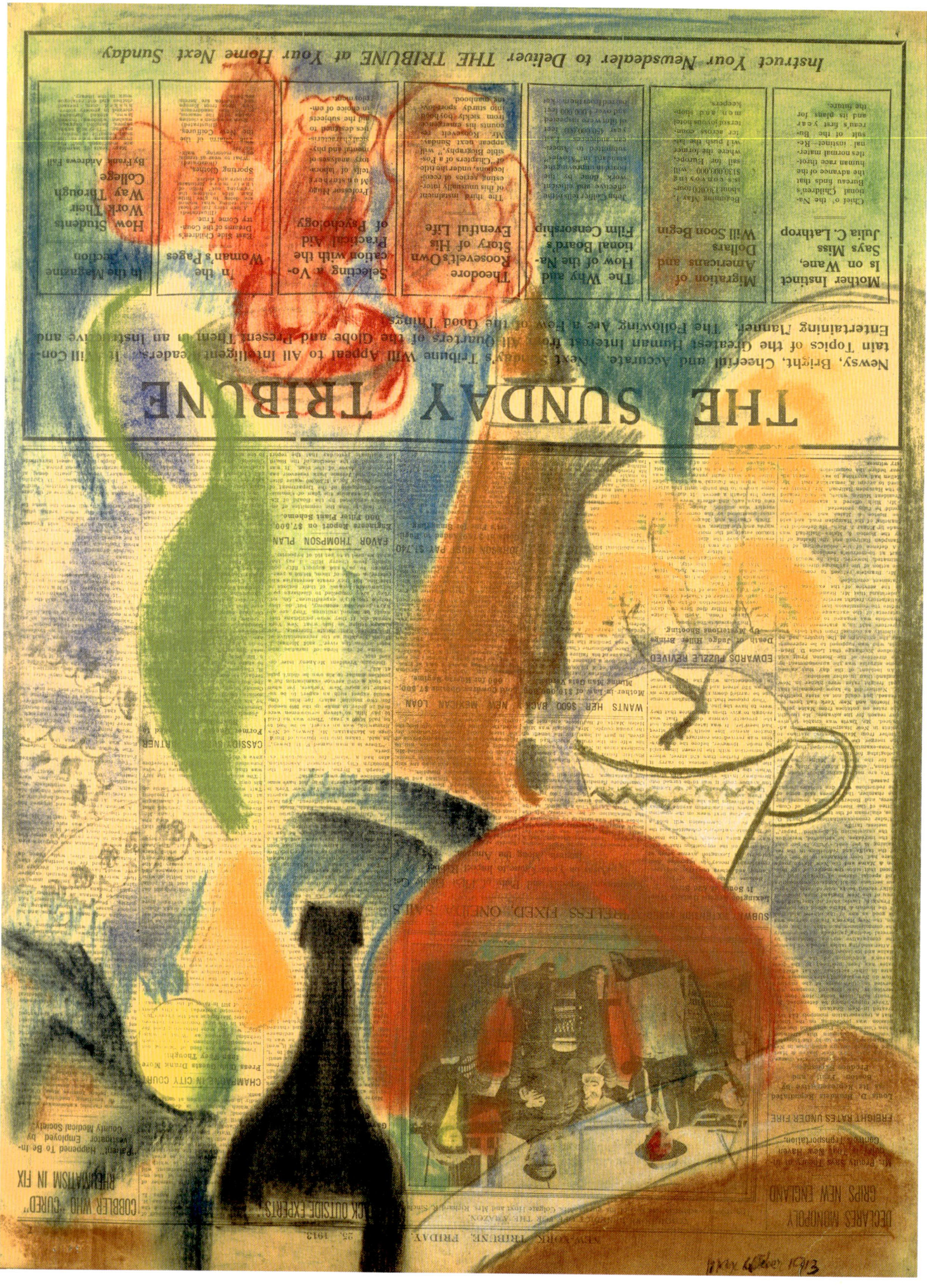

33

MAX WEBER

The Sunday Tribune

1913, pastel on newspaper,
22 ½ × 16 ⅜ (57.2 × 41.6), Private collection, New York

How is it that Picasso in Paris and Weber in New York conceived of the same strategy within months of each other? Each took a full page of newspaper, inverted it, and used it as a support-cum-background for a composition. Although Weber had lived in Paris from 1905 to 1908 and knew Picasso — indeed, he was influential in getting him his first exhibition in the United States — Weber was firmly planted in New York in 1913, as Picasso was in Paris.

Weber's *Sunday Tribune* is on a page of newspaper dated Friday, April 25, 1913. The two relevant works by Picasso are on newspaper pages dated December 8, 1912, and May 6, 1913 (pl. 6). Presuming that both artists used the newspapers soon after their publication, which is likely but not certain, then Weber's *Sunday Tribune* followed Picasso's first venture by a little over four months. Was this a matter of influence or coincidence? Weber could have come upon the idea independently, but he probably got wind of it from an avant-garde insider visiting New York to see the Armory Show, which ran from February 17 to March 15, 1913 (following the publication of Picasso's earlier newspaper source and preceding the publication of Weber's.

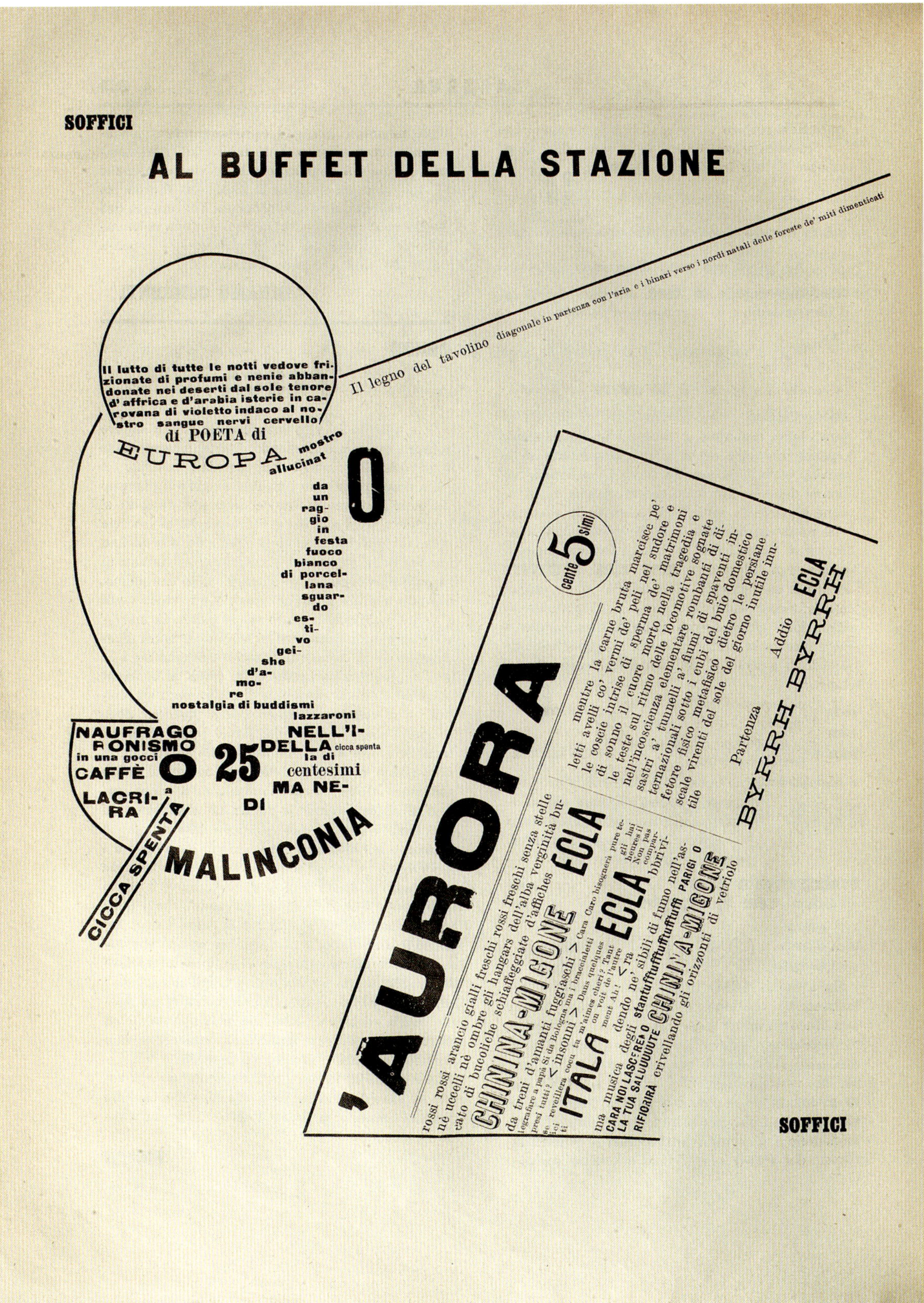

34

ARDENGO SOFFICI

Al buffet della stazione ***(In the railway café), in*** **Lacerba** ***2, no. 15***

August 1, 1914, photomechanical reproduction, 14⅜ × 21¼ (36.5 × 54), The Art Institute of Chicago, Ryerson and Burnham Libraries

The avant-garde journal *Lacerba* promoted futurist ideas, art, and poetry. Although *Al buffet della stazione* represents a traditional subject—a still life of a coffee cup and saucer, an extinguished cigarette (*cicca spenta*), and a newspaper bearing the masthead *[L]'Aurora*—it is otherwise unconventional. Neither painted nor drawn, Soffici's still life is made up of printed words, which spill over the cup's rim, run down its side, and fill the front page of a newspaper. Soffici created a word-picture as well as a free-word poem—dubbed *parole in libertà* (words in freedom) by Marinetti—evoking the stream-of-consciousness reflections of a person drinking coffee and reading a newspaper at a railway café.

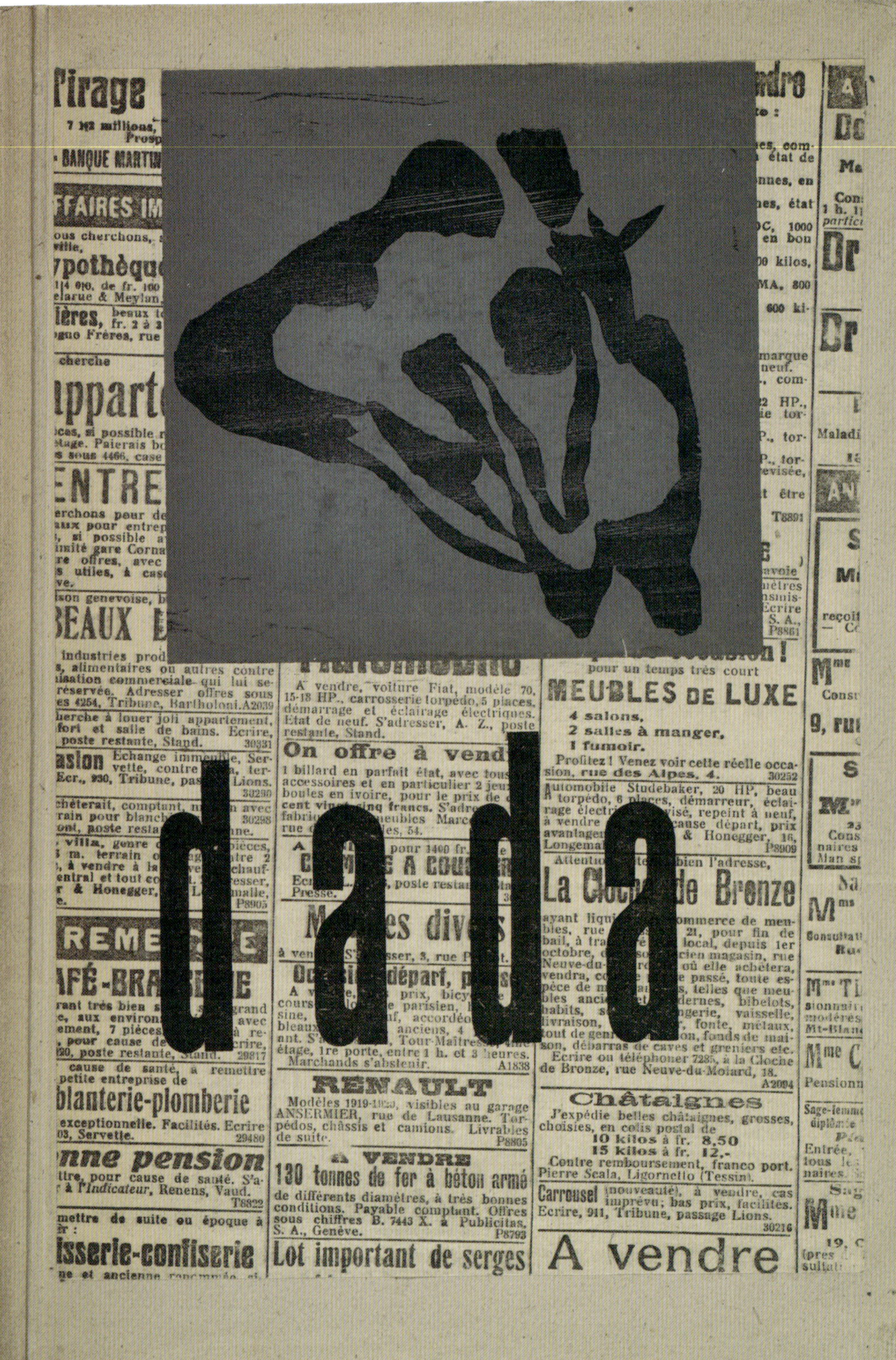

35

JEAN (HANS) ARP

***Cover of the journal* Dada, *no. 4–5:* Anthologie Dada**

(Zurich, 1919), woodcut on colored paper adhered to newspaper (deluxe edition), 10¾ × 7¼ (27.4 × 18.5), Beinecke Rare Book and Manuscript Library, Yale University

---

This deluxe edition of the *Anthologie Dada* underscores Dada's rupture with traditional fine-art practices. Both the deluxe and regular editions of the anthology feature Arp's original woodcut on the cover. But only the deluxe edition includes real newspaper as well. Instead of offering a fancy leather binding to purchasers of the superior and more costly edition, Arp and the book's editor, Tristan Tzara, opted for lowly and ephemeral newspaper—a decidedly antideluxe approach.

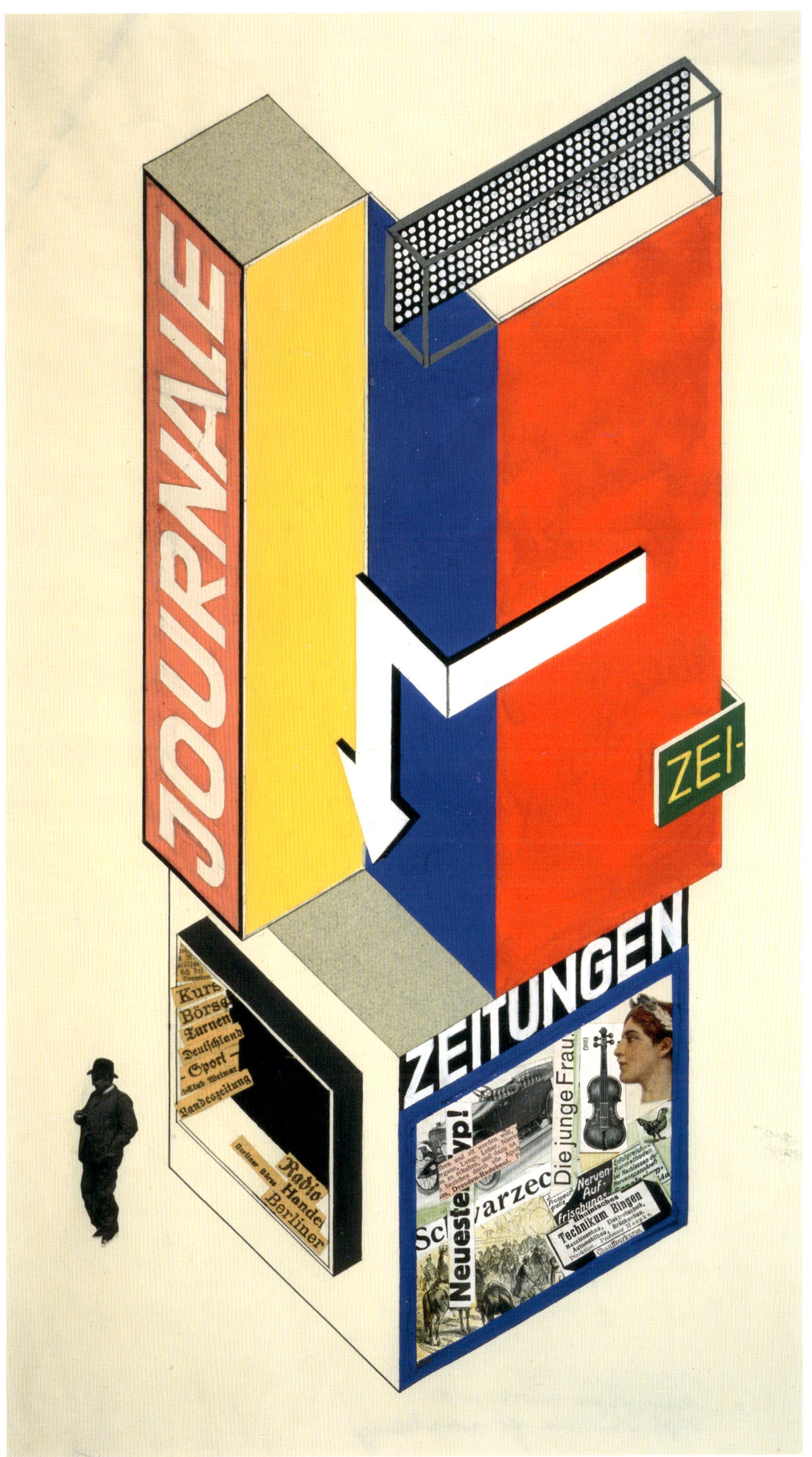

36

HERBERT BAYER

Design for a Newspaper Kiosk

1924, tempera, paper, and collage over graphite on paper, 25⅜ × 13⅝ (64.5 × 34.5), Bauhaus-Archiv Berlin

Bayer's plan for a newspaper stand reveals a more than passing knowledge of de Stijl and Russian constructivism. It also suggests a familiarity with designs for kiosks by such Russian artists as Aleksei Gan and Gustav Klutsis. Made while Bayer was still a student at the Bauhaus, the design is dominated by two rectangular units, painted red, blue, yellow, and pink, that overhang a cubicle, its left side featuring an open frame with rows of titles clipped from newspapers and magazines, and its right side collaged with clippings from advertisements. The words *Zeitungen* (newspapers) and *Journale* (magazines) in white letters are aligned horizontally and vertically, and a bright white arrow aims itself (and the viewers' eyes) downward to the newsstand.

Hal Foster aptly describe Bayer's advertising structures as "imagin[ing] what architecture will be in a mass-mediated society, how virtual it will become when the old imperative of shelter succumbs to the new priority of publicity, when structure is refashioned as sign" (Bergdoll and Dickerman 2009, 181). Bayer's design for a newspaper kiosk is just such an imagining—a supersized advertisement masquerading as a kiosk.

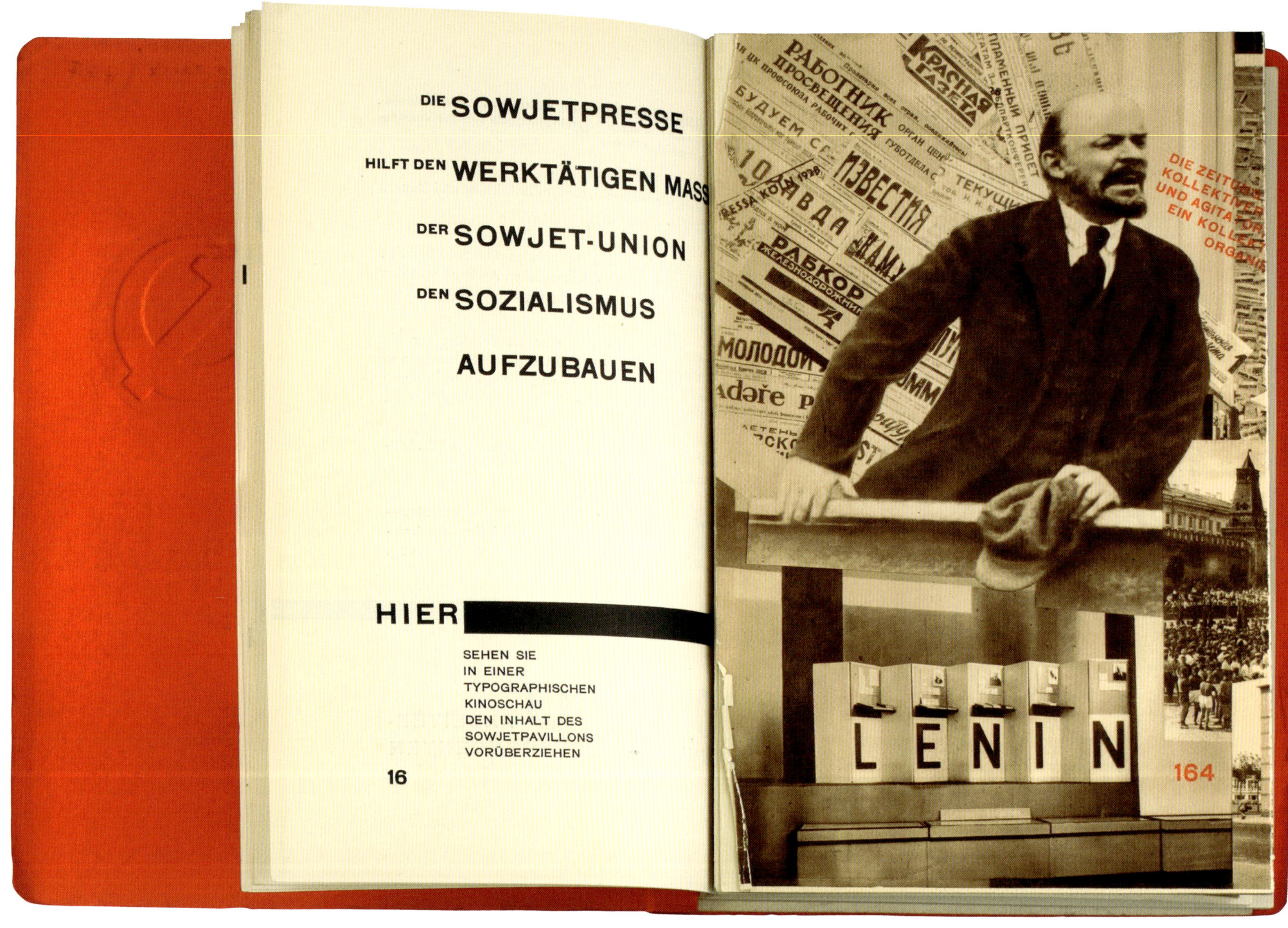

37

EL LISSITZKY AND SERGEI SEN'KIN

Katalog des Sowjet-Pavillons auf der Internationalen Presse-Ausstellung *(Catalogue of the Soviet Pavilion at the International Press Exhibition)*

(Cologne, 1928), concertina volume with photomechanical reproductions, closed: 8 ¼ × 6 (21 × 15.2); fully extended: 8 ¼ × 91 ⅛ (21 × 231.5), Collection Merrill C. Berman

38

SPANISH 20TH CENTURY

L'Opinió

1932, rotogravure, 18 7/8 × 13 3/4 (47.9 × 34.9), Collection Merrill C. Berman

---

Silhouetted in a contour line, a young newsboy holds copies of *L'Opinió*, a center-left Catalonian newspaper published in Barcelona from 1928 to 1934. A tray of letterpress type serves as the design's backdrop, as if ready for printing the front page of *L'Opinió*. According to Deborah Roldán at the Fundación Juan March, "this seemingly innocuous advertising poster was also one of political propaganda and served the dual purpose of advertising not only a leftist newspaper but its agenda as well, exhorting men to go out and vote 'left' in the coming elections." The exhortation is made explicit in the paper's motto, visible to the right of the masthead. Carrying the date September 23, 1932, the paper would have been published a month before the first democratic elections in Catalonia, which resulted in an overwhelming victory for the left.

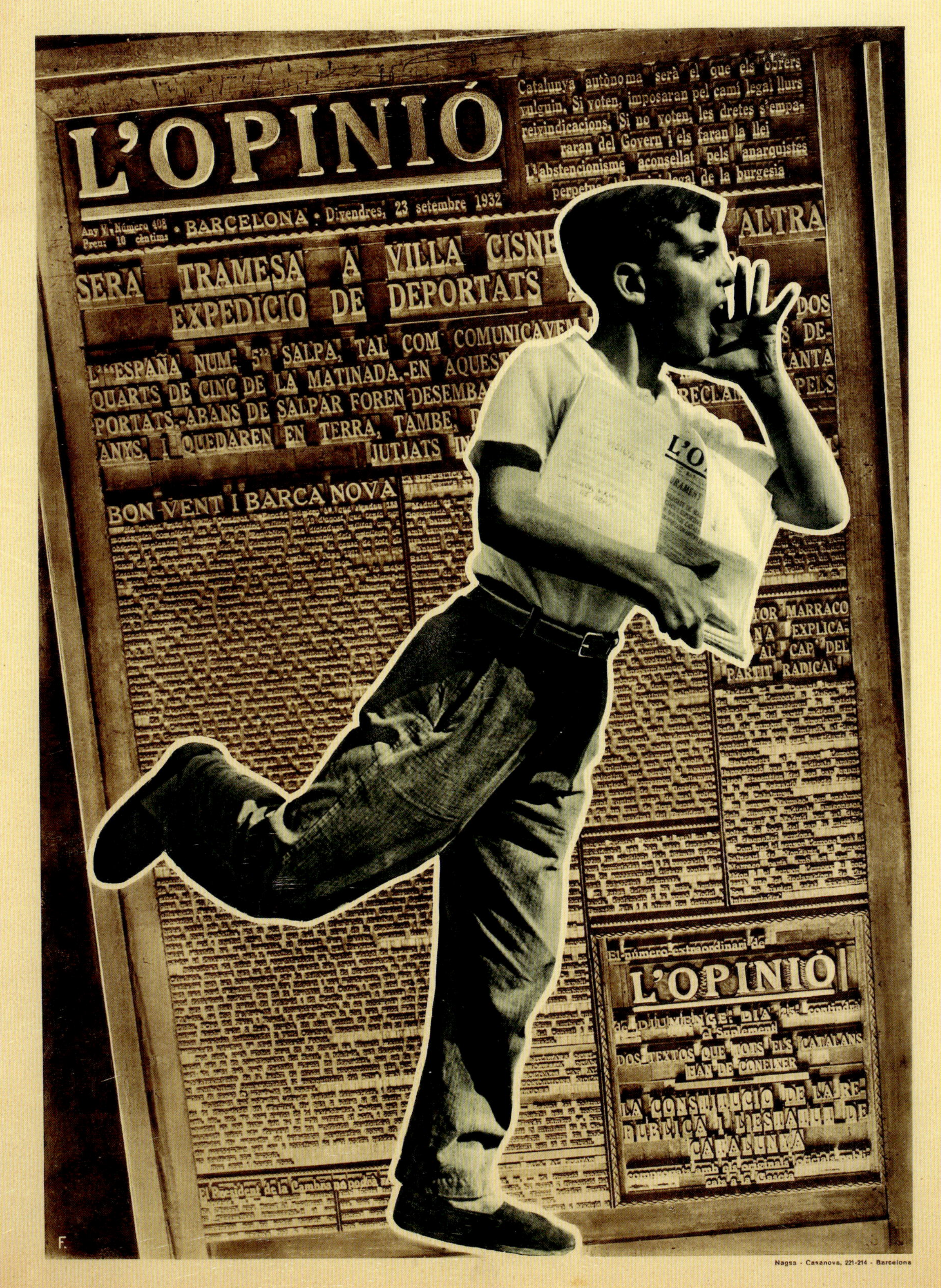

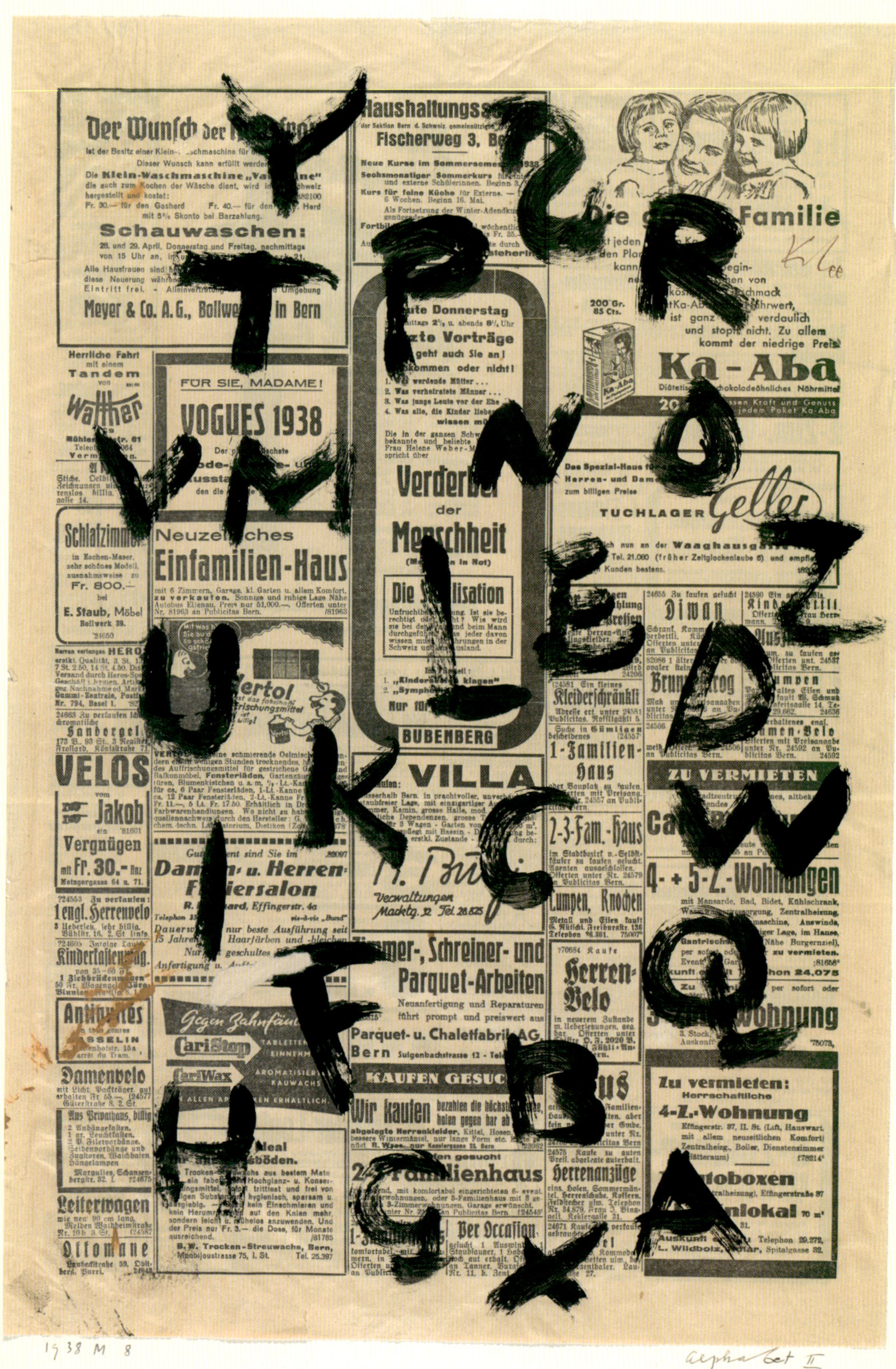

39

PAUL KLEE

Alpha bet II

1938, pigmented paste on newspaper, 19 ¼ × 13 (49 × 33), Zentrum Paul Klee, Bern

Each letter in Klee's dashed-off alphabet is like a jaunty stick figure let loose on a regulated typographical field—the field's mechanical type serving as a foil to the artist's spontaneous lettering.

Scores of Klee's paintings include newspaper, though it usually underlies layers of paint and is visible only on close inspection. In this and another alphabet work in the collection of the Zentrum Paul Klee in Basel, pages from the *National Zeitung* remain prominent. Indeed, Klee seems to have been as inspired by the newspaper's typography, as was Picasso in his *Head of a Man with a Moustache* (pl. 6).

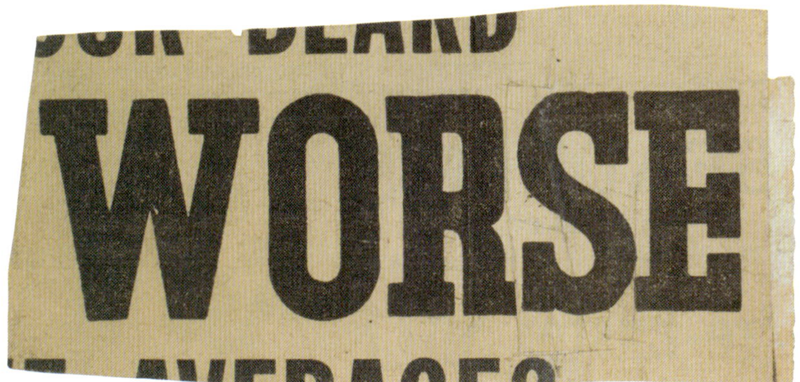

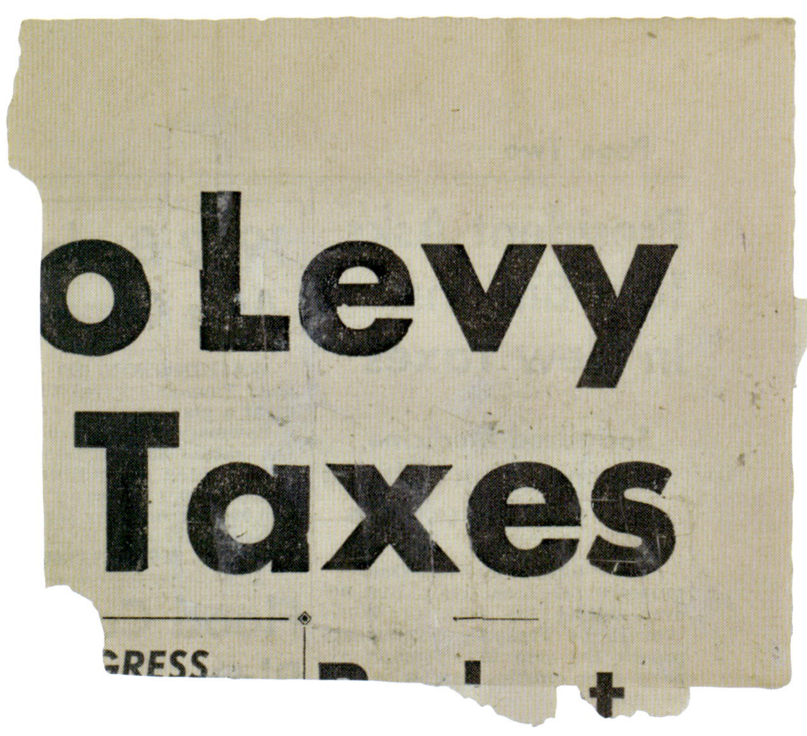

40

JAMES CASTLE

three untitled newspaper fragments

c. 1930 / 1950, cut and re-adhered newspaper, dimensions vary, James Castle Collection and Archive

It is unlikely that Castle thought of these newspaper fragments as works of art. Different from his drawings and constructions, they were conceptual in nature, based on an intense fascination with letters and words.

His procedure was as follows: Castle would tear fragments from newspapers, typically focusing on a single word or phrase. He then would excise small sections of letters, for example, a serif from an *E* or a bend from an *S*. Last he would reverse the procedure, refitting the excised sections back into place. Except for telltale incision marks, each newspaper fragment would end up looking much as it had at the outset. The practice takes on almost yogic dimensions, considering that Castle engaged in it for decades.

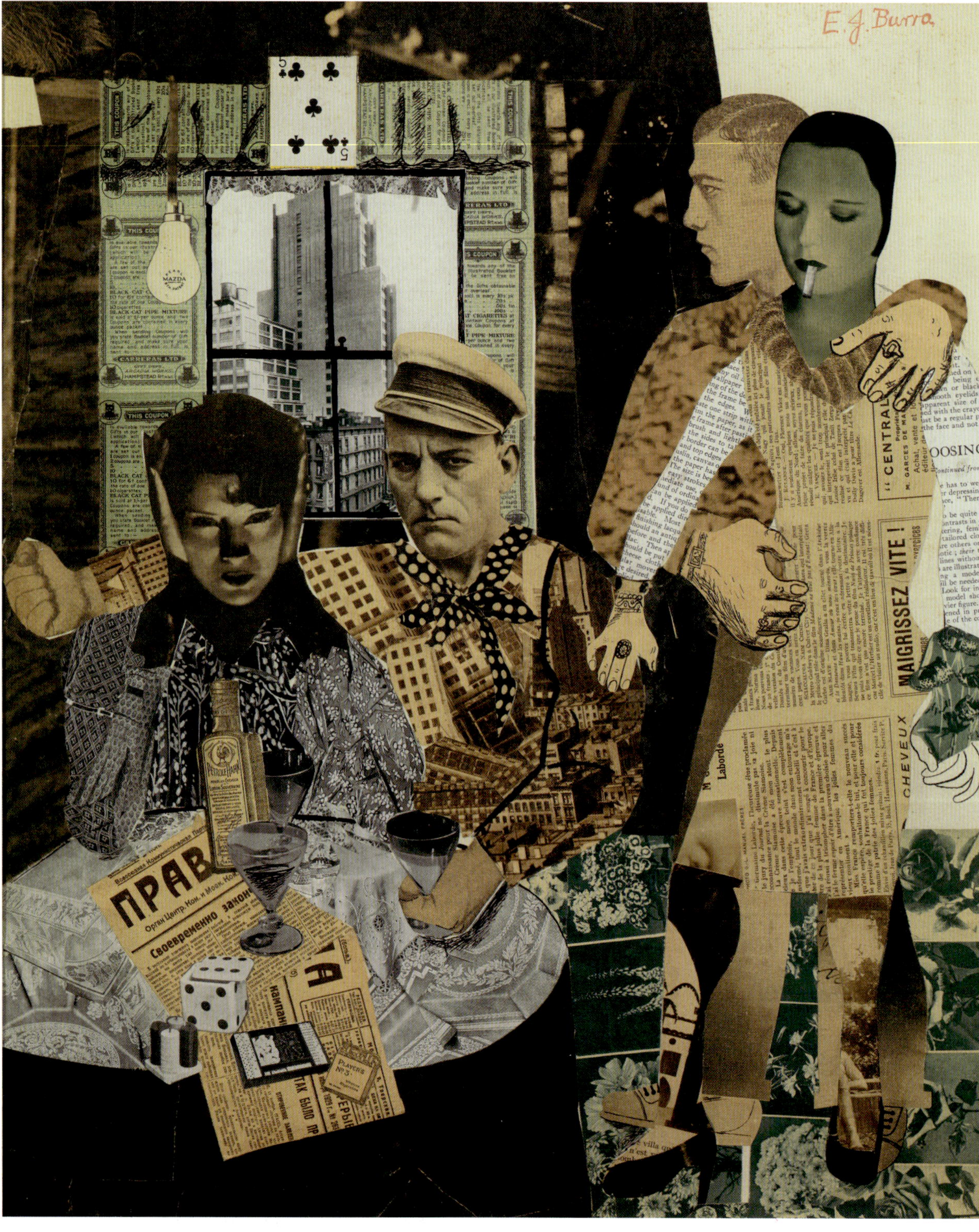

41

EDWARD BURRA

Composition Collage

1929, collage and ink on paper, 18¾ × 15½ (47.6 × 39.4), Private collection

---

Burra's collage contains clippings from an array of sources, including the Russian newspaper *Pravda* on the café table. The dress of the standing woman was taken from a French newspaper and features an article about Germaine Laborde, Miss France of 1928. Where the woman's waistline curves inward, an advertisement announces "MAIGRISSEZ VITE!" (Lose weight fast!). (*Plus ça change, plus c'est la même chose.*) The man embracing her from behind bears the cutout face of Primo Carnera, an Italian boxing champion. And at the café table on the left two figures bear the faces of American silent-film stars Louise Brooks and Lon Chaney.

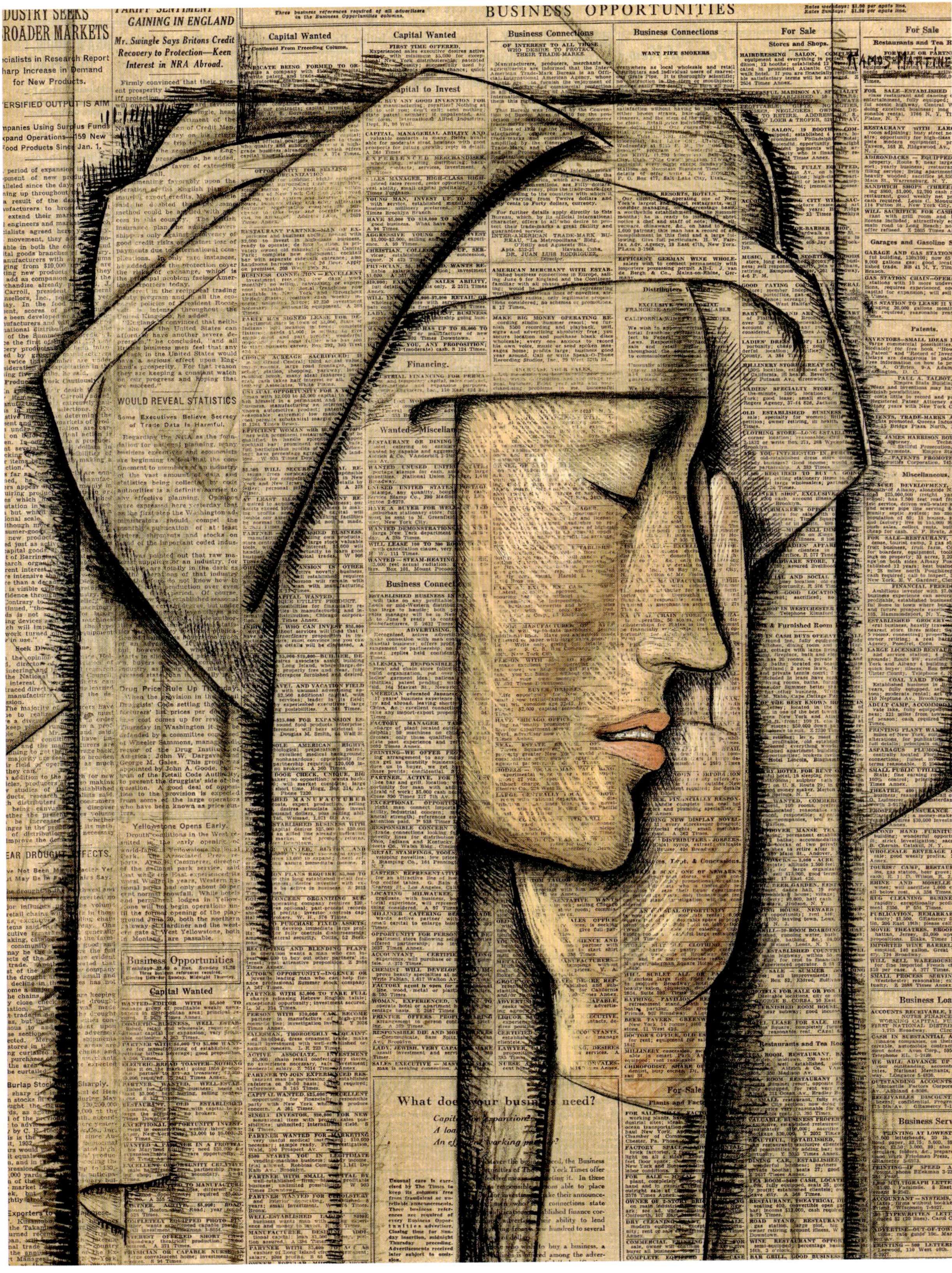

42

ALFREDO RAMOS MARTINEZ

Head of a Nun

1934, tempera on newspaper, 20 ½ × 15 ½ (52 × 39.4), Madeline and Bruce Ramer Collection

One would hardly expect the image of a nun to turn up on a newspaper page largely concerned with business opportunities and job listings. Ramos Martinez may have been underlining the tension between the spiritual and the secular, or he may simply have liked the way the newspaper columns lend structure to the nun's veil and add atmosphere to the composition overall.

Ramos Martinez's career got an important boost when the philanthropist Phoebe Hearst, mother of newspaper tycoon William Randolph Hearst, visited Mexico City in 1899. She happened upon some of Ramos Martinez's work and arranged to meet the young artist, whom she took under her wing and supported for the next seven years, enabling him to move to Paris. In 1910 he returned to Mexico, where he established himself as an artist, and then moved to Los Angeles in 1929. He continued to make easel paintings and murals in California as well as works on newspaper, including this head of a nun that relates to a mural he made for a chapel at the Santa Barbara Cemetery.

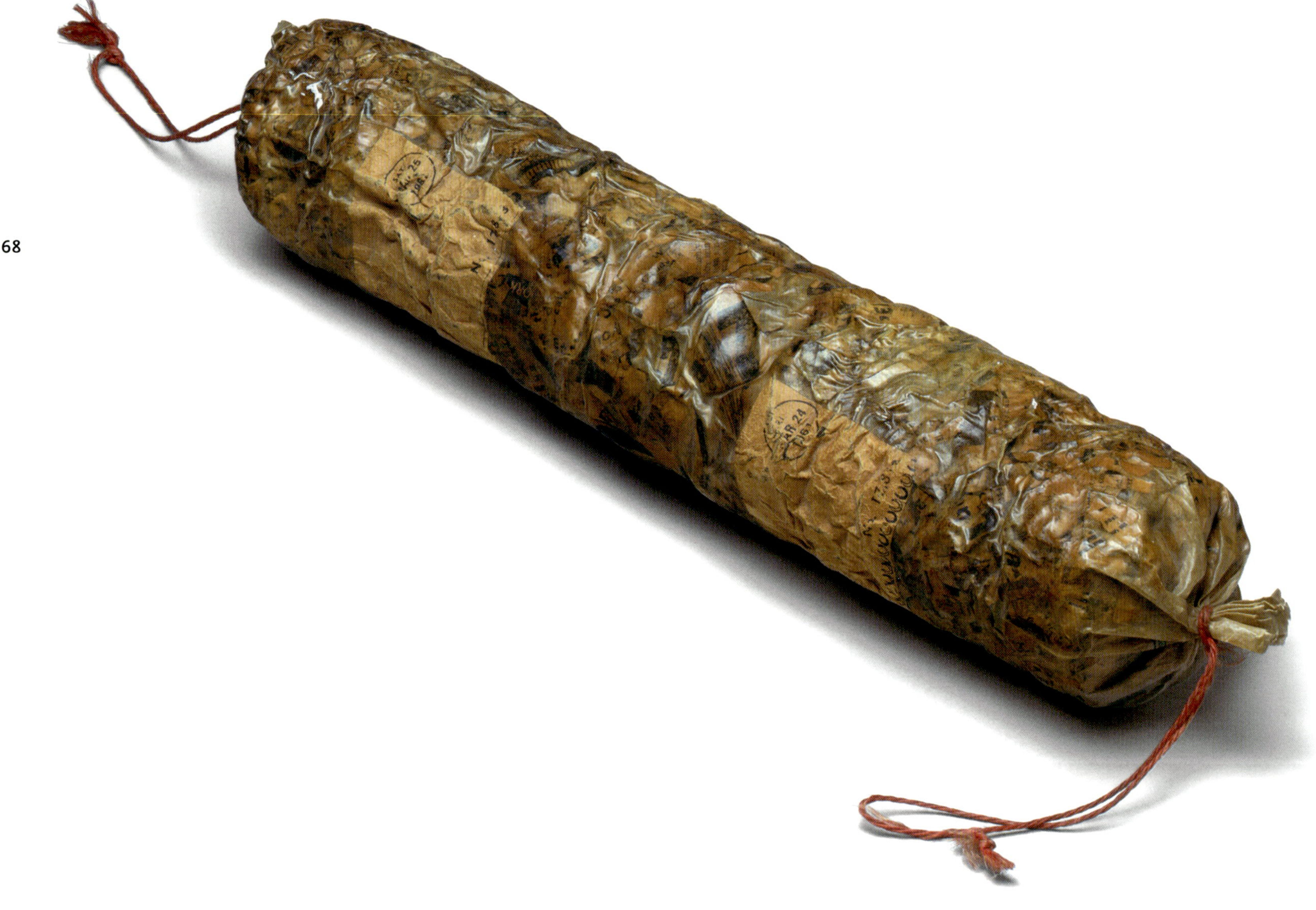

43

DIETER ROTH

Literaturwurst (Daily Mirror)

1961, newspaper, water, gelatin, and spices in sausage casing, 18 × 5 (45.7 × 12.7), Barbara Wien, Berlin

Rightly or wrongly, sausage makers are notorious for using lesser or even dubious cuts of meat. Roth turned to sausage making in the 1960s and 1970s, employing such customary ingredients as spices, water, and gelatin. But in place of ground meat, he substituted pages from books or magazines he disdained or whose authors he wished to needle. His sources ranged from *Der Spiegel* to Günther Grass' *Tin Drum*. Equally unorthodox, he marketed the Literaturwursts as artist's books.

The very first, *Literaturwurst (Daily Mirror)*, is the only one to incorporate newspaper, namely the British tabloid the *Daily Mirror*. It is further distinguished for being the only Literaturwurst made personally by Roth and prepared using a traditional animal-intestine casing. (Subsequent wursts were fabricated by trained technicians who used plastic casings.) Roth gave his prized *Literaturwurst (Daily Mirror)* to the artist Daniel Spoerri, who kindly returned it years later. Roth subsequently bestowed it on its present owner.

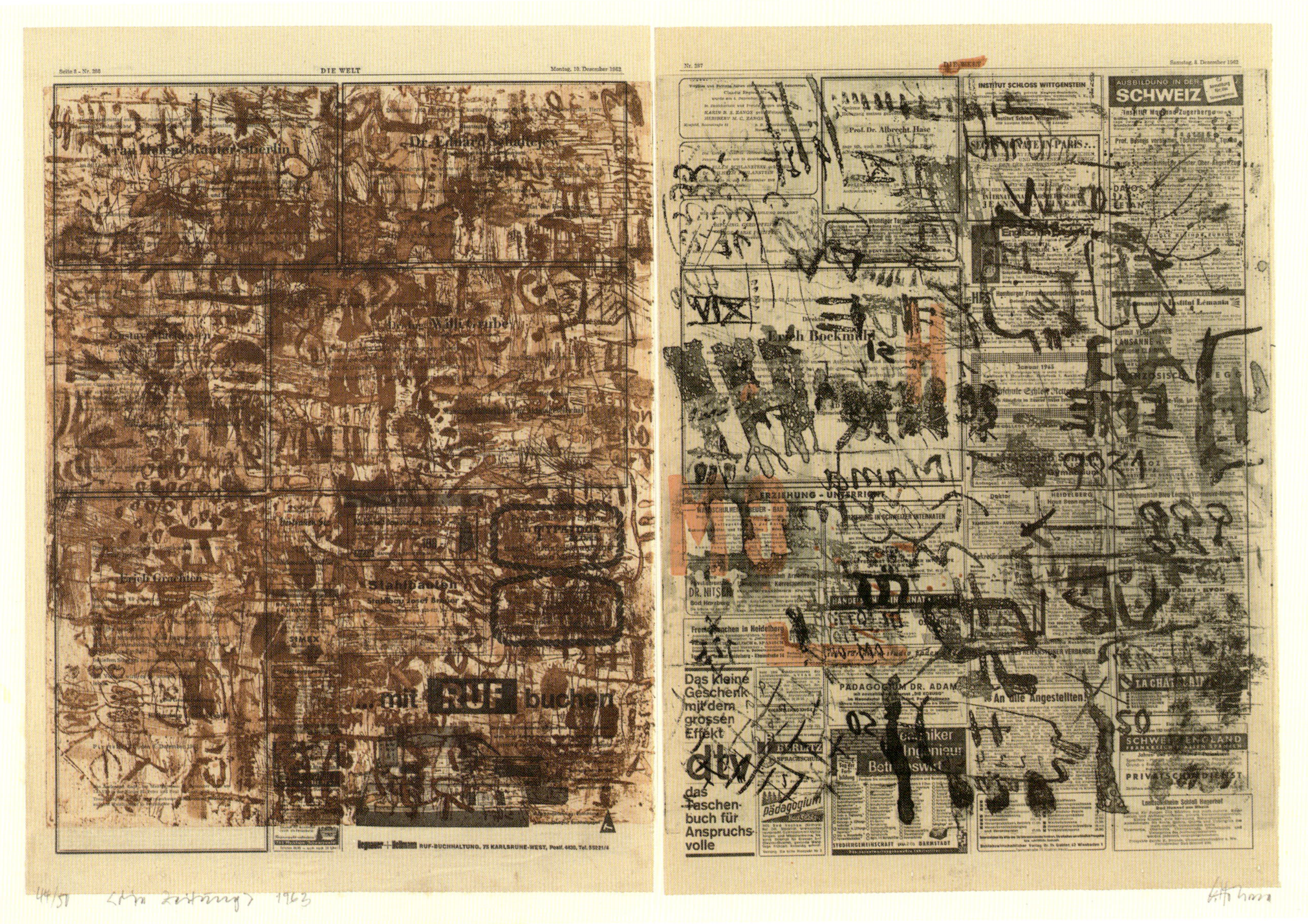

44

GERHARD HOEHME

Die Zeitung (Newspaper)

1963, etching and aquatint with hand-coloring, printed on two sheets of newspaper, mounted on paper, 23 5/8 × 33 3/4 (60.1 × 85.6), National Gallery of Art, Washington, Gift of Ruth Cole Kainen, 2012

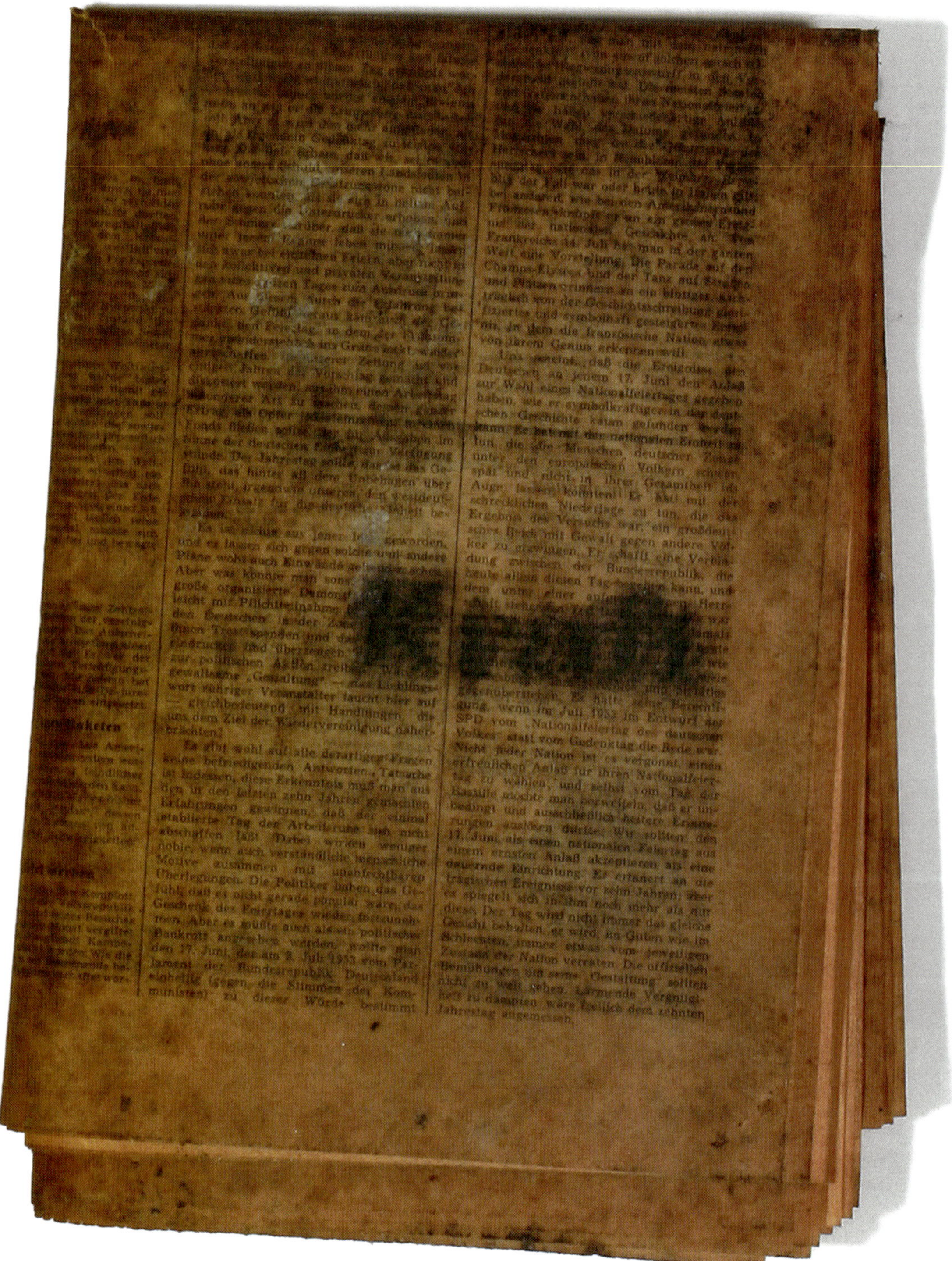

45

JOSEPH BEUYS

Kraft

1963, ink on fat-impregnated newspaper (folded), 12 ¼ × 8 ⅞ × ⅞ (31.2 × 22.5 × 2.2), Museum Schloss Moyland, Van der Grinten Collection

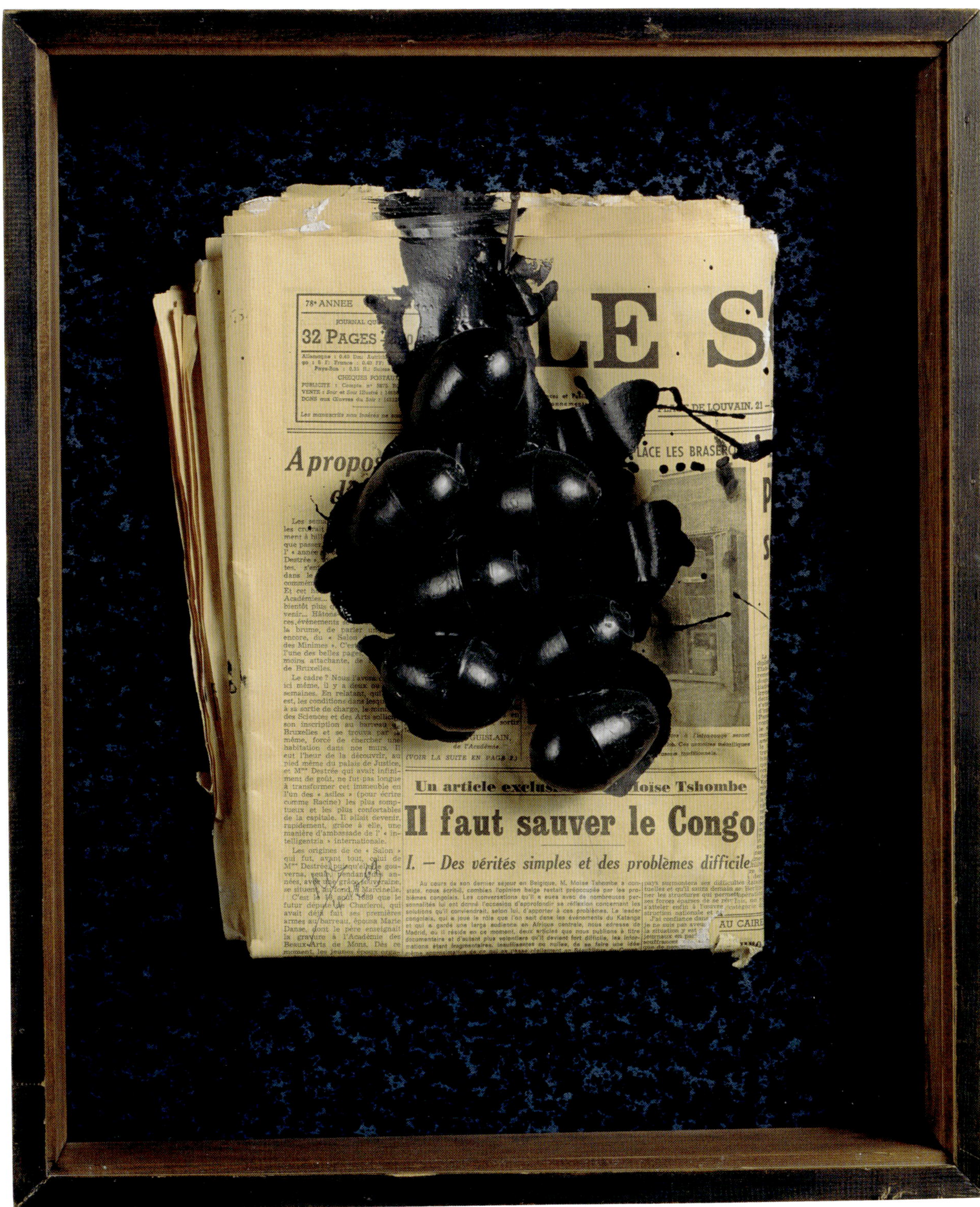

46

MARCEL BROODTHAERS

Le problème noir en Belgique

(The black problem in Belgium)

1963, newspaper, manufactured eggs, paint, metal nail, and gesso on prepared backing; artist's frame: 19⅝ × 16⅛ × 3 (50 × 41 × 7.5), Private collection, The Netherlands

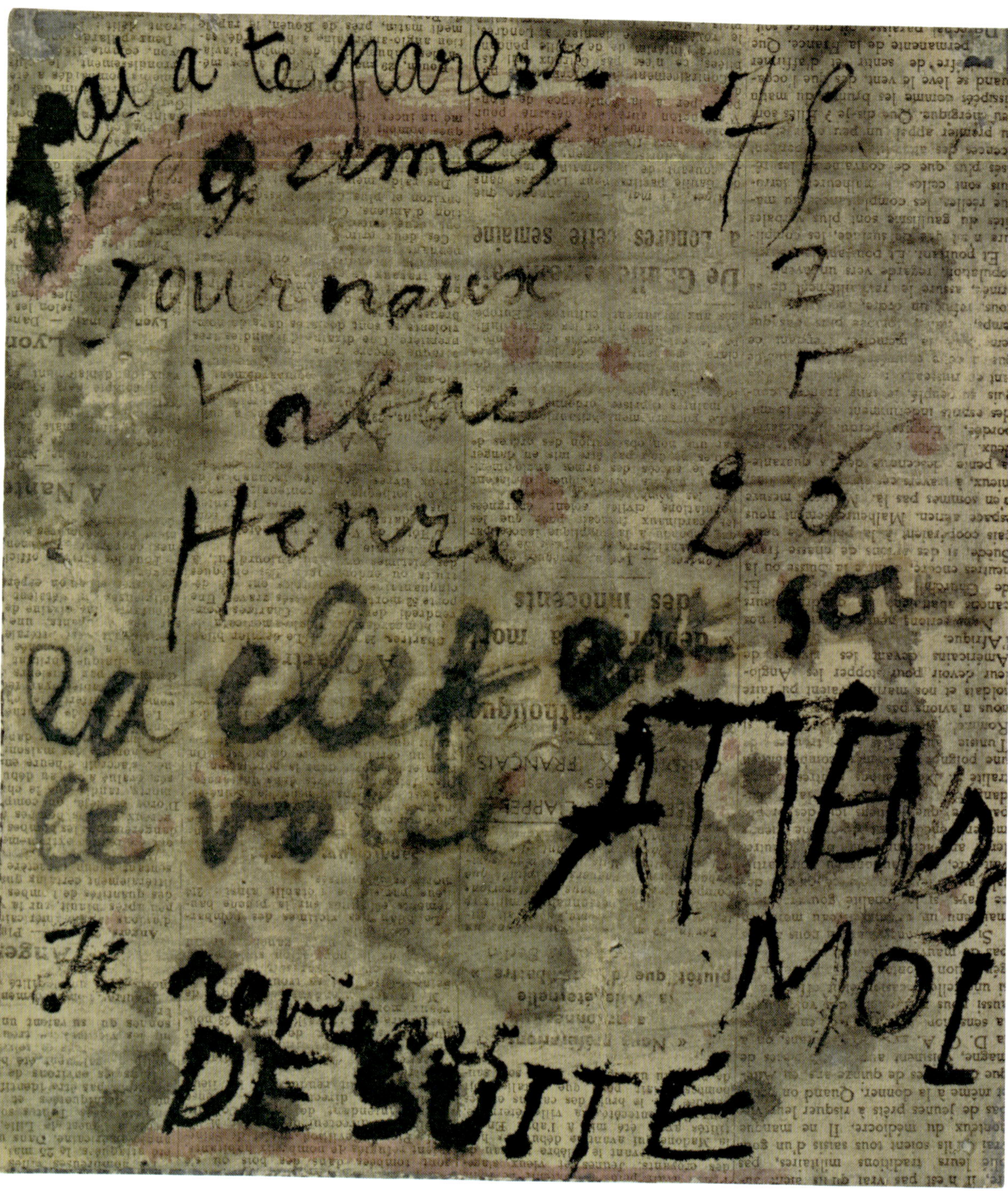

47

JEAN DUBUFFET

Message: La clef est sous le volet *(Message: The key is under the shutter)*

1944, ink on newspaper, 8⅛ × 7 (20.6 × 17.8), The Museum of Modern Art, New York, Gift of Mary Callery, 1974

It takes scrutiny, but the dates May 23, 25, and 29 can be found amid the newsprint type that underlies this work—one of a series of *Messages* that Dubuffet made in 1944. Those dates reveal that the newspaper was published shortly before D-Day (June 6) while France was still under German occupation. Crammed around a shopping list and a column of numbers, Dubuffet's jottings seem to have been penned in haste and with urgency: *J'ai a te parler, légumes, journaux, tabac, Henri, la clef est sous le volet, ATTENDS MOI, je reviens DE SUITE* (I have to talk to you, vegetables, newspapers, tobacco, Henri, the key is under the shutter, wait for me, I will be back soon).

A bit of headline (inverted) near the paper's center reads "mort des innocents" (death of innocents), a reminder that this cryptic message could carry grave implications and was written during extraordinary and precarious times.

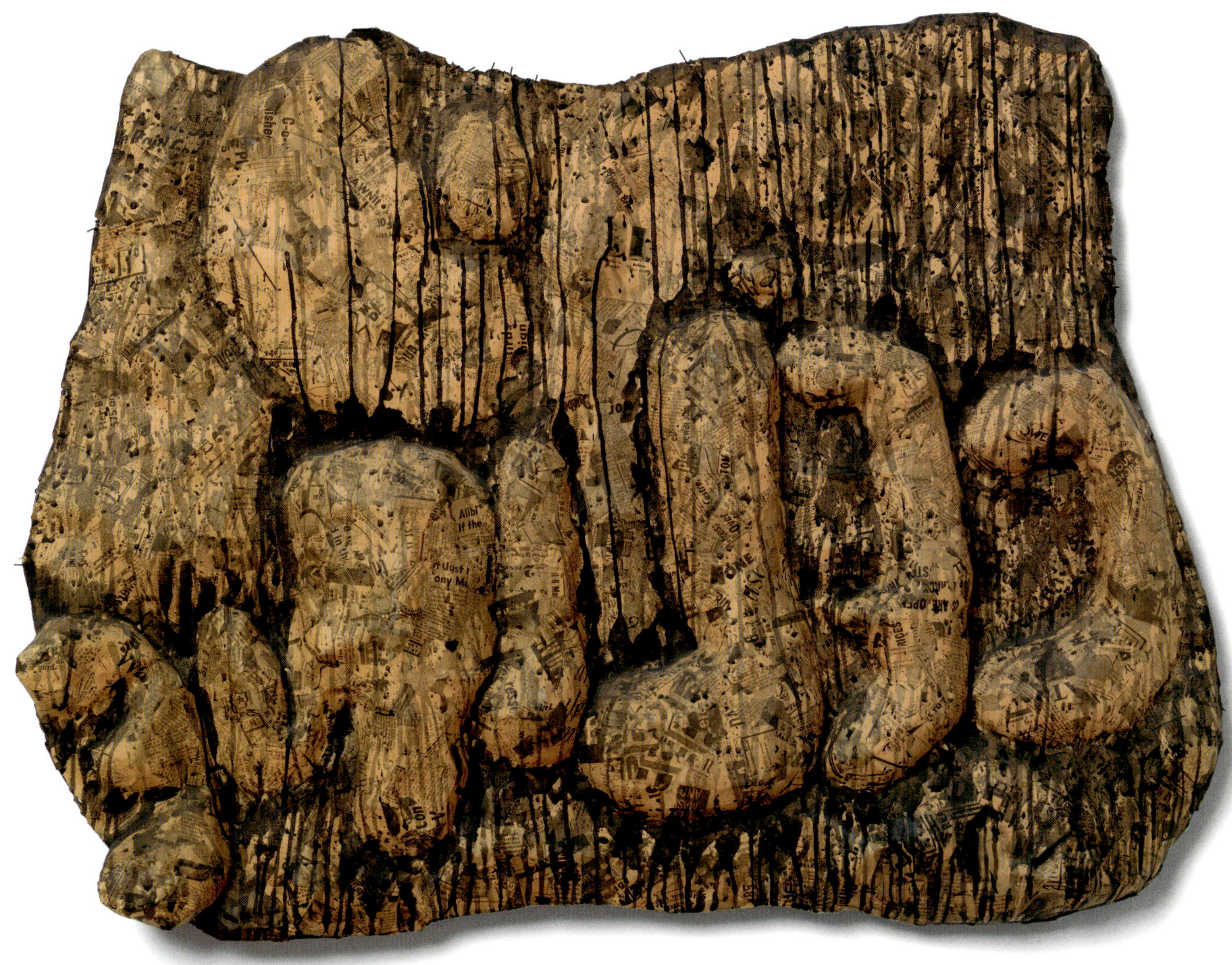

48

CLAES OLDENBURG

C-E-L-I-N-E, Backwards

1959, newspaper soaked in wheat paste over wire frame, painted with casein, 30 × 40 × 3 (76.2 × 101.6 × 7.6), Glenstone

Don't be fooled. Oldenburg is an A-R-T-I-S-T. It may seem as if he was thumbing his nose at aesthetic decorum in *C-E-L-I-N-E, Backwards*, but the truth is more complicated. The black paint that dribbles over the relief's bulbous letters produces (in the artist's words) a "vertical linear effect." He calls his tearing of the newspaper into strips a "chance operation" but notes that he selected pages carefully, not for "what they said, but the fact that they had some forms on them, letter forms and so on, and photographs that would make [the piece] work." He favored the movie pages for their "masses of blacks" and found the *Daily News* to be too gray—"stingy with their ink" in his estimation—whereas the *New York Post* offered photographs, heavy headlines, and thick type. If Oldenburg's molded relief calls to mind the ugly duckling of fairy tale, the artist sees its potential for exceptional beauty.

"Céline" in the work's title refers to the French writer Louis-Ferdinand Céline, whose talent Oldenburg admired but whose reputation as a Nazi sympathizer and anti-Semite made him a "negative character." "So in a simplistic way," stated Oldenburg, "I indicated that he was undesirable by making him backwards."

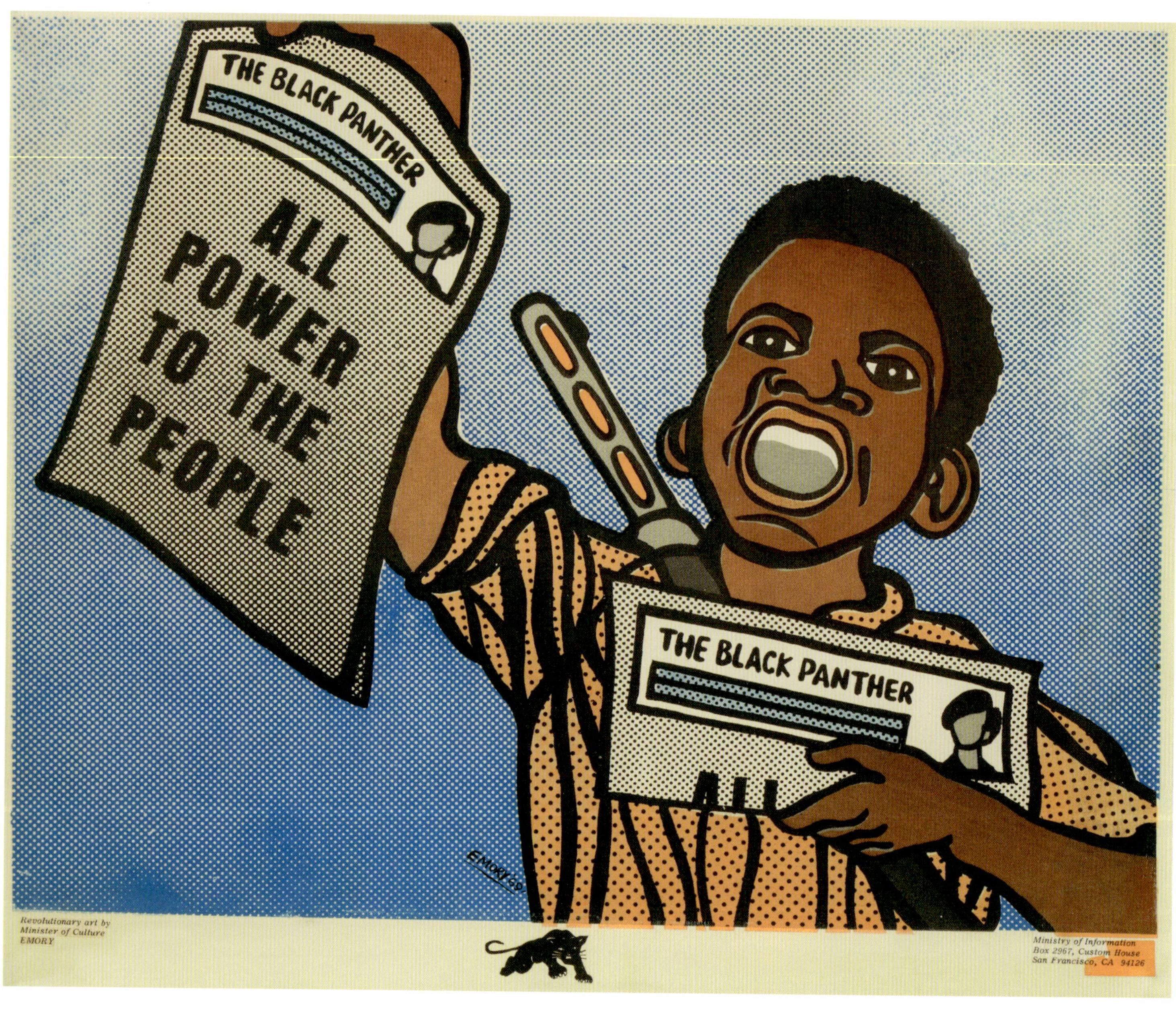

49

EMORY DOUGLAS

All Power to the People

1969, offset lithograph, 15 × 22 ½ (38.1 × 57.2), Collection of Alden and Mary Kimbrough

---

Rather than play down this work's reproductive nature, Douglas played it up—flooding the background and the newsboy's shirt with halftone and Ben-day dots, much like the approach of Roy Lichtenstein. But in the late 1960s, when Lichtenstein's pop images were being displayed in art galleries and museums, Douglas' posters could be seen plastered on the walls of urban slums.

Beginning in 1967 and for the next twelve years, Douglas was the Black Panthers' official "revolutionary artist and minister of culture," responsible for translating the party's insurgent vision into forceful images. The boy hawking newspapers in *All Power to the People* holds the *Black Panther* paper aloft, a rifle is slung over his shoulder, and his well-muscled arm underscores his identity as an empowered young man.

50

LAURIE ANDERSON

New York Times, Horizontal / China Times, Vertical

1976 (first conceived 1971), woven newspaper, 22⅝ × 14½ (57.5 × 36.8), Los Angeles County Museum of Art, Ralph M. Parsons Fund

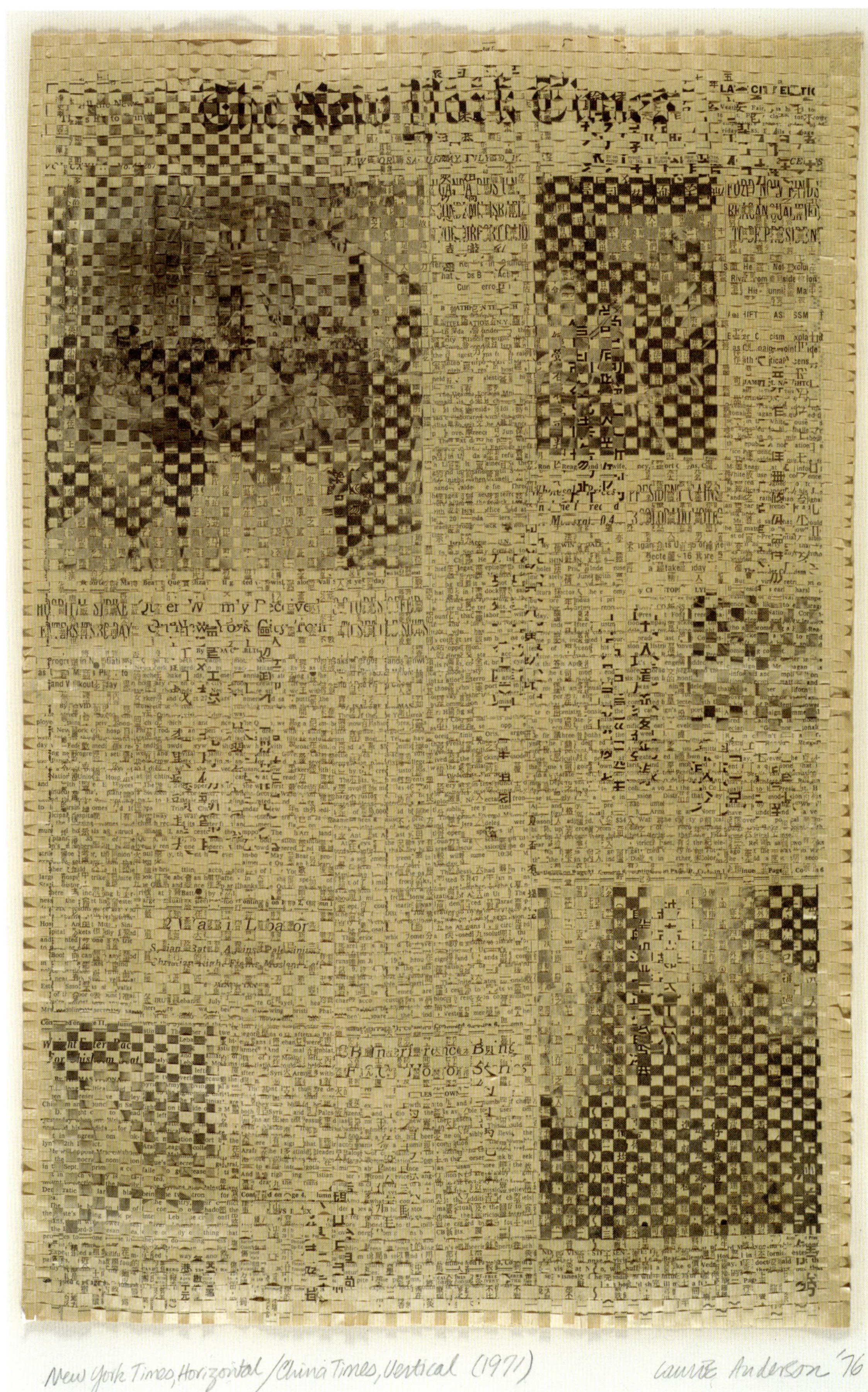

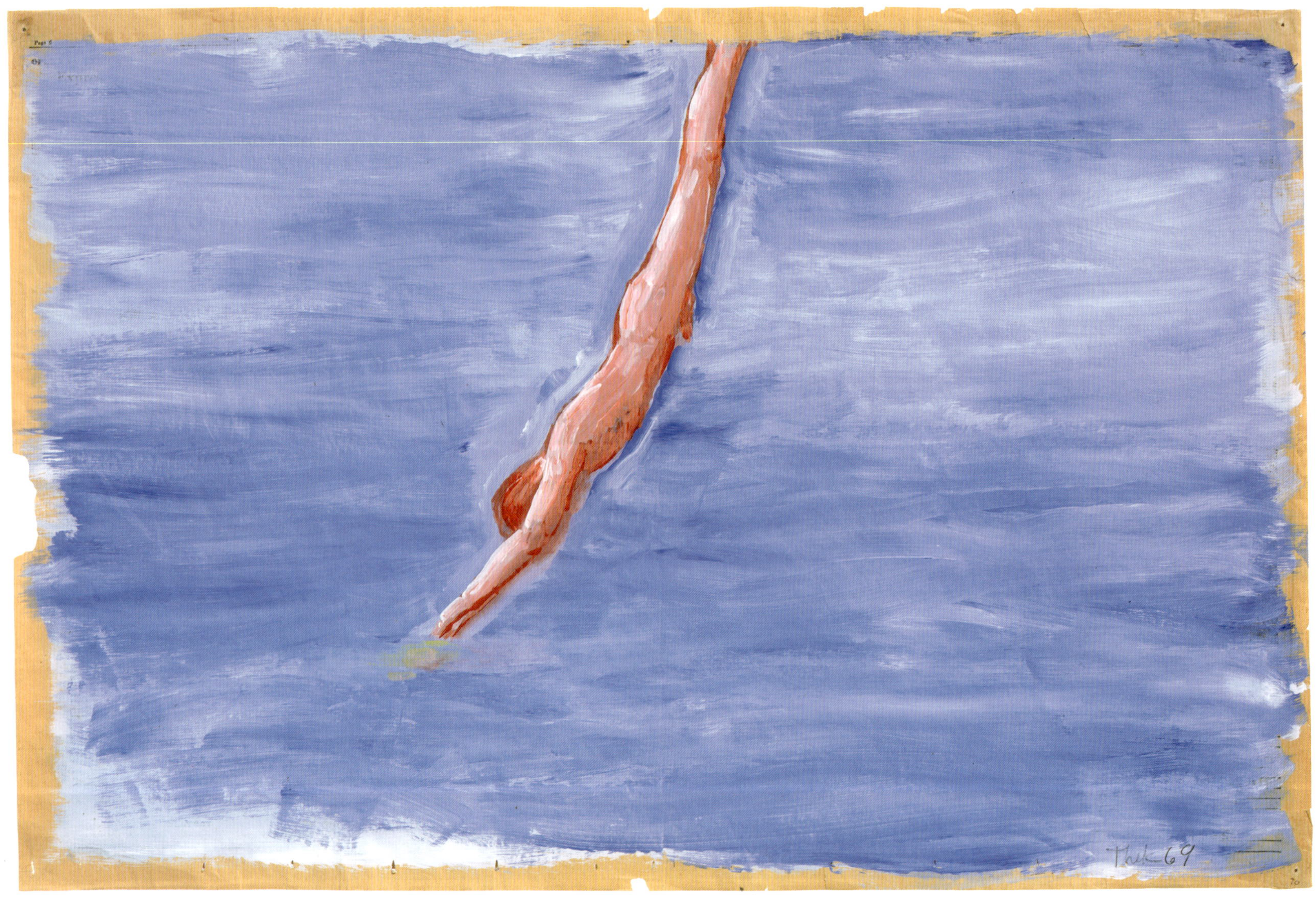

51

PAUL THEK

Untitled (Diver)

1970, acrylic on newspaper, 23 × 29 (58.4 × 73.7), Collection of Gail and Tony Ganz

The newsprint that underlies *Untitled (Diver)* was almost entirely obscured by Thek, suggesting that his interest in the newspaper as a material had little to do with its content. Rather, it was cheap and accessible and among the castoff materials he favored. Presumably Thek also liked the way the newsprint paper buckles in response to wet paint. Though thin and relatively weightless, it ably supports the image of a man plunging into an expanse of blue undulating water.

(Although this work is inscribed "69" at the lower right, it was almost certainly made in 1970, at the same time as a related work painted on a July 1970 page of the *International Herald Tribune*.)

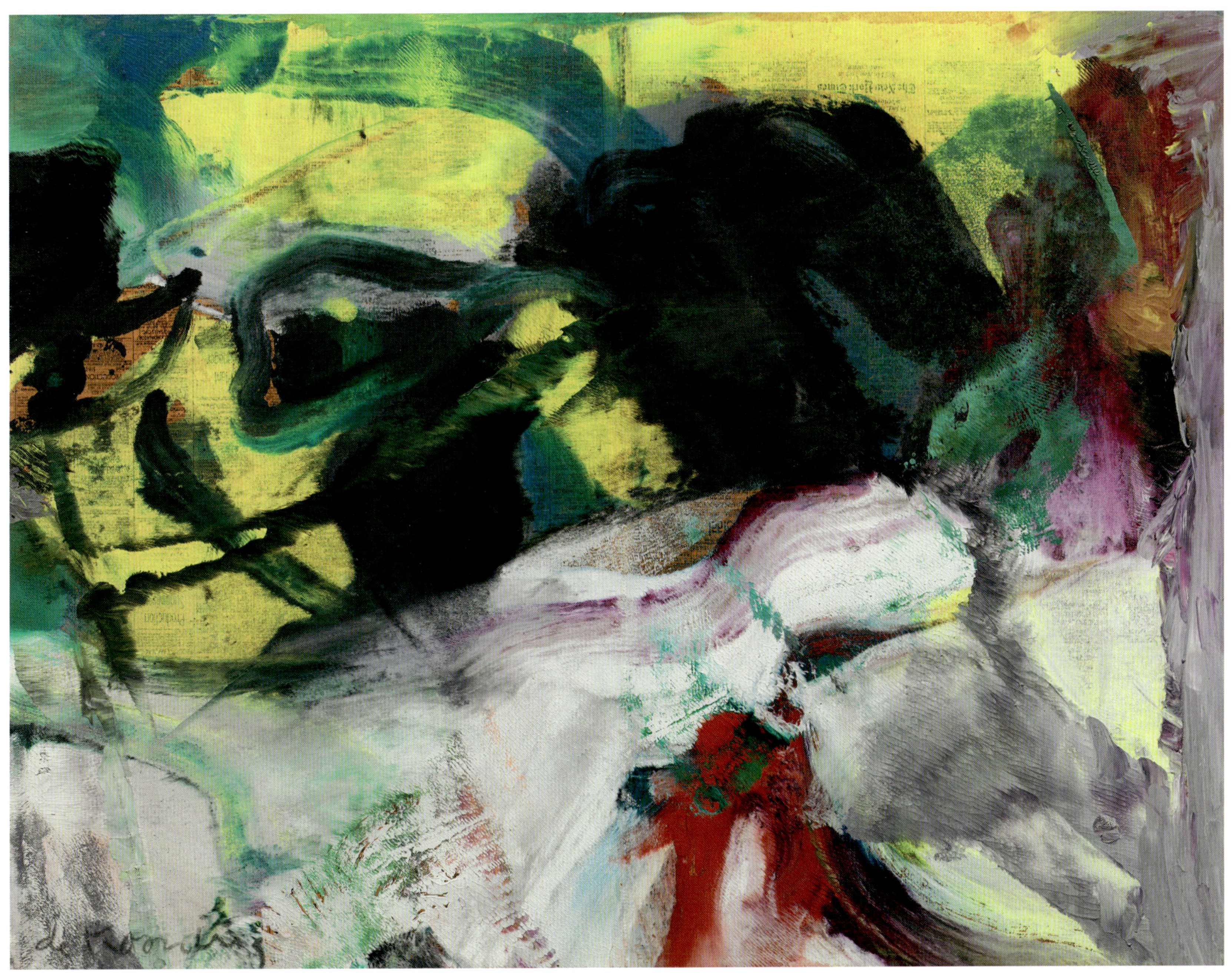

52

WILLEM DE KOONING

Untitled

1976, oil on newspaper mounted to canvas, 23 × 29 (58.4 × 73.6), National Gallery of Art, Washington, Gift of Ruth Cole Kainen, 2012

To retard drying, de Kooning would often press pages of newspaper onto his still-wet canvases, a practice that evolved into a strategy in three paintings, all of which incorporate text and images offset from newspapers (*Attic*, 1949, Metropolitan Museum of Art; *Gotham News*, 1955, Albright-Knox Art Gallery; and *Easter Monday*, 1955–1956, Metropolitan Museum of Art). De Kooning later revived—and reversed—the strategy in the 1960s and 1970s, creating works that feature paint offset onto newspaper. These later works are sometimes referred to as "countertypes" but more often as "oil transfers." The gray traces of newsprint bring an altogether different type of energy to these works, producing passages that crackle with crisp detail and buzz with the sound of voices.

X-ray fluorescent imaging of the National Gallery's oil transfer reveals that its support is a double-page spread from the *New York Times* published on Sunday, March 21, 1976.

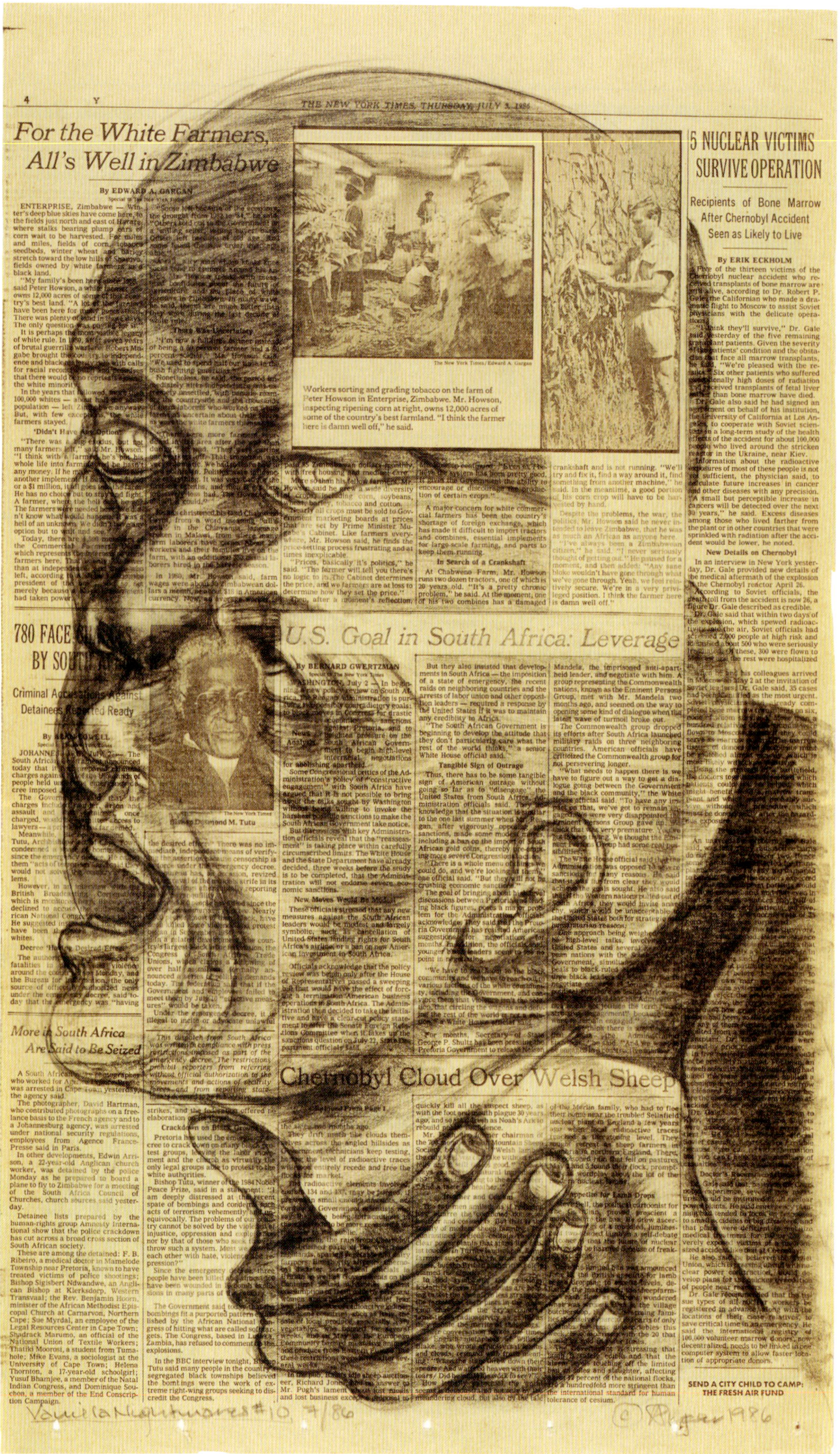

53

ADRIAN PIPER

Vanilla Nightmares #10

1986, charcoal and oil crayon on newspaper, 22 × 13¾ (55.8 × 34.9), Collection Walker Art Center, Minneapolis, T. B. Walker Acquisition Fund, 2004

Looming large on a page of the July 3, 1986, edition of the *New York Times*, Piper depicted a black man clutching at the throat of a white man. She also highlighted a centrally placed headline on the page: "U.S. Goal in South Africa: Leverage." The relevant article deals with the Reagan administration's policy of "constructive engagement" with South Africa's apartheid regime. But the tables could be turned, and the headline could be read as a reference to the goals of black South Africans and their plan to gain "leverage" or advantage. The means to do so, or so the drawing implies, might be by force.

Near the top of the page Piper additionally highlighted a picture of black workers sorting tobacco on a Zimbabwean farm and one of Peter Howson, the farm's white owner, inspecting ripening corn. An adjacent column reports that "despite the problems, the war, the politics, Mr. Howson said he never intended to leave Zimbabwe, that he was as much an African as anyone here." Howson continued: "Any sane bloke wouldn't have gone through what we've gone through. Yeah, we feel relatively secure. We're in a privileged position. I think the farmer here is damn well off." Is he dissembling? Does he let slip more than a hint of anxiety in his claim to feel "relatively secure"?

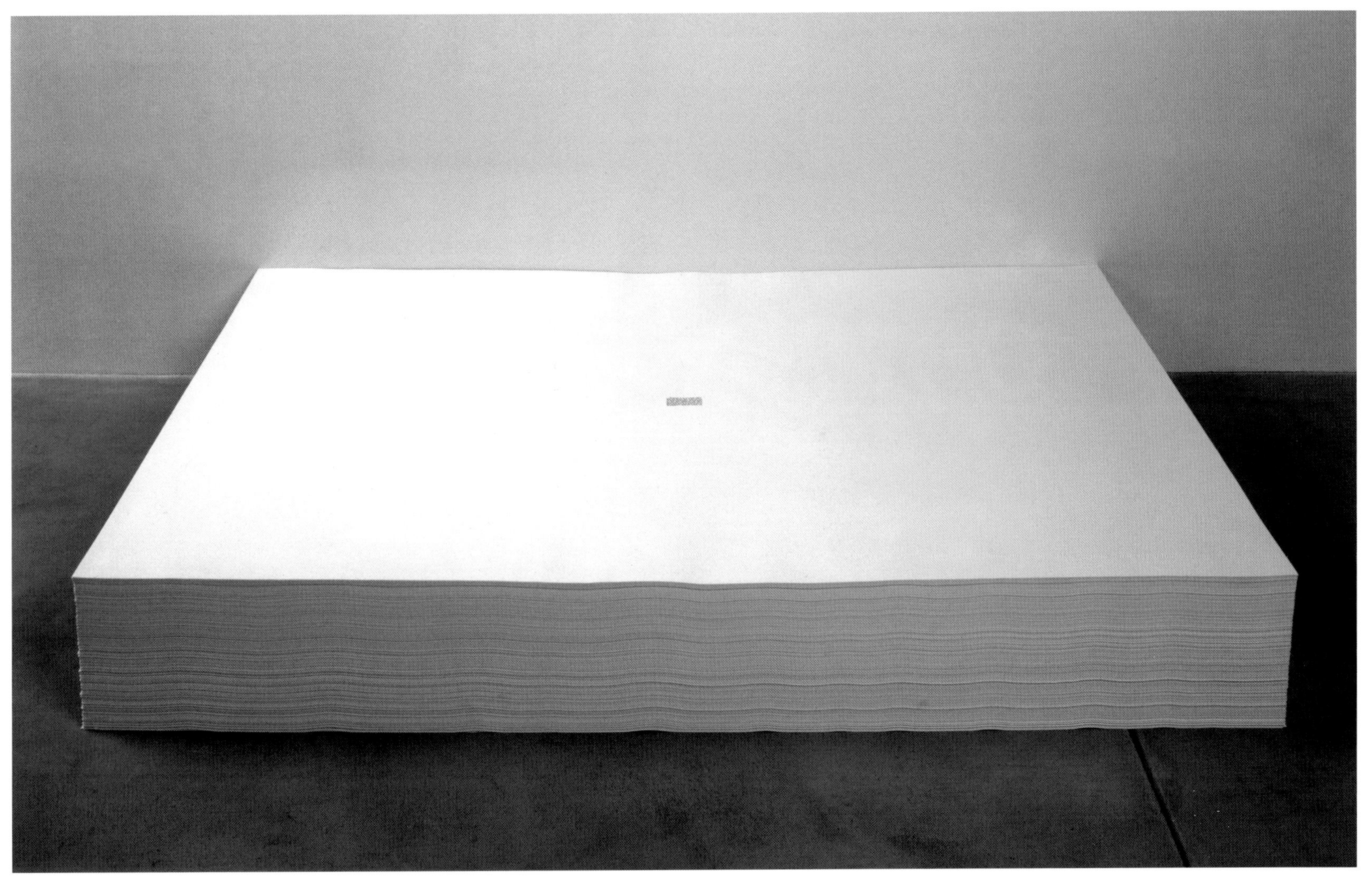

54

FELIX GONZALEZ-TORRES
"Untitled"
1991, offset print on paper (endless copies), 8 ½ (at ideal height) × 42 × 58 (21.6 × 106.7 × 147.3), EG Collection, Milan

The offset prints that make up Gonzales-Torres' stack are identical, each featuring two excerpts from articles published in the *New York Times*. The excerpts present contradictory views on the practice of profiling and expose its slipperiness. A law-enforcement official maintains that "it's very hard to know who's dangerous and who's not," while a spokesman for the Drug Enforcement Administration boasts that "an agent can spot a drug dealer the way a woman can spot a deal at the supermarket" (more profiling). The texts are printed separately—on the front and back of each sheet—echoing the very nature of a newspaper, where a story printed on one side of a page might contradict another on its reverse.

Wherever the stack is displayed, the prints are available for taking. Thus visitors get to breach the "do not touch" rule in addition to the tacit "do not take" rule. Like Marinetti's with his gambit on the front page of *Le Figaro*, Gonzalez-Torres capitalized on an establishment institution's ability to disseminate a message widely.

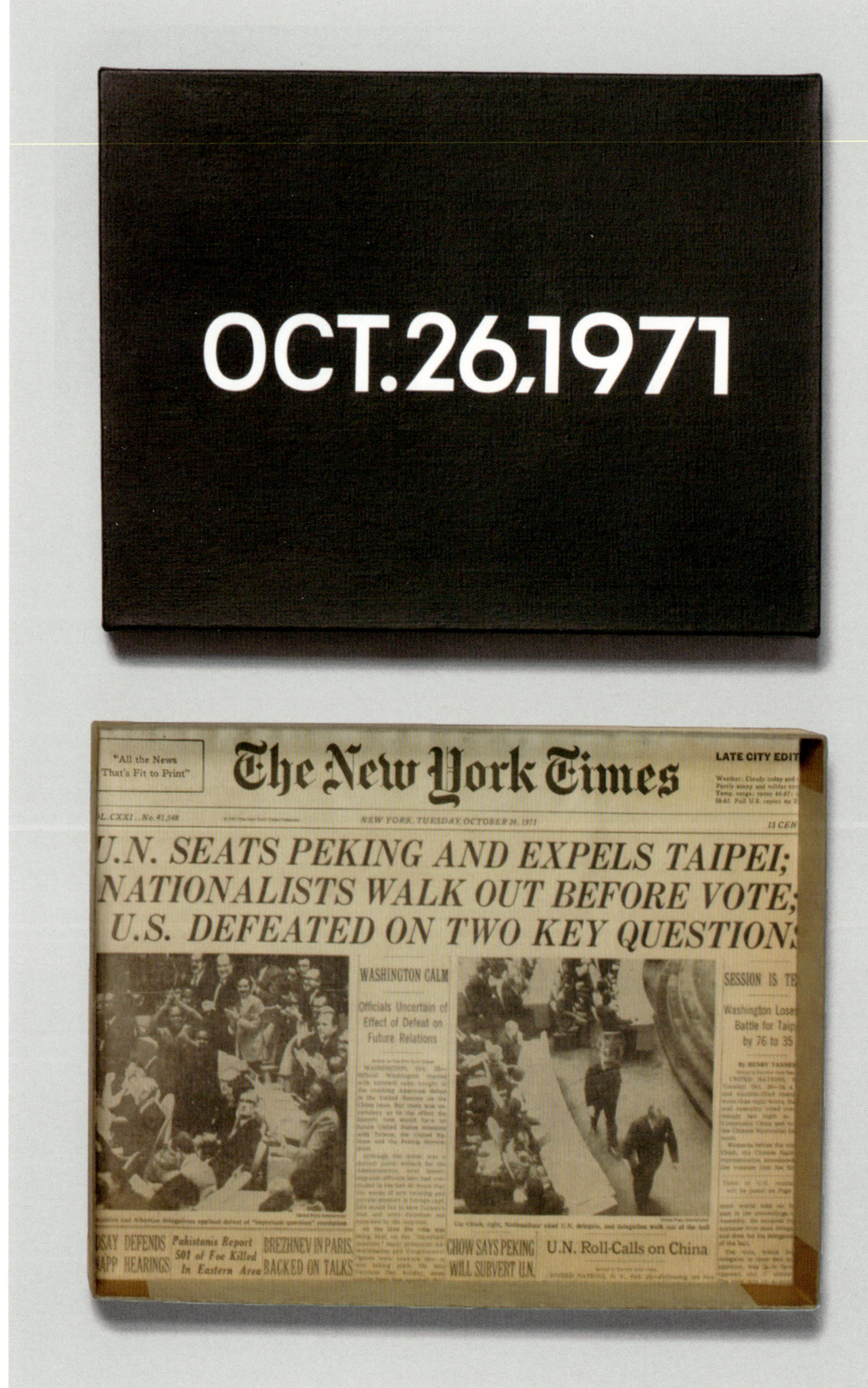

55

ON KAWARA

OCT. 26, 1971 *from* Today *series*

1971, liquitex on canvas; newspaper in cardboard box; painting: 10¼ × 13⅛ (25.9 × 33.2), box: 10¾ × 13⅝ × 1¾ (27.3 × 34.4 × 4.4), Hirshhorn Museum and Sculpture Garden, Smithsonian Institution, Joseph H. Hirshhorn Purchase Fund, 2007, The Panza Collection

In white paint on a dark monochrome ground, On Kawara meticulously transcribed the date on which this painting was made. If he had not completed it by the close of that day, he would have destroyed it. Kawara's "date paintings" typically come housed in handmade cardboard boxes lined with newspaper, in this case a portion of the *New York Times* published on October 26, 1971, its headline announcing the United Nations vote to seat communist China and expel the Chinese Nationalist Party. The newspaper not only reaffirms the date of the painting but reifies the idea of time and place.

Kawara's first "date painting" was made on January, 4, 1966, and in the following eight years he made 250 to 300 per year, thereafter averaging about 80 to 90 annually. He continues his campaign to the present (the works are collectively known as the *Today* series) but apparently with no ultimate goal in mind. If we were to assign it one, it might well be constancy.

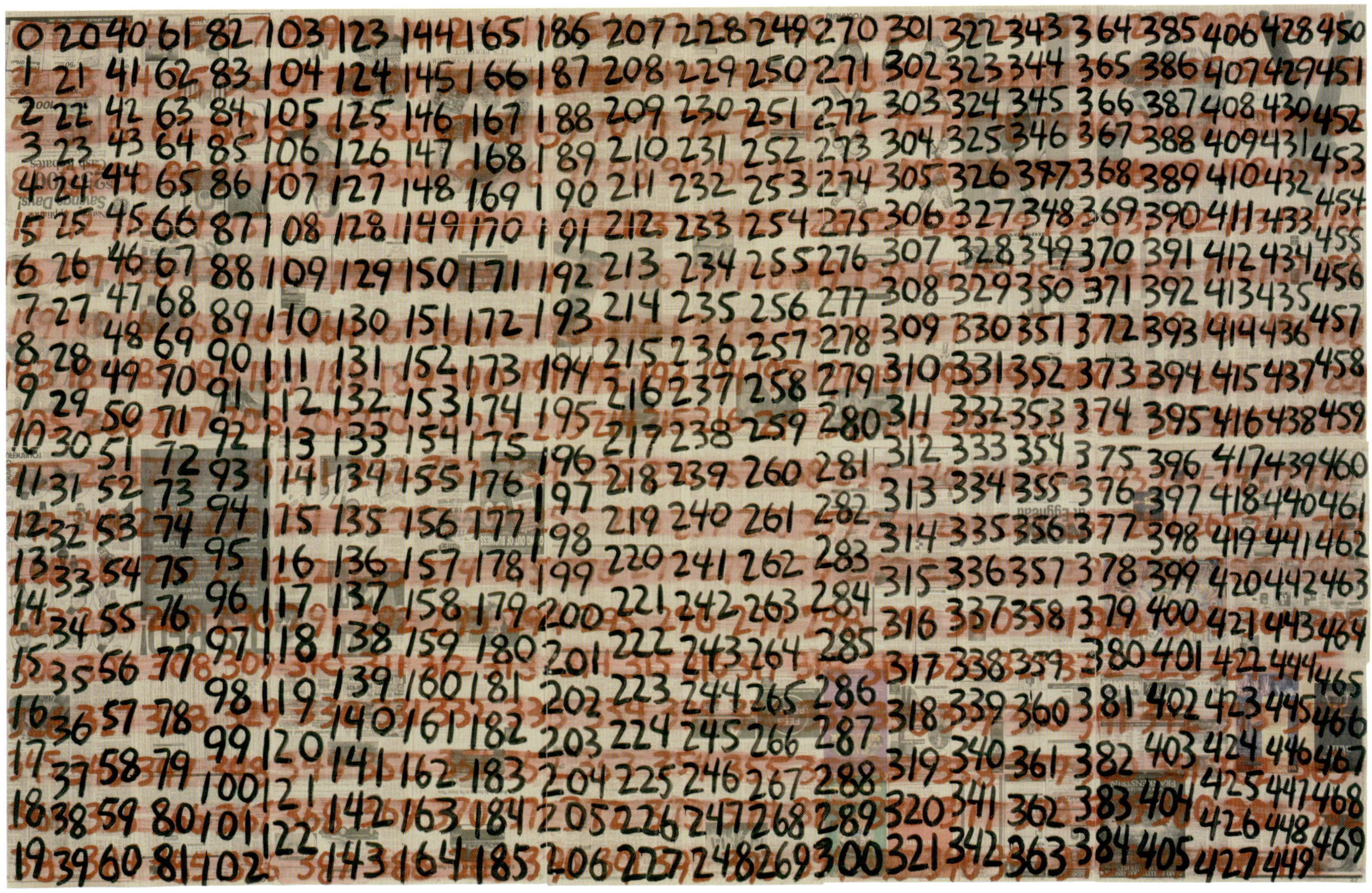

56

MEL BOCHNER

Counting: Intransitive (Red and Black)

1994, oil on twenty sheets of newspaper, 88 × 136 (223.5 × 345.4), Collection of the artist

It would be like Bochner to add a linguistic teaser to a work's title. Red and black refer to the numbers that traverse *Counting: Intransitive.* But red and black also conjure up a familiar riddle: "What is black and white and red all over?" The answer is the newspaper, and the riddle hinges on "red" and "read" being homophones. Here the wordplay is simple, comparable to Picasso's play on the phrase *Le Jou* in *Guitar, Sheet Music, and Glass* (pl. 2). As for the use of "intransitive" in the title, an intransitive verb takes no subject, and indeed nothing here is being counted. Counting itself is the work's subject.

Competing options produce what Bochner refers to as "mental static." We can choose to read the red numbers that advance left to right or the black numbers that advance top to bottom. The newspaper ground also puts a notational system into play: the English language, which reads left to right. Yet Bochner undermines reading by inverting the sheets of newspaper. Some prominent words stand out: "Egghead" (above the black 356); "Savings Days!" (below the black 24); and, notably, in large letters, "RED!" (below the black 76). But this is purely a matter of chance. Also by chance there is a lapse—numbers 290 through 299 are missing from the black series. Bochner attributes this to human error, proving his oft-repeated point that all invented systems, no matter how ostensibly logical, are not entirely dependable.

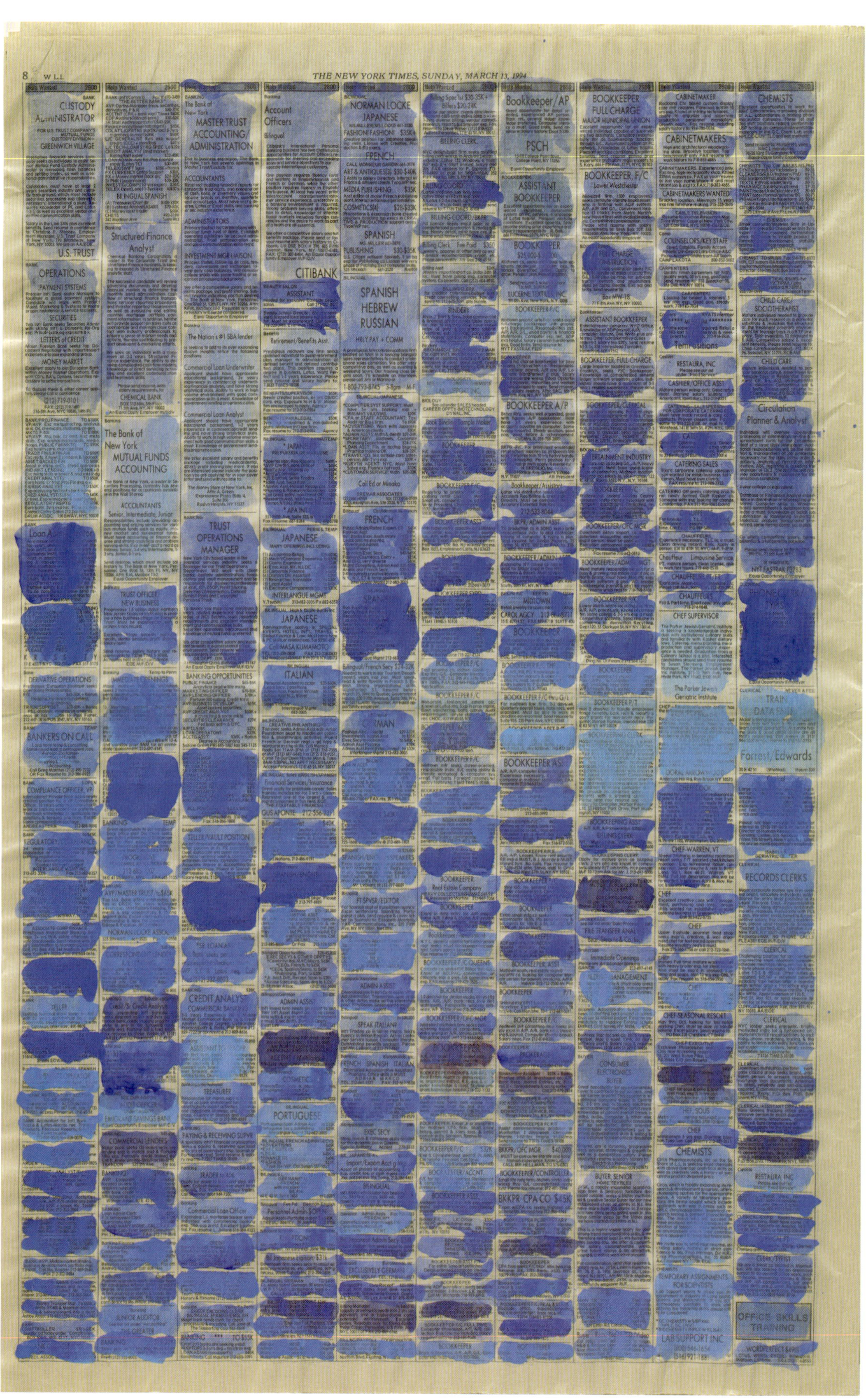

57

STEPHEN DEAN

Untitled (Help Wanted Full Page)

1994, watercolor on newspaper, 22 ¼ × 14 (56.6 × 35.6), National Gallery of Art, Washington, Gift of Werner H. and Sarah-Ann Kramarsky, 2000

Dean identified a readymade grid on a help wanted page of the March 13, 1994, edition of the *New York Times*. In the individual spaces allotted for ads, he deposited aqueous pools of blue watercolor ranging from deep ultramarine to light cerulean, pumping color onto a page that was wanting in that regard. The Old Gray Lady, nickname of the *New York Times*, was among the last newspapers to adopt color, not doing so until October 16, 1997, when a color photograph appeared on its front page.

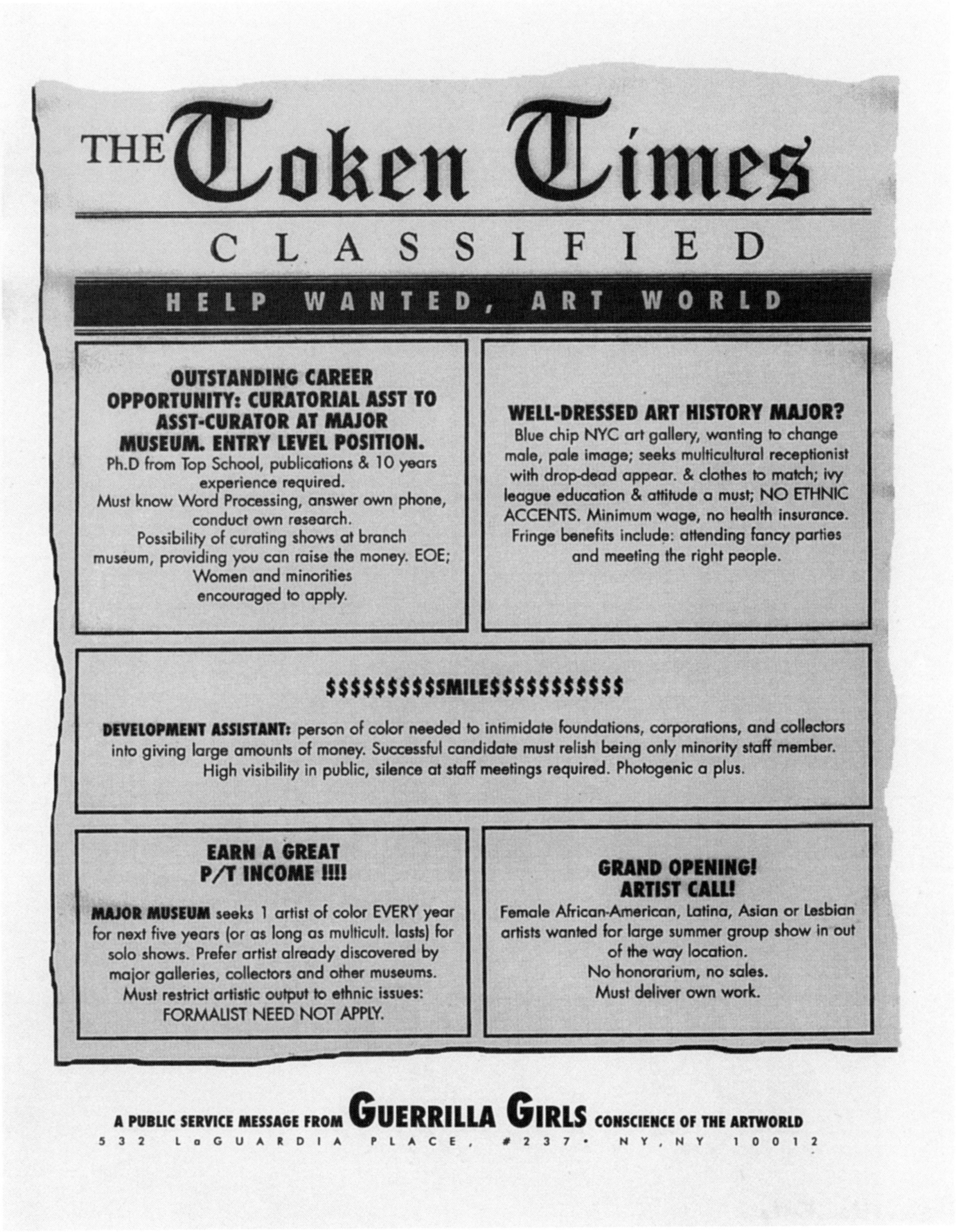

THE Token Times

CLASSIFIED

HELP WANTED, ART WORLD

OUTSTANDING CAREER OPPORTUNITY: CURATORIAL ASST TO ASST-CURATOR AT MAJOR MUSEUM. ENTRY LEVEL POSITION.
Ph.D from Top School, publications & 10 years experience required.
Must know Word Processing, answer own phone, conduct own research.
Possibility of curating shows at branch museum, providing you can raise the money. EOE; Women and minorities encouraged to apply.

WELL-DRESSED ART HISTORY MAJOR?
Blue chip NYC art gallery, wanting to change male, pale image; seeks multicultural receptionist with drop-dead appear. & clothes to match; ivy league education & attitude a must; NO ETHNIC ACCENTS. Minimum wage, no health insurance. Fringe benefits include: attending fancy parties and meeting the right people.

$$$$$$$$$SMILE$$$$$$$$$$$

DEVELOPMENT ASSISTANT: person of color needed to intimidate foundations, corporations, and collectors into giving large amounts of money. Successful candidate must relish being only minority staff member. High visibility in public, silence at staff meetings required. Photogenic a plus.

EARN A GREAT P/T INCOME !!!!

MAJOR MUSEUM seeks 1 artist of color EVERY year for next five years (or as long as multicult. lasts) for solo shows. Prefer artist already discovered by major galleries, collectors and other museums. Must restrict artistic output to ethnic issues: FORMALIST NEED NOT APPLY.

GRAND OPENING! ARTIST CALL!
Female African-American, Latina, Asian or Lesbian artists wanted for large summer group show in out of the way location.
No honorarium, no sales.
Must deliver own work.

A PUBLIC SERVICE MESSAGE FROM **GUERRILLA GIRLS** CONSCIENCE OF THE ARTWORLD
532 LaGUARDIA PLACE, #237 • NY, NY 10012

58

GUERRILLA GIRLS

The Token Times

1995, offset lithograph, 22 × 17 (55.9 × 43.2), National Gallery of Art, Washington, Gift of the Gallery Girls in support of the Guerrilla Girls, 2007

Since their founding in 1985, the Guerrilla Girls have raised awareness (and eyebrows) in the art world. Their "public service messages" may be couched in humor, but they are aimed to make people squirm.

A selection of classified ads in the so-called *Token Times* exposes patent examples of bias and tokenism: a "blue chip NYC art gallery" looking for a "well-dressed art history major" with "drop-dead appear. & clothes to match" for job as a receptionist (those with ethnic accents need not apply); an organization looking for a person of color "to intimidate foundations, corporations, and collectors into giving large amounts of money"; and a major museum seeking "1 artist of color EVERY year for next five years (or as long as multicult. lasts) for solo shows. Prefer artist already discovered by major galleries, collectors, and other museums. Must restrict artistic output to ethnic issues: FORMALIST NEED NOT APPLY."

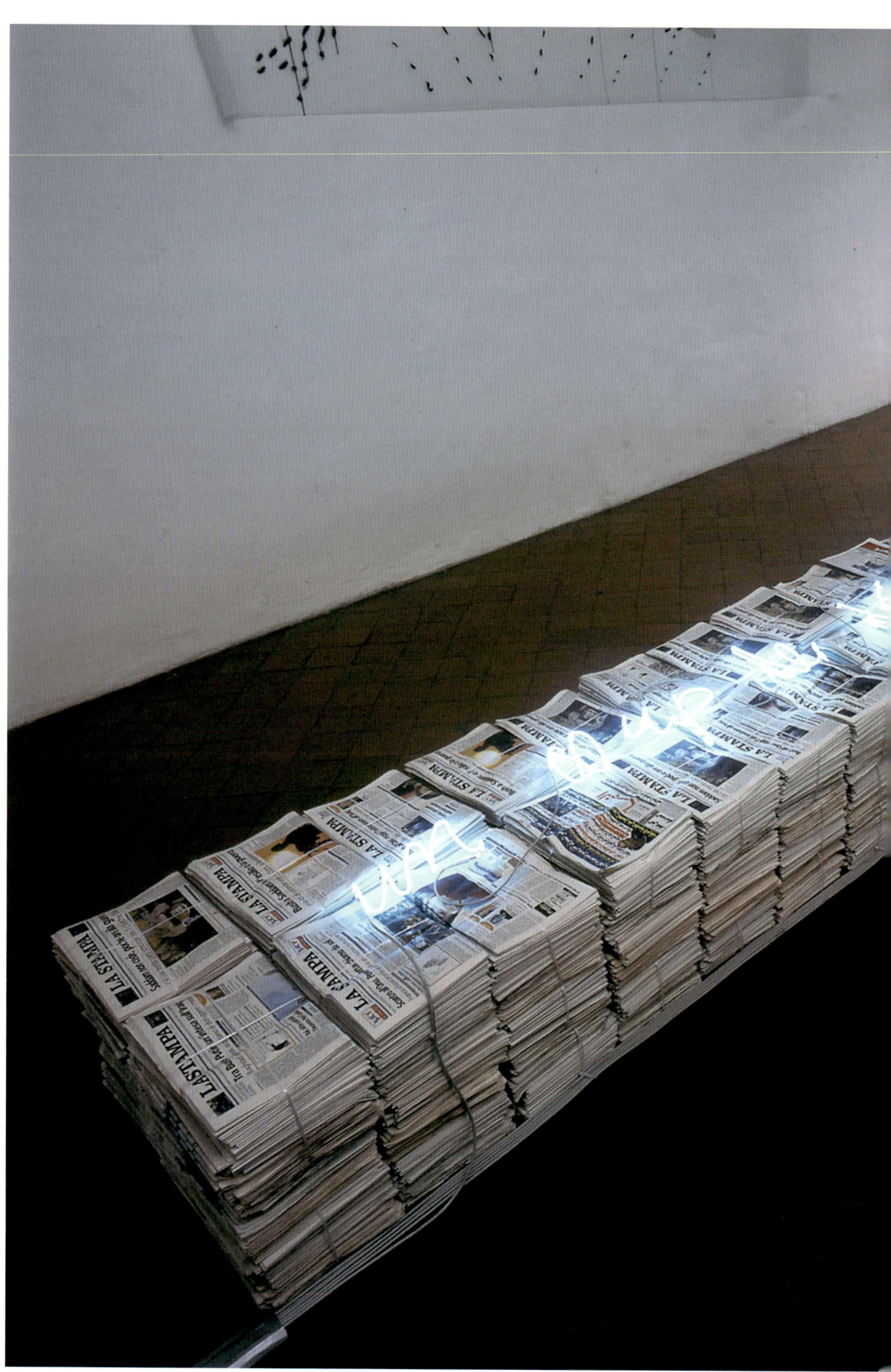
LA STAMPA

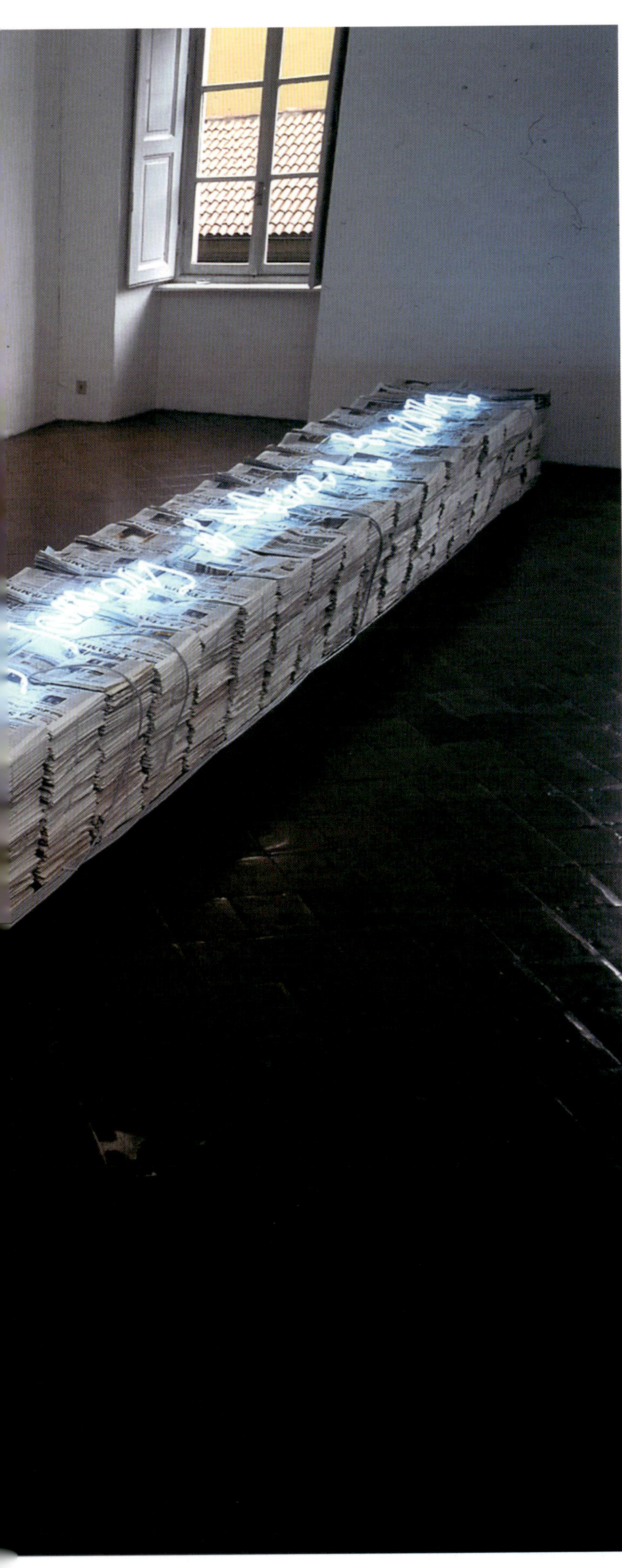

59

MARIO MERZ

À Mallarmé

2003, newspapers and neon,
21⅝ × 283½ × 31½ (55 × 720 × 80),
Collezione Merz, Turin

60

MARINE HUGONNIER

Art for Modern Architecture (Homage to Ellsworth Kelly)

2005, set of seven collages on newspaper, each: 22 7/8 × 15 (58.1 × 38.1), National Gallery of Art, Washington, Gift of the Collectors Committee, 2009

Two events dominated news reports on the front pages of the Palestinian newspaper *Al-Ayyam* during the week of November 1, 2004: Yasser Arafat's health failed, and the United States held its presidential election. Hugonnier "covered" these and other events by pasting over the photographs on *Al-Ayyam*'s front pages that week. Inspired by Ellsworth Kelly's ambition to make art for modern architecture, Hugonnier excised cuttings from Kelly's book, *Line Form Color* (published 1999), and used them as collage elements, integrating them into the "architecture" of the modern newspaper.

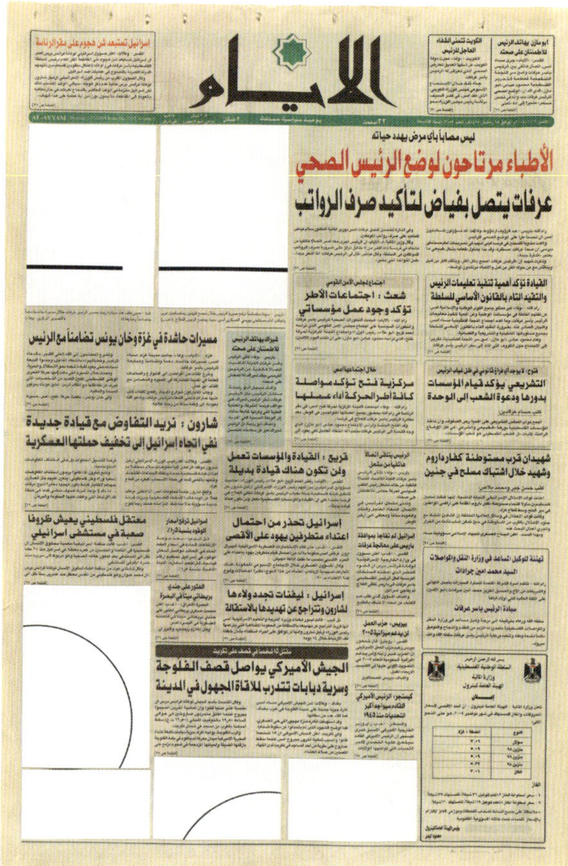

الأيام

ليس مصابا بأي مرض يهدد حياته

الأطباء مرتاحون لوضع الرئيس الصحي

عرفات يتصل بفياض لتأكيد صرف الرواتب

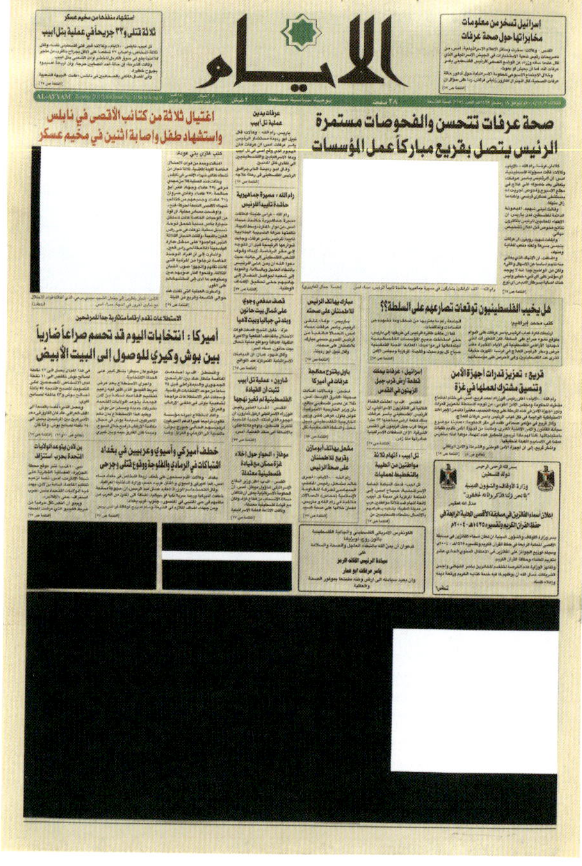

الأيام

صحة عرفات تتحسن والفحوصات مستمرة

الرئيس يتصل بقريع مباركاً عمل المؤسسات

اغتيال ثلاثة من كتائب الأقصى في نابلس

واستشهاد طفل وإصابة اثنين في مخيم عسكر

أميركا: انتخابات اليوم قد تحسم صراعاً ضارياً بين بوش وكيري للوصول الى البيت الأبيض

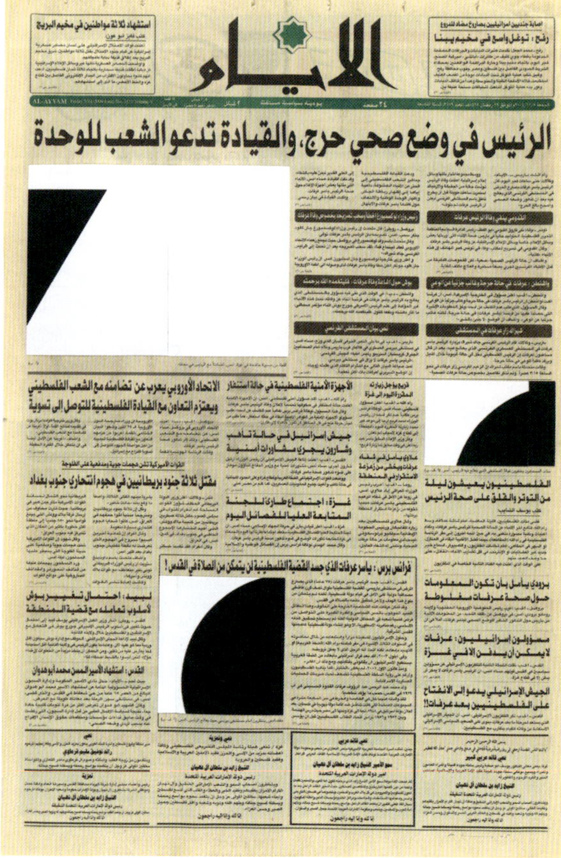

الأيام

الرئيس في وضع صحي حرج، والقيادة تدعو الشعب للوحدة

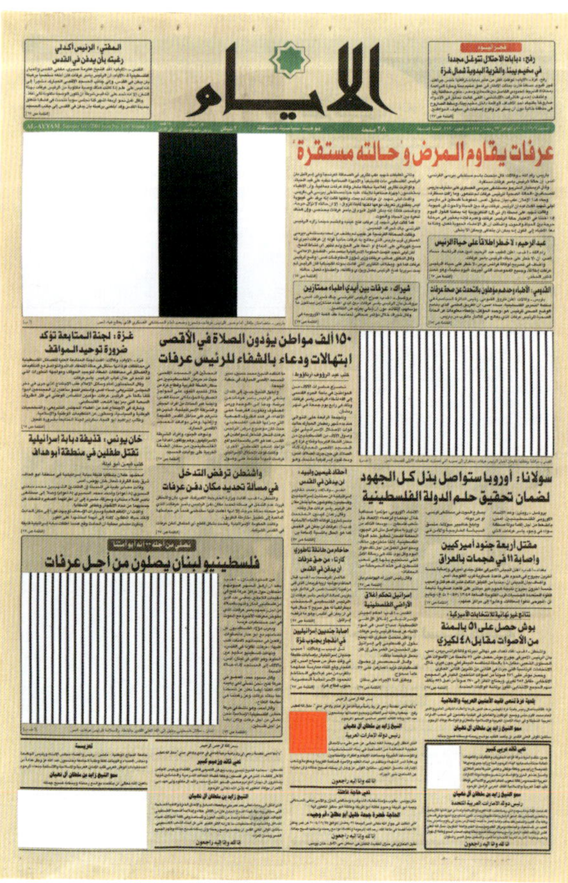

الأيام

عرفات يقاوم المرض و حالته مستقرة

١٥٠ ألف مواطن يؤدون الصلاة في الأقصى

ابتهالات ودعاء بالشفاء للرئيس عرفات

فلسطينيو لبنان يصلون من أجل عرفات

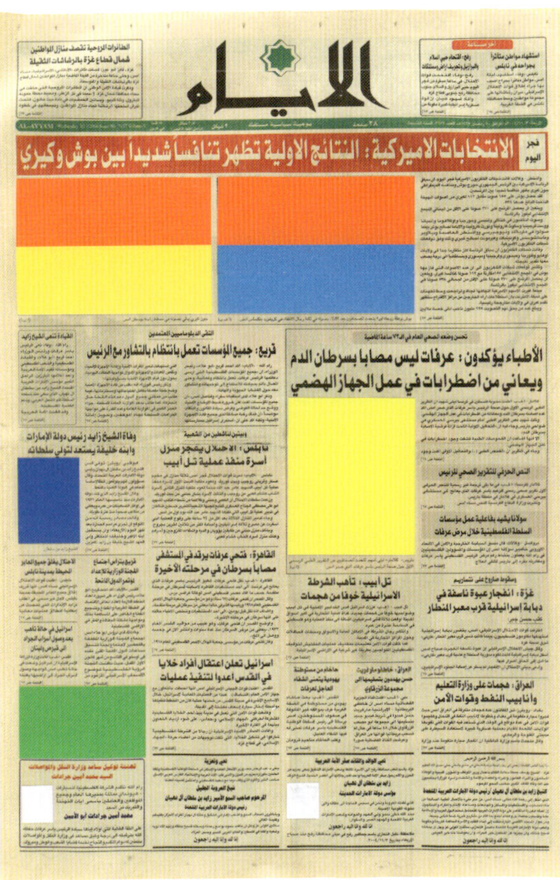

الأيام

الانتخابات الاميركية: النتائج الاولية تظهر تنافسا شديدا بين بوش وكيري

الأطباء يؤكدون: عرفات ليس مصابا بسرطان الدم ويعاني من اضطرابات في عمل الجهاز الهضمي

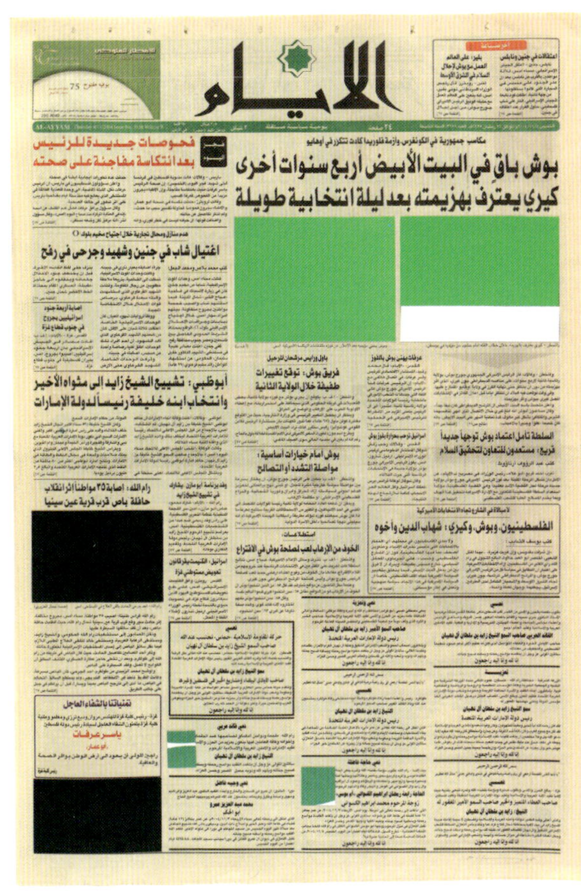

الأيام

بوش باق في البيت الأبيض أربع سنوات أخرى
كيري يعترف بهزيمته بعد ليلة انتخابية طويلة

فحوصات جديدة للرئيس بعد انتكاسة مفاجئة على صحته

اغتيال شاب في جنين وشهيد وجرحى في رفح

أبوظبي: تشييع الشيخ زايد الى مثواه الأخير وانتخاب ابنه خليفة رئيسا لدولة الإمارات

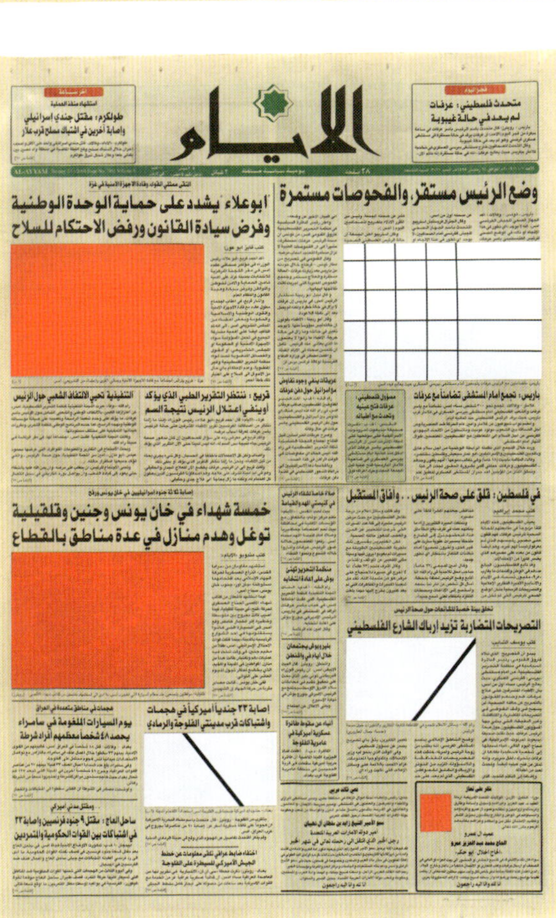

الأيام

وضع الرئيس مستقر، والفحوصات مستمرة

ابو علاء يشدد على حماية الوحدة الوطنية وفرض سيادة القانون ورفض الاحتكام للسلاح

خمسة شهداء في خان يونس وجنين وقلقيلية
توغل وهدم منازل في عدة مناطق بالقطاع

التصريحات المتضاربة تزيد ارباك الشارع الفلسطيني

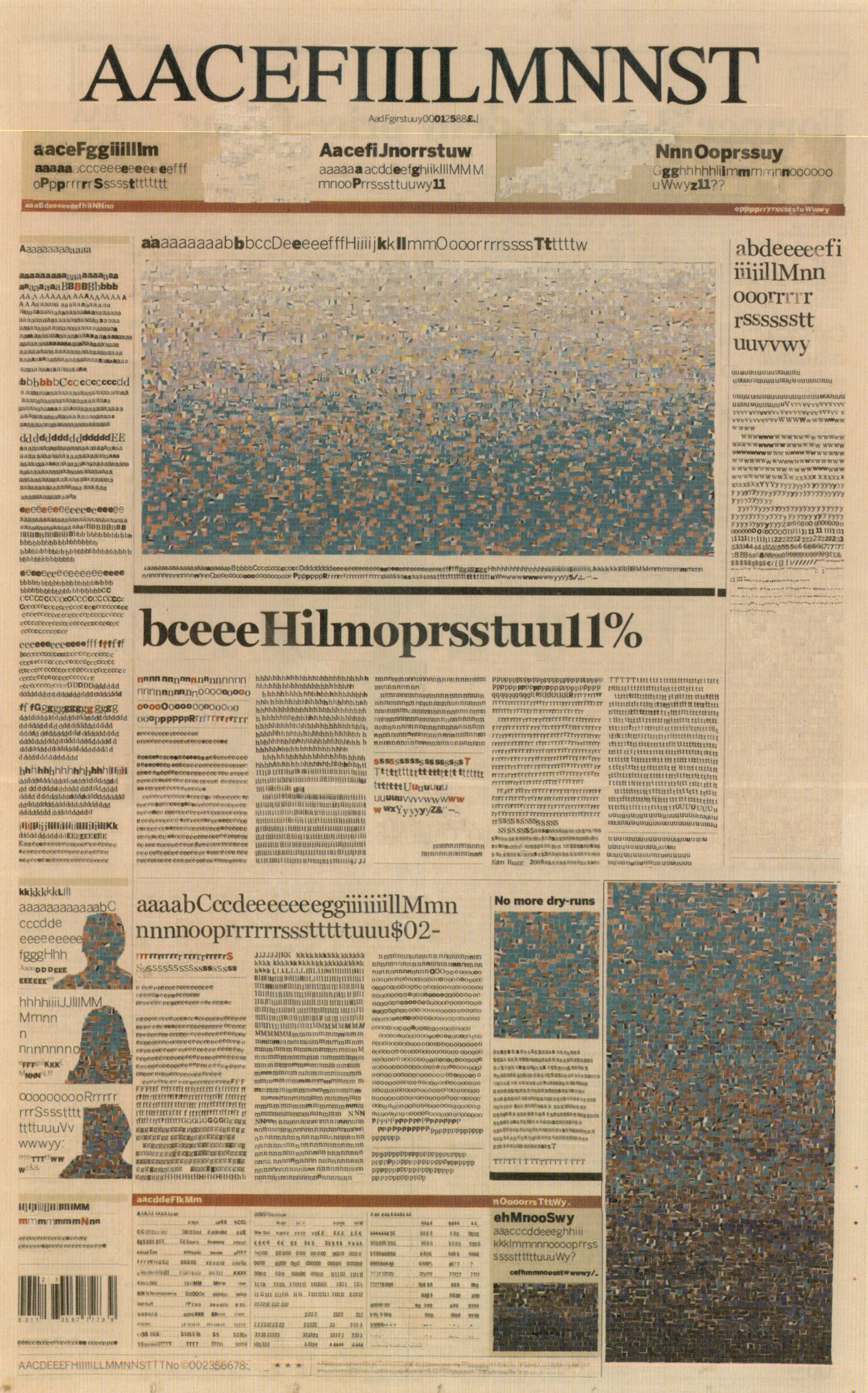

61

KIM RUGG

No More Dry-Runs

2008, cut-and-rearranged newspaper, 23 ⅝ × 14 ¾ (60 × 37.5), National Gallery of Art, Washington, Gift of the Collectors Committee, 2009

Rugg painstakingly excised each and every character of the August 8, 2008, edition of the *Financial Times* and rearranged them in alphabetical order — a radically anachronistic practice in the age of digital technology, recalling outmoded movable-type printing. By alphabetizing the text (note that the *Financial Times*' masthead has been reordered from *A* to *T*) Rugg also obscured and invalidated the news.

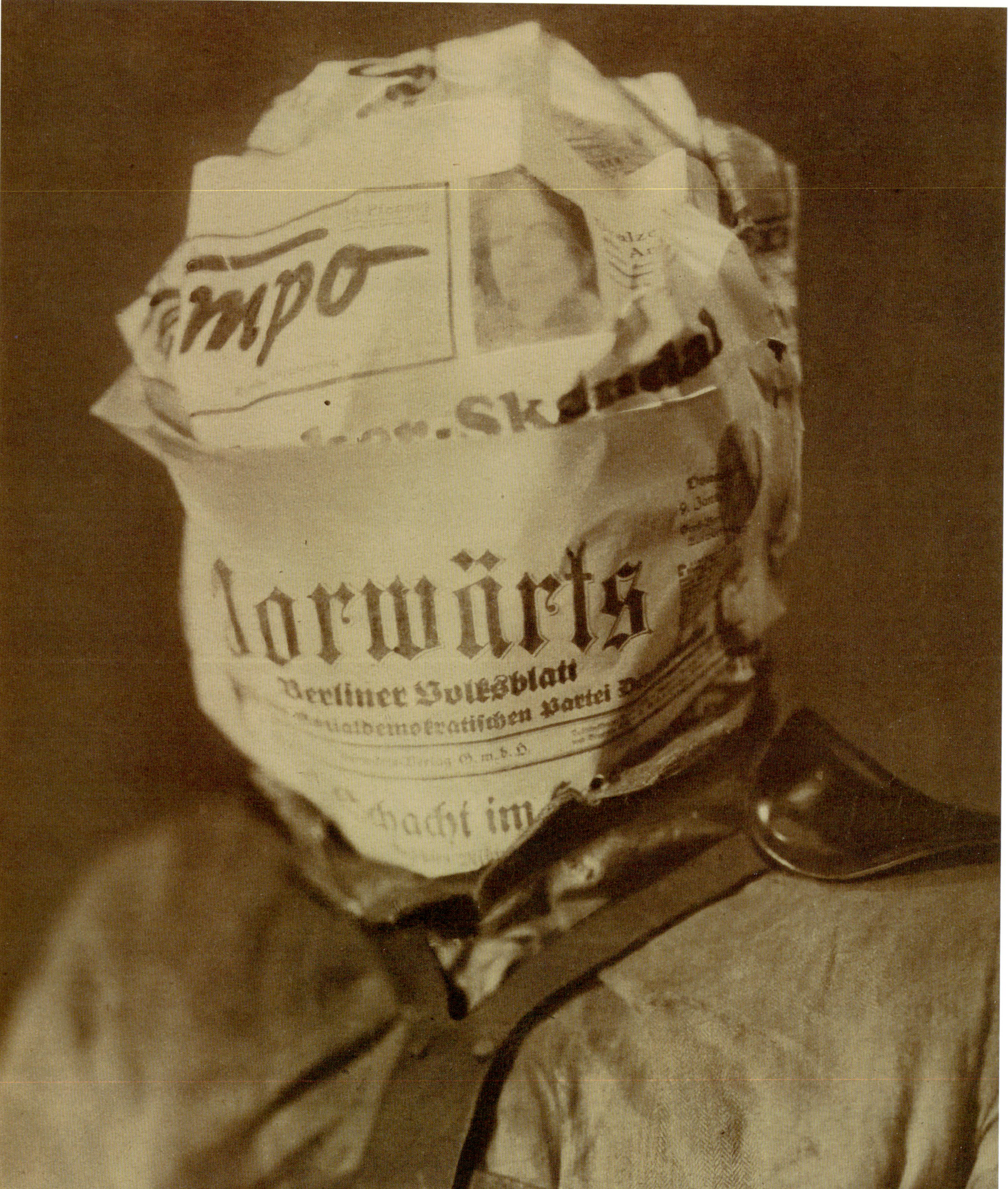
orwärts
Berliner Volksblatt

RIPPED FROM THE HEADLINES

Sarah Boxer

"...I brandish my knife, like a poultry butcher. The virgin folds...await the introduction of a weapon, or paper cutter, in order for possession to take place."
Stéphane Mallarmé, 1895

It is the clash of headlines and ads, news and weather. The optical buzz of the set type, the straight columns bringing superficial order to what Walter Benjamin called a "scene of...literary confusion."[1] It is the newspaper's dailiness and its air of impersonality. Its urgency and crassness. It is what the nineteenth-century poet Stéphane Mallarmé termed its "spectacular vulgar advantage...the multiplication of copies...the print run."[2] It is the way the newspaper circulates and gets used for fish wrap. The way it contains and defines a day. It is the factory-fresh smell of the factory-printed paper. The way papers are stacked and bundled, thrown on doorsteps and sold at newsstands. It is the size of the page, the crinkle of the sheets, the ink on your fingers. The types of type. The datelines and bylines. And the blunt lingo of the newsroom and the composing room. The hed. The lede. Kerning and carding. H & J. TKTKTKTK. Agate type. Dummy type. Thumbsucker. Q-hed. The news hole. The nut-graf. The banner. The kicker. The jump. The slug. The slot. The widows and orphans. The morgue.

The Battle Is On!

On October 9, 1912, Pablo Picasso wrote to Georges Braque: "I am using your latest papery and powdery procedures. I am in the process of imagining a guitar."[3] In the next month or so, Picasso produced *Guitar, Sheet Music, and Glass* (pl. 2). One of the most shocking things about it, notably missing from the work's conventional title, was the belligerent scrap of newspaper headline, "La Bataille s'est engagé" (The battle is on), which had been cut from *Le Journal*'s headline announcing a new skirmish in the Balkan War.[4] As Picasso's biographer John Richardson points out, "This *papier collé* is celebrated for the headline featured in it...which continues to stir up controversy."[5]

What does Picasso's lopped headline mean? Or, as Richardson asks, "With whom was battle... joined? With warmongers and nationalists? With philistines and reactionaries?" With "the Section d'Or" (an exhibition organized by the Duchamp brothers, which Picasso and Braque steered clear of) and with the Salon cubists represented there? Or with "the only living artists he regarded as his peers: Matisse and Braque"?[6]

Perhaps the enemy was not even human. Maybe the war was against what Picasso called (in the letter to Braque just mentioned) "our horrible canvas."[7] Or against the idea of a canvas having any unified, concentrated meaning. Theodor Adorno, along these lines, proposed that collage was a step toward art's self-destruction. "Affixed debris," he wrote, using a violent metaphor, "cleaves visible scars in the work's meaning."[8]

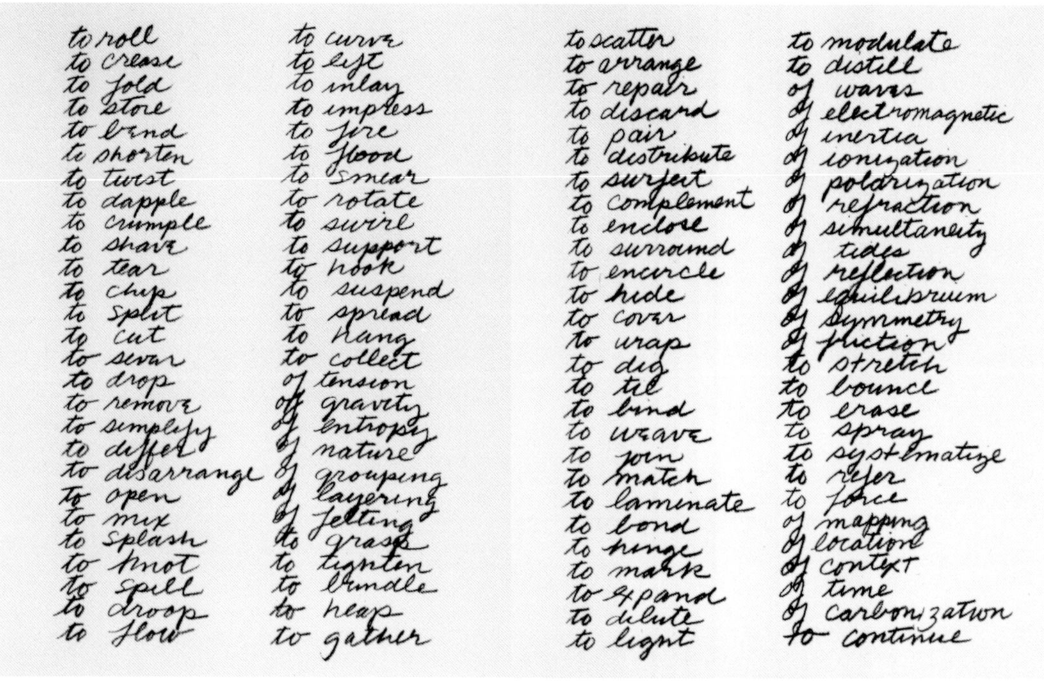

1

FIG. 1 Richard Serra, *Verb List*, 1967–1968, graphite on two sheets of paper, The Museum of Modern Art, New York, Gift of the artist in honor of Wynn Kramarsky

FIG. 2 Pablo Picasso, *Table with Bottle, Wineglass, and Newspaper* (also known as *Un coup de thé*), 1912/1913, newspaper, charcoal, and gouache on paper, Musée national d'art moderne, Centre Georges Pompidou, Paris, Gift of Henri Laugier

Curiously, Richardson's list of possible combatants, and everyone else's for that matter, leaves out one obvious adversary: the newspaper. Isn't it possible that Picasso was declaring war on the newspaper?

Maybe I am hypersensitive about printed newspapers because they are now endangered,[9] or because I used to work for one,[10] or both, but when I see art incorporating newspapers, I see a war against the once-composed page. I see the newspaper tortured: cut, gutted, minced, diced, snuffed, silenced, defiled, mocked, tarred, drowned, bound, gagged.

When I look at newspaper art, if there is such a thing, I am reminded of the violent *Verb List* (fig. 1) that Richard Serra wrote in 1967–1968, which begins: "to roll, to crease, to fold, to store, to bend, to shorten, to twist, to dapple, to crumple, to shave, to tear, to chip, to split, to cut, to sever, to drop, to remove, to simplify, to differ, to disarrange."[11]

In every piece of art that incorporates newspaper I think you can detect a clear contest for survival—between the newspaper as news medium and the newspaper as art medium. If the newspaper works as an art medium, it has surrendered as a news medium, at least in the work in which it appears. It doesn't matter if the news scraps can be read or not. Whatever purposes that newspaper served in its old life must be muffled. Whatever rapid decisions were made to compose that paper's stories, ads, headlines, typefaces, and layout must be undone so that a new order can emerge. An eye for an eye, a medium for a medium. Only from the decomposed bits of a newspaper can a new composition rise. Voilà, violence!

Casus Belli

But why would Picasso go after the newspaper for his art? Maybe it has something to do with his veneration of the poet Mallarmé, who disparaged newspapers (and loved books). In the essay "The Motivation of the Sign," Rosalind Krauss notes that Mallarmé scourged the newspaper for its "column upon column of monotonous gray type"; for "the monstrous amorphousness of an open, flat sheet, as distinct from the precious folds made available by the pages of a book"; and for its layout being "dictated by power" rather than by any other considerations, such as aesthetic ones.[12]

A prime piece of evidence supporting the idea that Picasso's use of the newspaper has something to do with Mallarmé is the *papier collé* Picasso made sometime after December 4, 1912, titled *Table with Bottle, Wineglass, and Newspaper* (fig. 2), which includes a bit of a newspaper headline, "UN COUP DE THÉ" (cut from the longer headline "UN COUP DE THÉÂTRE")—most likely a punning reference to Mallarmé's poem "Un coup de dés jamais n'abolira le hasard" (A throw of the dice will never abolish chance). That poem, Krauss argues, can be read as a point-by-point "reproach" to the newspaper: the "typographic spacing and diversity" of the poem "refuse the monotony of the column of gray print"; the "poetic lines [that] must be read across the gulf of the book's central fold" combat the crude, open, flat sheet; and the "dispersal of the poem's title across the first eleven pages acts to interweave the master typography of the 'headline' into the protracted body of the text."[13] (Picasso's clever choice of a piece of *newspaper* to refer to a poem that is a *reproach to newspaper* is a gorgeous bit of irony!)[14]

But wait. Hasn't Krauss just admitted, by using the term *headline* (albeit with scare quotes), that Mallarmé, the supposed archenemy of newspapers, actually borrowed something from the newspaper, something very much like a headline, for his poem? In fact, Mallarmé used several sizes and weights of type as well as some *italic* type, just as newspapers do to distinguish heads from subheads and headlines from one another. How then could this poem be a reproach? Because, Krauss suggests, the headline—decapitated, so to speak—does not act as a real newspaper headline but rather is woven into the text so as to create "wave after wave of poetic sound."[15]

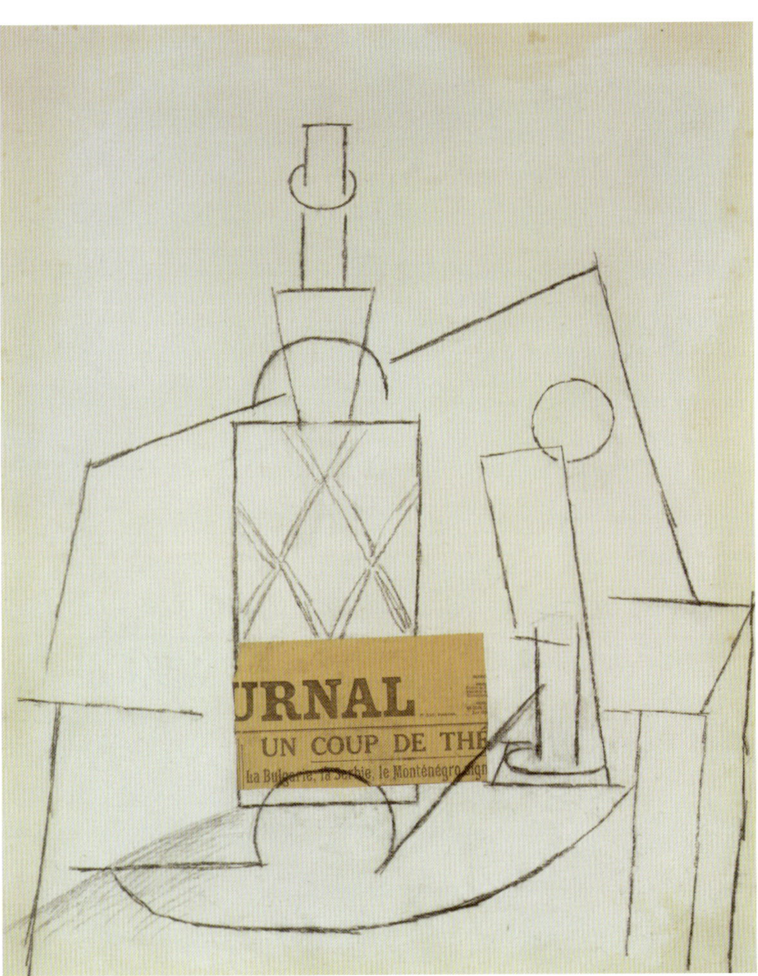

2

Le Hasard

Perhaps. And yet the first time I saw the varieties of type in that poem, I thought *newspaper type*. The first time I saw the big words LE HASARD in a constellation of smaller type, I thought BANNER HEADLINE (fig. 3). Mallarmé may have hated the newspaper, but he sure seems to have envied it, too, however secretly.

In "The Semiology of Cubism," Yve-Alain Bois notes that "Mallarmé's attitude toward the 'low' is more ambiguous than generally believed. His friend Georges Rodenbach recalled, for example, that Mallarmé loved posters, which 'should set the example for books, for they are a kind of printed intonation [*une sorte d'intonations imprimées*],' the various sizes and shapes of their typographic characters mimicking the various volumes and tones of speech and 'nuancing thought.'"[16] And in *The Book as Instrument: Stéphane Mallarmé, the Artist's Book, and the Transformation of Print Culture,* Anna Sigrídur Arnar augments this thought, pointing to Mallarmé's "guarded admiration for the newspaper's uncanny ability to structure disparate and even contradictory bits of information."[17] With this in mind, you can detect in Mallarmé's disparagement of, say, the newspaper's "spectacular vulgar advantage... the multiplication of copies," a flush of jealousy.

And this jealousy seems even more blatant in the case of Picasso's *papiers collés*. In his use of real, scandalous scraps, Picasso was not simply showing (in a covert debate with one of his literary heroes) "that the newspaper can... be made to yield... the very qualities Mallarmé condemned it for lacking," as Krauss puts it;[18] he was also appropriating for himself some of the things in the newspaper that he, like Mallarmé, envied and wanted.

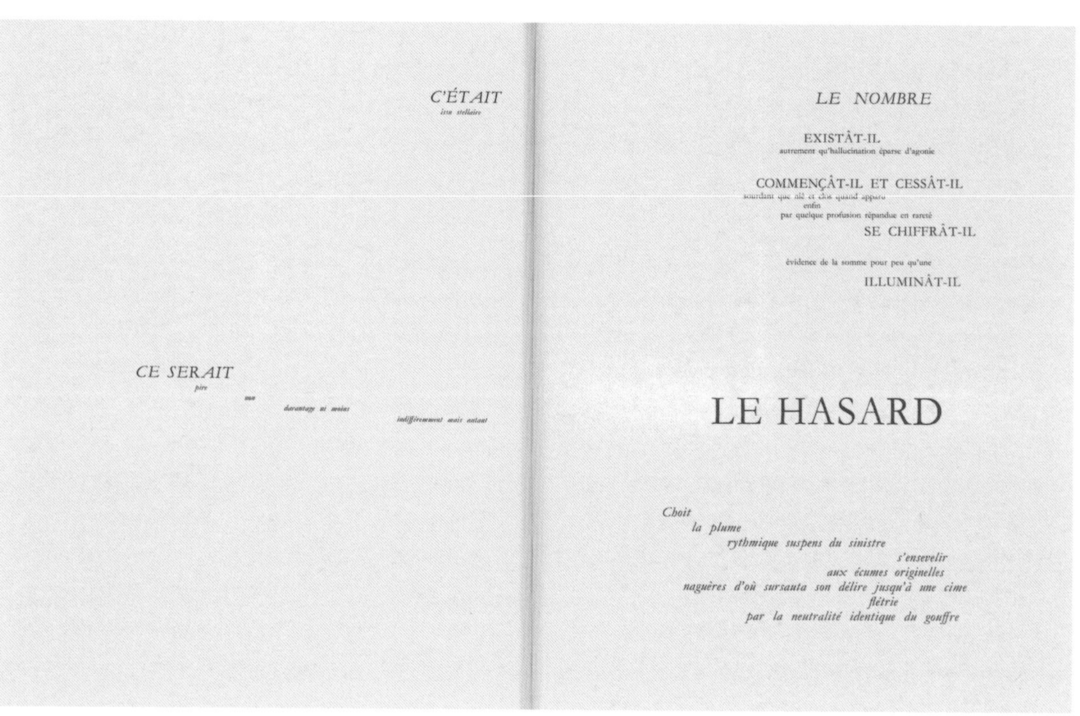

C'ÉTAIT
issu stellaire

CE SERAIT
pire
non
davantage ni moins
indifféremment mais autant

LE NOMBRE

EXISTÂT-IL
autrement qu'hallucination éparse d'agonie

COMMENÇÂT-IL ET CESSÂT-IL
sourdant que nié et clos quand apparu
enfin
par quelque profusion répandue en rareté
SE CHIFFRÂT-IL

évidence de la somme pour peu qu'une
ILLUMINÂT-IL

LE HASARD

Choit
la plume
rythmique suspens du sinistre
s'ensevelir
aux écumes originelles
naguères d'où sursauta son délire jusqu'à une cime
flétrie
par la neutralité identique du gouffre

3

FIG. 3 Stéphane Mallarmé, two-page spread from *Un coup de dés jamais n'abolira le hasard* (1897; Paris, 1914)

FIG. 4 Front page of *The World*, June 15, 1904, evening edition

If you look carefully at art that involves newspaper, you will see that much of the aggression against the newspaper is not so much vindictive as rivalrous—one medium sparring closely with another. Newspapers, after all, are not mere scrap material but everyday objects that are attractive, useful, popular, and diverting. (Mallarmé published his art criticism in newspapers, just as, two generations later, Picasso turned to the papers to read about art exhibitions and bullfights.) And newspapers—unlike, say, flowered wallpaper or faux bois paper—are composed objects, full of words and pictures that are so powerfully attractive that they can potentially steal attention from the work of art that incorporates them. To read, or not to read; that is the tension.[19]

The Spoils of War

Every work of newspaper art thus carries, I think, not only a reforming or sadistic impulse, a desire to make the newspaper yield, but also a whiff of envy. There is always something that the artist wants from the newspaper. But what exactly?

For nearly half a century, the usual explanation for Picasso's and Braque's resort to newspapers, and to collage itself (whether scraps of sheet music or wallpaper or whatever), was "the need for renewed contact with 'reality' in face of the growing abstractness of Analytical Cubism."[20] In 1959, though, Clement Greenberg challenged this, proposing that what Picasso and Braque wanted from these *flat* scraps was (surprisingly) a renewed contact with pictorial *depth:* "By its greater corporeal presence and its greater extraneousness, the affixed paper or cloth serves... to push everything else into a more vivid *idea* of depth."[21]

More recently scholars have emphasized how Picasso and Braque exploited the signifying potential of the words on the scraps of paper or even of the scraps themselves. In other words, when Picasso cut up a newspaper, he was after some particular thing in its scraps. But (again) what? Headlines? Puns? News? Words? Letters?

Patricia Leighten, discussing the *papier collé Glass and Bottle of Suze* (1912), suggests that it was the news stories themselves that Picasso wanted. He destroyed the newspaper to put together his own, creating a new "matrix of meaning" to replace the one he cut up, one intended to challenge the "visual conventions" of "public 'order' and 'unity.'"[22] His collages attacked the newspaper's order so as to present an anarchic yet readable representation of Picasso's own alleged anarchist views.

Robert Rosenblum, by contrast, suggests that what Picasso wanted to steal from the newspaper was the fun and fungibility of individual words. To be fully appreciated, he writes, cubist collages "must often be *read* as well as *seen*"—read not so much for their stories as for their puns.[23] So, when Picasso cut up *Le Journal* and served up *jou* or *jour* (day), he also suggested *jeu* (game) and *jouer* (to play) as well as *joie* (joy) and *jouir* ("to enjoy or, in sexual slang, to come"). When he juxtaposed *urnal* (urinal) with *un coup de thé*, making pee from tea or tea from pee, the bathroom humor was fully intended.[24] Similarly, when Juan Gris permitted "only the letters EAU [water] to show on the label" of a red wine bottle "(originally a B*eau*jolais, B*eau*ne, or Bord*eau*x)," he was performing "his own Cubist version of The Miracle at Cana," turning wine into water.[25] Remember, Rosenblum writes, Picasso and his band were members "of that literary generation which included the greatest punster in the history of Western literature, James Joyce."[26]

The Wine Dark Sea

And punning wasn't all they shared. Picasso's joyfully cannibalistic relationship to his materials was strikingly like Joyce's. Just as Picasso's friends would hunt down wallpaper for his collages, so Joyce, while working on *Ulysses* (from 1914 to 1921), far away from Dublin, would ask friends to send him materials—cheap novelettes, penny hymnals, and trigonometry books. Above all, he needed newspapers, "notably, the *Freeman's Journal* and *Evening Telegraph* for June 16, 1904," which, as R. Brandon Kershner notes, "would be woven directly into the texture of the novel":[27] Gerty's recollection of an advertisement for pills that cure drunkenness came from a real ad printed in the *Weekly Freeman* on June 11, 1904. Bloom's "Bath of the Nymph" came from an issue of *Photo Bits*. The bicycle race in "Wandering Rocks" was in the June 17, 1904, edition of the *Irish Independent*.[28] And news of the *General Slocum* ferry disaster, which occurred on New York City's East River on the morning of June 15, 1904 (and remained the city's largest disaster for a century, until 9/11), might have come from just about any newspaper dated June 15, 1904, or June 16, 1904 (fig. 4).[29] So, yes, James Joyce and the cubists were brothers in scavenging as well as brothers in punning—lusting after what Mallarmé called "just Language, playing."[30]

But to read the scavenged scraps of newspaper in the works of Picasso, Braque, and Gris *just* for the words and wordplay is to miss much of their importance. For Krauss, as for Bois, the *papiers collés* do more than deploy language (Leighten) or play with language (Rosenblum); they demonstrate how visual representation is *like* language, how the newspaper scrap, whether it's read or not, can be wordlike in its ability to take on different, often opposite, meanings in varying contexts.

Picasso uses the "buzz of tiny letters, black flecks on white," to represent not only the buzz of conversation, or "the sound of voices," as Krauss writes, but also to represent "the look of scumbled paint," which in turn conjures "the effect of air."[31] Or to represent "bubbles of soda, stripes of shadow, rays of sun." Or "the graining of wood." Or opacity and transparency. Or figure and ground. Or flatness and depth. Or historical depth. Or a turning in space. Or pure poetry—the *prêt, prêt, prêt* of bubbles rising to the top of a siphon bottle.[32] Picasso thus proved that news-

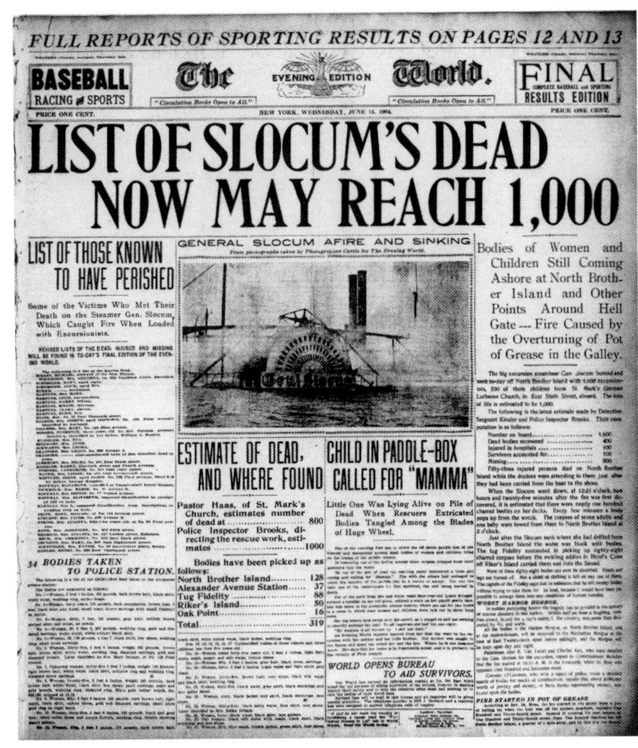
FULL REPORTS OF SPORTING RESULTS ON PAGES 12 AND 13

BASEBALL
RACING & SPORTS

The Evening Edition World.

FINAL
COMPLETE BASEBALL and SPORTING
RESULTS EDITION

PRICE ONE CENT.

NEW YORK, WEDNESDAY, JUNE 15, 1904.

PRICE ONE CENT.

LIST OF SLOCUM'S DEAD
NOW MAY REACH 1,000

LIST OF THOSE KNOWN
TO HAVE PERISHED

Some of the Victims Who Met Their Death on the Steamer Gen. Slocum, Which Caught Fire When Loaded with Excursionists.

REVISED LISTS OF THE DEAD, INJURED AND MISSING WILL BE FOUND IN TO-DAY'S FINAL EDITION OF THE EVENING WORLD.

34 BODIES TAKEN
TO POLICE STATION.

GENERAL SLOCUM AFIRE AND SINKING

ESTIMATE OF DEAD,
AND WHERE FOUND

Pastor Haas, of St. Mark's Church, estimates number of dead at 800
Police Inspector Brooks, directing the rescue work, estimates 1000

Bodies have been picked up as follows:

North Brother Island	128
Alexander Avenue Station	37
Tug Fidelity	88
Riker's Island	50
Oak Point	16
Total	319

CHILD IN PADDLE-BOX
CALLED FOR "MAMMA"

Little One Was Lying Alive on Pile of Dead When Rescuers Extricated Bodies Tangled Among the Blades of Huge Wheel.

WORLD OPENS BUREAU
TO AID SURVIVORS.

Bodies of Women and Children Still Coming Ashore at North Brother Island and Other Points Around Hell Gate—Fire Caused by the Overturning of Pot of Grease in the Galley.

The big excursion steamboat Gen. Slocum burned and sank to-day off North Brother Island with 1,600 excursionists, 500 of them children from St. Mark's German Lutheran Church, in East Sixth Street, aboard. The loss of life is estimated to be 1,000.

The following is the latest estimate made by Detective Sergeant Kinsler and Police Inspector Brooks. Their computation is as follows:

Number on board	1,600
Dead bodies recovered	400
Injured in hospitals	100
Survivors accounted for	100
Missing	800

WORST HARBOR HORROR.

FIRE STARTED IN POT OF GREASE.

4

paper, in his hands, could be made to yield the things Mallarmé suggested they were lacking—depth, opacity, polysemy, transmutation.[33]

Road Rage

To follow the endless sign-play in a collage requires not only rigorous decoding but also a restless mind and a free-floating gaze—a mind and gaze, come to think of it, very like that of a newspaper reader. Here then is another possible target of the artist's newspaper envy: not the object itself or the sign-play it enables but how the object is actually consumed. A newspaper reader is a kind of literary flâneur, taking in headlines, zipping around the display page, jumping to the "jump," looking down columns to scan a story, noticing eye-catching ads between sips of coffee and getting dressed. As Walter Benjamin put it, "Nothing binds the reader more tightly to his paper than this all-consuming impatience."[34]

This restless gaze must have been one of the things that attracted the futurists to newspapers, too, because for them impatience and speed (along with a disdain for museums, libraries, peace, and women) were cardinal virtues. And speed was closely connected to violence. In the "Founding and Manifesto of Futurism" (published in 1909) (pl. 1), Marinetti tells how his impatience, his road rage, led to his destructive credo: while he was speeding in his car outside Milan, he veered into a muddy ditch to avoid hitting two slow cyclists "wobbling" on the street "like two lines of reasoning." It was while he was submerged in this "Maternal ditch," this "factory drain," that, as Marinetti tells it, he "gulped down" the "bracing slime" and emerged "a filthy and stinking rag" with a blind and joyful destructiveness in his heart: "Art...can be nothing if not violence, cruelty, and injustice."[35]

Although the futurists used many of the same newspaper-torture techniques that Picasso did—mostly cutting and pasting—the tone of their works, as well as what they actually got out of the newspapers they cut up, is different, especially after 1914. They didn't care as much for the buzzy visual texture, the clever puns, or the polyphonic structure of newspapers as for their dynamism and lack of focus. As Christine Poggi writes, they were more interested in exploring "the freedom to scatter words dynamically about the page, to stretch and deform verbal elements...to create visually expressive patterns" and to arouse "diffuse sensations."[36]

In *Al buffet della stazione* (In the railway café) (1914; pl. 34), as Poggi writes, Ardengo Soffici juxtaposed a piece of newspaper, a cup of coffee, and "a spent cigarette," all made of words, with a saucer, also composed of words that had been clipped, it seems, from various sources and assembled into a puzzling poem: "shipwreck in the irony of the cigarette butt in a drop of coffee 25 cents black tear of melancholy."[37] In other words, he made a tempest in a tea saucer.

In other futurist collages, such as Carlo Carrà's *Pursuit* (*Inseguimento*) (1915; pl. 5), the pieces of newspaper are crushed under speeding machines—horses, wheels, or whatever—which are also made largely of newspaper. In Umberto Boccioni's *Charge of the Lancers* (1915), the newspaper may have something to say, but its bits get lost in a stampede of horses and spears. No time to read. No time to pun. Gotta fight. Words a blur.

In *Manifestazione interventista* (Interventionist demonstration) (fig. 5), Carrà uses strips of newspaper and other printed matter to convey urgency and energy. It may be a poem, but it's also a paean to speed (the printed fragments form a wheel) and the blur of repetitive nonsense (*krrrrrudeele, EEVVIVAAA, REEE, HUHUHUHU, SIR ENE SIR ENE*). In this piece, the attitude toward the newspaper fragments seems to be: hey, if you can read these words, I must be moving too slowly. If you can decipher anything coherent in them, I'd better rev my engine a little louder. The only sense that shines through the blur is patriotism (at least two Italian flags are visible), a hint of flatulence ("flatulenze mori odori pesi calore"), the words *Sports* and *Strada,* the sound of the word *serene* turned into a siren wail (SIR ENE SIR ENE), and the banner of the *Corriere della Sera,* pretty much intact.

The closest patron saint here would be Guillaume Apollinaire, whose 1912 poem "Zone" reveled in the crassness of the paper:

FIG. 5 Carlo Carrà, *Manifestazione interventista* (Interventionist demonstration), 1914, pasted papers, charcoal, ink, and gouache on board, Mattioli Collection. Long-term loan to the Peggy Guggenheim Collection, Venice

You read the handbills, catalogues, posters that sing out loud and clear—

That's the morning's poetry, and for prose there are the newspapers,

There are tabloids lurid with police reports,

Portraits of the great and a thousand assorted stories.[38]

And so, the newspaper was loved and shredded for its street cred.

Bloody Fingerprints

The nonsense-making machine, which chewed up newspapers and spit out energetic poems and pictures, had a somewhat different feel in the hands of the Dadaists. In the early days of Dada, Hannah Höch said, "Our whole purpose was to integrate objects from the world of machines and industry in the world of art."[39] (The term *photomontage,* Dawn Ades notes, "had its origin in the adoption of the term . . . *montiert* or *montieren*"— both of which mean to assemble, as in an assembly line.)[40] It didn't matter whether these photomontages said anything coherent. In fact, it was better if they didn't, since they were meant to reflect what Richard Huelsenbeck, in his Dada Manifesto (1918), called "the frenzied cataract of life."[41]

The key thing was slumming with industry and trying to disorder mechanically made materials, such as bits of newsprint and magazine photos, cigarette butts and ticket stubs. For the Dadaists, "the tiniest authentic fragment of daily life says more than painting," Walter Benjamin wrote in his essay "The Author as Producer." "Just as the bloody fingerprint of a murderer on the page of a book says more than the text."[42]

But by the 1920s some Dadaists had become less entranced with fragmentation for fragmentation's sake. In the book *Les collages,* Louis Aragon described the moment that Heartfield stopped making explosive, chaotic Dada images from scraps of papers and photographs, such as *Life and Activity in Universal City at 12:05 Midday* (which he assembled with George Grosz, in 1919), and instead started making coherent political satire: "As he was playing with the fire of appearances, reality took fire around him. . . . John Heartfield was no longer playing. The scraps . . . that he formerly manouevred for the pleasure of stupefaction, under his fingers began to *signify.*"[43] And what they signified was almost always political villainy and, occasionally, something villainous about the newspapers themselves.

Consider Heartfield's 1930 photomontage showing a beaten-down man whose head is wrapped in pages from two newspapers — *Vorwärts,* the official organ of the Social Democratic Party, and *Tempo,* a mass-market tabloid — sheets that are made to look like the leaves of a head of cabbage (pl. 8). The text, printed in white type over the man's chest says, "Ich bin ein Kohlkopf. Kennt ihr meine Blätter?" (I am a cabbage head. Do you know my leaves?).

This photomontage could be read as just another bit of Dada nonsense, goofing around with language and image. Look, it's a man with a cabbage head! Or maybe it's a newspaper head!

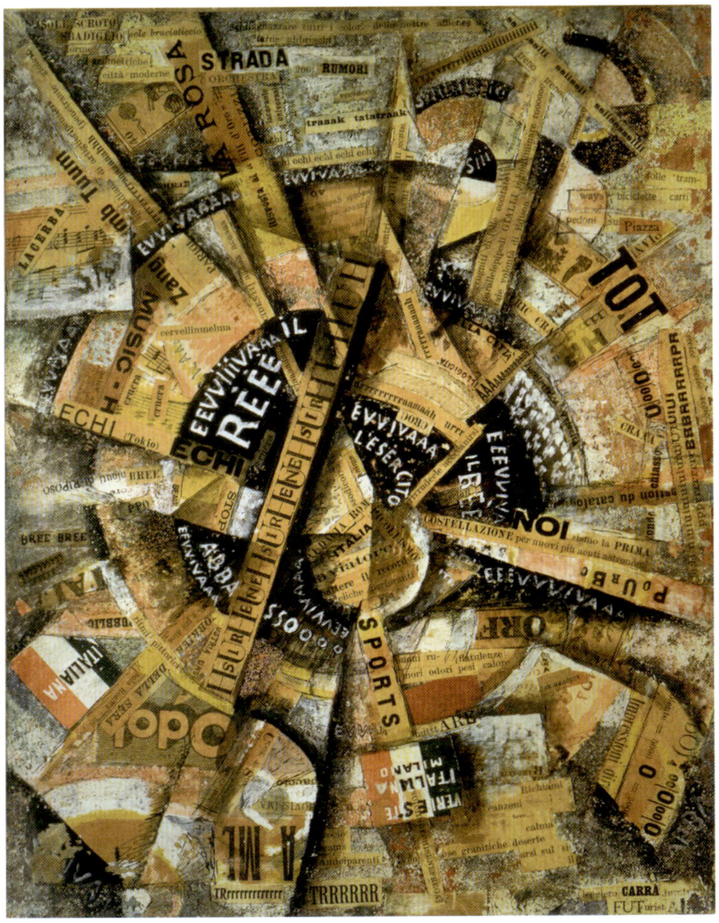

5

Or maybe they're the same thing! *Blätter* can mean either the leaves of a cabbage plant or the pages of a newspaper; and the phrase "I am a cabbage head" plays off the Prussian national anthem "I am a Prussian."[44] But beyond puns, there is a lesson, which Heartfield fairly shouts out in the work's title, *Wer Bürgerblätter liest wird blind und taub. Weg mit den verdummungsbandagen!* (Whoever reads bourgeois newspapers goes blind and deaf. Away with bandages that make you dimwitted!). It's so blunt you don't even have to look at the picture of a man blinded by newspapers to get it. You only have to read the caption below the picture.

So where in this attack on the newspaper is the kernel of envy? It's right there—clear as a caption. In fact, it is a caption! What Heartfield steals from the newspaper is its ability to come right out and say something precise and clear. He steals the weapon of the caption only to turn it on the newspaper itself. And here's the kicker. Heartfield published most of his collages in newspapers and magazines, including *Der Knüppel,* the German Communist Party's satirical weekly; the Communist newspaper *Die Rote Fahne;* and the illustrated weekly *Arbeiter Illustrierte Zeitung.*[45] He was a newspaper man himself.

Hostile Takeover

On the face of it, El Lissitzky and Sergei Sen'kin's series of photomontages for the Soviet pavilion at the Pressa exhibition (1928; pl. 37) echoes Heartfield's *I Am a Cabbage Head.* Like Heartfield, they use newspaper-type headlines to tell you what to think. But there the affinities tail off. Instead of turning the newspaper against itself, as Heartfield did, Lissitzky and Sen'kin have taken over the machinery of the newspaper to create their own. Their series of photomontages are in effect the pages of a newspaper that tell newspapers what newspapers are meant to do!

Publishing one's own news (or one's own newspaper) is a time-honored way for artists to steal something enviable from the newspaper for themselves—especially the newspaper's hold on "the truth" and its readers' attention and credulousness. In 1909, Marinetti published his Futurist Manifesto in an issue of *Le Figaro* (pl. 1). In 1945, Salvador Dalí published the *Dali News,* which included news only about himself (pl. 21). Yves Klein's *Dimanche—Le journal d'un seul jour* (1960), another mock newspaper, includes a picture of Yves Klein supposedly jumping out a window and concerns, yes, Yves Klein (pl. 22). In 1991, Robert Gober created his own page of the *New York Times* (pl. 29)—complete with soft, deckled edges, mismatched wedding announcements ("the women's sports pages," as a friend of mine calls them), and a (clearly fictional) story about his own death, written as a kind of light news item or *fait divers:* "Boy Drowns in Pool." It goes like this: "According to the initial police report the child's mother, Leah Gober, found her six year old son Robert late Monday evening face down in about three inches of water" (fig. 6).[46] Just like Marinetti.

And then there's *Bloom-Zeitung,* a faux issue of the German newspaper *Bild-Zeitung* created by Bazon Brock, Bernhard Jäger, and Thomas Bayerle, in honor of Bloomsday, the day commemorated by Joyce's *Ulysses,* June 16, 1904 (pl. 20). Distributed throughout Frankfurt on June 16, 1963, the fifty-ninth anniversary of Bloomsday, the *Bloom-*

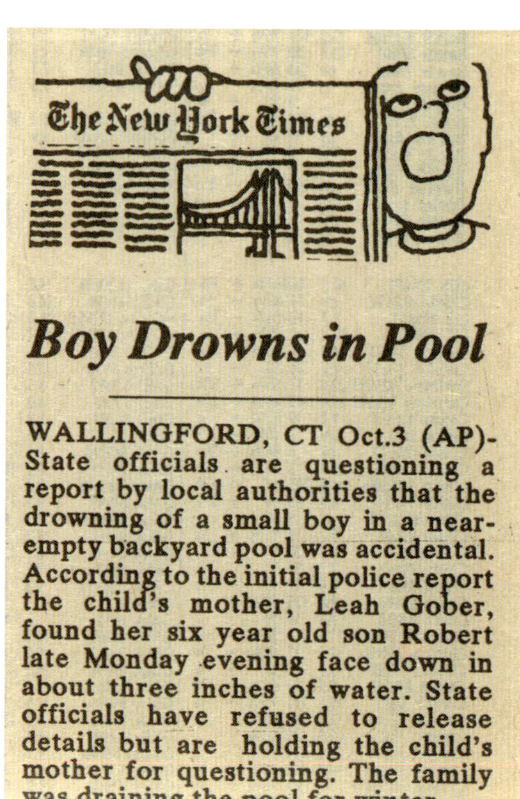
The New York Times

Boy Drowns in Pool

WALLINGFORD, CT Oct.3 (AP)- State officials are questioning a report by local authorities that the drowning of a small boy in a near-empty backyard pool was accidental. According to the initial police report the child's mother, Leah Gober, found her six year old son Robert late Monday evening face down in about three inches of water. State officials have refused to release details but are holding the child's mother for questioning. The family was draining the pool for winter.

6

FIG. 6 Detail from Robert Gober, *Untitled,* 1991. See also pl. 29

FIG. 7 Detail from Paul Thek, *Untitled (Diver),* 1970. See also pl. 51

Zeitung celebrated the day by replacing many of the nouns (and some of the verbs) in every advertisement, article, and headline with the name "Bloom." One story, "Bloom versunken," concerns a water disaster: "45-year-old 'Bloom' watched while his mother, his wife, and his 3-year-old daughter slid into the Weser River. While he was able to save his daughter, the car sank into the water with the other two 'Blooms.'" Thus was the *Bild-Zeitung* flooded with Blooms.

Waterboarding

What about artists who leave the newspaper whole? No cutting. No mocking. No wrapping. No stuffing. Are these artists also aggressing against the newspaper? In 1913, Picasso turned the newspaper page upside-down and used it as a sheet of drawing paper (pl. 6). So did Max Weber (pl. 33). For *Transmutation* (1916), Man Ray used a whole newspaper page as a backdrop and a foil for his puns and dirty jokes (pl. 7). It all was pretty tame.

Then the volume and the violence got turned up. By the 1950s, the newspaper wasn't so much an ever-ready drawing surface but a subject to be drowned out. In 1952, Robert Rauschenberg made *Asheville Citizen* by plastering an issue in black oil (pl. 16). In 1957, Jasper Johns embedded a newspaper in waxy encaustic (pl. 18). In 1962, Robert Morris, upset with news of the Cuban missile crisis, washed over it with layers of gray paint (pl. 19). In 1970, Paul Thek painted over a newspaper page until it was a pool of blue, impenetrable liquid, then added a diver plunging in (fig. 7). In 2002, Cy Twombly lathered black paint on an open page, leaving only the edges of the newspaper showing, and then, it seems, scraped into the paint to reveal little glints of newsprint underneath. In all these examples, the newspaper was literally liquidated.

The sixties were, arguably, the most violent decade in the war against newspapers. In 1968, five years after John F. Kennedy's assassination, Andy Warhol shot flowers at the surface of the November 22, 1963, issue of the *New York World-Telegram*—the one with the headline "PRESIDENT SHOT DEAD" (pl. 24).[47] In 1961, Dieter Roth diced and minced newspaper, mixed it with water,

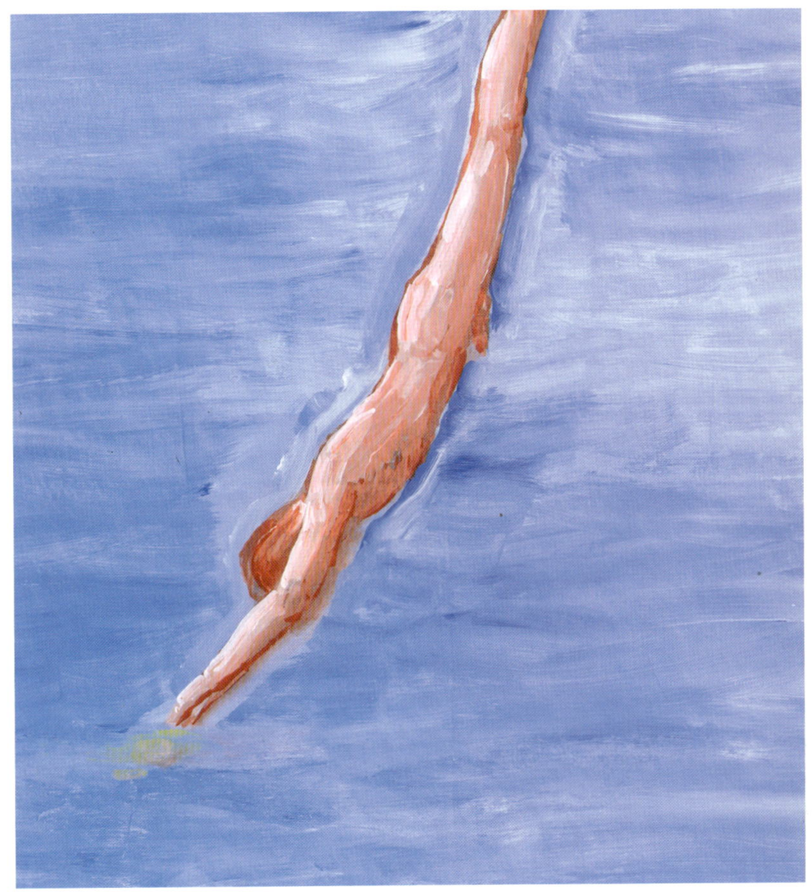

7

gelatin, and spices, stuffed it all in a sausage casing, and called it *Literaturwurst* (pl. 43). In 1963, the Belgian artist Marcel Broodthaers plopped a bunch of ink-covered plastic eggs (they actually look like black dung) onto a newspaper and titled the mess "Le problème noir en Belgique" (The black problem in Belgium), while totally messing it (pl. 46). (Broodthaers, by the way, is also known for taking Mallarmé's poem "Un coup de dés" and replacing all its words with black bars.) In 1963, Joseph Beuys branded a newspaper with the word *Kraft* (power) (pl. 45). In these last two cases it is notable that the artist took care to fold the newspaper before attacking it. Perhaps the open page looked just too vulnerable.

Folding Up Shop

The final frontier in the war against newspapers is folding and stacking. And this is a particularly subtle form of aggression, for although it does nothing to harm the surface of the paper, it returns the newspaper to an unreadable or preread state (much the way that Broodthaers' version of "Un coup de dés" does). The newspaper becomes a solid thing, a sculpture, frozen, impenetrable.

Robert Gober's newspaper stacks, such as *Newspaper* (1992) (pl. 28), which appear in several of his installations, fall into this category. So does Mario Merz's assemblage *À Mallarmé* (2003), which the critic Thomas Micchelli described as "bundled stacks of newspapers in Italian (Turin's *La Stampa*) and Arabic, counting down the days before Bush launched his war against Iraq"—topped off by a "quotation from Stéphane Mallarmé... emblazoned in blue neon tubing... *Un coup de dés jamais n'abolira le hasard*" (pl. 59).[48]

À Mallarmé is a summing-up work. The riverine ribbon of blue neon takes us from 2003, before the war in Iraq began (but after, it was said, the die had already been cast by George W. Bush), all the way back (via Mallarmé) to the dawn of newspaper art, with Picasso's *Un coup de thé*. So how should we understand this odd tribute to the poet whose famous hatred for the newspaper launched a hundred-year war against it?

Maybe those stacks of news with their Mallarmé icing are a message to the poet, telling him that the war against newspapers is over, that the papers have been defeated, turned into objects, in which all their objectionable (to Mallarmé) qualities have been muted. The stacks are mere tombs, and the neon tubing is a gravestone marker.

Or maybe it's just the opposite, a big heaping helping of newspapers served up to a man who hated them—a finger thumbed at the dead poet: In your face, Mallarmé!

Of course, there are other possible readings of this piece of newspaper art. Maybe Merz is telling Mallarmé that newspapers, which once were monstrously "open, flat sheets," have reformed since his day to become more like his sacrosanct books, at least in their thickness. They are now replete with those mysterious folds that Mallarmé found so inviting and so vulnerable. (Part of what Mallarmé loved about the folded pages of a book was the violence, the slicing open, that had to be done to them before they were read: "I brandish my knife, like a poultry butcher. The virgin folds of a new book, still, lend themselves to a sacrifice whose blood stained the edges of ancient volumes red; they await the introduction of a weapon, or paper cutter, in order for possession to take place.")[49]

Mallarmé, Merz might be saying, would be pleased to learn that in this way, too, newspapers have become like books. In the hands of artists, they have proven that they, too, can be thoroughly deflowered—cut, branded, drowned, mocked, dumped on, bound, gagged. If the violence done to an object is a measure of its value, then newspaper is now pure gold. See Jim Hodges' *Good News* (2008), an issue of the Arabic paper *Al Arab Al Yawm* covered in 24K gold (pl. 31).[50]

Flooding the Zone

I think I've used the term *newspaper art* more than once. Does that mean I think it's a genre? A medium? Maybe. And if pressed to say what's

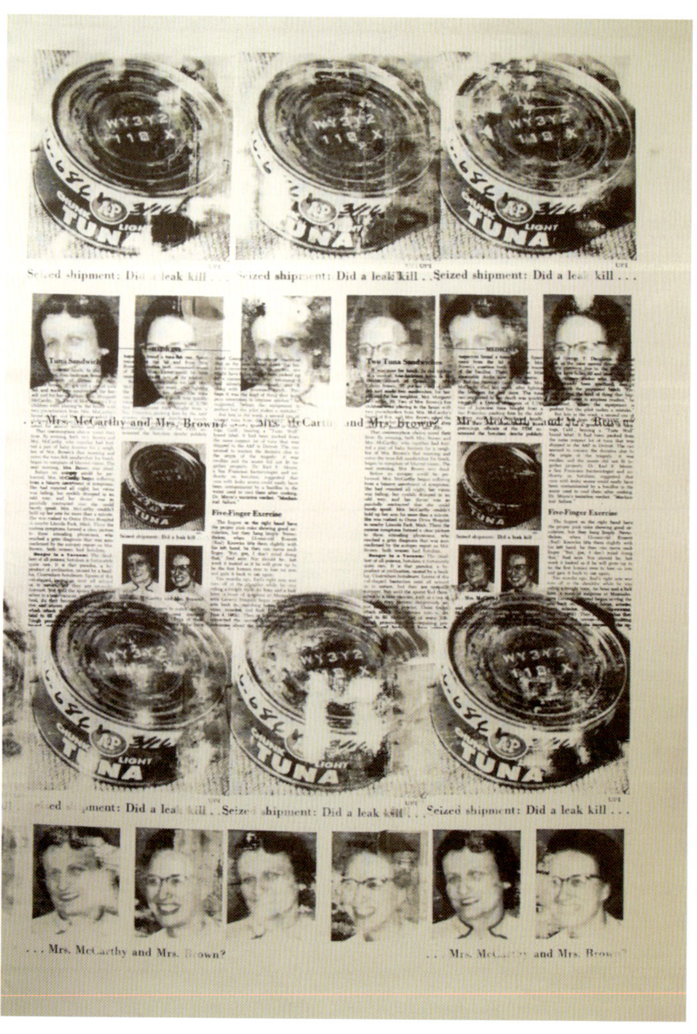

8

FIG. 8 Andy Warhol, *Tunafish Disaster*, 1963, silkscreen ink and silver paint on linen, Andrew and Denise Saul

FIG. 9 Pablo Picasso, *Siphon, Glass, Newspaper, and Violin*, 1912/1913, newspaper, hand-painted faux bois paper, paper, and charcoal, Moderna Museet, Stockholm

special about this medium, I'd say it is the violence toward the newspaper with a hint of envy shining through.

But there's something else—not so much a rule as a tendency. Have you noticed it yet?

The attraction to water and other liquids? The themes of immersion and drowning, shipwreck and flooding? The obsession with Bloomsday and *Ulysses*, which are themselves loaded with water imagery? (*Ulysses* includes not only more than one mention of the "snotgreen" sea and of peeing but several references to the *General Slocum* steamboat disaster).[51] From the car-in-the-ditch in Marinetti's manifesto to the car-in-the-river in *Bloom-Zeitung*, from Picasso's café drinks to Soffici's little "shipwreck" in a saucer, from Gris's unholy trick of turning wine to water to the total washouts of Morris and Thek, from Gober's "Boy Drowns in Pool" to Warhol's *Tunafish Disaster* (fig. 8), newspapers have fairly drawn the fluids out of artists. Or, to borrow a phrase from football and journalism (it was a favorite of Howell Raines, the editor of the *New York Times*, during the weeks following 9/11), these artists have "flooded the zone." Or, to put it as Picasso did after Apollinaire published pictures of some of his paper constructions, "The watertight barriers have been breached."[52]

Why so much water? Perhaps *Siphon, Glass, Newspaper, and Violin* (1912–1913), which is the most waterlogged collage I can think of—Rosenblum terms it "Picasso's deep-sea fishing" picture—can shed some light on the liquid obsession of newspaper artists (fig. 9). This newspaper collage features not only a full siphon bottle but also a violin whose bottom resembles a ship's anchor and, to top it off, a newspaper picture of a boat and line with its caption intact: "Comment on pose une ligne à 1000 mètres de fond" (How to lay a line at a thousand meters' depth). "Here, in a cross-section of the sea, almost Cubist in its schematic transparency," Rosenblum writes, the line from the boat "almost seems to attempt to anchor, with its plumb-line verticality, the swaying, teetering rhythms of the Cubist objects set afloat around it."[53] In the same *papier collé*, some of the newspaper scraps, as Krauss points

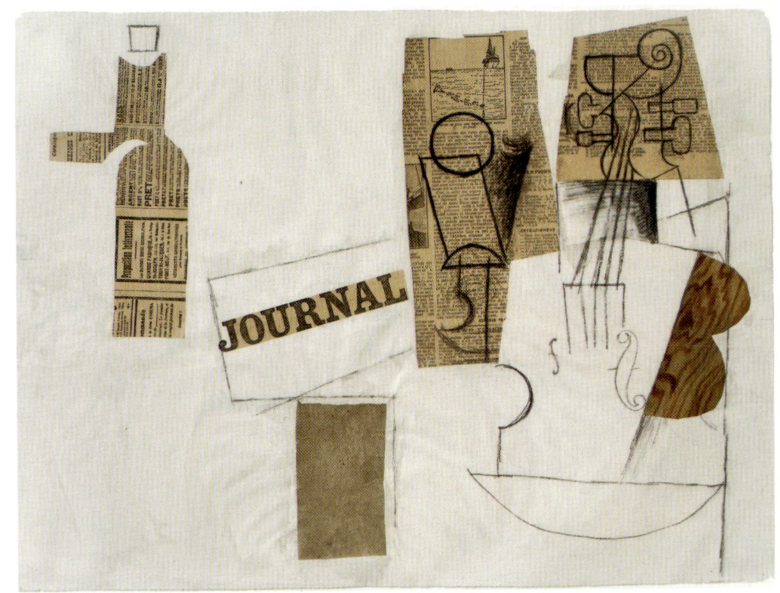

9

out, can be read as signs for liquid—the "glinting facets on the surface of water" and the "rising bubbles" in the siphon bottle.[54]

But even more important, Krauss notes, is the liquid way that signs like these circulate: "Each newsprint fragment forms the sign for a visual meaning; then . . . the sign re-forms and the meaning shifts . . . but never enduringly so."[55] Every meaning is liquid, constantly changing. And to appreciate this never-ending circulation, one must see fluently, or, you know, go with the flow.

Maybe then the water fixation of newspaper artists has to do with the liquidity of language. Or with the liquid look of newspapers and the liquid way they circulate. Or with the setting of the earliest newspaper collages. The café, after all, *is* a matter of liquids—coffee, tea, wine, beer, absinthe. But then why the fixation on the café? Because that is where three rivers join: the circulation of fluids, of newspapers, and of signs. It's where language is liquid and liquid is language and where loose lips sink ships. Here the violent contest between art and the newspaper dissolves, just where it started. Shipwrecks become conversation, tears are drowned, wine becomes water, tea turns to pee, and tempests return to their teapots.

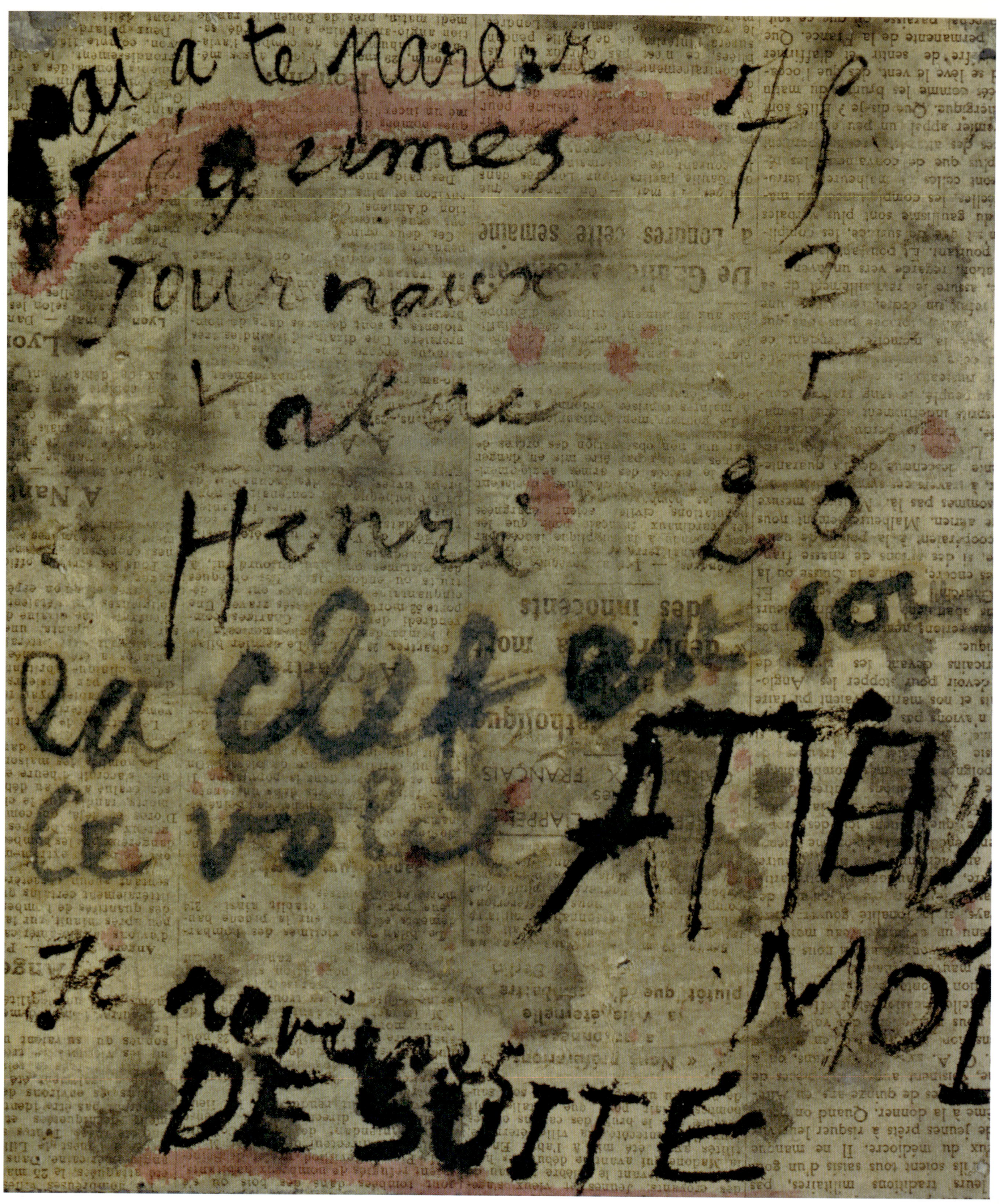
ai à te parler
Journaux
Henri
la clef
Je reviens
DE SUITE
MOI

NEWSPRINT AND NEWS TIME

Janine Mileaf and Matthew Witkovsky

"Yesterday's news is tomorrow's fish and chip wrapper."
Anonymous

"A newspaper is canned time."
Karl Kraus, 1923

When Pablo Picasso decided to include newspaper cuttings in his initial *papiers collés*, in 1912, the sight of a daily newspaper on a Parisian café table was standard fare. In the years culminating around World War I, newspaper reading in France expanded phenomenally.[1] Improved printing and communication technologies like half-tone reproductions, the rolling press, and telephones and radio fed the demand for immediate information about current events, propelling newspaper and magazine sales and furthering the preeminence of the newspaper in particular as the first truly mass medium.[2] The reading public had increased following an expansion of literacy made possible by mandatory education laws and because of legislation ensuring the freedom of the press.[3] As the American correspondent Harry Greenwall recalled in his memoirs, it was not uncommon for Parisians to read three to five newspapers per day—some for varying political points of view and others because they arrived at different hours.[4] The nature of the war itself was altered by the growth of the tabloid press, which delivered illustrated reports of activity from the front at a startling pace—and bore information daily to those at the front as well (fig. 1).

That a still life of a café scene in Picasso's day should include the paper, then, was no great shock. The surprise came instead from his deployment of newsprint to stand in for something other than the news (pl. 13). Certainly, the use of newsprint symbolized an everyday reality, but not in such a straightforward way; rather, it marked an intrusion of everydayness into the noble and enduring realm of art. Art historian Leo Steinberg noted that newsprint lent "a texture, a kind of precise energy within the field" of Picasso's collages.[5] The headlines in those works—large enough for a viewer to read, as Steinberg noted—gave the artist elements of language to be played around with, just as he teased visual signs (for wallpaper, guitar holes, or faces) away from their habitual referents. But beneath any puns or cryptic messages, the "precise energy" that Steinberg registered encoded the swift passing of time. Yellowing almost before one's eyes, newsprint carries a material currency only slightly greater than its validity as a bearer of fresh information. It returns written language, for thousands of years the consummate expression of a human striving to eternalize knowledge, to a state of perishability no better than that of ordinary market produce—or, tragically, that of young soldiers sent to the trenches. At the same time, such quickened awareness of mortality can paradoxically bring increased vigor and life, as the quickly fading energy of newsprint is transformed into the feverish excitement of creating a new language for art.

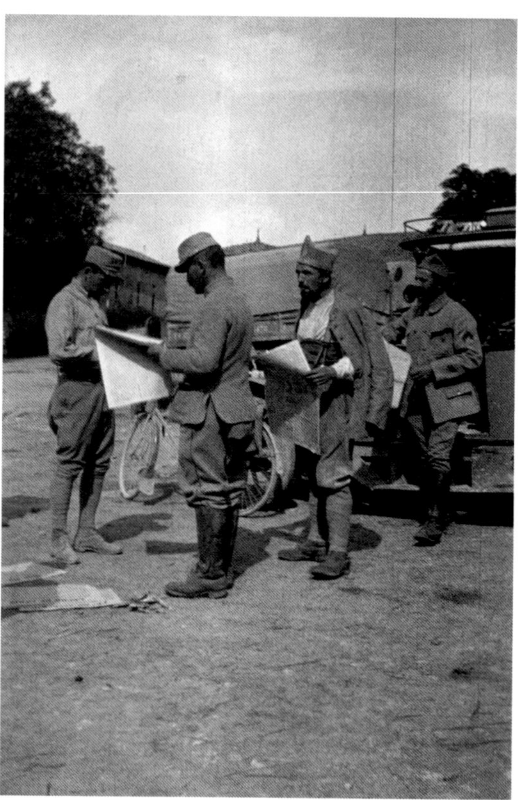

1

Filippo Tommaso Marinetti, leader of the Italian futurists, radiated vitality through the papers as well, although he adopted what appears to be a very different tactic than Picasso. Rather than infecting fine art with the news, Marinetti infiltrated the news and occupied it like a foreign body, heralding the Italian avant-garde "invasion" in a manifesto that he placed in 1909 in such signal dailies as *La Corriere della Sera* and, most prominently, on the front page of *Le Figaro*.[6] Where Picasso engaged the material character of newsprint, Marinetti applied himself to questions of distribution and consumption, undercutting the eternal nobility of fine art by making it headline news for a consumer audience.

What the paper-reading public was buying, however, was once again a heightened sense of its own mortality, a thrilling anxiety about the world as a quickly spent commodity. Marinetti's manifesto astutely exacerbated these fears, treating durable goods (automobiles, electric lights) with marvelous extravagance as perishable items and overlaying a quasi-biblical language of perdition and redemption onto scenes from the commodified everyday. "Death, domesticated, was overtaking me at every turn, gracefully holding out a paw," Marinetti writes in a preamble describing the thrill of a nocturnal automotive escapade undertaken with his fellow futurists, "or sometimes stretching out on the ground with a noise like that of grating jawbones, casting me velvety and tender looks from every puddle." A car wreck, which upends Marinetti into a bath of "good factory slime," serves as the rite of passage—a conflation of baptism and last rites—that prepares the actual manifesto, a set of declarations issued "to all the *living* men of the earth."[7]

The paired legacy of Picasso and Marinetti, as explored in this book, suggests a dual mode of interaction with the daily papers. On one hand are works that deal with the fragmentary everydayness of modern life through the material of newsprint itself; on the other are those that mimic or infiltrate the apparatus of newspaper publishing and its increasingly commodified public. These two paths through the twentieth century intersect regularly, however, and cannot be assigned neatly to Picasso or Marinetti, introductory examples notwithstanding. Picasso's costumes for the 1917 production of Jean Cocteau's ballet *Parade,* for example, derived from the "sandwichmen" who walked around Paris wearing advertising billboards, a close cousin to his conflation of men and newspapers in the collages, as Jeffrey Weiss has shown (pls. 6, 13).[8] Newsprint as material could easily serve to satirize news media. A staging soon afterward of *Les mamelles de Tirésias* (The breasts of Tiresias), a play by Guillaume Apollinaire, included knock-offs of Picasso's *Parade* costumes that featured bits of newspaper attached to "walking kiosks," an idea that resonated into the 1920s, as a sketch for a later production of Apollinaire's play in Prague reveals (fig. 2).[9] But again, the common denominator between material and institutional critique here is the perishable nature of commodified matter itself. News time, the temporal pace that structures all modernity, is caught between great currency and rapid obsolescence, instant immortality and sudden death.

Toward the end of the nineteenth century, poet Stéphane Mallarmé launched an attack on newspapers from a literary standpoint. His exalta-

FIG. 1 André Jeunet, *French soldiers reading Paris newspaper*, c. 1916, photograph, University of Louisville, Photographic Archives

FIG. 2 Otakar Mrkvička and Karel Teige, costume design for Guillaume Apollinaire's *Les mamelles de Tirésias* (The breasts of Tiresias), 1926, ink on paper, location unknown

FIG. 3 Albrecht Dürer, *Erasmus of Rotterdam*, 1526, engraving, National Gallery of Art, Washington, Rosenwald Collection

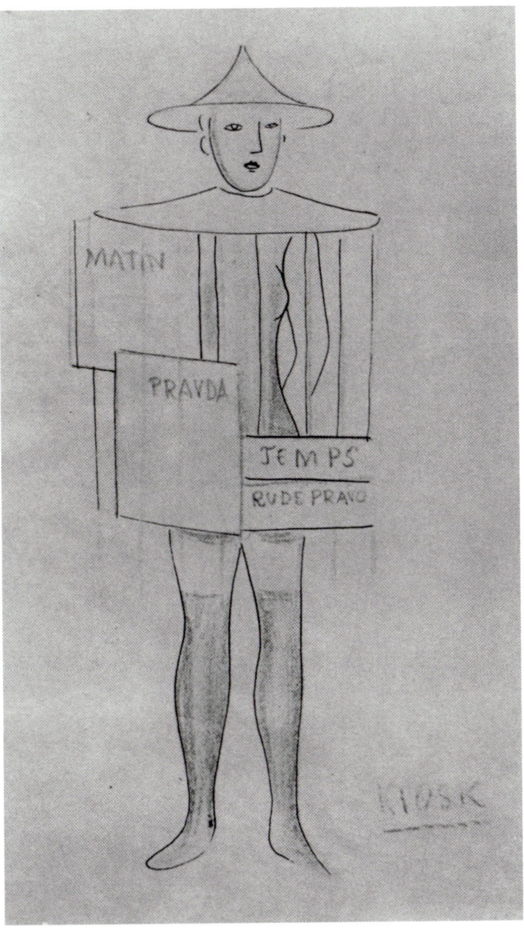

2

tion of the book centered on its substantive physical presence, which Mallarmé opposed to the thinness of the newspaper: flimsy, weightless, and repetitious to boot, a monotonous collection of "eternally unbearable columns, which are merely strung down the pages by hundreds."[10] Mallarmé also likened the news outright to a commodity, an emblem of the culture of disposability that had come to characterize bourgeois life.[11] The longevity of literature could never be attained by the "Paris editions," which "pulse in the unknown womb of the hour, shown in the pages as clear and evident."[12] The presumed clarity of the words on a newspaper page betrayed their nonliterary character.

Mallarmé further equated the public's ever-increasing demand for fresh information to a desire for fashionability, a false sense of life lived in an eternal present tense.[13] He sought to have literature escape this condition of ceaseless renewal: "The visual emblem of the tirelessly repeated column reflects the way the newspaper organizes time: today is nothing more than an indifferent replacement of yesterday, and a forerunner of tomorrow.... Literature, by contrast, makes a leap outside of time."[14] Although the gray-brown palette adopted by Picasso and Georges Braque certainly muddied the clarity of black-and-white journalism, their cuttings emphatically reintroduced the journalistic "now" into the visual field, perhaps in ironic reply to Mallarmé's very comments. Newsprint and news time were ubiquitous by the 1910s, and it made more sense to exaggerate their effects on human sensibility, as a means of commentary, than to seek to escape those effects. The "human newsstand" imagined in *Parade* or *Tiresias' Breasts* is but one of many figures, in and after those years, for an eclipse of humanism by the news. The tradition of contemplative penmanship symbolized by Erasmus writing in his den (fig. 3) had been superseded apparently overnight by humanoids literally made of newsprint, who circulated moreover in an environment plastered with newspapers as well (pls. 9, 10, 36). By the later 1920s, the image of society, or at least its more doubtful elements, as an empty media construct was part of the visual vernacular (pl. 41).

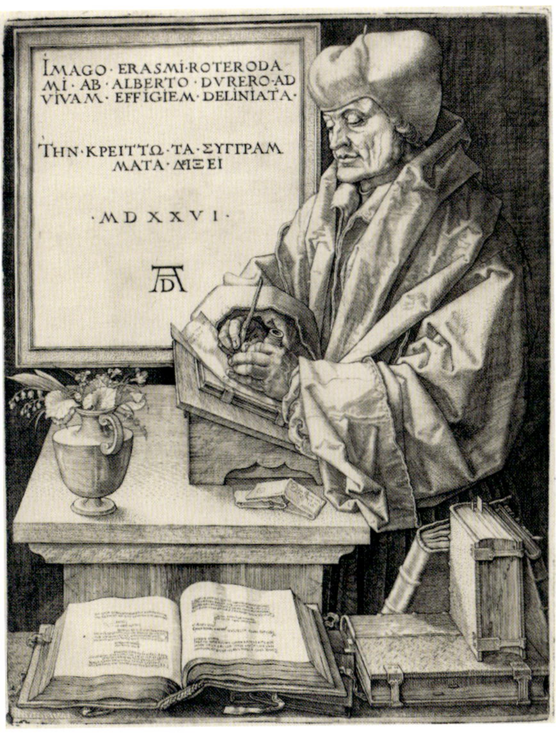

3

Critics Karl Kraus and Walter Benjamin engaged at close range with the threats of newsprint and news time. "The newspaper is an instrument of power," warned Benjamin in an essay on his Austrian colleague Kraus, who spent his life battling the degradation of human language brought about by journalism.[15] To fight that fire, Kraus developed his own incendiary device, the aphoristic barb: a pithy phrase that would lodge in the reader's mind like a newspaper headline, but with a caustic, punning force that carried lasting critical insight. In a 1923 collection of his aphorisms that he titled *Sprüche und Widersprüche* (*Dicta and Contradicta*), Kraus cast grave doubt on the veracity of newspaper reports, stating that they had "approximately the same relation to life as Tarot ladies to metaphysics."[16] He was irate at the corrupt use of language and the deployment of words as marketable items, yet he recognized the efficacy of the technique.[17]

John Heartfield similarly fought fire with fire in his montages for the *Arbeiter Illustrierte Zeitung,* or *AIZ,* treating images and phrases alike as explosive headliners. Another critic of the time, Adolf Behne, noted Heartfield's achievement in a suitably aphoristic encomium: "The photomontage of Heartfield: That is photography plus dynamite."[18] The *AIZ* had itself been founded to rival the mainstream press as a newspaper that would give laborers news and images filtered through the illuminating lens of "the worker's eye," rather than the blinkered view of ruling society.[19] Heartfield accordingly established a production team worthy of those at mainstream media outlets and delivered gravely witty indictments of Nazism week after week in tabloid images. Every time he "repurposed" a propaganda photograph, he pointed a finger not only at fascist politicians but at the media enterprise that glorified or ineffectively combated their lies. In one attack from 1930 (pl. 8), a rank-and-file citizen has presumably been led to his servile imbecility through repeated swaddling in unenlightening Socialist Party mastheads: "Whoever reads bourgeois newspapers goes blind and deaf. Away with bandages that make you dimwitted!" The materiality of newsprint here is allegorical, a figure for the regular press as a set of carceral institutions.

The same material could be rendered transparent, however, in ways that suggested an ideal of honesty in mass communications on which the very future of a class-conscious humanity depended. Thus the shadowy female figure in Semen Fridliand's 1929 montage *Die käufliche Presse* (The venal press), whose luminous innocence shines a light on (Western) press corruption even as her darkened eyes remain unable to see through it (pl. 32). So, too, the masterful exhibition installation of the Soviet pavilion at the 1928 exhibition *Pressa,* undertaken by a team of dozens led by designers El Lissitzky and Sergei Sen'kin, with its monumental billboards, props, and wraparound frieze titled "The Task of the Press Is the Education of the Masses" (pl. 37).[20] In the accompanying catalogue, a tour-de-force of bookmaking that itself echoes the functioning of newspapers in several respects, one spread shows a worker holding a newspaper in his hands as he observes his own face emerging from the printed page (fig. 4). The fusion of flesh and newsprint tends now in the opposite direction: the posthumanist individual is not rendered faceless and mindless by the news but instead inhabits its surface, for his productive life is what gives the news stuff and substance.

In place of Lissitzky and Sen'kin's forgotten figure of the reader as newspaper, Walter Benjamin suggested wresting control of the bourgeois press through a now famous phrase: "the author as producer."[21] Like Mallarmé, Benjamin saw the newspaper as one with the driving desires of commodity culture. He described the reader as "impatient" and the paper as responding to his "longing for daily nourishment," a need fulfilled by publishers, "who are constantly inaugurating new columns to address the reader's questions, opinions, and protests."[22] This collaboration between an insatiable public and accommodationist publishers could, however, put the reader in the position of definer, or "even a prescriber," of the form and function of the news.[23] A condemned era could be redeemed: "And it is at the scene of the limitless debasement of the word — the newspaper, in short — that its salvation is being prepared."[24] In an explicitly Marxist move, Benjamin called for the writer to reimagine his own labor

FIG. 4 El Lissitzky and Sergei Sen'kin, spread from *The Task of the Press Is the Education of the Masses,* in *Catalogue of the Soviet Pavilion at the International Press Exhibition* (Cologne, 1928). See also pl. 37

along the lines of the proletariat: "The place of the intellectual in the class struggle can be identified—or, better, chosen—only on the basis of his position in the process of production."[25]

Surrealism, a movement that claimed Benjamin's sympathies, also contained positions similar to his own on the relation of authorship to production that were importantly articulated with regard to newspapers as material and institutional creations. There was, first, the inalienable authenticity of newsprint, which delivered what Tristan Tzara called a consummate example of surrealist "shock" when integrated into works of fine art: "The affirmation of the ephemeral and of temporal and perishable materials," he wrote, "signaled the most poetic and revolutionary moment in the history of painting."[26] André Breton, referring to Picasso's constructed guitars of 1912 (some made of cut-and-pasted newspaper), similarly determined that he had "counted on this impoverishment, this dismemberment even," to embrace the "ultra-real" of his constructions.[27]

In his important essay of 1930, "The Challenge to Painting," Louis Aragon turned to Picasso's collages not for their insurrectionary potential as authentic in their instant datedness but for the way in which they foreshadowed an abandonment of authorial individuality in favor of a more purely intellectual and managerial creative role. For Aragon, the early experiments by Picasso pointed toward the irrelevance of individual facture as a means of commentary on the governing structures of modern life:

> One can imagine a time when the painters who no longer mix their own colors will find it infantile and unworthy to apply the paint themselves and will no longer consider the personal touch, which today still constitutes the value of their canvases, to possess anything more than the documentary interest of a manuscript or autograph. One can imagine a time when painters will no longer even have their color applied by others and will no longer draw. Collage offers us a foretaste of this time.[28]

"A manufactured object can equally well be incorporated into a painting, it can constitute the painting in itself," Aragon continued, setting Picasso up as the precursor to Marcel Duchamp and his readymades, as well as automatist procedures of assembly undertaken by Max Ernst and other surrealists at the time of Aragon's writing.[29]

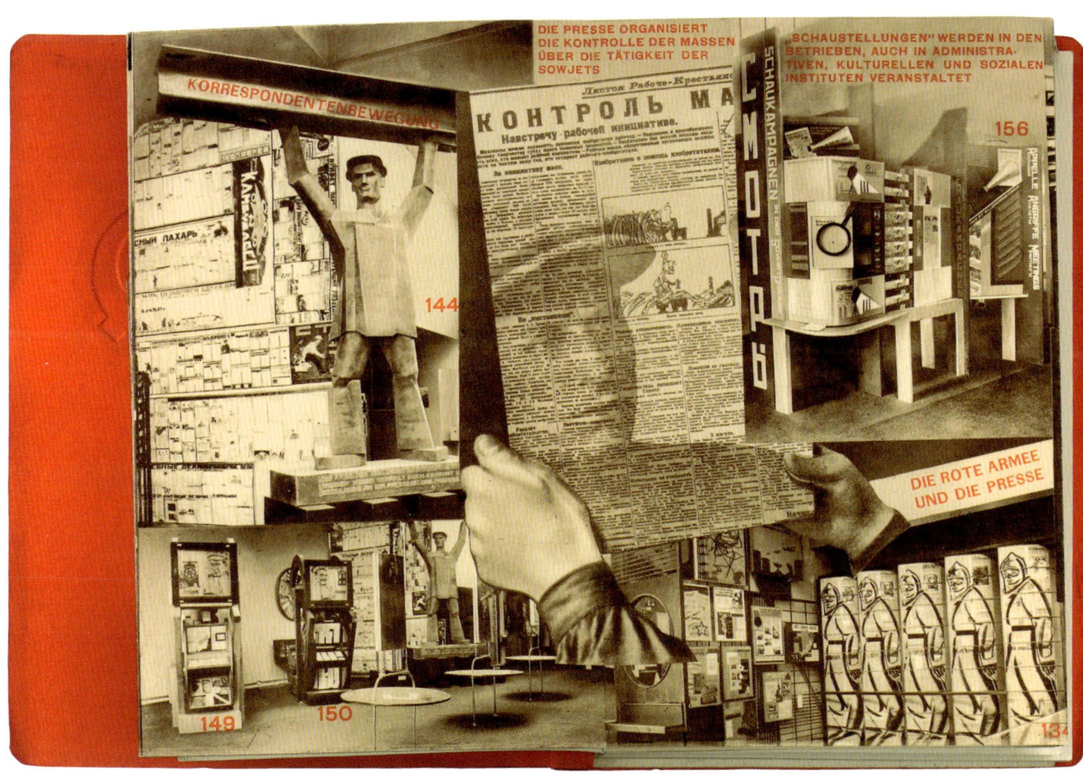

4

Artists making use of the newspaper in subsequent decades abolished any remaining faith in its informational capacity while forging strategies that, as in Aragon's telling, married the material of newsprint to an analysis of institutions of the news.

The illegibility of newspaper text is a signal feature of postwar vanguard art. In place of the fragments seen in cubist or Dada collage, the sheets deployed as substrate in the 1940s through the 1970s are rendered unreadable by wrapping, stacking, weaving, or simply being painted over. Perhaps by historical coincidence, in the same decades newspapers themselves became a totalized screen of information as they took on the format of a fully professionalized, corporate authority. In democratic nations, the largest papers became monolithic symbols of truthfulness, investigative questioning, and objectivity, while in coercive regimes, state-run newspapers placed a mendacious curtain between government and the public, crystallizing citizens' use of doublespeak to structure their daily thoughts. The description offered by journalism historians Kevin Barnhurst and John Nerone for postwar dailies in the West could in fact be applied universally: "In both text and image, the emergent modern newspaper required the effacing of the persona of the journalist, who might have a name (registered in a byline), but who did not have a point of view, a set of values, or (usually) a style of writing. The modern journalist and photojournalist became experts, not authors."[30]

A similar transition from author to expert emerged in advanced art during the 1960s — but the totalization of the news field can be seen already twenty years earlier. The marks that largely or fully obscure newsprint can be aggressively, even rudely individuated, as with Jean Dubuffet, who spews his anti-authoritarian self across the battlefield report of a wartime daily (pl. 47); or they can be almost excessively civilized, as in the variously refined brushstrokes of Robert Rauschenberg, Jasper Johns, or Paul Thek that veil whole newspaper spreads (pls. 16, 18, 51). The perishability of newsprint is at times literalized — consider the *Literaturwurst (Daily Mirror)* made by Dieter Roth in 1961 (pl. 43) — and at times allegorized as the ultimate instance of a breakdown in representation — see Robert Morris' early thought piece, *Crisis (Act of War: Cuba)* (pl. 19). Uniting this variety of purpose is a shift from the topical and publicly oriented uses, in earlier art, of headlines and legible news fragments to the news as a field of privatized information — a situation that matches not just changes in the newsroom but also the abandonment of the public sphere, including by newspaper readers.[31]

Marcel Broodthaers' early provocation piece *Le problème noir en Belgique* (The black problem in Belgium) (1963; pl. 46) is thus exceptional for the period in its polemical public address. Broodthaers here uses a newspaper headline to create a punning alignment between racist Belgian "benevolence" toward its recently liberated colony ("The Congo Must Be Saved") and the "ink spilled" over race issues in the artist's native country, the land of mussels and fries. For the most part, by contrast, explaining informational clues left visible in the shrouded or scumbled matter of postwar art requires a good deal of decipherment.[32] Legible content has generally been displaced from the artworks to their titles, which also read less like headlines than pronouncements balancing between the oracular and the evidentiary. *Asheville Citizen, Newspaper.* (The work by Broodthaers is, again, exceptional in this context, whereas the one by Rauschenberg, *Asheville Citizen* [pl. 16], may have received even this plain title only after it left the artist's hands.)

To suppress the news was also to focus on its impact in more categorical terms. Such thinking led in the 1960s and after to a renewed engagement with the news as a set of institutions, often in echo of the pioneering interventions by Marinetti in 1909. Art went into the newsroom even as the newsroom was brought into spaces of art. As an example of the former, Adrian Piper conceived of the printed form of her performance character in the series *Mythic Being* (1973–1975) as a personal advertisement to be placed in the newspaper, on the model of ad space taken out for artworks by Dan Graham, Ed Ruscha, Judy Chicago, and Piper herself beginning in the later 1960s.[33] Appearing in the weekly *Village Voice* newspaper approximately once each month from October 1973 until February 1975, Piper's seven-

FIG. 5 Adrian Piper, *Mythic Being, Ad #12*, published in *Village Voice*, August 29, 1974, Museum of Modern Art, New York

FIG. 6 David Lamelas, *Office of Information about the Vietnam War at Three Levels: The Visual Image, Text, and Audio*, 1968, installation view at the *LXXXIV Biennale di Venezia, Venice*, 1968, Courtesy the artist and Sprüth Magers, London-Berlin

teen-part series featured the artist as an Afroed, cigar-smoking male of indeterminate sexual orientation speaking through text bubbles that were in fact taken from Piper's teenage diaries (fig. 5). Difficult to "read" in her self-image yet provocatively clear in her words, Piper succeeded in turning the newspaper page into a private-public forum on personal identity and coming of age as an artist outside the dominant race and gender.

A crowning example of the newsroom entering the space of art, meanwhile, was conceived by David Lamelas for the 1968 Venice Biennale (fig. 6). Lamelas erected a glass-walled office in the Argentine pavilion, in which he installed office furniture, a telephone connection, a tape recorder, and a telex machine connected to the Italian news agency ANSA (Agenzia Nazionale Stampa Associata). For the duration of the Biennale, a female assistant hired by Lamelas received dispatches regarding the Vietnam War via telex, affixing the wire stories on a wall for viewing and also reading them aloud to visitors over the telephone while simultaneously recording her speech. *Office of Information about the Vietnam War at Three Levels: The Visual Image, Text, and Audio* was a sculptural work investigating the production of

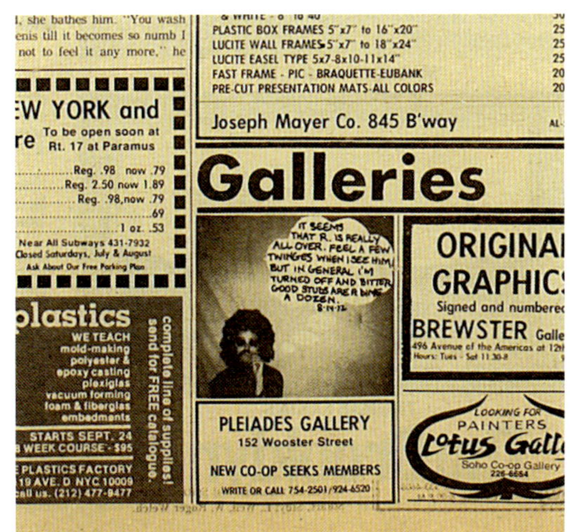
l, she bathes him. "You wash
enis till it becomes so numb I
not to feel it any more," he

PLASTIC BOX FRAMES 5"x7" to 16"x20" 25
LUCITE WALL FRAMES 5"x7" to 18"x24" 25
LUCITE EASEL TYPE 5x7-8x10-11x14" 25
FAST FRAME - PIC - BRAQUETTE-EUBANK 20
PRE-CUT PRESENTATION MATS-ALL COLORS 20

Joseph Mayer Co. 845 B'way

EW YORK and
re To be open soon at Rt. 17 at Paramus
Reg. .98 now .79
Reg. 2.50 now 1.89
Reg. .98,now .79
.69
1 oz. .53
Near All Subways 431-7932
Closed Saturdays, July & August
Ask About Our Free Parking Plan

Galleries

IT SEEMS THAT R. IS REALLY ALL OVER. FEEL A FEW TWINGES WHEN I SEE HIM, BUT IN GENERAL I'M TURNED OFF AND BITTER. GOOD STUDS ARE A DIME A DOZEN.
8-14-72

ORIGINAL
GRAPHICS
Signed and numbered
BREWSTER Galle
496 Avenue of the Americas at 12th
Hours: Tues - Sat 11:30-8

plastics
WE TEACH
mold-making
polyester &
epoxy casting
plexiglas
vacuum forming
foam & fiberglas
embedments
STARTS SEPT. 24
WEEK COURSE - $95
PLASTICS FACTORY
19 AVE. D NYC 10009
call us. (212) 477-9477
complete line of supplies!
send for FREE catalogue.

PLEIADES GALLERY
152 Wooster Street
NEW CO-OP SEEKS MEMBERS
WRITE OR CALL 754-2501/924-6520

LOOKING FOR
PAINTERS
Lotus Gall
Soho Co-op Gallery
226-6654

5

social space through media relay systems: wire services, newspapers, and radio and television stations, all of which normally find their endpoint in homes or businesses. It treated principally information delivery rather than content. The choice of the Vietnam War should hardly be discounted on that ground, for it was paradigmatic, in Lamelas' view, of the divisiveness occasioned by newspaper reading. "One of the things that always impressed me," Lamelas recounted recently about the role of newspapers in his childhood, "was that this printed matter,

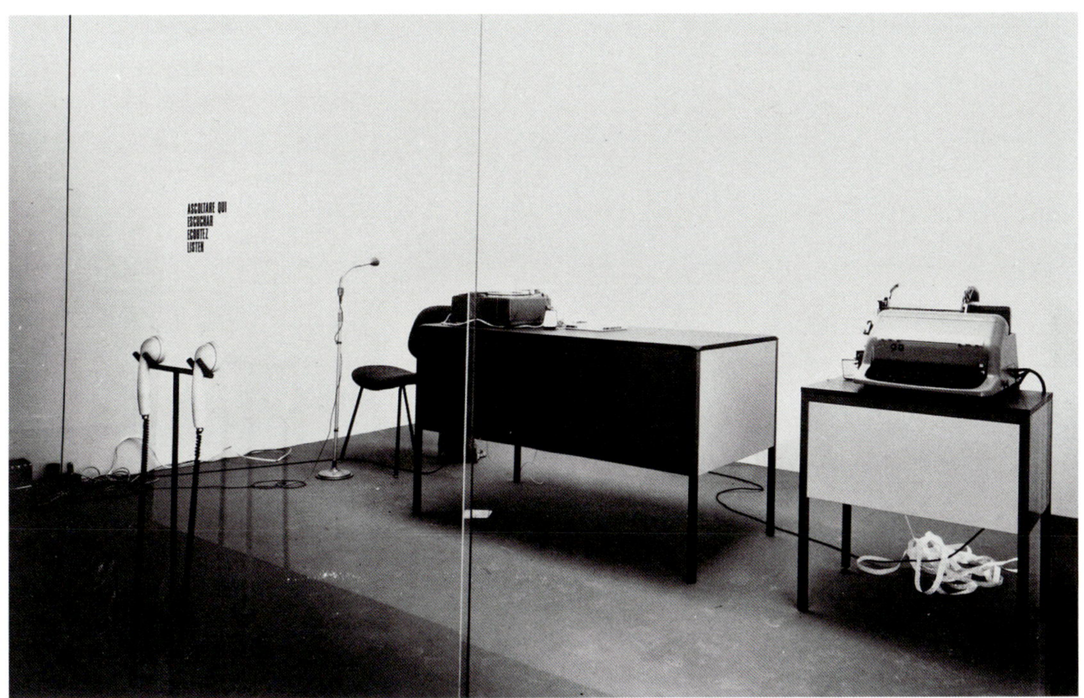

6

which consisted of text and photographs, provided information that could have been the subject of fighting between members of the family; someone would take one political point of view and someone else would take a different point of view, another person was interested in the cinema listings, another was interested in the fashions, and my mother was interested in the recipes. So it was interesting that people were picking up different segments of that printed matter. But all it was was text and photography, and I realized it was something I wanted to analyse because it was such a simple thing that created such a phenomenon."[34]

On Kawara's "date paintings," which the artist has been making since January 4, 1966, under the umbrella title *Today,* offer another prime example of newsprint and news time brought categorically into the space of art. Where Lamelas was concerned with social relations, Kawara emphasizes individual existence in the world, and he accordingly accentuates the importance of his own location in making each painting, although in a singularly laconic way. Place has long been as important as time for artists using newsprint: it had to be Milan and Paris for Marinetti, it had to be Asheville, North Carolina, for Rauschenberg in the era of Black Mountain College, and it had to be Brussels for Broodthaers. Kawara makes his art while constantly on the move, but this peripatetic creativity leads him to emphasize locale all the more. As Mark Godfrey has discussed with reference to Kawara's series *I Got Up* (1968–1979), the many sets of picture postcards that Kawara stamped with that phrase (and the precise minute and hour of his awakening) and sent off during his travels permit a comparative reading of cultural assumptions in various locations; Godfrey opposes, for example, a preference for "native" representations in a French-made postcard of Senegal to a British postcard showing a fully modern scene in nearby Sierra Leone.[35] Kawara sent both postcards in early March 1973, just days after he had made the painting shown here (fig. 7) while passing through the not-too-distant Canary Islands.

Unlike his postcard images, which Kawara sent through the mail unconcealed even by an envelope, the newspapers that tie date and location together in the paintings are fully hidden, for they serve as a meticulously pasted lining to boxes that Kawara constructs to house his finished canvases. Yet this paper lining is present to the paintings' maker and their owners, and it may be exhibited as well. Expressive where the paintings are mute, these newsprint containers, like the postcards, point up local political positions but also the symbolic value of local newspapers

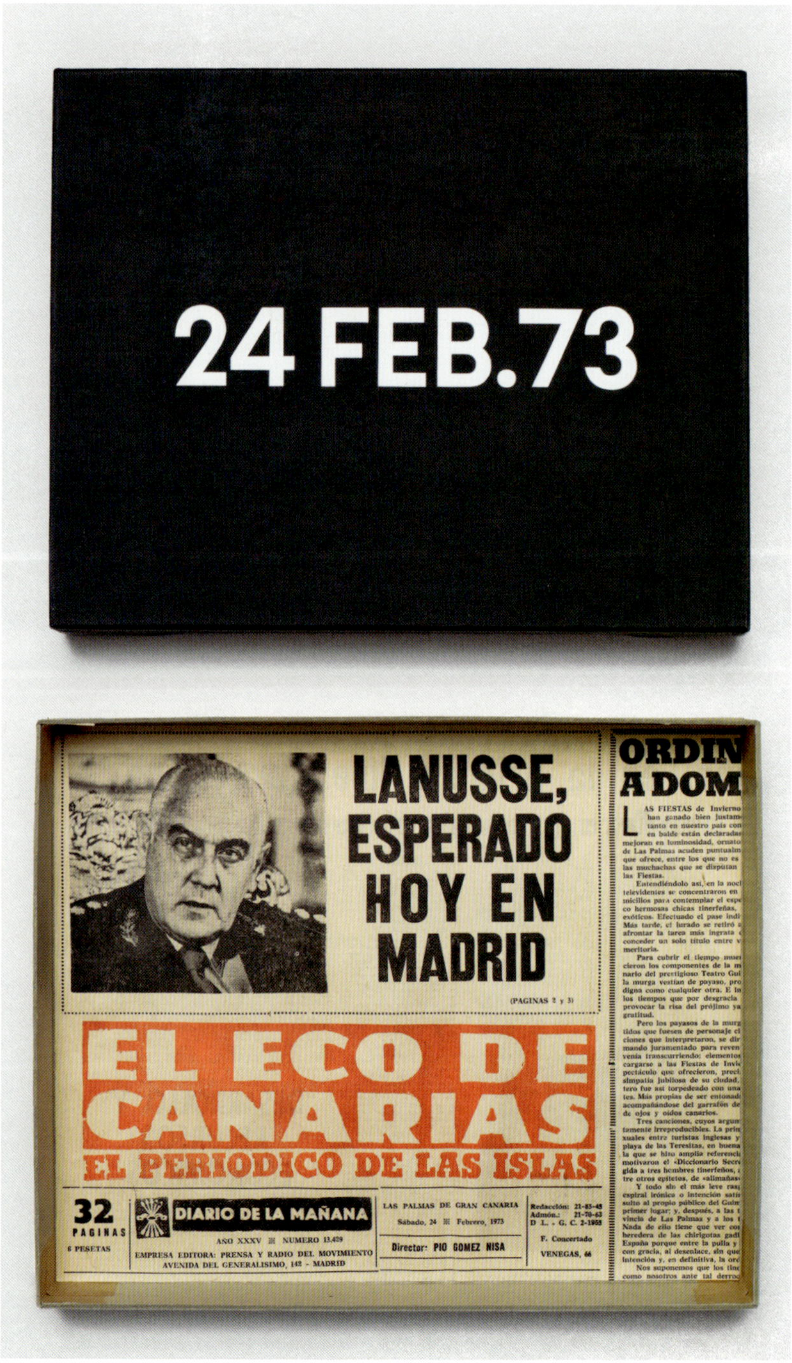

7

FIG. 7 On Kawara, *24 Feb. 1973*, 1973, Courtesy the artist and David Zwirner, New York

more generally. The choice of *El Eco de Canarias,* a prominent Spanish morning paper attached to the labor union movement — still in opposition in 1973, during the final years of the Franco regime — may certainly be considered significant. The paper trumpets a visit to Spain by Agustín Lanusse, like "Generalissimo" Franco a soldier, but quite exceptionally one who had presided over epochal democratic reforms in his native Argentina, in a headline that bears directly on Kawara's project: "Lanusse Expected *Today* in Madrid" (emphasis added). Just as important, however, is the modernist solidity of the newspaper's typeface, its masthead styled in echo of the Republican graphics of the Civil War era.[36] That sense of historical continuity embedded in graphic design endows this paper, which lasted from 1963 to 1983 and brought the unionist movement out from underground after Franco's death, with great local relevance — and the news, today more than ever, remains emphatically local.

In a lengthy letter to his dealers Paul Maenz and Gerd de Vries, likely written three months after Kawara's date painting, German artist Hans-Peter Feldmann discussed his important series of *Bilderbücher* (Picture books) (1968–1975) in terms of a similar conflict between the forms taken by traditional artistic authorship and those that served information delivery. Feldmann had created the books out of a desire to contest authenticity and originality, he explained, and he expressed the hope that in the future he might find a thoroughly anonymous and ephemeral diffusion for these images — which Feldmann variously created and collected from previously published sources, without indicating which was which — through the mass media:

> [When I started] I had to consider in what form to present my photos and it was very important that they be reproduced and printed. . . . And if I should begin to make my books [the *Bilderbücher*] into objects, then I would be doing something I absolutely do not want to do. Something totally false. [I would rather] continue to make my pictures but have them appear *only* in others' publishing outlets such as magazines, books, illustrated daily newspapers etc. This would be an original idea and would no doubt interest a lot of people if I did it long enough. But I would find that as false as emphasizing the object character of my books. Those things fall for me in the realm of aesthetics and its attendant ethics and I'm very sensitive to that. We've been ordering our thoughts and desires according to those things for long enough now and you already know what comes out of that.[37]

To be alive, in the 1960s and 1970s, meant to forestall fixity, and ironically the papers — the very medium that Mallarmé had found tedious in its repetitive format — could be seen to offer that life-giving variety: whether in the differentiated social discourse they could generate in people's homes or in the variety of inflections to be found in local news offices (Douglas Huebler's *Location Piece 6 — National,* 1970, joins up with Kawara's work in this regard; pl. 25) or more basically in the existential affirmation that they brought simply by appearing, day after day. But this vitality came, as it had a half-century earlier, against the backdrop of mass death, and artists' fascination with newspapers registered once again the awareness of mortality conveyed so acutely by newsprint and news time.

The obituary is for that reason the most important section in any paper — the modern-day *vanitas* — and it is not surprising that artists engaging with newspapers over the past decades have often been fascinated with obituary announcements, whether in their regular place (pl. 27) or on the front page (pl. 24). The general state of mourning for newspapers in so much recent work can be seen as an extension of this elegiac emphasis on passing and commemoration, expressed in everything from the stacks and timelines by Felix Gonzalez-Torres to Gabriel Orozco's *Obit* (2008), specifically drawn from newspaper phrases or headlines (fig. 8).

Life hangs in the balance in Sarah Charlesworth's three works about the kidnapping of Italian prime minister Aldo Moro from her series *Modern History,* showing the front pages of forty-five Italian and international newspapers on April 21, 1978, following Moro's abduction one month previously by members of the ultraleft terrorist faction Red Brigade. Moro, architect of a "historic compromise" among the leading parliamentary parties at the beginning of March, is pictured seated with a wise but dejected air, on the thirty-sixth day of his captivity, under a homemade banner that undulates as, one assumes, it is held upright by his captors (pl. 26). The tightly cropped photograph, released by the terrorists one day after they had claimed to have killed their prisoner, shows Moro listing to one side while he holds a copy of *la Repubblica* newspaper from the day before, with a front-page article speculating on the veracity of reports of his assassination. His demeanor suggests an ironic self-awareness, but it would be difficult to say whether this is in response to maneuvering by his captors for the terms of his release—though certainly, for a politician who had gained fame as an able reconciler of political differences, his sudden fall into powerlessness at the bargaining table could prompt a knowing smile. The sardonic tilt of his lips and eyebrows might just as likely suggest Moro's sense that his past and future had collapsed at this moment. To the abyssal regression of images that fascinated Charlesworth—newspapers of newspapers, time suspended through an endless recycling of imagery—one might oppose the quickening of time that is possible when one holds another's life in one's hands. Moro is dead, then alive, then already dead again, and he knows it. Not three weeks later, his body was found inside a Renault hatchback on a Roman side street, wrapped in a blanket and riddled with bullet holes.[38]

One of the more recent works using newspapers that carries greatest impact is *9/12 Front Page,* a piece by Feldmann that gathers 151 daily newspapers from around the world, all published one day after the terrorist attacks of September 11, 2001. First shown (only in part) seven years later in New York, in the exhibition *Archive Fever,* the work presented what the curator, Okwui Enwezor, called "a provocation" in its pure activity of collecting incendiary images of "iconographic shock and spectacle" without further commentary.[39] *9/12 Front Page* recalls other projects by Feldmann, among them *100 Jahre,* a set of portrait photographs of individuals aged one to one hundred, and *Die Toten,* a lineup of ninety re-photographed images of dead men. In all three cases, individuality (of corpses, birthdays, newspaper formats) is played against conformity to a framework of convention on one hand and the limitless subjects and means of commemoration on the other.

Like most works of art-as-archive, *9/12 Front Page* mimics archival procedure while manipulating archival goals; archivists rarely worry about round numbers or space constraints, for example, while Feldmann permits one hundred of the

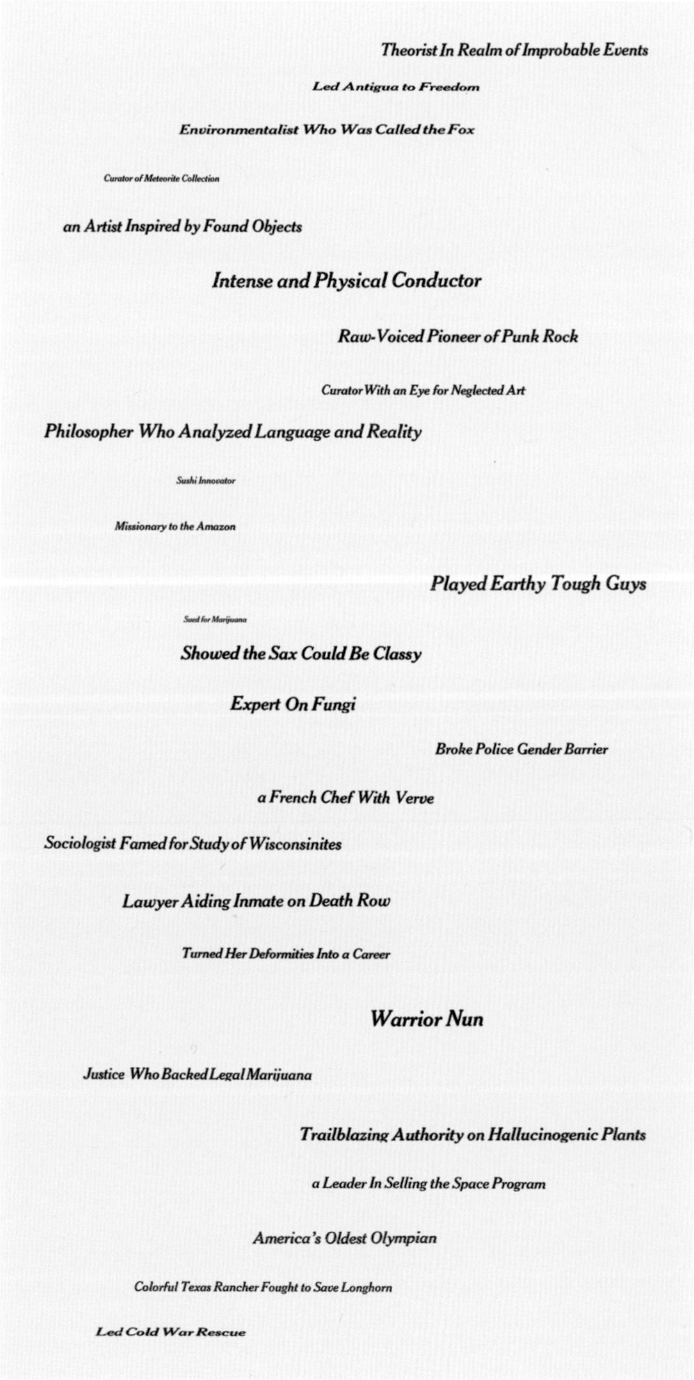

Theorist In Realm of Improbable Events
Led Antigua to Freedom
Environmentalist Who Was Called the Fox
Curator of Meteorite Collection
an Artist Inspired by Found Objects
Intense and Physical Conductor
Raw-Voiced Pioneer of Punk Rock
Curator With an Eye for Neglected Art
Philosopher Who Analyzed Language and Reality
Sushi Innovator
Missionary to the Amazon
Played Earthy Tough Guys
Sued for Marijuana
Showed the Sax Could Be Classy
Expert On Fungi
Broke Police Gender Barrier
a French Chef With Verve
Sociologist Famed for Study of Wisconsinites
Lawyer Aiding Inmate on Death Row
Turned Her Deformities Into a Career
Warrior Nun
Justice Who Backed Legal Marijuana
Trailblazing Authority on Hallucinogenic Plants
a Leader In Selling the Space Program
America's Oldest Olympian
Colorful Texas Rancher Fought to Save Longhorn
Led Cold War Rescue

8

FIG. 8 Gabriel Orozco, *Obit,* 2008, ink jet print, Courtesy the artist and Marian Goodman Gallery, New York

newspapers to be shown at a time if there isn't room for more. He does ask, however, that the piece be hung in a separate gallery to evoke a funerary chapel. Pacing such an installation, one is invited to compare strategies of information delivery from one front page to the next. A few papers on September 11 gave the front page over fully to a single image, while others, by far the majority, played a monumental overview of the destruction against smaller, anecdotal scenes of individual grief and horror — or simply other news stories or advertisements. Headlines about "the world" are tallied in Feldmann's work against those discussing only America, while the papers in Arabic draw special attention, their layout and pictures taking on inordinate weight alongside texts in what is for most of Feldmann's audience an unreadable language. Naturally, encountering the work in an art exhibition, one is prone to reflect as well on point of view and to assume that it was not by coincidence that *Le Monde* chose a shot of the catastrophe that foregrounded the Statue of Liberty, the great French gift to America.

All this comparative analysis, which is also the basic stuff of art historical training, nevertheless falters in contemplating such a massive, sudden, and still recent event. The effect of standing surrounded by one hundred or more newspapers emblazoned with images of colossal destruction is nearly overwhelming. Framed and aligned on the walls, a false sense of precision attaches to these selected pages that echoes the slick corporate geometry of the Twin Towers yet manages to make even more outrageous their hideous disfiguration. Ultimately, *9/12 Front Page* appears as a cynical work, a high-culture echo of the reduction of all political conflict to a media event that governs contemporary existence. The delusion of thorough or manageable knowledge is blown apart in these pictures, again and again, then papered over through statistical sampling, in a sadly fitting echo of a world that seeks answers to matters of life and death with polls and surveys. This is not news, but it is still shocking.

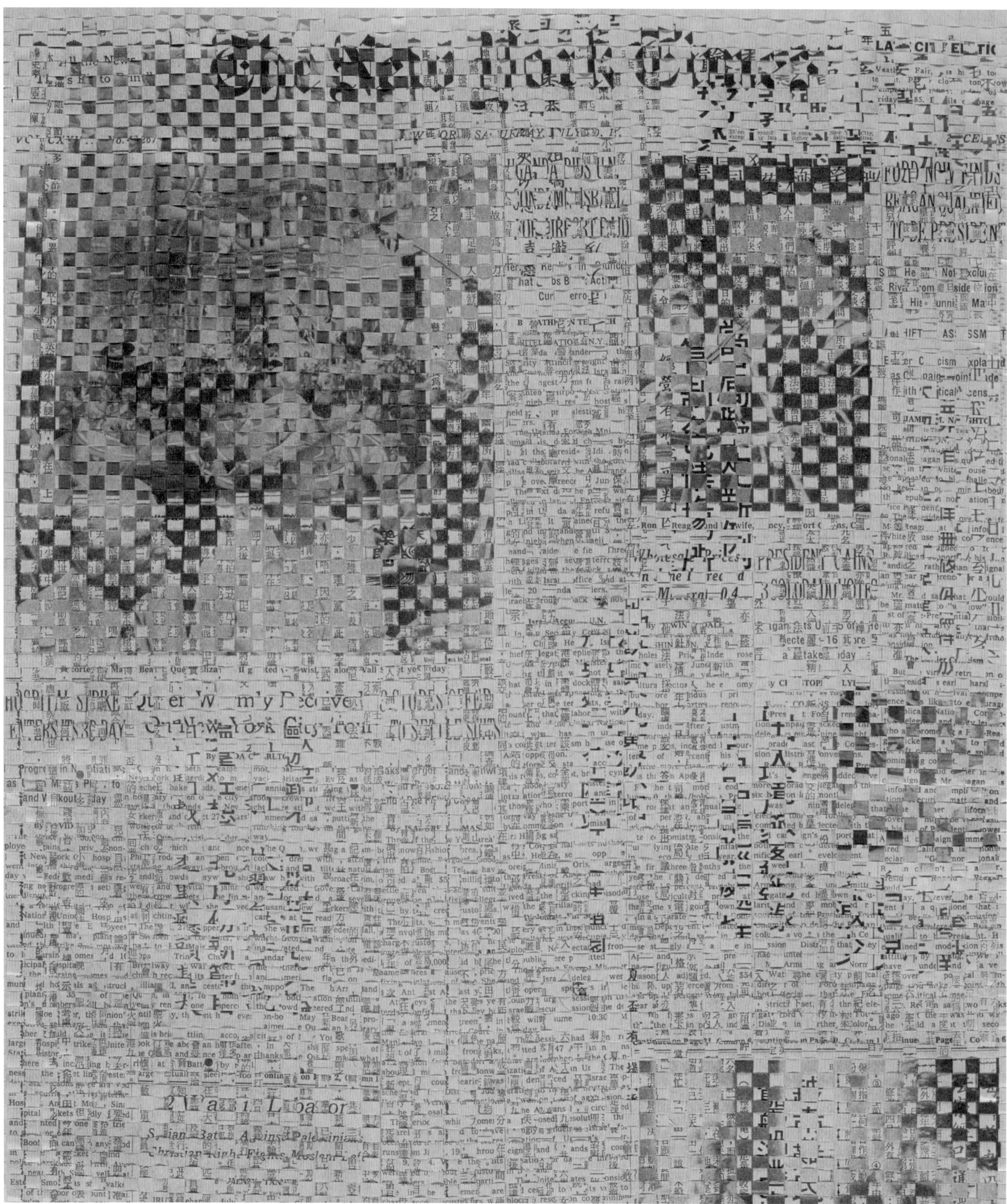

INFLEXIONS OF THE TIMES: NEWSPAPER IN THE ERA OF ART

Christine Poggi

"You can't always paint rotten oranges. My ambition is to do good journalism."
Robert Rauschenberg, 1961

Newspaper appears in the art of our time as a disruptive emissary of the world "outside," signaling the sphere of public life with its ever-accelerating flows of information, opinion, and advertising. Addressed to mass audiences, newspapers are inherently reproducible and heterogeneous, condensing within their hierarchically ordered pages the texts and visual imagery of numerous authors, photographers, and illustrators, many of whom remain anonymous. This interplay of voices and styles generates the complex temporality of the newspaper, indexing a "single day" in the contingent form of a montage of elements gathered from different places and time zones, sometimes with a delay of a day or more. A typical newspaper includes headlines of immediate interest, columns devoted to developing issues, multipart or narrative features, stock market reports, a repertoire of images including documentary photographs, hand-drawn political cartoons, comics and advertising, announcements of past, current, and future events, as well as forecasts (the weather, economic trends, horoscopes...) and corrections of past errors. Thus, although the newspaper seems to capture a unified moment of history writ large, its dailiness is produced through the nexus of divergent series of nonsynchronous temporalities, organized through a gridded and largely repetitive but variable structure. A hastily composed trace of an expanded "present" whose time signature includes the past and future, the newspaper is always already incomplete and fragmentary, a vector of dynamic mass cultural processes caught in midstream. Its very form and materiality embody flux, speed, transience, and multiplicity.

Post–World War II works of art take account of this layered and folded (multi-pli, many-folded), complex (woven together, intertwined), and temporally disjunctive morphology by putting newspaper to a wide range of uses. In the early part of the twentieth century, artists interpolated cut and torn pieces of newspaper into pictorial works of art, where they took up residence as (more or less) planar elements. It was this very planarity that for Clement Greenberg demonstrated the subordination of the newspaper as a dissonant fragment of "reality" to the unified, self-reflexive dimension of the pictorial field.[1] But already in Pablo Picasso's collages, newspaper was sometimes fixed to the surface in ways that pointed to its folds, wrinkles, and depth, as well as to its double-sidedness. In *Violin* of fall 1912, for example, a single cut through a section of newspaper produces two shaped elements: one, pasted to the center left, offers the simplified profile of the violin's body, while its partner, flipped over and displaced to the upper right, functions as a (fig-

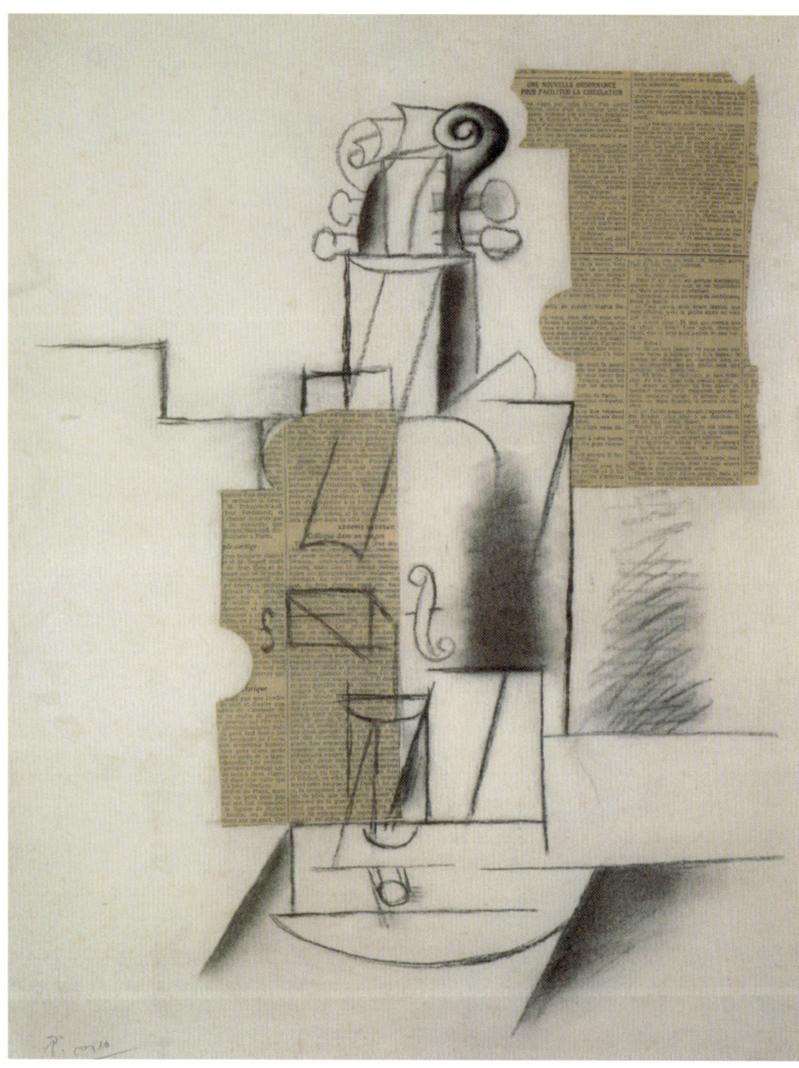

1

ured) ground, allowing the violin's opposing profile to emerge as a "negative" shape (fig. 1). This oscillation of figure and ground not only destabilizes the classical coherence of the depicted object but also alludes to local operations of reading, which often involve turning the page, finding the cut and displaced segment of a continuing text within a new configuration of columns, and then turning back to follow a different story. Layering appears in other early collages as a means of establishing literal spatial relations (or their subversion): in *Head of a Man,* also of fall 1912, Picasso superimposed an overturned *T*, probably cropped from a newspaper headline, onto a rectangular section of newsprint that signifies the abstracted frontal plane of a man's face (fig. 2). Yet the inverted *T*, a humorously simplified, ready-made "sign" for the man's nose, interrupts the diagonal arris drawn across the underlying facial plane; the rigidly symmetrical, frontally sited nose thus appears, impossibly, *over* the profile view implied by the arris. In other collages, Picasso sometimes pins or glues pieces of newspaper to the pictorial ground in ways that emphasize their irregularity and depth, as well as the fragile or imperfect adherence of overlapping planes. And in several works, newspaper plays a fully three-dimensional role. *Construction with a Guitarist* of 1913, an ephemeral installation that now exists only as a photograph, comprised a drawn and painted guitarist holding a real (but inverted) guitar with arms made of crudely cut, folded, and pinned newspaper. The newspaper elements emerge from the vertically suspended picture plane into the "real" space of the viewer, as cantilevered, figural objects with sufficient density to cast shadows. Visitors to Picasso's studio could hardly miss noticing the material identity of the newspaper arms with the ordinary, folded newspaper lying on the "still life" table below.

In cubist works such as these, as well as in other European and American early twentieth-century collages and montages, cut, torn, and frequently superimposed newspaper elements instantiate complex figure-ground relations. Hannah Höch's photomontages of the years following World War I, Raoul Hausmann's *Salomo Friedländer (Mynona)* of 1919 (pl. 9), Eugen Batz's *Contrast Study* of 1929/1930 (pl. 15), and Arthur Dove's *The Critic* of 1925 (pl. 10) exemplify this practice, which exploits the fact that a piece of newspaper arrives already figured, marked with columns of text and images. In many of these works, artists employ variations in typography and in the color of disparate newspaper fragments, and/or alter the orientation of lines of text to create overlapping, interfused patterns or to enhance a sense of movement, as Höch did in *Dada-Rundschau* of 1919 (p. 14, fig. 5).

Ellsworth Kelly's *Head with Beard* of 1949, with its shape cut from a piece of newspaper rotated to create an off-kilter grid, distills this process (pl. 14). Working freely from memory with the intention of making a quick self-portrait, Kelly isolated and transformed a complex three-dimensional motif (which refers not only to himself but to the French

FIG. 1 Pablo Picasso, *Violin*, 1912, pasted newspaper and charcoal on paper, Musée national d'art moderne, Centre Georges Pompidou, Paris, Gift of Henri Laugier

FIG. 2 Pablo Picasso, *Head of a Man*, 1912, pasted newspaper and ink on paper, Lille Métropole Musée d'art moderne, d'art contemporaine, et d'art brut, Gift of Geneviève and Jean Masurel

FIG. 3 Ellsworth Kelly, *Ubu*, 1949, oil on canvas, Private collection. Currently on loan to the Philadelphia Museum of Art

genre of the artist's self-portrait with "barbe" or "booque") into a deceptively simple, flattened silhouette. Seven internal cutouts produce eyes, one ear, nostrils, mouth, and philtrum (the medial cleft between the bottom of the nose and the mouth), thereby establishing a literal correspondence between the openings or "voids" in the head and those in the newspaper.[2] As in many cubist works, these cutouts generate a series of positive-negative, figure-ground reversals that Kelly would develop further in a subsequent group of painted, cutout reliefs in wood and string. *Head with Beard* should also be seen in relation to *Ubu,* a contemporary painting of a Picasso- and Brancusi-inspired head executed through quasi-automatic drawing that seeks to allow chance to collaborate in the making of the image (fig. 3). In *Ubu,* curved lines trace the passage of the head's exterior contour into its

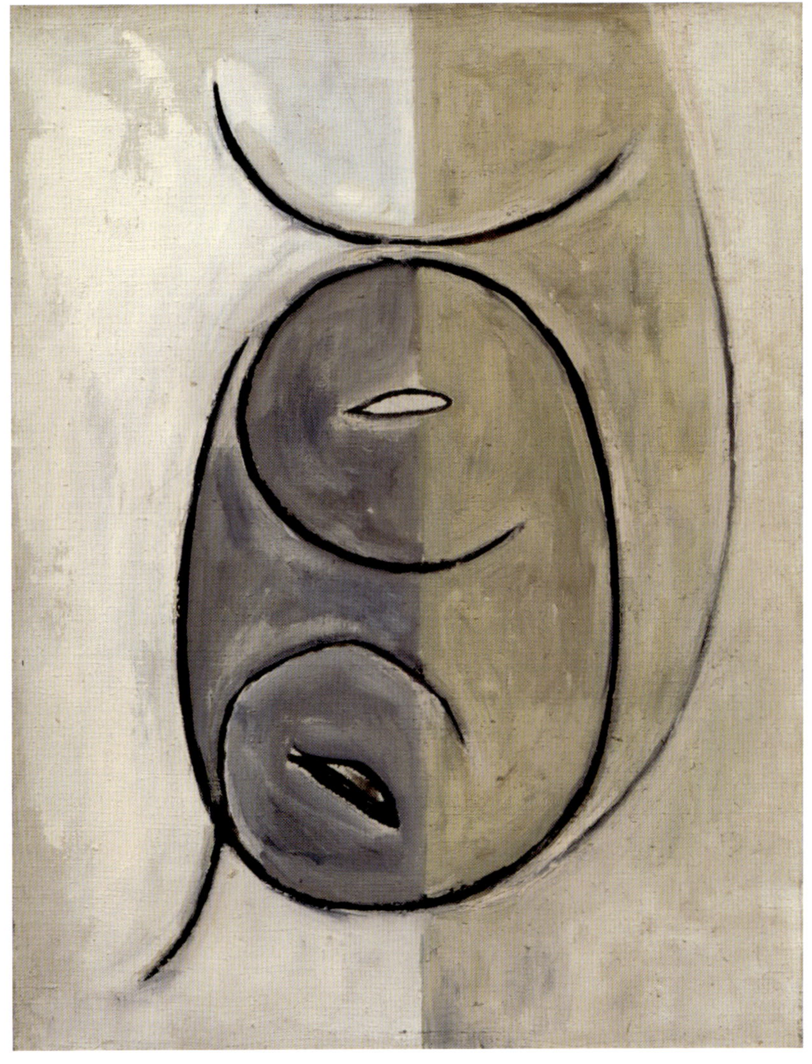

3

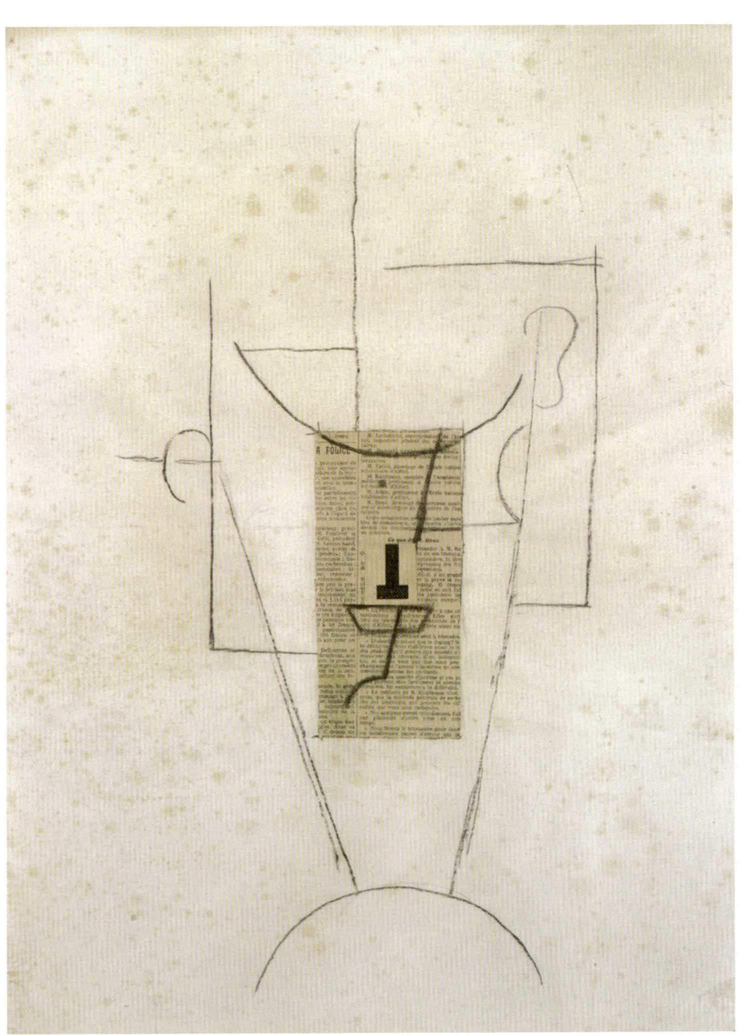

2

interior, where a loop articulates the lower part of the face (à la Constantin Brancusi), while mouth and eye become equivalent, mutable signs (as they often were in Picasso's work). The circular flow of these lines creates a sense of turning, encouraging the viewer to read the head right side up as well as upside down and to observe the change in affective value that occurs as the lower aperture alternates between a tense, distorted mouth (when the work is seen upright) and a slanted eye rendered in profile (when the work is viewed upside down). Right side up, the head rises from the curve of the neck; inverted, the oval head floats over the curve of the shoulders against a pictorial field divided into yellow-ocher and blue-gray zones; this meeting of warm and cool tones suggests the encounter of two figures, as in Brancusi's *The Kiss,* where the shared, elliptical contour of a frontal eye overruns the interior mark of scission that defines and links the profiles of an embracing couple.

Head with Beard operates with a similar economy of means, incorporating chance in the form of a piece of English newspaper and the contingent stories and layout it presents, rather than in the form of a seemingly uncensored (but reworked and overdrawn) biomorphic line. Seeking an impersonal technique that would suppress individual expression and compositional decision-making, as well as conventional notions of beauty, Kelly (who had been spending time with John Cage in Paris) opened his work to the world of ordinary chance occurrences and real objects: "I wanted an outdoor source rather than a personal handwriting like Johns and De Kooning, artists whose work I admire. I wanted to bring in the outside, to let nature be the decision maker."[3] Newspaper—no doubt among the "paper fragments in the street" that Kelly mentions as liberating him from "the need to compose"—provided an "outdoor source" par excellence.[4] In addition to enhancing the objectivity of the work, the use of newspaper establishes a literal sense of scale, here tuned to that of the depicted motif. An already flat element, it also serves to counteract any tendency to read the image illusionistically, as a volume in space. Yet even as the newspaper remains rigorously planar against the gray-blue ground, its rotated axis seems to loosen the anatomical siting of the facial features, which, as in *Ubu,* begin to float and turn, the nostrils, philtrum, and mouth swerving against the tide of cascading newsprint. One of those chance encounters sought by Kelly seems to occur in the "Police and Court" section at the right, which reports the recovery of a gray steel boat that had broken free of its mooring.

If newspaper in early twentieth-century art was often cut, ripped, creased, puckered, layered, folded, pinned, glued, inverted, enlarged, and repositioned, in post–World War II art it would be crumpled, stacked, rolled, wrapped, shredded, nailed, cast in metal, simulated, defaced, accumulated, submerged in various substances, and put into motion. The earlier approach tended to produce a sense of rupture within what was still understood as a two-dimensional pictorial field of representation by juxtaposing mass-produced newspaper and hand-drawn elements or by emphasizing the collision and recombination of disparate newspaper fragments (along with other collage elements), even in the absence of traditional drawing. In such works, the displaced piece of newspaper oscillates between its status as a readymade, material fragment of the outside world, to be alternately read and viewed, and its new status as a pictorial and textual signifier within an aesthetic domain. Even the monumentally scaled Soviet pavilion for the Pressa exhibition in Cologne in 1928, designed by a team of thirty-eight artists headed by El Lissitzky and Sergei Sen'kin, employs figurative and symbolically shaped elements, along with fragmentation and juxtaposition, to intensify the viewer's experience (pl. 37). Its magnified, intercut, and projecting sections, which include six diagonally mounted, crisscrossing "transmission belts" that evoke the mechanical power of the rolling press, charge the ideological message with historical dynamism. Similarly, the 112-page exhibition catalogue, also designed by Lissitzky and Sen'kin, comprises eighteen accordion-style foldouts that stage the process of reading as a temporal sequence of opening and closing, folding and unfolding, pleated pages. These pages can also stand up, as if an activated mode of reading demands an upright, gravity-defiant posture of book and reader alike. (Photographs of the post-revolutionary period in the Soviet Union frequently show newspapers pinned to the walls of workers' clubs, where they invite collective acts of reading and authorship.) In the opening foldout of the catalogue, Lissitzky offers a lesson in revolutionary reading. The image superimposes a cutout photograph of Vladimir Ilyich Lenin standing at a podium over a backdrop of radiating vectors of text that seem to have been culled from socialist newspapers and pamphlets. Leaning forward to address the masses (pictured at the lower right), Lenin brings the typographically varied words that surround him to life, his oral performance enacting the animation of text sought by the Pressa exhibition and catalogue. Printed in red capital letters against the black and white of

FIG. 4 Robert Rauschenberg, *Untitled*, as exhibited at the Stable Gallery exhibition, New York, 1954, five-panel black painting, c. 1951. Photograph by Robert Rauschenberg

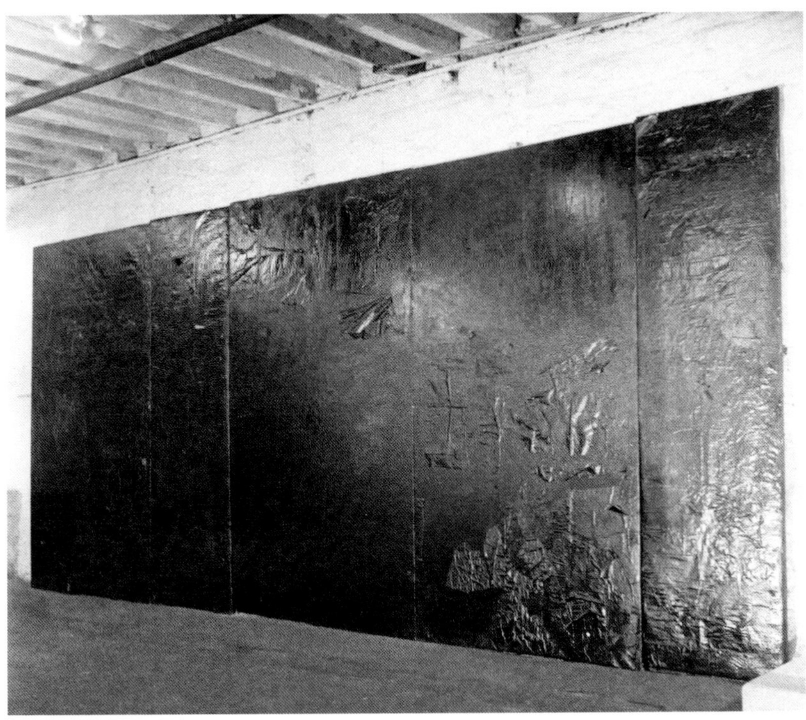

4

the other texts, the phrase that emanates directly from Lenin's mouth quotes a line from his 1901 essay, "Where to Begin?" It advocates the founding of an all-Russian political newspaper as a vehicle for the education and organization of the masses: "A newspaper is not only a collective propagandist and a collective agitator, it is also a collective organizer."[5] Because of Lissitzky's emphasis on vivified oral rhetoric as a means of interpellating a revolutionary collectivity, indeed of bringing this collectivity into being, the slogans and fragments of newspaper text remain legible, figure and ground never entirely fusing or reverting to sheer materiality.

By contrast, newspaper in much post–World War II European and American art tends to be treated less as a vehicle of rhetorical persuasion or figure-ground formal play than as a physical substance whose thick, stratified structure yields similarly thick, stratified works. If Lissitzky presents the newspaper as a means of generating revolutionary consciousness leading to action, artists in the capitalist West tend to construe its power as an effect of a commercial mass culture, or even as a material remnant of this culture that could be put to new, and at times critical, uses. Reviving a sense of the tactility of the newspaper/work of art as an object inhabiting (and inhabited by) the world of everyday life was often central to their aims. Whereas artists including Picasso (*Head of a Man with a Moustache,* 1913; pl. 6), Max Weber (*The Sunday Tribune,* 1913; pl. 33), and Paul Klee (*Alpha bet II,* 1938; pl. 39) had occasionally employed an entire sheet of newspaper as an already figured ground for a drawing or painting, Rauschenberg would introduce newspaper as a means of nearly obliterating the figure-ground distinction in a series of highly textured black paintings in 1951–1953. In some of these works, glossy black enamel paint drenches a multipart surface that ripples, creases, and puckers from embedded layers of newspaper. *Untitled,* one of the largest of these works, originally comprised five contiguous panels of differing width that could be arranged in variable sequences (fig. 4). Isolated, *informe* islands of textural incident seem to coalesce and drift in currents across these panels, as if they were mobile, evanescent forms suspended in a vast aqueous environment. According to Calvin Tomkins, Rauschenberg made these works by randomly dropping glue-soaked, torn sheets of newspaper onto his canvases, implying that he worked in a horizontal mode.[6] If this is true, his process recalls and negates that of Jackson Pollock, converting the highly romantic, individualized gesture of dripping and flinging skeins of thinned paint from the ends of brushes and sticks onto a horizontally unrolled and uncut, pristine canvas to that of ripping and gluing messy sheets of newspaper to a set of objectlike, serially displayed surfaces. Whereas Pollock's tangled web of lines and pooled paint seems to hover in space against an indeterminate, partly dematerialized ground, Rauschenberg's engagement with newspaper, treated as the detritus of everyday life, makes the ground itself the object of both visual and tactile apprehension. In *Untitled,* the newspaper constitutes a densely worked, variable surface, redolent of the street. Yet its vast scale and the play of reflected light across its pulsed expanse also evokes the liquid, luminous effects of Claude Monet's *Waterlilies,* with their intimations of spatial depth, which *Untitled* paradoxically achieves through the opacity of viscous black enamel.

Rauschenberg's *Asheville Citizen* (c. 1952) varies the procedure of building up the surface with torn fragments of newspaper by submerging entire double-sheet spreads *between* layers of black matte paint (pl. 16). As the artist has stated, the newspaper's counterpoint of rectilinear columns and illustrations, and its aleatory juxtapositions (like those of real life), was a source of inspiration for him.[7] Yet *Asheville Citizen* subdues any sense of merely random juxtaposition through a sober, complex balancing of literal, depicted, and found geometries and a muted tonality of black and brown. Two contiguous, open pages of newspaper, laid horizontally across the lower-middle section of the work (the one at right is cropped at the painting's edge), emerge from the thick black paint into visibility. These pages bridge the gap between the painting's two superimposed base panels, so that lines of text running vertically carry the eye across the horizontal divide. This intersection of vertical and horizontal edges produces a Mondrian-like, decentered composition of interlocking rectangles and one small square at the middle-right edge, a composition echoed by that of the newspaper's rectilinear pattern and its internal fold; at the same time, the relation of thickly painted upper and lower black quadrants to the central section with revealed newspaper yields a tripartite organization of vertically superimposed fields that stretch from edge to edge. The thin, mottled washes of brown and black paint that stain the central section only partly obscure the text, which bears the classified and sports sections of the *Asheville Citizen* from Friday, August 3, 1951 (at right), and Saturday, March 29, 1952 (at left), introducing a subtle sense of temporal disjunction. Here the newspaper functions to bind physical support and text/image into a dissonant but highly structured formal unity, which at six feet in height assumes (male) bodily proportions. Yet the newspaper also retains its identity as a displaced representative of the raucous, unpredictable world outside the studio. Newspaper thus operates as a kind of hinge in the gap between art and life in *Asheville Citizen*. As Walter Hopps has observed, many of the photographs Rauschenberg took of the black paintings at Black Mountain College situate them before doorways or abutting doorframes. He further claims that "more than simple scaling devices, they suggest human presence and establish a literal conjunction of abstract art and the physical factum of everyday life."[8] Placed in or before architectural thresholds that invite passage, the black paintings also gesture toward the chiastic crossing of inside and outside, a movement replicated (folded, bent back) in the newspaper's intrication of folded and layered pages that convert every outside into an inside, and vice versa.

Jasper Johns' *Newspaper* of 1957 intensifies this tendency to conflate the material ground and readymade figure/image by taking the newspaper as both support and subject (pl. 18). Splaying an opened newspaper with a visible central crease across his canvas, the artist then covered this already figured, textured, and divided ground with highly activated but discrete strokes and slashes of gray encaustic along with touches of white. Hardening as it cools, wax encaustic is a medium that allowed Johns to work quickly without the risk of blurring the brushstrokes laid on in earlier stages.[9] The result is a strangely reified, layered surface, with fluidly applied smears and daubs of encaustic congealing into low relief but nonetheless retaining a vestigial sense of the translucence and warmth of human skin. Despite Johns' apparent speed of execution, his allover, almost casual approach to painting suggests cool detachment. The choice of gray also contributes to this objectifying effect. As the artist explains, "The encaustic paintings were done in gray because to me this suggested a different kind of literal quality that was unmoved or unmovable by coloration and thus avoided all the emotional dramatic quality of color. Black and white is very leading. It tells you what to say or do. The gray encaustic paintings seemed to me to allow the literal qualities of the painting to predominate over any of the others."[10] Yet the embedded newspaper, a similarly literal presence that surfaces through the veil of encaustic, introduces a note of ambiguity. Here is the object itself, centered within a somewhat larger pictorial field as if it were a figure posed against a neutral ground or an entire image bordered by a mat or frame. The non-hierarchical field of brushstrokes largely ignores this figure/ground

FIG. 5 Jasper Johns, *The Dutch Wives*, 1975, encaustic and newspaper on canvas (two panels), Collection of the artist

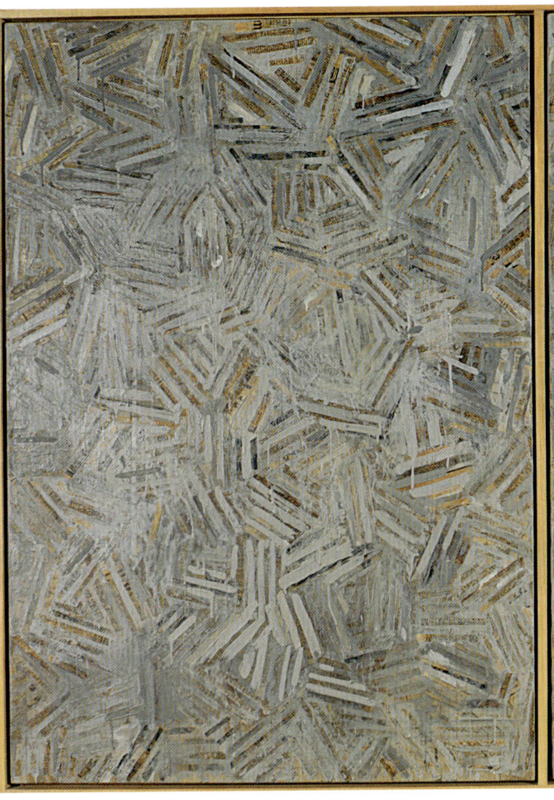
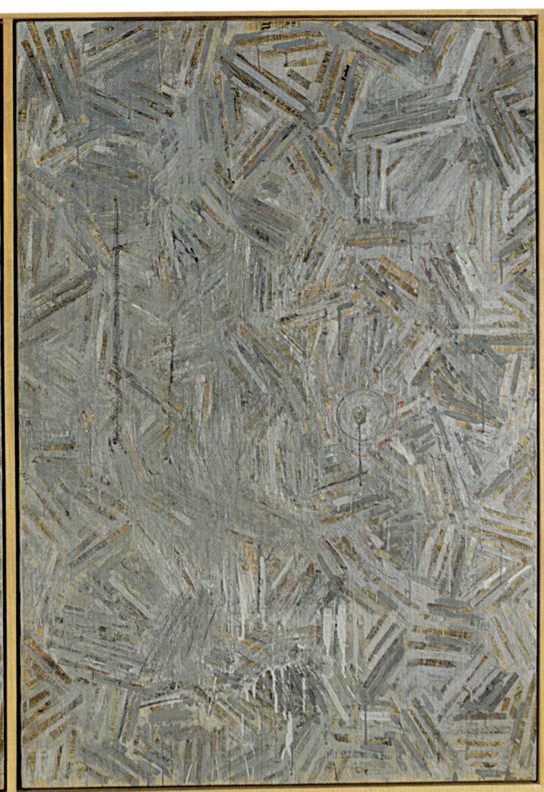

5

distinction, however, so that the newspaper registers as a latent disruptive force, a token of everyday, public life that charges the surface with dissonance and rupture. As such, it troubles our sense that what lies beneath or within a stratified structure reveals a more private or immediate moment of subjective expression—perhaps a first, spontaneous notation or sketch—whereas the reworked exterior represents its "public," more finished face. Johns' *Newspaper* renders such familiar distinctions strangely inoperative.

In later works such as the two-panel *Dutch Wives* of 1975, Johns would further blur the boundary between the purportedly personal, unique brushstroke and the public, mass-produced writing of the newspaper (fig. 5). Discrete, repetitive, manual procedures create an allover crosshatching pattern out of strips of intercalated newsprint and gray encaustic, the latter applied so thickly that it sometimes drips across the surface. Remarkably, the two panels do not simply resemble or even mirror each other but instead constitute nearly identical copies, the same strips of newsprint appearing in the same locations on each panel.[11] The reproducibility of the newspaper invades the realm of gesture painting, even as replicated clusters of distinct strokes evoke (without quite instantiating) a series of indexical handprints.

Writing in the now famous essay "The Legacy of Jackson Pollock" in 1958, Allan Kaprow claimed that through the freedom afforded by the artist's painting technique, Pollock had succeeded in breaking with tradition, moving beyond the canvas to "fill the world with itself," to engage the "stuff of his art as a group of *concrete facts* seen for the first time."[12] For Kaprow, Pollock's example posed two alternatives: to continue in the same vein by making variations of his aesthetic in the medium of painting or to abandon painting altogether in order to become "dazzled by the space and objects of our everyday life, either our bodies, clothes, rooms, or, if need be, the vastness of Forty-Second Street. Not satisfied with the *suggestion* through paint of our other senses, we shall utilize the specific substances of sight, sound, movements, people, odors, touch. Objects of every sort are materials for the new art: paint, chairs, food, electric and neon lights, smoke, water, old socks, a dog, movies, a thousand other things which will be discovered by the present generation of artists."[13] This encomium, however, draws on the example of Rauschenberg, Johns, and John Cage even more than it does on that of Pollock. Although Kaprow's list of ordinary objects and substances the artist might find dazzling does not mention newspaper, many of his earliest assemblages and environments make liberal use of this material. *Untitled* of late 1959 confronts the viewer with a heap of individually crumpled pages of newspaper, held up by a buried central structure comprising a stepladder, chicken wire, and tape (fig. 6).[14] An oxymoronic monument to ephemera, Kaprow's precarious structure intimates collapse and dispersal; and indeed, after a given exhibition it is dismantled and swept away. Here Pollock's elegant, dancelike movements and gestures are reduced to a set of familiar, deskilled techniques: collecting newspaper, rolling and crushing it into balls, and then piling, wedging, and taping them into place. The repetitive, even compulsive nature of the process (probably carried out by a group) conflates the accumulation of commodities and of waste, of form and *informe,* as the interlocking sides of capitalist production.

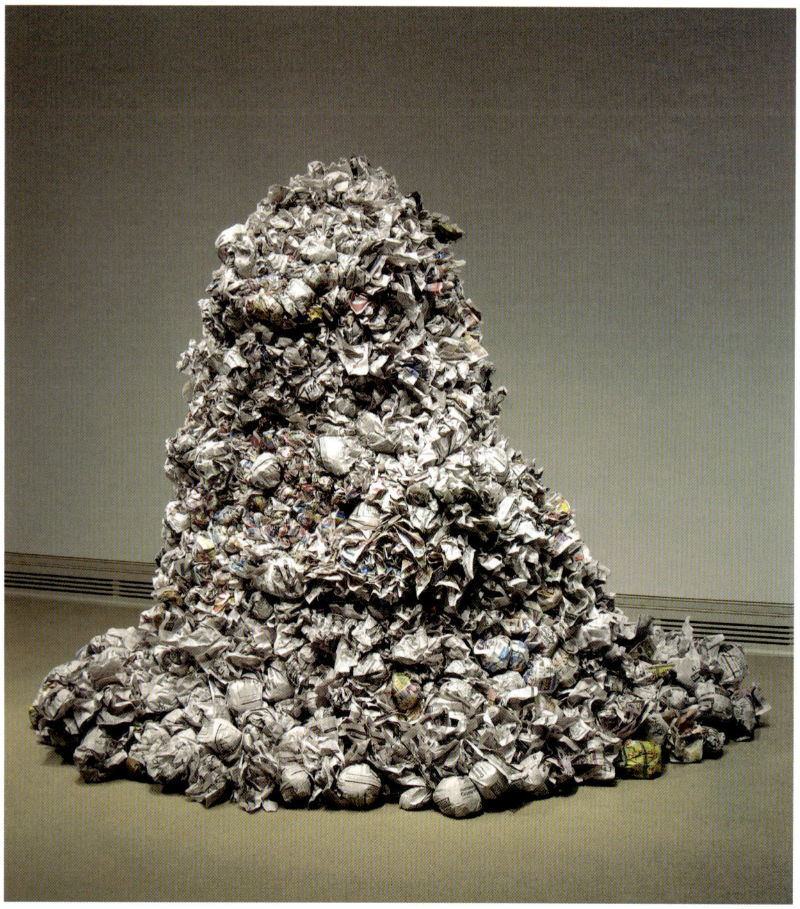

6

The late fifties and early sixties saw the proliferation of assemblages and large-scale environments, some featuring vast quantities of newspaper, a cheap, malleable material that evoked the chaotic world of everyday collective experience. Carolee Schneemann's *Newspaper Event,* held on January 29, 1963, at the Judson Dance Theater in New York, exemplifies this moment (fig. 7). Newspaper was scattered across the stage floor and hung from lines running across the rafters, creating an immersive environment that the dancers could engage with improvised actions. As Schneemann explained, "I wanted touch, contact, tactile materials, shocks—boundaries of self and group to be meshed and mutually evolving."[15] A series of eight basic instructions, focusing on specific parts of the body and related physical, spatial, or interactive aims, choreographed what remained an essentially open, rhizomatic structure: "LEGS-FACE. Your effort is to become horizontal in space." Many of the instructions called for horizontal, constantly changing, rootlike entanglements: crawling, burrowing, rolling around, becoming flat, stretching out, making a link in space between other performers. These actions entailed a series of transformations, from assuming assertive, vertical positions to adopting limp, horizontal positions, from making a pinnacle of newspaper (of "ludicrous proportions"—perhaps like Kaprow's *Untitled*) to becoming as small as possible and then large again—like Alice in Wonderland.[16] The presence of a mobile, layered, antiform newspaper "ground" enhanced the gravity-bound, multi-directional, responsive character of the dancers' movements. Rather than serving as a static backdrop or an illusionistic scene, newspaper literally engulfed the space: an influx from the street intensified by the process of accumulation and defamiliarized by its new context.

If Kaprow's *Untitled* and Schneemann's *Newspaper Event* intervened in the cycle of a newspaper's life by accelerating and conjoining its moments of accumulation and disposal, Arman (Armand Pierre Fernandez) sought to arrest its final stage: gathering and reframing what had already been thrown out. In assembling

FIG. 6 Allan Kaprow, *Untitled*, 1959 (re-created 2008), stepladder, chicken wire, newspaper, tape, dimensions variable, Ackland Museum, University of North Carolina at Chapel Hill (re-created at each venue according to the artist's instructions)

FIG. 7 Carolee Schneemann, *Newspaper Event*, January 29, 1963, photograph of performance, Judson Dance Theater, New York, for eight performers, a few benches, stools, or small chairs, and a pile of newspapers stacked at least four feet high

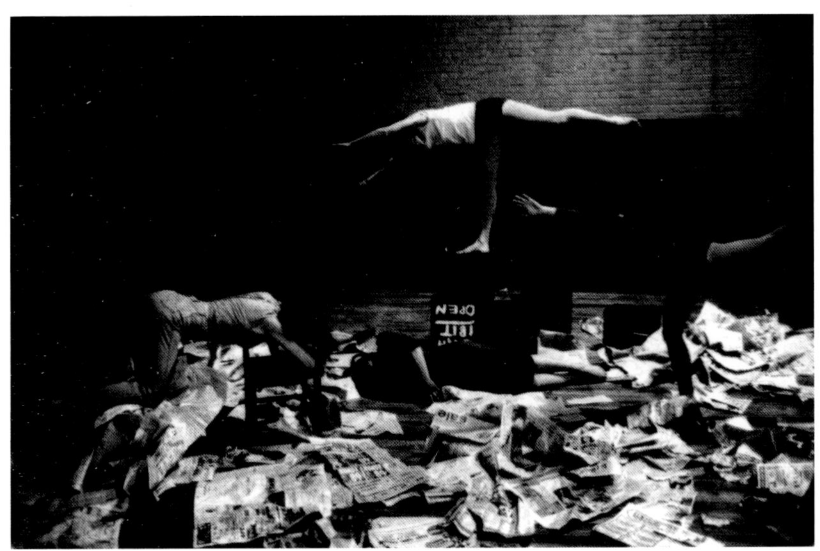

7

his first *Poubelles* (Trash cans), Arman worked as an urban archaeologist, discovering facts about a given society by what he could find littering its streets or festering in its garbage bins. *Grand déchets bourgeois* (Large bourgeois trash), of 1959–1960, re-presents the rubbish of the upper class in a glass and wood display case, where it can be viewed from several sides as if it were a scientific specimen or a commodity in its own right (fig. 8). Folded, crushed, and mangled pieces of newspaper figure prominently among the cigarette butts, spent matches, wine bottle wrappers, corks, tin cans, striped tie, crumpled cloth, tampon box, cotton balls, old towels, and plastic packaging. The warning on a torn and folded envelope inscribed "Photos [ne pas] plier" (Photos—don't bend) at the bottom right has clearly been ignored. Arman recalls that Rauschenberg, who first viewed the *Poubelles* at an exhibition in New York in 1961, objected that they were too random and automatic to be art.[17] Although Arman did not engage in the kind of complex formal play that structures Rauschenberg's black paintings and combines, he did carefully sift through the trash he gathered from gutters, trashcans, outdoor markets, and even the galleries that showed his work, removing organic material that would rot and smell. He then layered the remaining refuse in the cases, taking care in *Grand déchets bourgeois* to position a few telling fragments against the glass and to create an allover scattering of red, yellow, and blue within a general field dominated by the browns and black of aging newspaper.

Even without the decaying food and other organic substances, the trash in Arman's vitrines speaks of the body, rendering visible its processes and routines: eating, drinking, smoking, attending to hygiene, dressing, reading the newspaper, and so forth. Also responding to the growing prevalence of disposable commodities but directly engaging rotting material and its repellent odors as a vehicle of irony, German-Swiss artist Dieter Roth launched the series *Literaturwurst* (Literature sausage) in 1961. Each of the books "published" in the series was made by rigorously following a traditional sausage recipe, using all the spices, water, gelatin, onions, garlic, and fat but replacing the meat with the shredded scraps of a reviled newspaper, magazine, or book. Roth cooked up the first *Literaturwurst* with a copy of the wildly popular British tabloid the *Daily Mirror,* stuffing the mixed ingredients into a sausage casing and binding it at either end with red string (pl. 43). A repellent object, this literary work conflates the process of consuming the *Daily Mirror* with that of eating a rather greasy, oversized sausage. As the artist explained, "From time to time I take books I can't stand or from authors I want to annoy and make: sausages c. 40 cm long, 8 cm thick, should end up as an edition of 50, titles on the outside, signed, numbered, DM100."[18]

The notion of turning the ephemeral, commodified pages of a mass cultural tabloid into a "book" that takes the shape of a decaying sausage is obviously satirical. Roth further emphasized the leveling potential of such an intervention by issuing instructions, along with nationally varied recipes, so that "fresh meat" was replaced with "one fresh, delicate book" and "one small, fresh, fatty book" in an Italian recipe and "a pound of fresh book" in a Creole recipe. Participants were encouraged to "sell and soil and slice and save and save and do whatever else you wish without restriction!" to their *Literaturwurst.* The expanding series culminated in 1974 with *Georg Wilhelm Friedrich Hegel's Work in 20 Volumes,* fabricated by the collector Hanns Sohm according to the artist's instructions. The twenty "volumes" were presented as if in a slaughterhouse, suspended from

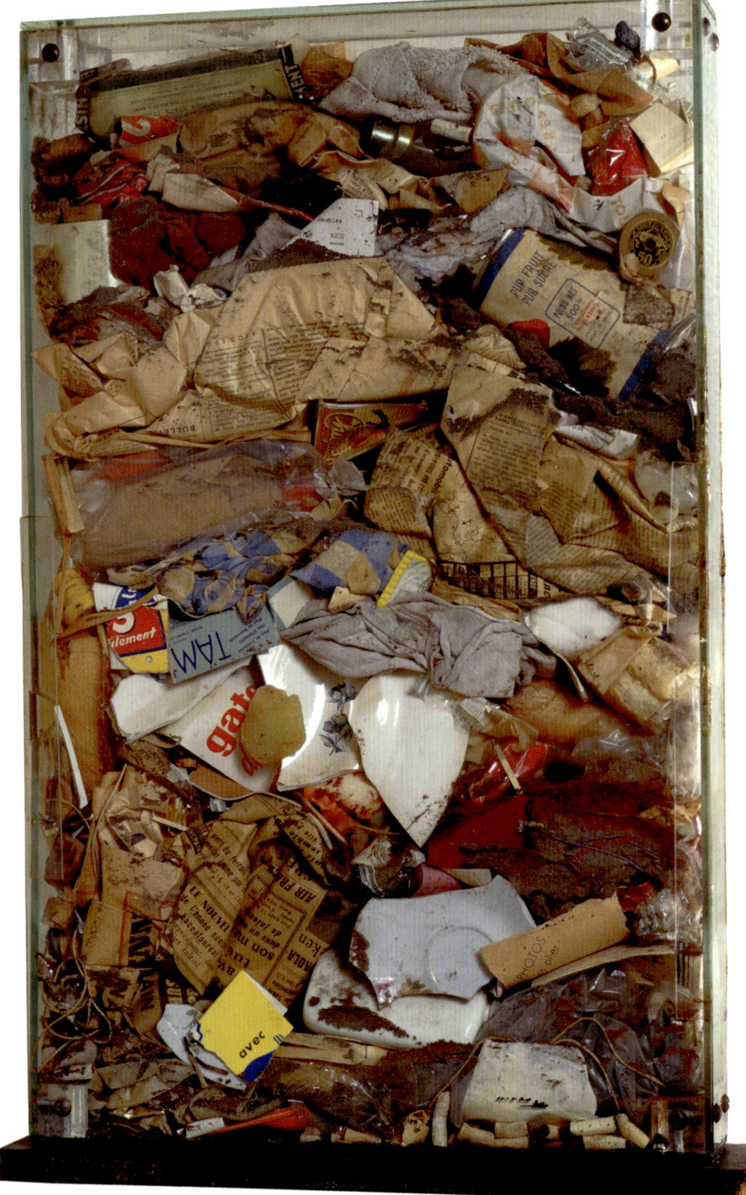

8

FIG. 8 Arman, *Grand déchets bourgeois* (Large bourgeois trash), 1959–1960, accumulation of trash arranged in a glass and wood box, Collection Christo, New York

FIG. 9 Chryssa, *Folded Newspaper*, 1963, in three editions, anodized aluminum, several parts, Private collection

a wooden frame in two rows.[19] Other related pieces such as *Daily Mirror Book* and *Book 3a,* both of 1961, resulted in relatively more conventional volumes with bound pages made out of the cut, sometimes inverted or angled, and resequenced sheets of the *Daily Mirror* and various Icelandic newspapers, respectively. The *Daily Mirror Book,* in a reduced format of under an inch square, acquires a new thickness owing to its accumulated pages. Like Lissitzky and Sen'kin's Pressa catalogue, it readily stands up with its pages unfurled, although it has abandoned all aspiration to constituting a new, revolutionary collectivity. Instead such books circulated through the international avant-garde networks established by Fluxus. Yet Roth's newspaper books exemplify the principle of "active" reading, and their reliance on transmission through the medium of simple verbal instructions that promote collective forms of authorship still operates within the expanded legacy of the historical avant-gardes of the twenties.

During what has been called her "newspaper period" (1958–1962), Chryssa (Chryssa Vardea Mavromichali) issued a series of works that similarly reconfigure the readymade structure of the daily, in some cases producing an edition of "books."[20] After the Cycladic Books, a set of stark, geometric, plaster or clay reliefs produced by casting the interior fold of a cardboard box, Chryssa turned her attention to the hierarchically organized, multipage structure of the newspaper. Her *Newspaper Book* of 1962 comprises twenty-two lithographic "newspaper images," each a meditation on the composition of columns and type characteristic of a specific page: *Front Page, Real Estate Page, Classified Ads, Classified Ads with Space, Weather Maps, Crosswords,* and so forth. As rendered by Chryssa, these images assume a rigorously abstract, geometric order, varied by the intrusion of unexpected typographical or design elements: a large ampersand and vertically aligned letters spelling "SPACE" (in *Real Estate Page*) or hand-drawn smudges and squiggles and the word "BORDER" (in *Front Page*). Seeking to integrate these diverse pages in a single, unified work, Chryssa executed *Folded Newspaper* in 1963 from a Sunday edition of the *New York Herald Tribune* (fig. 9). She began by cutting and recombining the stereotyped metal plates used in the process of printing the newspaper so as to form a new mold. (Some of these metal plates had already served to print sections of *Newspaper Book.*) Chryssa then sent the resulting composition of intermixed texts and graphics, culled from eight different pages, to a foundry to be cast in two metals, bronze and anodized aluminum. Thus reproduced, *Folded Newspaper* mimics the generic, gridded structure of the newspaper, with its typography, columns, charts, and folds, while disrupting the integrity and expected order of the page: the crossword puzzle intrudes into the space just below the masthead, the blank strip we expect at the bottom of a page runs through the middle, the scale of the upright page is double that of its horizontal counterpart, the columns are sometimes misaligned, and the void intervals between them take on an exaggerated sculptural presence. Most significantly, Chryssa gives us a folded newspaper, one whose layers establish literal depth. This is a paper that appeals to tactile sensations, inviting us to handle, turn, unfold, and refold its embossed pages, or at least frustrating our desire to do so; it is also a newspaper that, however reified in its Duchamp-like boxed edition, refers explicitly to the mutability of horizontal and vertical reading positions.

Given the power of the modern mass media during this period, no reconfiguration of a major newspaper could appear as a neutral act. Chryssa's juxtaposition of the *New York Herald Tribune*'s inverted and upside down masthead with the classifieds, financial report, and crossword puzzle, for example, upsets the newspaper's normative order and authority and also brings the usually latent nexus of political power and commercial interests clearly into view. Joseph Beuys' 1963 *Kraft* (force, power, authority, military power, effect of law) also addresses the theme of power or force, situating the newspaper in a contested historical zone (pl. 45). In Beuys' earlier cabinet assemblage *Stag Hunt* of 1961, fifteen bundles of newspaper bound by twine in a cross formation (which was then overpainted in brown paint) serve as "batteries" of accumulated energy and ideas.[21] Similarly, *Kraft* treats newspaper as a material emblem of concentrated political and cultural capital, including the fraught question of national identity. Like the brown crosses that marked the newspaper batteries in *Stag Hunt,* the word *Kraft,* inscribed in deep black charcoal, impresses the folded newspaper with its symbolic force: indeed it appears in Gothic script, a typeface often seen as archetypally German. For Beuys, "Kraft" was a highly resonant term, signifying the life force that surges forth in the creation of art. As he once stated: "Die einzig revolutionäre Kraft is die Kraft der menschlichen Kreativität..., die einzig revolutionäre Kraft is die Kunst" (The only revolutionary force is the force of human creativity..., the only revolutionary force is art).[22] By writing *Kraft* onto this bundle of newspaper, the artist seems to have wanted to infuse the cold, materially motivated analysis of political and economic questions with generative force, with creative warmth and vitality, thereby making the newspaper over into art. Beuys may also have wanted to recuperate the word "Kraft" from its use by the National Socialists, where it referred to the spontaneous, irrepressible drive of Germany toward expansion and world domination.[23]

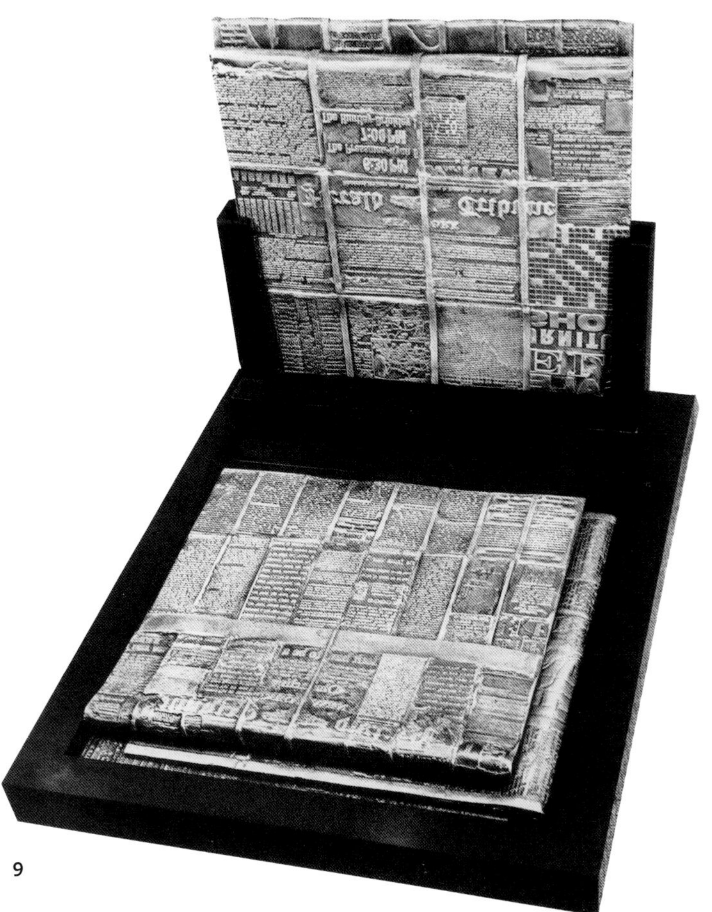

9

The principal story visible in this folded paper, which perhaps should be seen merely as symptomatic of a broader, postwar national crisis, addresses the need to find a powerful symbol (*symbol kräftiger*) of German history in the form of a national holiday, like the French July 14, and the creation of such a holiday on June 17, the "Day of German Unity."[24] Ironically, however, this date commemorates the violent suppression of an anti-Communist construction workers' uprising in East Berlin in 1953, and the Communists in the German Parliament therefore opposed its selection. On the tenth anniversary of these events—and after the erection of the Berlin Wall—the fracturing of Germany into East and West must have represented a highly symbolic, and at least partly self-inflicted, national trauma to Beuys. Seen in this context, the term "Kraft," itself an emblem of official state violence, assumes its full charge. Beuys alluded to this violence by blackening the newspaper with charcoal and by adding a few scattered bits of gesso that suggest ash, giving the work a charred appearance. The word "Kraft" can also be read as a burnt inscription, which inevitably evokes the terror of Nazi newspaper burnings in the 1930s and the branding of prisoners in the camps. As a gesture of healing the trauma and death it represents in a quasi-corporeal manner, Beuys also soaked the newspaper in melted fat, thereby effecting a literal infusion of warmth and new energy. But like charcoal, fat is a disturbing organic substance that may connote life-saving energy to Beuys (who claims that he was once saved by nomadic Tatars who wrapped his body in fat and felt when his Nazi plane was downed in 1943 in the Crimea) but that also recalls the residue of burnt bodies in concentration camps. A truly disturbing work, *Kraft* engages the symbols and materials of German national history, seeking a homeopathic inoculation against its multiple wounds rather than an explicit reckoning with history.

Executed in the same year, Marcel Broodthaers' *Le problème noir en Belgique* (The black problem in Belgium) refers to the continuing conflict in Congo, a former Belgian colony (pl. 46). A headline in the lower section of a folded copy of *Le Soir* reads, "Il faut sauver le Congo" (We must save the Congo), and promises two articles by Moïse Tshombe, the Belgian-supported African leader of a pro-Western faction in the Congolese civil war. In 1960, the year Congo became an independent republic under Prime Minister Patrice Lumumba, Tshombe had himself elected president of the mineral-rich province of Katanga in a secessionist move supported by European businesses eager to avoid nationalization of their mines. When United Nations forces overthrew the rebels after the brutal murder of Lumumba, Tshombe went into exile in Spain, where he agitated for his return and for a federalist solution to the "difficult problems" of Congo.[25] Broodthaers' *Le problème noir en Belgique* presents the popular Francophone newspaper nailed to a mottled support board backed by wood as if it were a political manifesto nailed to a splattered wall or Martin Luther's Ninety-Five Theses nailed to the door of the Castle Church in Wittenberg. A swarming mass of plastic eggs, drenched in shiny black paint, spills down from the newspaper's nailed upper edge. These eggs evoke the threat of further violence in the colonies, of forces that Belgian colonialism has unleashed and that it can no longer contain. The distant problems of Congo erupt in visceral form, like a pot of mud thrown in the public's face, disrupting illusions of Belgium's benevolent neo-colonialism and of the seemingly objective reporting of *Le Soir*.

Later works, including Laurie Anderson's *New York Times, Horizontal/China Times, Vertical* (1971/1976) also allude to current political events and crises (pl. 50). Anderson first executed this piece in 1971, weaving the front pages of the two *Times* together along horizontal and vertical axes, effecting a rapprochement of the two national papers during the intensifying, seemingly irresolvable war in Vietnam. (The *China Times* of the People's Republic of China was published in Taiwan in traditional Chinese. It also issued a US edition in San Gabriel, California.) Although Anderson's interlacing of the two front pages respects the vectors of English and Chinese reading, the work nevertheless interrupts their physical and semantic unity, producing a strangely blurred, shimmering image in which general patterns of columnar text broken by photographs can still be detected. The chiastic, relational movement of the cut strips, flowing from outside to inside and back, constantly redraws boundaries and thresholds, and reminds of us of newspaper's mobile, heterogeneous, and intertextual status within a global communications network. Replicated in 1976 for inclusion in an exhibition, *New York Times, Horizontal/China Times, Vertical* folds together not only the two newspapers but the two historical moments (1971 and 1976), thereby calling attention to the dramatic changes in Sino-American relations that occurred during these years.

In the works considered here, newspaper appears as a layered multiplicity, whose folds, creases, depth, and double-sidedness register the temporal and material inflexions of a public "outside" as it constitutes a reconfigured "inside."[26] Writing in the 1890s, the symbolist poet Stéphane Mallarmé had opposed the debased, commercial writing of the newspaper to the pure, rarified writing of poetry in part owing to the operation of the fold: whereas the newspaper offered its thin, open pages to a mass public, the "spiritual book" revealed the hidden, mysterious contents of its thick, folded pages only to the discerning reader, whom Mallarmé characterized as the book's first lover.[27] According to this paradigm, the newspaper, a cheap commodity, "its full sheet on display," becomes an emblem of sheer exteriority, a material surface without depth or meaning. In contrast, the book, even after its folds have been cut by its first reader, remains virginal, marked but intact, "inviting one to open or close the page, according to the master."[28] For Mallarmé, poetry provides the occasion to reanimate the letter, to vanquish chance word by word, by motivating the relation of sound and meaning as well as the visual appearance of words on the page.[29] Mallarmé's aspirations are most fully realized in his poem of 1897, "Un coup de dés jamais n'abolirà le hasard" (A throw of the dice will never abolish chance). Here the horizontal flow of typographically varied words across a series of double pages evokes analogies with a musical score while also at times assuming pictorial form to suggest a listing boat and a constellation. Such devices lead readers to turn the page even as they convert the darkness of scattered letters into a luminous "alphabet of stars."[30]

As we have seen, the works of many post–World War II artists contest the antinomies that structure Mallarmé's aesthetic, so that the folds and layered depths of the newspaper generate the very mobility and formal-syntactical complexity that Mallarmé attributed only to the book. And rather than defeat chance through a poetic motivation of language, many artists employ newspaper precisely because its organization encompasses both the iterability of the grid and aleatory juxtapositions. Mario Merz's 2003 *À Mallarmé* refers to the symbolist poet's most famous work explicitly (pl. 59). Two rows of twenty-five stacks of bound newspaper in varying layers of brown, tan, gray-white, and beige (suggesting bricks or other building materials) lie side by side on the floor.[31] The stacks create a low wall or barrier that stretches more than twenty-three feet across the museum floor, topped by a wild tangle of electrical cord and neon tubing. Close inspection reveals that this neon spells out "Un coup de dés jamais n'abolirà le hasard" in cursive, thereby infusing the newspaper stacks with a Beuysian sense of accumulated energy while also connoting both commercial advertising and barbed wire. The newspapers, comprising mostly Turin's daily *La Stampa* as well as three Arabic papers, feature American president George W. Bush issuing a bold ultimatum to the ONU (the Italian acronym for the United Nations) in the days leading up to the American-led invasion of Iraq. Aglow in blue neon, the words "Un coup de dés jamais n'abolirà le hasard" refer ironically to Mallarmé's verbal constellation, which here invokes not the luminous work of poesis but the "throw of the dice" posed by Bush's politics and endlessly repeated in the bundles of newspaper. Yet even as they assume shape as a violently reinforced, rectilinear boundary or limit, a barrier to passage, Merz's newspaper stacks reveal their fragile contingency, heterogeneity, and openness to new configurations. Paradoxically, *À Mallarmé* invites the viewer-participant to engage in a post-Mallarméan reading of the newspaper(s) and their neon countertext. Such an encounter acknowledges the public exteriority of mass-produced newspaper as a vehicle of political and economic power while simultaneously inflecting and multiplying its folds, thresholds, and inclusions.

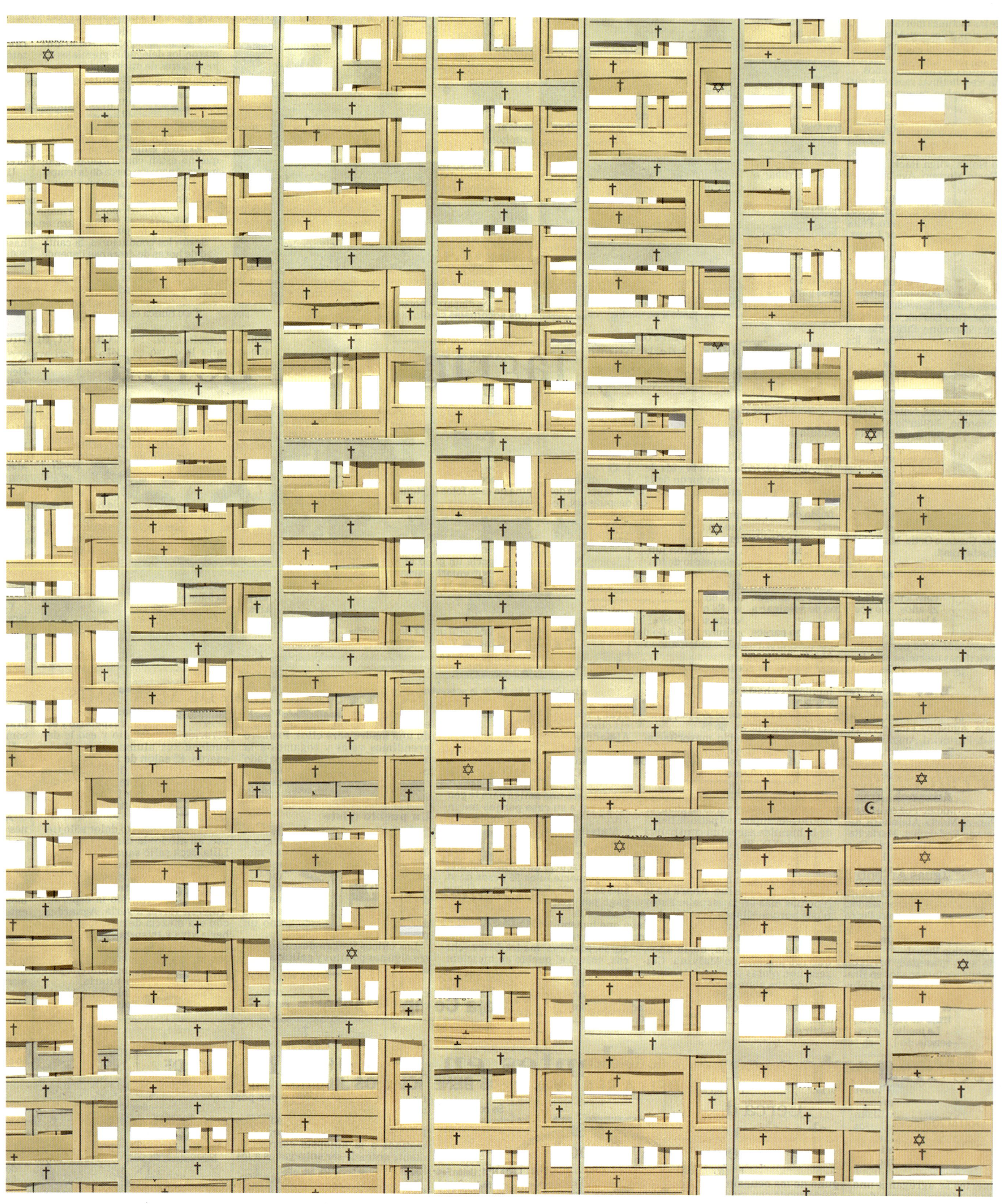

NOTES

Reading the Newspapers, 1909–2009

Taken from the seventh episode of *Ulysses* ("Aeolus"), set in the newsroom of the *Freeman's Journal* and *Evening Telegraph*, my epigraph plays on the biblical passage, "Sufficient unto the day is the evil thereof" (Matthew 6:34). Although *Ulysses* was not published until 1922, Joyce began working on the novel in 1914, not long after Marinetti published his manifesto in *Le Figaro* and Picasso incorporated newspaper into *papiers collés*.

1. "Est-il besoin de dire que nous laissons au signataire toute la responsabilité de ses idées singulièrement audacieuses" (Needless to say, we leave to the signatory full responsibility for his singularly audacious ideas). For a discussion of the disclaimer, see Jeffrey T. Schnapp, "A Preface to Futurism (on the 100 year anniversary of the publication of the *Foundation and Manifesto of Futurism*)," *Modernism/Modernity* 16, no. 2 (April 2009): 203–209.

2. Marinetti evidently reserved the narrative account, which he wrote in late 1908, for *Le Figaro*. Though the narrative is commonly referred to as the preamble or prologue, both are misnomers since the narrative not only precedes but follows the manifesto. After publication in *Le Figaro*, the narrative and manifesto were thereafter called the "Founding and Manifesto of Futurism." For the earlier publications of the manifesto, see Christine Poggi, *Inventing Futurism: The Art and Politics of Artificial Optimism* (Princeton, 2009), 4–5n14.

3. The missing paragraphs have received scant attention. All are from the Founding text, not the manifesto. First column, end of paragraph 6: "comme un cadavre dans sa bière, mais je ressuscitai soudain sous le volant—couperet de guillotine—qui menaçait mon estomac"; first column, after paragraph 8: "Et nous chassions, tels de jeunes lions, la Mort au pelage noir tacheté de croix pâles, qui courait devant nous dans le vaste ciel mauve, palpable et vivant. / Et pourtant nous n'avions pas de Maîtresse idéale dressant sa taille jusqu'aux nuages, ni de Reine cruelle à qui offrir nos cadavres tordus en bagues byzantines!... Rien pour mourir si ce n'est le désir de nous débarrasser enfin de notre trop pesant courage! / Nous allions écrasant sur le seuil des maisons les chiens de garde, qui s'aplatissaient arrondis sous nos pneus brûlants, comme un faux-col sous un fer à repasser. / La Mort amadouée me devançait à chaque virage pour m'offrir gentiment la patte, et tour à tour se couchait au ras de terre avec un bruit de mâchoires stridentes en me coulant des regards veloutés du fond des flaques"; first column, end of paragraph 15 and continuing: "qui me rappelle la sainte mamelle noire de ma nourrice soudanaise! / Comme je dressai mon corps, fangeuse et malodorante vadrouille, je sentis le fer rouge de la joie me percer délicieusement le coeur. / Une foule de pêcheurs à la ligne et de naturalistes podagres s'était ameutée d'épouvante autour du prodige. D'une âme patiente et tâtillonne, ils élevèrent très haut d'énormes éperviers de fer, pour pêcher mon automobile, pareille à un grand requin embourbé. Elle émergea lentement en abandonnant dans le fossé, telles des écailles, sa lourde carrosserie de bon sens et son capitonnage de confort / On le croyait mort, mon bon requin, mais je le réveillai d'une seule caresse sur son dos tout-puissant, et le voilà ressuscité, courant à toute vitesse sur ses nageoires. / Alors,"; second column, end of paragraph 4 after eleven-point manifesto and continuing: "Voulez-vous donc vous empoisonner? Voulez-vous donc pourrir? / Que peut-on bien trouver dans un vieux tableau si ce n'est la contorsion pénible de l'artiste s'efforçant de briser les barrières infranchissables à son désir d'exprimer entièrement son rêve?" For the French version of the Founding, see "Fondation et manifeste du futurisme (1909)—Marinetti," in Giovanni Lista, *Futurisme: Manifestes, proclamations, documents* (Lausanne, 1973), 85–89.

4. The original handwritten text includes the missing paragraphs, as do the leaflets that Marinetti sent to newspapers and journals immediately following its publication in *Le Figaro*. Given that the Founding included the missing paragraphs before and after its appearance in *Le Figaro*, logic suggests that the decision to make the cuts was not Marinetti's. Giovanni Lista, "Genesis and Analysis of Marinetti's 'Manifesto of Futurism,' 1908–1909," in *Futurism*, ed. Didier Ottinger (Centre Pompidou, Paris, 2009), 81n38.

5. The title of this catalogue and related exhibition plays on the title of Robert Hughes' popular BBC television series (1980) and the book based on that series, *The Shock of the New: Art and the Century of Change* (London, 1980). Interestingly, Ian Dunlop, not Robert Hughes, was the first to use the title; see Dunlop's *The Shock of the New: Seven Historic Exhibitions of Modern Art* (London, 1972).

6. See Didier Ottinger, "Cubism + Futurism = Cubofuturism," in Ottinger 2009, 20. See also Schnapp 2009, 207.

7. It should be noted that Anne Baldassari questions whether *Guitar, Sheet Music, and Glass* was Picasso's first newspaper *papier collé.* See Anne Baldassari, *Picasso Working on Paper,* trans. George Collins (London, 2000), 65–67.

8. Eddie Wolfram, *History of Collage: An Anthology of Collage, Assemblage and Event Structures* (London, 1975), 9; Hendel Teicher, ed., *Cut-Outs and Cut-Ups: Hans Christian Andersen and William Seward Burroughs* (Irish Museum of Modern Art, Dublin, 2008), 95; Baldassari 2000, 16, figs. 26–28, 34, 36, 40.

9. Clement Greenberg, "The Pasted-Paper Revolution," *Art News* 57, no. 5 (September 1958): 47–48.

10. Robert Rosenblum, "Picasso and the Coronation of Alexander III: A Note on the Dating of Some *Papiers Collés,*" *Burlington Magazine* 113, no. 823 (October 1971): 604–606.

11. Robert Rosenblum, "Picasso and the Typography of Cubism," in *Picasso in Retrospect,* ed. Roland Penrose and John Golding (London, 1973), 49–75. Rosenblum briefly introduced the topic in 1960. See Rosenblum, *Cubism and Twentieth-Century Art* (New York, 1960), 64, 72, 96, 121.

12. Rosenblum 1973, 51. For an image of the top portion of *Le Journal* published on November 18, 1912, see Kirk Varnedoe and Adam Gopnik, *High and Low: Modern Art and Popular Culture* (Museum of Modern Art, New York, 1990), 26, fig. 7.

13. Jeffrey Weiss, *The Popular Culture of Modern Art: Picasso, Duchamp, and Avant-Gardism* (New Haven, 1994), 11.

14. Patricia Leighten is the most forceful proponent of this view. See Leighten, "Picasso's Collages and the Threat of War, 1912–1913," *Art Bulletin* 67, no. 4 (December 1985): 653–672; and Leighten, *Re-Ordering the Universe: Picasso and Anarchism, 1897–1914* (Princeton, 1989).

15. Leighten 1985, 664.

16. William Rubin, *Picasso and Braque: Pioneering Cubism* (Museum of Modern Art, New York, 1989), 28.

17. Jeffrey Weiss, e-mail to author, December 16, 2011.

18. Picasso used newspaper as a material for cutouts, scale models, sketches, and fully realized works at least until 1963. In the 1930s he created plaster casts of crumpled newspapers, which Brassaï captured in photographs a decade later. In 1935 he conceived a poem, "Maxima au sol," composed by stringing together unrelated passages from the December 8, 1935, edition of *Le Journal.* For a thorough examination of Picasso's lifetime engagement with the newspaper, see Baldassari 2000.

19. Comtesse de Tramar, *L'amour obligatoire, les étapes de la vie d'une femme, la carrier de l'homme* (Paris, 1909). Passages visible in the newspaper ad include: "extrait de la table des matières / la femme dans ses rapports avec son mari / lits communs / lit séparés / les révélations de l'intimité / secrètes répulsions / la femme qui rencontre trop tard son idéal / les petites déceptions fruit défendu / l'amant représailles / l'amour en dehors du mariage / le règne de l'amour et la blonde / l'âge des passions / la femme de 30 ans."

20. Aaron Freundschuh, "'New Sport' in the Street: Self-Defence, Security and Space in Belle Epoque Paris," *French History* 20, no. 4 (December 2006): 424–441.

21. Lewis Kachur reports that both of the ads were published in *Le Journal: MOTO (Automobiles MOTOBLOC)* on October 16, 1913, p. 9, and *L'amour obligatoire* on December 12, 1913, p. 9. Kachur e-mail to author, March 28, 2011.

22. On the subject of public posting and advertising around the turn of the century, see Varnedoe and Gopnik 1990, 249–250; and the chapter "Prenez-garde à la Peinture" in Weiss 1994, esp. 61–65.

23. Edward F. Fry, *Cubism* (New York, 1966), 31. Rosenblum 1973, 64.

24. Marianne W. Martin points out the non-militaristic appearance of the riders, in Martin, *Futurist Art and Theory: 1909–1915* (Oxford, 1968), 199. For an in-depth examination of the work, see Flavio Fergonzi, "Carlo Carrà, *Pursuit (Horse and Rider); Inseguimento (Cavallo e cavalieri),* 1915," in *The Mattioli Collection: Masterpieces of the Italian Avant-Garde; Catalogue Raisonné* (Milan, 2003), 217–229.

25. The pictures of the women clustered at the top right (moving clockwise from top, as captioned) are the actresses Florence Shirley, Juliette Day, and Janet Beecher. They overlap a larger rectangle that frames Carroll McComas, pictured with her hands resting on her lap.

26. Francis Naumann, "Cryptography and the Arensberg Circle," *Arts Magazine* 51, no. 9 (May 1977): 127–133. For more on Man Ray and cryptography, see Kenneth R. Allan, "Metamorphosis in *391*: A Cryptographic Collaboration by Francis Picabia, Man Ray, and Erik Satie," *Art History,* 34, no. 1 (February 2011): 102–125.

27. In a detailed discussion of *Transmutation,* Francis Naumann suggests that "Dou" (lower right) might refer to Arthur Wesley Dow, a specialist in pictorial composition whose writings Man Ray knew. See Francis M. Naumann, "Man Ray and America: The New York and Ridgefield Years: 1907–1921" (PhD diss., City University of New York, 1988), 246–249.

28. My reading of *Dada Rundschau* is indebted to these analyses: Maud Lavin, *Cut with the Kitchen Knife: The Weimar Photomontages of Hannah Höch* (New Haven, 1993), 35–37; Maria Makela, "By Design: The Early Work of Hannah Höch in Context," in *The Photomontages of Hannah Höch,* ed. Maria Makela and Peter Boswell (Walker Art Center,

Minneapolis, 1996), 61, pl. 2; and Brigid Doherty, "Berlin," in *Dada*, ed. Leah Dickerman (National Gallery of Art, Washington, 2005), 105–107.

29. Jochen Hung, e-mail to author, October 5, 2011. I am grateful to Hung for his overall guidance on the subject of German newspapers.

30. For a discussion of Heartfield and AIZ, see David Evans, *John Heartfield, AIZ: Arbeiter-Illustriete Zeitung, Volks Illustrierte, 1930–38* (New York, 1992), 9–41; and Maud Lavin, "Heartfield in Context," in *Clean New World: Culture, Politics, and Graphic Design* (Cambridge, 2001), 12–25. For a discussion within the broader context of German publications of the period, see Sherwin Simmons, "Picture as Weapon in the German Mass Media, 1914–1930," in *Art and Journals on the Political Front, 1910–1940*, ed. Virginia Hagelstein Marquardt (Gainesville, FL, 1997), 142–182.

31. Extensive analyses of the Cabbagehead can be found in Nancy Ann Roth, "The Politics of Collaboration: Brothers, Friends, the Party, and the Performance of John Heartfield, 1915–1938" (PhD diss., City University of New York, 1996), 238–247; and Sabine Tania Kriebel, "Revolutionary Beauty: John Heartfield, Political Photomontage, and the Crisis of the European Left, 1929–1938" (PhD diss., University of California, Berkeley, 2003), 75–84.

32. David Evans described the Cabbagehead as wearing the uniform of the Reichsbanner Schwarz-Rot-Gold (Black, red, gold banner of the Reich), a right-wing paramilitary force affiliated with the Social Democratic Party, which Simmons and Kriebel restated (Simmons 1997, 173; Kriebel 2003, 79). Kriebel has since expressed doubt, believing instead that he is wearing the harness of a common laborer. Sabine Kriebel, e-mail to author, August 19, 2010. This seems a more likely scenario. The Cabbagehead may obediently mouth the Reichsbanner party line, but looks too apprehensive to face the risk of fighting. His weary posture seems to say it all.

33. Kriebel 2003, 78.

34. "Hjalmar oder Das washsende Defizit" (Hjalmar or the growing deficit), *AIZ* 13, no. 14 (April 5, 1934), 224; and "Neudeutscher Kraft-akt" (New German strong-man act), *AIZ* 13, no. 49 (December 6, 1934), 800. Both reproduced in Evans 1992, 203, 275.

35. For a discussion of *Tempo*, see Jochen Hung, "'Der deutschen Jugend!' The Newspaper *Tempo* and the Public Discourse on the 'Young Generation,'" presented at the German History Society Annual Conference 2011, King's College London, September 8–10, 2011, http://www.jochenhung.de/academic/papers/Deutsche%20Jugend/Deutsche%20Jugend.html (accessed January 16, 2012). Hung's talk is forthcoming in *Beyond Glitter and Doom: The Contingency of the Weimar Republic* (2012).

36. The quotation is cited in Douglas Kahn, *John Heartfield: Art and Mass Media* (New York, 1985), 73.

37. For more about Friedländer in relation to Hausmann and for an analysis of Hausmann's portrait of Friedländer, see Timothy O. Benson, *Raoul Hausmann and Berlin Dada* (Ann Arbor, MI, 1987), 10–12, 134–144. For more about Friedländer in relation to Höch, see Peter Chametzky, *Objects as History in Twentieth-Century German Art: Beckmann to Beuys* (Berkeley, 2010), 55–56, 77. Friedländer is named in a text fragment in Hannah Höch's famous *Schnitt mit dem Küchenmesser Dada (Cut with the Kitchen Knife Dada)* (1919–1920), pasted onto the forehead of Albert Einstein.

38. The prominent letters *e Pe* seem to match those in *Le Petit Journal*'s masthead. That masthead coincidentally appears in another work in this catalogue: Semen Fridliand, *Die käufliche Presse* (pl. 32).

39. Cortissoz wrote: "The United States is invaded by aliens, thousands of whom constitute so many acute perils to the body politic. Modernism is of precisely the same heterogeneous alien origin and is imperilling the republic of art in the same way." Royal Cortissoz, *American Artists* (New York, 1932), 18.

40. Debra Bricker Balken, *Arthur Dove: A Retrospective* (Addison Gallery of American Art, Andover, MA, 1997), 32.

41. Richter also used newspaper in at least three related works: *Invasion* (1944–1945); *Liberation of Paris* (1945–1946); and *Stalingrad* (1946). See Stephen C. Foster, ed., *Hans Richter: Activism, Modernism, and the Avant-Garde* (Cambridge, MA, 1998), 269, pl. 1, 10.

42. Cynthia Jaffee McCabe, *Hans Richter's "Stalingrad (Victory in the East)"* (Hirshhorn Museum and Sculpture Garden, Washington, 1980), unpaginated.

43. Rosalind Krauss compares newsprint's lines of type to "stippled flecks of graphite" and sees the newsprint fragments in Picasso's *papiers collés* as circulating signs, which "submit [themselves] to meaning, but never enduringly so." Krauss, *The Picasso Papers* (London, 1998), 26–27.

44. Author's telephone conversation with Ellsworth Kelly, April 5, 2011.

45. Kelly was living in Belle Île, Brittany, when he made *Head with Beard (Self-Portrait)*. He recalls that his mother would mail him copies of the *Herald Tribune*, but apparently here he used a Chicago newspaper, perhaps the *Chicago Tribune*. Kelly speculates that it may have been given to him by one of the English-speaking sailors who docked at Belle Île. Conversation with Kelly, April 5, 2011.

46. Quoted in Calvin Tomkins, *Off the Wall: Robert Rauschenberg and the Art World of Our Time* (Garden City, NY, 1980), 72.

47. Picasso made numerous works on pages from *Paris-Soir* in the early forties, time and again incorporating the daily crosswords (*les mots croisés*).

48. Joan Retallack, ed., *Musicage: Cage Muses on Words, Art, Music* (Hanover, NH, 1996), 121.

49. Kathan Brown, *Ink, Paper, Metal, Wood: Painters and Sculptors at Crown Point Press* (San Francisco, 1996), 225.

50. Tomkins 1980, 72.

51. For an examination of Johns' early work in the light of Cézanne, see Kathryn A. Tuma, "The Color and Compass of Things: Paul Cézanne and the Early Work of Jasper Johns," in *Jasper Johns: An Allegory of Painting, 1955–1965*, ed. Jeffrey Weiss (National Gallery of Art, Washington, 2007), 170–187.

52. Asked about the appeal of the newspaper, Johns explained that it brought "a different kind of information" to his work and lent an "intellectually different focus" to the viewing experience. He went on to speculate that it probably also had to do with a "kinetic response" in that "what you are used to doing with a newspaper is turning [the pages]." Johns, interview with David Bourdon from 1977, in Kirk Varnedoe, ed., *Jasper Johns: Writings, Sketchbook Notes, Interviews* (New York, 1996), 161–162. See also Druick's essay in James Rondeau and Douglas Druick, *Jasper Johns: Gray* (The Art Institute of Chicago, 2007), 86. The Art Institute's catalogue inspired me to think about the color gray in relation to the newspaper.

53. The work is widely reproduced, including in Weiss 2007, 212.

54. James Meyer, *Minimalism: Art and Polemics in the Sixties* (New Haven, 2001), 78.

55. Quotation from Julia Bryan-Wilson, *Art Workers: Radical Practice in the Vietnam War Era* (Berkeley, 2009), 118.

56. Bryan-Wilson 2009, 98.

57. For a description and further images, see Arturo Schwarz, *Man Ray: The Rigour of Imagination* (New York, 1977), 27–30, figs. 12, 13.

58. *Bloom-Zeitung*'s inside pages are devoid of articles and items and take the form of a poster that spells out "BLOOM" in huge black letters, interspersed with phrases honoring Joyce's protagonist, for example: "Wer aber ist Bloom? Du und Sie! / Wer war Bloom? Er und wir! / Wer wird Bloom sein? Ihr und Es!" (But who is Bloom? Thou and you! Who was Bloom? He and we! Who will Bloom be? You guys and it!).

59. "Bloom im Bild," *Der Spiegel* 27 (July 3, 1963), available at *Spiegel Online*, http://www.spiegel.de/spiegel/print/d-45144085.html (accessed January 16, 2012).

60. Like Marinetti, Dalí also saw his writing published on the front page of a mass-media newspaper, Barcelona 's *La Publicitat*, in the form of a series of articles ("*Documental París—1929*") published in 1929.

61. John Martin, "Ballet Premier of 'Mad Tristan,'" *New York Times*, December 16, 1944, 19.

62. "C'est alors que je réaliserai mon rêve de toujours : devenir journaliste-reporter!"

63. For an image of the manifesto, which was produced as a multiple, see Elizabeth Armstrong and Joan Rothfuss, *In the Spirit of Fluxus* (Walker Art Center, Minneapolis, 1993), 24.

64. Each of the eleven newspapers incorporates *V TRE* within its title, a nonsense term coined by the conceptual artist and composer George Brecht, apparently inspired by a malfunctioning neon sign. Examples include *Vaccum TRapEzoid* (March 1965); *Vaudeville TouRnamEnt* (July 1965); and *Vaseline sTREet* (May 1966). The letters *cc* appended to the title of the first four issues (1964) refer to Brecht, according to a code devised by George Maciunas and in keeping with Maciunas' belief that individual artist names should be sublimated to the collective spirit of Fluxus. See Simon Anderson, "Fluxus Publicus," in Armstrong and Rothfuss 1993, 38–61.

65. This is Warhol describing his response to news of the assassination: "When President Kennedy was shot that fall, I heard the news over the radio while I was alone painting in my studio. I don't think I missed a stroke…that was the extent of my reaction.…I'd been thrilled having Kennedy as president…but it didn't bother me that much that he was dead." Andy Warhol and Pat Hackett, *POPism: The Warhol '60s* (New York, 1980), 60.

66. Hal Foster, *The First Pop Age: Painting and Subjectivity in the Art of Hamilton, Lichtenstein, Warhol, Richter, and Ruscha* (Princeton, 2012), 110.

67. Foster 2012, 148.

68. A copy of Huebler's typewritten letter to Kynaston McShine, dated June 6, 1970, was sent to me by Lucy Gallun, curatorial assistant, Department of Photography, The Museum of Modern Art.

69. Lisa Phillips, "Sarah Charlesworth: Rite of Passage," in Louis Grachos and Susan Fisher Sterling, *Sarah Charlesworth: A Retrospective* (SITE Santa Fe, 1998), 41. The exhibition was *January 5–31, 1969*, organized by Seth Siegalaub. See Alexander Alberro, *Conceptual Art and the Politics of Publicity* (Cambridge, MA, 2003).

70. I am grateful to Gabriel Pérez-Barreiro for discussing Macchi's work with me and reviewing this section of the essay.

71. Jeffrey Weiss concisely states the case that "few sentiments of art criticism are as familiar as the charge 'modern art is a hoax.'" See Weiss 1994, xv.

72. In an instance of life imitating art, the *New York Times* published its first same-sex "commitment" announcement a decade later, in September 2002.

73. "Gober Art Is More than Queer—It's a Hoax," *Catholic League for Religious and Civil Rights*, http://catholicleague.biz/printer.php?p=Release&id=290 (accessed September 9, 2011). The quotation is William Donohue's.

74. Weiss 1994, 45.

75. André Billy, *Apollinaire vivant* (Paris, 1923), 92, quoted in Weiss 1994, 45.

76. David Cottington, "Cubism, Aestheticism, Modernism," in *Picasso and Braque: A Symposium*, ed. William Rubin, Kirk Varnedoe, and Lynn Zelevansky (Museum of Modern Art, New York, 1992), 69.

77. Conversation with Fred Tomaselli, October 22, 2011.

78. For the quotation and more, I thank Hugh Price, Director of Operations and Planning for the Production Department, *Washington Post*.

79. Erika Wolf suggests that Fridliand's montage may have been the inspiration for John Heartfield's Cabbagehead. For a discussion of Fridliand and *Ogonëk*, see Wolf, "Selected New Acquisitions," *Zimmerli Journal* 2 (Fall 2004): 106–117; and Wolf, "The Soviet Union: From Worker to Proletarian Photography," in *The Worker Photography Movement (1926–1939): Essay and Documents*, ed. Jorge Ribalta (Madrid, 2011), 32–46.

80. Curiously, the image published in *Ogonëk* does not match the image in *Foto-Auge*. The masthead for *Le Figaro* lands on the woman's chin in the magazine, for instance, and below her chin in the book; *Le Petit Parisienne*'s masthead lands on her nose in the magazine and on her mouth in the book.

Ripped from the Headlines

1. Walter Benjamin, "The Newspaper" (1934), in *Walter Benjamin: Selected Writings*, ed. Michael W. Jennings, Howard Eiland, and Gary Smith, trans. Rodney Livingstone, vol. 2 (Cambridge, MA, 1996), 741.

2. Stéphane Mallarmé, "The Book as Spiritual Instrument" (1895), in *Divagations*, trans. Barbara Johnson (Cambridge, MA, 2007), 228.

3. Anne Umland, *Picasso Guitars, 1912–1914* (Museum of Modern Art, New York, 2011), 20. The original quotation is: "Je emploie tes derniers procédés paperistiques et pusièreux. Je suis en train de imaginer une guitare et je emploie un peu de pusière contre notre orrible toile." It is not clear whether Picasso was referring to the *papier collé* or one of the constructions.

4. The full headline from *Le Journal* is "La Bataille s'est engagée furieuse sur les lignes de Tchataldja." It's unclear why Picasso removed the last *e* of *engagée*. Perhaps to agree (in gender) with the *jeu* (game) that's suggested by *jou* and so to suggest "The game is on."

5. John Richardson, with the collaboration of Marilyn McCully, *A Life of Picasso*, vol. 2: 1907–1917 (New York, 1996), 250.

6. Richardson 1996, 252.

7. Umland 2011, 35n11. "Je emploie un peu de pusière contre notre orrible toile."

8. In *Aesthetic Theory*, trans. Robert Hullot-Kentor (Minneapolis, 1997), 155, Theodor W. Adorno suggests that collage is a war on "the artwork as a nexus of meaning." He defines collage as "the inner-aesthetic capitulation of art to what stands heterogeneously opposed to it," and he laments that with collage, "art thereby begins the process of destroying the artwork as a nexus of meaning. For the first time in the development of art, affixed debris cleaves visible scars in the work's meaning."

9. "Philip Meyer, in his book *The Vanishing Newspaper* (2004), predicts that the final copy of the final newspaper will appear on somebody's doorstep one day in 2043." Eric Alterman, *New Yorker*, March 31, 2008.

10. I worked as an editor, reporter, and critic at the *New York Times* from 1989 to 2006.

11. Bernice Rose, Michelle White, and Gary Garrels, eds., *Richard Serra Drawing: A Retrospective* (Menil Collection, Houston, 2011), 86–87.

12. Rosalind Krauss, "The Motivation of the Sign," in *Picasso and Braque: A Symposium*, ed. William Rubin, Kirk Varnedoe, and Lynn Zelevansky (Museum of Modern Art, New York, 1992), 276.

13. Krauss 1992, 276.

14. Krauss 1992, 278. Krauss writes that Picasso's *Un coup de thé* "punningly signals a field skewered to the surface by a headline that slyly summons forth 'Un Coup de dés' in what is perhaps an ironic echo."

15. Krauss 1992, 276.

16. Yve-Alain Bois, "The Semiology of Cubism," in Rubin, Varnedoe, and Zelevansky 1992, 203.

17. Anna Sigrídur Arnar, *The Book as Instrument: Stéphane Mallarmé, the Artist's Book, and the Transformation of Print Culture* (Chicago, 2011), 228. "Mallarmé devoted substantial analysis to the structure of the newspaper page in a number of key essays published in the 1890s. These essays reveal his guarded admiration for the newspaper's uncanny ability to structure disparate and even contradictory bits of information. Moreover, he recognized that the newspaper's artificial packaging of text demanded particular skills from the reader and that it thus provided valuable lessons for writers seeking relevance in the democratic age. Indeed, the consumer-oriented newspaper offered a degree of mobility and freedom that Mallarmé deemed worth exploring—even harnessing—for the modern book, including the final version of *Un coup de dés*."

18. Krauss 1992, 281.

19. One of the most heated debates about cubist collage has to do with the question of whether and how to read the newspaper pieces in it. See, e.g., Rosalind Krauss, *The Picasso Papers* (London, 1998); and Patricia Leighten, "Cubist Anachronisms: Ahistoricity, Cryptoformalism, and Business-as-Usual in New York," *Oxford Art Journal* 17, no. 2 (1994): 91–102.

20. Clement Greenberg, "Collage" (1959), in *Art and Culture: Critical Essays* (Boston, 1965), 70.

21. Greenberg 1965, 75.

22. Leighten 1994, 99.

23. Robert Rosenblum, "Picasso and the Typography of Cubism," in *Picasso in Retrospect,* ed. Roland Penrose and John Golding (New York, 1973), 50.

24. Rosenblum 1973, 51–52.

25. Rosenblum 1973, 56–57.

26. Rosenblum 1973, 50–51.

27. The way Joyce scrounged for materials for his novel *Ulysses* (which has a whole chapter, "Aeolus," set in a newsroom and punctuated by headlines) was strikingly similar to Picasso's way of getting collage materials. On January 5, 1920, Joyce wrote to Mrs. William Murray asking for "a bundle of other novelettes and any penny hymnal you can find." In 1921, he wrote to his friend Frank Budgen asking for "any ragged, dirty, smudged, torn, defiled, effaced, dogeared, coverless, undated, anonymous misprinted book on mathematics or algebra or trigonometry or Euclid from a cart." R. Brandon Kershner, *The Culture of Joyce*'s Ulysses (New York, 2010), 85–86. Compare that with Duncan Grant's account (to Clive Bell) of Picasso: "I promised to take him a roll of old wallpapers which I have found in a cupboard of my hotel and which excited him very much as he makes use of them frequently and finds [them] very difficult to get. He sometimes tears small pieces off the wall." Richardson 1996, 250.

28. Kershner 2010, 85–89.

29. On Wednesday morning, June 15, 1904, a group from St. Marks Evangelical Lutheran Church, at 325 East Sixth Street in New York City, boarded the *General Slocum* for a trip up the East River. Just before 10:00 a.m., a fire started in the ship's forward section. The crew tried to put it out, but the hoses were rotten. The lifeboats were inaccessible, and the life preservers useless: the cork in them had long-since disintegrated into fine dust so that they either fell apart or, worse, absorbed water and dragged their wearers—mostly women and children—beneath the surface of the river. Most of the passengers were, like the majority of Americans in 1904, unable to swim. Ultimately, 1,021 people died by fire or drowning. After the disaster, the survivors couldn't bear to remain in the neighborhood, then known as Little Germany. They moved uptown, and the church became a synagogue, which it remains to this day. See Edward T. O'Donnell, *Ship Ablaze: The Tragedy of the Steamboat "General Slocum"* (New York, 2003). For the comparison between the *Slocum* disaster and the events of September 11, 2001, see N. R. Kleinfield, "As 9/11 Draws Near, a Debate Rises: How Much Tribute Is Enough?" *New York Times*, September 2, 2007, p. 1.

30. Mallarmé, "The Mystery in Letters" (1896), in *Divagations*, 2007, 235.

31. Krauss 1998, 26.

32. Krauss 1998, 26, 27, 28, 33, 38, 41, 49, 50.

33. Krauss 1992, 281.

34. Benjamin, "The Newspaper," in *Selected Writings*, 1996, 741. "The fact that nothing binds the reader more tightly to his paper than this all-consuming impatience, his longing for daily nourishment, has long been exploited by publishers."

35. F. T. Marinetti, "The Founding and Manifesto of Futurism," in *Futurism: An Anthology*, ed. Lawrence Rainey, Christine Poggi, and Laura Wittman (New Haven, 2009), 49–53.

36. Christine Poggi, *In Defiance of Painting: Cubism, Futurism, and the Invention of Collage* (New Haven, 1992), 28, 219.

37. Poggi 1992, 219.

38. Krauss 1992, 277.

39. Dawn Ades, *Photomontage* (London, 1993), 13.

40. Ades 1993, 23. George Grosz and John Heartfield would often stamp the abbreviation "*mont.*" on their works instead of a signature.

41. Ades 1993, 26.

42. Walter Benjamin, "The Author as Producer" (1934), in *Selected Writings*, 1996, 774.

43. Ades 1993, 42.

44. David Evans, *John Heartfield, AIZ: Arbeiter-Illustrierte Zeitung, Volks Illustrierte, 1930–38* (New York, 1992), 44.

45. Ades 1993, 43.

46. The pictures were published in the *New York Times* in the 1960s, and the texts were published in the *Times* in the 1990s.

47. Warhol made *Flash—November 22, 1963,* not in the year that John F. Kennedy was shot (which Warhol remembered for "the way the television and radio were programming everybody to feel so sad") but in 1968, the year Warhol himself was shot. Warhol's recollection of that event connects his shooting with Kennedy's: "As I was coming down from my operation, I heard a television going somewhere and the words 'Kennedy' and 'assassin' and 'shot' over and over again. Robert Kennedy had been shot, but what was so weird was that I had no understanding that this was a *second* Kennedy assassination—I just thought that maybe after you die, they rerun things for you, like President Kennedy's assassination." Molly Donovan, "Where's Warhol? Triangulating the Artist in the Headlines," in *Warhol: Headlines* (National Gallery of Art, Washington, 2011), 16–17.

48. Thomas Micchelli, "Life on Mars: 55th Carnegie International," *Brooklyn Rail* (September 2008).

49. Mallarmé, "The Book as Spiritual Instrument" (1895), in *Divagations*, 2007, 229.

50. Speaking of gold, Krauss points out the "strange chronological convergence between the rise of the inconvertible token money of the postwar economy" (the abandonment of the gold standard) and "the birth of the non-referential sign" (the way newspaper scraps and other collage elements can stand in for different things). Krauss 1998, 6. To turn newspaper into gold then, as Hodges does, is a way to reverse this historical process, to freeze the free-floating, non-referential signs.

51. The *Slocum* disaster is alluded to in the following episodes in *Ulysses*: "Lestrygonians," "The Wandering Rocks," and "Eumaeus." "The Wandering Rocks" contains four distinct references, the longest of which reads: "Terrible affair that General Slocum explosion. Terrible, terrible! A thousand casualties. And heart-rending scenes. Men trampling down women and children. Most brutal thing. What do they say was the cause? Spontaneous combustion: most scandalous revelation. Not a single lifeboat would float and the firehose all burst. What I can't understand is how the inspectors ever allowed a boat like that.... I thought we were bad here." James Joyce, *Ulysses* (New York, 1934), 239. For annotations on all references to the *Slocum* disaster, see Don Gifford and Robert T. Seidman, Ulysses *Annotated: Notes for James Joyce's* Ulysses, 2nd ed., rev. and enl. by Don Gifford (Berkeley, 1988), 186–187, 262, 273, 552.

52. Richardson 1996, 254. "The watertight barriers have been breached. Now we are delivered from Painting and Sculpture.... Art will at last be fused with life, now that we have at last ceased to try to make life fuse with art."

53. Rosenblum 1973, 60.

54. Krauss 1998, 48–49.

55. Krauss 1998, 25–26.

Newsprint and News Time

1. Louis Guéry, *Visages de la presse: La présentation des journaux des origines à nos jours* (Paris, 1997), 103. For example, by 1914 about 4.5 million copies of the four major French newspapers were printed each day.

2. Richard Terdiman claims the newspaper as the first authentic *mass* medium, stressing its commodity status as a commercial enterprise beginning in the 1830s. He further notes that, already from 1830 to 1880, newspaper production had increased by 4,000 percent. See his "Newspaper Culture," in *Discourse/Counter-Discourse: The Theory and Practice of Symbolic Resistance in Nineteenth-Century France*, ed. Richard Terdiman (Ithaca, NY, 1985), 118, 129–135.

3. Guéry 1997, 103.

4. "I believe I am right in stating that worked out mathematically, Paris possesses more newspapers per ratio to the population than any city in the world." Harry J. Greenwall, *Scoops: Being Leaves from the Diary of a Special Correspondent* (New York, 1923), 211, and referenced in Ronald Weber, *News of Paris: American Journalists in the City of Light Between the Wars* (Chicago, 2006), 5.

5. Leo Steinberg, commentary, in *Picasso and Braque: A Symposium*, ed. William Rubin (Museum of Modern Art, New York, 1992), 77.

6. On the different versions of the manifesto, see Jeffrey Schnapp, "A Preface to Futurism," *Modernism/Modernity* 16, no. 2 (2009): 203–209.

7. F. T. Marinetti, "The Founding and Manifesto of Futurism," in *Futurism: An Anthology*, ed. Lawrence Rainey, Christine Poggi, and Laura Wittman (New Haven, 2009), 50, 51.

8. Jeffrey Weiss, *The Popular Culture of Modern Art: Picasso, Duchamp, and Avant-Gardism* (New Haven, 1994), 170–190.

9. Weiss 1994, 249–250; the "walking kiosk," by Serge Férat, took its cue from Apollinaire's suggestion of a newsstand with one human arm. For more on the Czech staging of Apollinaire's play, see Matthew S. Witkovsky, "Avant-Garde and Center: Devětsil in Czech Culture, 1918–1938" (PhD diss., University of Pennsylvania, 2002).

10. Stéphane Mallarmé, "The Book: A Spiritual Instrument" (1895), trans. Bradford Cook, in *Stéphane Mallarmé: Selected Poetry and Prose*, ed. Mary Ann Caws (New York, 1982), 83.

11. See Christine Poggi, "Mallarmé, Picasso, and the Newspaper as Commodity," *In Defiance of Painting: Cubism, Futurism, and the Invention of Collage* (New Haven, 1992), 141–163.

12. Mallarmé, "Action Restricted" (1895), trans. Mary Ann Caws, in Caws 1982, 80.

13. Ellen Wayland-Smith, "Passing Fashion: Mallarmé and the Future of Poetry in the Age of Mechanical Reproduction," *MLN* 117 (2002): 887–907.

14. Wayland-Smith 2002, 901.

15. Walter Benjamin, "Karl Kraus" (1931), in *Walter Benjamin: Selected Writings*, ed. Michael W. Jennings, Howard Eiland, and Gary Smith, trans. Rodney Livingstone, vol. 2 (Cambridge, MA, 1996), 440.

16. Karl Kraus, Aphorism 411, in Kraus, *Dicta and Contradicta*, trans. Jonathan McVity (Champaign, IL, 2001), 51.

17. For more on Kraus' use of language, see Jonathan McVity, "The Twist: *Dicta and Contradicta* in Context," in Kraus 2001, 129–160.

18. Adolf Behne, "Künstler des Proletariats, Nr. 16," *Eulenspiegel* 6 (June 1931): 95, reprinted in Roland März and Gertrud Heartfield, *John Heartfield: Der Schnitt entlang der Zeit: Selbstzeugnisse, Erinnerungen, Interpretationen* (Dresden, 1981), 186.

19. The classic expression of a class-conscious seeing in this context (actually published in *Der Arbeiter-Fotograf*, the companion magazine to *AIZ*) is Edwin Hoernle, "Das Auge des Arbeiters" (1930), reprinted as "The Working Man's Eye" in *Germany:*

The New Photography, 1927–33, ed. David Mellor (London, 1978), 47–49. For a recent, theoretically informed account of Heartfield's work for *AIZ,* see Sabine Kriebel, "Manufacturing Discontent: John Heartfield's Mass Medium," *New German Critique* 107 (Summer 2009): 53–88.

20. See Jeremy Aynsley, "Pressa Cologne, 1928: Exhibitions and Publication Design in the Weimar Period," *Design Issues* 10, no. 3 (1994): 52–76.

21. The phrase "author as producer" (*der Autor als Produzent*) can be traced through several essays by Benjamin collected in Jennings, Eiland, and Smith 1996. It first appeared in "Diary from August 7, 1931 to the Day of My Death" (501–506), then in the brief notice entitled "The Newspaper" (1934) (741–742), which he repeated verbatim in the groundbreaking text, "The Author as Producer" (768–782), written in the spring of 1934 but not published during Benjamin's lifetime.

22. Benjamin, "Newspaper," in Jennings, Eiland, and Smith 1996, 741.

23. Benjamin, "Newspaper," in Jennings, Eiland, and Smith 1996, 741.

24. Benjamin, "Newspaper," in Jennings, Eiland, and Smith 1996, 742.

25. Benjamin, "Author as Producer," in Jennings, Eiland, and Smith 1996, 773.

26. Tristan Tzara, "Le papier collé ou le proverbe en peinture" (1931), reprinted as "The Pasted Paper or the Proverb in Painting," in *The Surrealists Look at Art,* ed. Pontus Hultén (Venice, CA, 1990), 218, 220.

27. André Breton, "Picasso in His Element" (1933), translated in *Surrealism and Painting,* ed. Simon Watson Taylor (New York, 1972), 109, and quoted in Ann Umland, *Picasso Guitars, 1912–1914* (Museum of Modern Art, New York, 2011), 33.

28. Louis Aragon, "La peinture au défi" (1930), reprinted as "The Challenge to Painting" in Hultén 1990, 55–56.

29. Aragon in Hultén 1990, 57. Aragon was not speaking particularly of newsprint, which figured rarely in surrealist work. One notable exception is Hans Arp's *Mutilé et apatride* (1936), a papier-mâché construction that figured in the *Exposition surréaliste d'objets* at the Galerie Charles Ratton, Paris, in 1936.

30. Kevin G. Barnhurst and John Nerone, *The Form of News: A History* (New York, 2001), 19–21.

31. By around 1960, newspaper consumption had moved from café racks and walls in the street to the breakfast and dinner tables of private homes, especially in the United States. A 1961 marketing study commissioned by the Newsprint Information Committee, *Daily Newspaper and Its Reading Public,* found that 90 percent of American newspapers were read in the home whereas only 1 percent were read in restaurants.

32. Scholarship on Jasper Johns and Robert Rauschenberg excels in this regard; see, e.g., Jonathan Katz, "The Art of Code: Jasper Johns and Robert Rauschenberg," in *Significant Others: Creativity and Intimate Partnership,* ed. Whitney Chadwick and Isabelle de Courtivron (New York, 1992), 189–207; and Katz, "Jasper Johns' *Alley Oop:* On Comic Strips and Camouflage" (2009), accessible online at http://www.queercultural-center.org/Pages/KatzPages/Katzoops.html.

33. Cherise Smith, "Re-Member the Audience: Adrian Piper's Mythic Being Advertisements," *Art Journal* 66, no. 1 (2007): 57. The description of Piper's work in this essay draws in its particulars on Smith's article.

34. David Lamelas, interview by Fay Nicholson, in *Nottingham Visual Arts Magazine,* July 8, 2009, http://www.nottinghamvisualarts.net/articles/jul08/274/outside-frame-interview-david-lamelas (accessed September 2011).

35. For more on Kawara and tourism, see Mark Godfrey, "Across the Universe," in *Light Years: Conceptual Art and the Photograph, 1964–1977,* ed. Matthew S. Witkovsky (Art Institute of Chicago, 2011), 59–60.

36. Information on *El Eco de Canarias* obtained through Jable: Archivo de Prensa digital, a service of the Universidad de Las Palmas de Gran Canaria, http://jable.ulpgc.es/jable/ (accessed August 2011).

37. Hans-Peter Feldmann to Paul Maenz and Gerd de Vries, undated, probably June 1973, Paul Maenz Papers, Getty Research Institute, ser. 2, box 15, fol. 11.

38. Robin Erica Wagner-Pacifici gives a theoretically astute interpretation of events in her book, *The Moro Morality Play: Terrorism as Social Drama* (Chicago, 1986), stressing the media ritual that claimed Moro as its victim, in the service of false public catharsis and real political standstill.

39. Okwui Enwezor, *Archive Fever: Uses of the Document in Contemporary Art* (New York, 2008), 30.

Inflexions of the Times: Newspaper in the Era of Art

1. Clement Greenberg, "The Pasted-Paper Revolution," *Art News* 57, no. 1 (September 1958): 46–49, 60–61. Greenberg discusses a series of devices, including a trompe-l'oeil nail and loop of rope, stenciled lettering, sand, and pasted papers, as means of "specifying the very real flatness of the picture plane so that everything else shown on it would be pushed into illusioned space by force of contrast. The surface was now *explicitly* instead of implicitly indicated as a tangible but transparent plane" (p. 48). Ultimately, such elements "begin to change places in depth with one another, and a process is set up in which every part of the picture takes its turn at occupying every plane, whether real or imagined, in it" (p. 48). Greenberg thus conceives the picture plane both as a literal, physical surface and as a cultural artifact whose flatness must be staged and signified. This occurs through a relational network of elements "shuffling and shuttling between surface and depth" (p. 48).

2. Ellsworth Kelly identified these features in a communication to the author, September 19, 2011.

3. Ellsworth Kelly, cited in *Ellsworth Kelly: Works on Paper,* ed. Diane Upright (Fort Worth Art Museum, 1987), 14.

4. Ellsworth Kelly, "Notes from 1969," in *Theories and Documents of Contemporary Art: A Sourcebook of Artists' Writings,* ed. Kristine Stiles and Peter Selz (Berkeley, 1996), 92.

5. Vladimir I. Lenin, "Where to Begin?" *Iskra,* no. 4 (May 1901): 1, in *V. I. Lenin Collected Work,* vol. 5, ed. Victor Jerome, trans. Joe Fineberg and George Hanna (London, 1961), 22. *Iskra* (Spark), the official organ of the Russian Social Democratic Labor Party, was founded by Lenin in Leipzig in 1900. Iskra's motto, "From a spark a fire will flare up," was a line written by Alexander Odoevsky in response to a poem Alexander Pushkin addressed to Dekabrists (Decembrists), a group that staged an unsuccessful anticzarist revolt in 1825.

6. Calvin Tomkins, *Off the Wall: Robert Rauschenberg and the Art of Our Time* (Garden City, NY, 1980), 71.

7. Walter Hopps, *Robert Rauschenberg: The Early 1950s* (Menil Collection, Houston, 1991), 68.

8. Hopps 1991, 62. See also the discussion of the black paintings' desublimated references to the body's daily functions and smells, including the expulsion of excrement, as registered through the repetitive dailiness of newspaper in Helen Molesworth, "Before *Bed,*" *October* 63 (Winter 1993): 68–82.

9. Jasper Johns, quoted in Emile de Antonio and Mitch Tuchman, *Painters Painting: A Candid History of the Modern Art Scene, 1940–1970* (New York, 1984), 97.

10. Jasper Johns, quoted in Joseph E. Young, "Jasper Johns: An Appraisal," *Art International* 13, no. 7 (September 1969), 51.

11. James Rondeau, "Jasper Johns: Gray," in James Rondeau and Douglas Druick, *Jasper Johns: Gray* (Art Institute of Chicago, 2007), 59.

12. Allan Kaprow, "The Legacy of Jackson Pollock," *Art News* 57, no. 2 (October 1958): 56.

13. Kaprow 1958, 56–57.

14. Kaprow's *Untitled* appeared in the Reuben Gallery show *Below Zero,* held from December 18, 1959, to January 5, 1960. Participants included Rauschenberg, Claes Oldenburg, Jim Dine, George Brecht, Ray Johnson, Jean Follet, and George Segal.

15. Carolee Schneemann, *More than Meat Joy: Complete Performance Works and Selected Writings,* ed. Bruce McPherson (New York, 1979), 33.

16. Schneemann 1979, 34–35.

17. Arman mentions the violence of Rauschenberg's response in several interviews. See Arman, interview by Susan Hapgood, in *Neo-Dada: Redefining Art, 1958–62* (American Federation of Arts, New York, 1992), 110; and Arman, "L'Archéologie du future," interview by Daniel Abadie, in *Arman* (Galerie nationale du Jeu de Paume, Paris, 1998), 51: "Tout à coup, en plein milieu du vernissage, Rauschenberg m'a attaqué de front et m'a dit... Je suis très déçu de voir cette exposition, surtout ces boîtes avec des objets dedans. L'accumulation par hasard, ce n'est pas de l'art, c'est de la chance" (All at once, in the middle of the opening, Rauschenberg attacked me directly and said... I am very disappointed to see this exhibition, especially these boxes with objects in them. Chance accumulation, this is not art, it is chance).

18. Dieter Roth to Hanns Sohm, spring 1964, quoted in Dirk Dobke, Dieter Roth, and Thomas Kellein, *Dieter Roth Books + Multiples* (Baden, Switzerland, 2004), 9.

19. *Roth Time: A Dieter Roth Retrospective,* ed. Theodora Vischer and Bernadette Walter, texts by Dirk Kobke and Bernadette Walter (Museum of Modern Art, New York, 2004), 74–75.

20. Pierre Restany, *Chryssa* (New York, 1978), 33.

21. See the discussion of *Stag Hunt* in Caroline Tisdall, *Joseph Beuys* (Solomon R. Guggenheim Museum, New York, 1979), 80–83.

22. Joseph Beuys, cited in Volker Harlan, *Soziale Plastik: Materialien zu Joseph Beuys* (Achberg, Germany, 1984), 59.

23. For example, Kraft durch Freude (Strength through Joy) was a state-controlled leisure organization established to promote the benefits of National Socialism.

24. My thanks to Judith Brodie, who shared her handwritten transcription of visible portions of the newspaper text with me. She further notes that the newspaper is most likely the *Frankfurter Allgemeine Zeitung,* which Beuys often used.

25. Georges Nzongola-Ntalaja, *The Congo from Leopold to Kabila: A People's History* (London, 2002), 94–140. See also Ludo De Witte, *The Assassination of Lumumba,* trans. Ann Wright and Renée Fenby (London, 2001).

26. For a discussion of "inflexion" as "the genetic element of the variable curve or fold," which shows that "no exact and unmixed figure can exist," see Gilles Deleuze, *The Fold: Leibniz and the Baroque,* trans. Tom Conley (Minneapolis, 1993), 14. Inflexion thus refers to a new conception of the object in which "fluctuation of the norm replaces the permanence of a law; where the object assumes a place in a continuum of variation; where industrial automation or serial machineries replaced stamped forms" (19).

27. See especially Stéphane Mallarmé, "Le livre: instrument spirituel" (1895), in *Oeuvres complètes,* ed. Henri Mondor and G. Jean-Aubry (Paris, 1945), 378–382. See also the discussion of Mallarmé's attitudes toward the newspaper and book in Christine Poggi, "Mallarmé, Picasso, and the Newspaper as Commodity," *Yale Journal of Criticism* 1, no. 1 (Fall 1987): 133–151. See also Christine Poggi, *In Defiance of Painting: Cubism, Futurism, and the Invention of Collage* (New Haven, 1992), 141–163.

28. Mallarmé, "Le livre: instrument spirituel" (1895), in Mondor and Jean-Aubry 1945, 380–381.

29. Stéphane Mallarmé, "Le mystère dans les lettres" (1896), in Mondor and Jean-Aubry 1945, 387.

30. Mallarmé, "L'action restreinte" (1895), in Mondor and Jean-Aubry 1945, 370.

31. In one version, the installation of this piece included twenty-four stacks in two rows. Another version offered a curved configuration of stacks, while in others the stacks were supported by glass partitions.

BIBLIOGRAPHY

Ades, Dawn. *Photomontage.* London, 1993.

Adorno, Theodor W. *Aesthetic Theory.* Translated by Robert Hullot-Kentor. Minneapolis, 1997.

Alberro, Alexander. *Conceptual Art and the Politics of Publicity.* Cambridge, MA, 2003.

Albers, Josef. *Search Versus Re-Search: Three Lectures by Josef Albers at Trinity College, April, 1965.* Hartford, CT, 1969.

Allan, Kenneth R. "Metamorphosis in *391:* A Cryptographic Collaboration by Francis Picabia, Man Ray, and Erik Satie." *Art History* 34, no. 1 (February 2011): 102–125.

Alterman, Eric. "Out of Print: The Death and Life of the American Newspaper." *New Yorker.* March 31, 2008.

Anderson, Simon. "Fluxus Publicus." In *In the Spirit of Fluxus,* edited by Elizabeth Armstrong and Joan Rothfuss, 38–61. Walker Art Center, Minneapolis, 1993.

Apgar, Garry, Shaun O'L. Higgins, and Colleen Striege. *The Newspaper in Art.* Spokane, 1996.

Aragon, Louis. "La peinture au défi." 1930. Reprinted as "The Challenge to Painting." In *The Surrealists Look at Art: Eluard, Aragon, Soupault, Breton, Tzara,* edited by Pontus Hultén, 47–72. Venice, CA, 1990.

Arman. "L'Archéologie du future." Interview by Daniel Abadie. In *Arman,* 37–63. Galerie nationale du Jeu de Paume, Paris, 1998.

Armstrong, Elizabeth, and Joan Rothfuss. *In the Spirit of Fluxus.* Walker Art Center, Minneapolis, 1993.

Arnar, Anna Sigrídur. *The Book as Instrument: Stéphane Mallarmé, the Artist's Book, and the Transformation of Print Culture.* Chicago, 2011.

Ault, Julie, ed. *Felix Gonzalez-Torres.* Göttingen, 2006.

Aynsley, Jeremy. "Pressa Cologne, 1928: Exhibitions and Publication Design in the Weimar Period." *Design Issues* 10, no. 3 (1994): 52–76.

Baker, Nicholson. "Deadline: The Author's Desperate Bid to Save America's Past." *New Yorker,* July 24, 2000.

———. *Double Fold: Libraries and the Assault on Paper.* New York, 2001.

Baldassari, Anne. *Picasso Working on Paper.* Translated by George Collins. London, 2000.

Balken, Debra Bricker. *Arthur Dove: A Retrospective.* Addison Gallery of American Art, Andover, MA, 1997.

Barnhurst, Kevin G., and John Nerone. *The Form of News: A History.* New York, 2001.

Behne, Adolf. "Künstler des Proletariats, Nr. 16." *Eulenspiegel* 6 (June 1931): 95. Reprinted in Roland März and Gertrud Heartfield, *John Heartfield: Der Schnitt entlang der Zeit: Selbstzeugnisse, Erinnerungen, Interpretationen,* 185–186. Dresden, 1981.

Benjamin, Walter. "The Author as Producer." In "1931–1934," vol. 2, pt. 2, of *Walter Benjamin: Selected Writings,* edited by Michael W. Jennings, Howard Eiland, and Gary Smith, 768–782. Translated by Edmund Jephcott. Cambridge, MA, 1996.

———. "Karl Kraus." In "1931–1934," vol. 2, pt. 2, of *Walter Benjamin: Selected Writings,* edited by Michael W. Jennings, Howard Eiland, and Gary Smith, translated by Rodney Livingstone, 433–458. Cambridge, MA, 1996.

———. "Newspaper." In "1931–1934," vol. 2, pt. 2, of *Walter Benjamin: Selected Writings,* edited by Michael W. Jennings, Howard Eiland, and Gary Smith, translated by Rodney Livingston, 741–742. Cambridge, MA, 1996.

Benson, Timothy O. *Raoul Hausmann and Berlin Dada.* Ann Arbor, MI, 1987.

Bergdoll, Barry, and Leah Dickerman. *Bauhaus, 1919–1933: Workshops for Modernity.* Museum of Modern Art, New York, 2009.

Berggruen, Olivier, Max Hollein, and Ingrid Pfeiffer, eds. *Yves Klein.* Schirn Kunsthalle Frankfurt, 2004.

Billy, André. *Apollinaire vivant.* Paris, 1923.

Blocker, Antonia. *Kim Rugg: Don't Mention the War.* Mark Moore Gallery, Santa Monica, CA, 2007.

Boaden, James. "Black Painting (with Asheville Citizen)." *Art History* 34, no. 1 (February 2011): 166–191.

Bochner, Mel. "Mel Bochner in Conversation with James Meyer." In Johanna Burton, *Mel Bochner: Language, 1966–2006,* 133–142. Art Institute of Chicago, 2007.

———. *Solar Systems and Rest Rooms: Writings and Interviews, 1965–2007.* Cambridge, MA, 2008.

Bois, Yve-Alain. "The Semiology of Cubism." In *Picasso and Braque: A Symposium,* edited by William Rubin, Kirk Varnedoe, and Lynn

Zelevansky, 169–208. Museum of Modern Art, New York, 1992.

Bourneuf, Annie. "A Refuge for Script: Paul Klee's Square Pictures." In *Bauhaus Construct: Fashioning Identity, Discourse, and Modernism,* edited by Robin Schuldenfrei and Jeffrey Saletnik, 105–124. London, 2009.

Breton, André. "Picasso in His Element." 1933. Translated in *Surrealism and Painting,* edited by Simon Watson Taylor. New York, 1972.

Brougher, Kerry, and Philippe Vergne. *Yves Klein: With the Void, Full Powers.* Hirshhorn Museum and Sculpture Garden, Washington, 2010.

Brown, Kathan. *Ink, Paper, Metal, Wood: Painters and Sculptors at Crown Point Press.* San Francisco, 1996.

———. *John Cage: Visual Art: To Sober and Quiet the Mind.* San Francisco, 2000.

Bryan-Wilson, Julia. *Art Workers: Radical Practice in the Vietnam War Era.* Berkeley, 2009.

Butler, Cornelia. *Figure 3: Paul Sietsema.* Museum of Modern Art, New York, 2009.

Cahan, Susan E. *I Remember Heaven: Jim Hodges and Andy Warhol.* Contemporary Art Museum St. Louis, 2007.

Castagnoli, Pier Giovanni, Ida Gianelli, and Beatrice Merz. *Mario Merz.* Fondazione Merz, Turin, 2006.

Causey, Andrew. *Edward Burra: Complete Catalogue.* Oxford, 1985.

Celant, Germano. *Claes Oldenburg: An Anthology.* Solomon R. Guggenheim Museum, New York, 1995.

Chametzky, Peter. *Objects as History in Twentieth-Century German Art: Beckmann to Beuys.* Berkeley, 2010.

Charlesworth, Sarah. *Modern History (Second Reading).* New 57 Gallery, Edinburgh, 1979.

Cohen, Arthur A. *Herbert Bayer: The Complete Work.* Cambridge, MA, 1984.

Cortissoz, Royal. *American Artists.* New York, 1932.

Cottington, David. "Cubism, Aestheticism, Modernism." In *Picasso and Braque: A Symposium,* edited by William Rubin, Kirk Varnedoe, and Lynn Zelevansky, 58–72. Museum of Modern Art, New York, 1992.

Crow, Thomas. "Saturday Disasters: Trace and Reference in Early Warhol." In *Modern Art in the Common Culture,* 49–65. New Haven, 1996.

De Antonio, Emile, and Mitch Tuchman. *Painters Painting: A Candid History of the Modern Art Scene, 1940–1970.* New York, 1984.

De Witte, Ludo. *The Assassination of Lumumba.* Translated by Ann Wright and Renée Fenby. London, 2001.

Deleuze, Gilles. *The Fold: Leibniz and the Baroque.* Translated by Tom Conley. Minneapolis, 1993.

Dickerman, Leah. *Dada.* National Gallery of Art, Washington, 2005.

Dietrich, Dorothea. *The Collages of Kurt Schwitters: Tradition and Innovation.* Cambridge, 1993.

Dobke, Dirk, Dieter Roth, and Thomas Kellein. *Dieter Roth Books + Multiples: Catalogue Raisonné.* Baden, Switzerland, 2004.

Doherty, Brigid. "Berlin." In *Dada,* edited by Leah Dickerman, 87–112. National Gallery of Art, Washington, 2005.

Donovan, Molly. *Warhol: Headlines.* National Gallery of Art, Washington, 2011.

Doswald, Christoph, ed. *Press Art: Sammlung Annette und Peter Noble.* Kunstmuseum St. Gallen, Switzerland, 2010.

Dunlop, Ian. *The Shock of the New: Seven Historic Exhibitions of Modern Art.* London, 1972.

Durant, Sam, ed. *Black Panther: The Revolutionary Art of Emory Douglas.* New York, 2007.

Elderfield, John. *Kurt Schwitters.* London, 1985.

Elger, Dietmar. *Felix González-Torres.* 2 vols. Sprengel Museum Hannover, 1997.

Enwezor, Okwui. *Archive Fever: Uses of the Document in Contemporary Art.* New York, 2008.

Evans, David. *John Heartfield, AIZ: Arbeiter-Illustriete Zeitung, Volks Illustrierte, 1930–38.* New York, 1992.

Fanés, Félis. *Dalí: Mass Culture.* Museo Nacional Centro de Arte Reina Sofía, Madrid, 2004.

Fergonzi, Flavio. "Carlo Carrà, *Pursuit* (*Horse and Rider*); *Inseguimento* (*Cavallo e cavaliere*), 1915." In *The Mattioli Collection: Masterpieces of the Italian Avant-Garde; Catalogue Raisonné,* 217–229. Milan, 2003.

Flood, Richard, and Frances Morris, eds. *Zero to Infinity: Arte Povera, 1962–1972.* Walker Art Center, Minneapolis, 2001.

Fogle, Douglas. *Life on Mars: 55th Carnegie International.* Carnegie Museum of Art, Pittsburgh, 2008.

Foster, Hal. "Death in America." *October* 75 (Winter 1996): 37–59.

———. *The First Pop Age: Painting and Subjectivity in the Art of Hamilton, Lichtenstein, Warhol, Richter, and Ruscha.* Princeton, 2012.

Foster, Stephen C., ed. *Hans Richter: Activism, Modernism, and the Avant-Garde.* Cambridge, MA, 1998.

Freundschuh, Aaron. "'New Sport' in the Street: Self-Defence, Security and Space in Belle Epoque Paris." *French History* 20, no. 4 (December 2006): 424–441.

Fry, Edward F. *Cubism.* New York, 1966.

Gifford, Don, and Robert T. Seidman. Ulysses Annotated: *Notes for James Joyce's* Ulysses, 2nd edition, revised and enlarged by Don Gifford. Berkeley, 1988.

Catholic League for Religious and Civil Rights. "Gober Art Is More than Queer— It's a Hoax." http://www.catholicleague.org/gober-art-is-more-than queer%E2%80%94it%E2%80%99s-a-hoax/ (accessed March 16, 2012).

Godfrey, Mark. "Across the Universe." In *Light Years: Conceptual Art and the Photograph, 1964–1977,* edited by Matthew S. Witkovsky, 57–65. Art Institute of Chicago, 2011.

Grachos, Louis, and Susan Fisher Sterling. *Sarah Charlesworth: A Retrospective.* SITE Santa Fe, 1997.

Green, Lynn, George Melly, and Andrew Causey. *Edward Burra.* Hayward Gallery, London, 1985.

Greenberg, Clement. "Collage." 1959. Reprinted in *Art and Culture: Critical Essays,* 70–83. Boston, 1965.

———. "The Pasted-Paper Revolution." *Art News* 57, no. 5 (September 1958): 46–49, 60–61.

Greenough, Sarah. *Modern Art and America: Alfred Stieglitz and His New York Galleries.* National Gallery of Art, Washington, 2000.

Greenwall, Harry J. *Scoops: Being Leaves from the Diary of a Special Correspondent.* New York, 1923.

Guéry, Louis. *Visages de la presse: La présentation des journaux des origines à nos jours.* Paris, 1997.

Hapgood, Susan. *Neo-Dada: Redefining Art, 1958–62.* American Federation of Arts, New York, 1992.

Harlan, Volker. *Soziale Plastik: Materialien zu Joseph Beuys.* Achberg, Germany, 1984.

Hendricks, John. *Fluxus Codex.* Detroit, 1988.

Hess, Thomas B. "8 Excellent, 20 Good, 133 Others." *ARTnews* 48 (Janaury 1950): 34–35, 57–58.

Higgins, Shaun O'L., and Colleen Striegel. *Press Gallery: The Newspaper in Modern and Postmodern Art.* Spokane, 2005.

Hoernle, Edwin. "Das Auge des Arbeiters." 1930. Reprinted as "The Working Man's Eye." In *Germany: The New Photography, 1927–33,* edited by David Mellor, 47–49. London, 1978.

Hopps, Walter. *Robert Rauschenberg: The Early 1950s.* Menil Collection, Houston, 1991.

Horowitz, Frederick A., and Brenda Danilowitz. *Josef Albers: To Open Eyes: The Bauhaus, Black Mountain College, and Yale.* London, 2006.

Hughes, Robert. *The Shock of the New: Art and the Century of Change.* London, 1980.

Hugonnier, Marine. *A Film Trilogy.* Philadelphia Museum of Art, 2007.

Hultén, Pontus. *Futurismo e futurismi.* Palazzo Grassi, Venice, 1986.

Hung, Jochen. "'Der deutschen Jugend!' The Newspaper *Tempo* and the Public Discourse on the 'Young Generation.'" Paper presented at the German History Society Annual Conference 2011, King's College London, September 8–10, 2011, http://www.jochenhung.de/academic/papers/Deutsche%20Jugend/Deutsche%20Jugend.html (accessed January 16, 2012).

Jenkins, Janet, ed. *The Photomontages of Hannah Höch.* Walker Art Center, Minneapolis, 1996.

Johns, Jasper. Interview by David Bourdon, 1977. In *Jasper Johns: Writings, Sketchbook Notes, Interviews,* edited by Kirk Varnedoe, 155–162. New York, 1996.

Joyce, James. *Ulysses.* 1922. Reprint, New York, 1934.

Kahn, Douglas. *John Heartfield: Art and Mass Media.* New York, 1985.

Kaprow, Allan. "The Legacy of Jackson Pollock." *Art News* 57, no. 2 (October 1958): 24–26, 55–57.

Katz, Jonathan. "The Art of Code: Jasper Johns and Robert Rauschenberg." In *Significant Others: Creativity and Intimate Partnership,* edited by Whitney Chadwick and Isabelle de Courtivron, 189–207. New York, 1992.

———. "Jasper Johns' *Alley Oop:* On Comic Strips and Camouflage." 2009. http://www.queerculturalcenter.org/Pages/KatzPages/Katzoops.html (accessed February 1, 2012).

Kelly, Ellsworth. "Notes from 1969." In *Theories and Documents of Contemporary Art: A Sourcebook of Artists' Writings,* edited by Kristine Stiles and Peter Selz, 92–93. Berkeley, 1996.

Kershner, R. Brandon. *The Culture of Joyce's* Ulysses. New York, 2010.

Kotz, Liz. *Words to Be Looked At: Language in 1960s Art.* Cambridge, MA, 2007.

Kraus, Karl. "Aphorism 411." In *Dicta and Contradicta,* translated by Jonathan McVity, 51. Champaign, IL, 2001.

Krauss, Rosalind. "The Motivation of the Sign." In *Picasso and Braque: A Symposium,* edited by William Rubin, Kirk Varnedoe, and Lynn Zelevansky, 261–286. Museum of Modern Art, New York, 1992.

———. *The Picasso Papers.* London, 1998.

Kriebel, Sabine. "Manufacturing Discontent: John Heartfield's Mass Medium." *New German Critique* 107 (Summer 2009): 53–88.

———. "Revolutionary Beauty: John Heartfield, Political Photomontage, and the Crisis of the European Left, 1929–1938." PhD diss., University of California, Berkeley, 2003.

Kyle, Chris R., and Jason Peacey. *Breaking News: Renaissance Journalism and the Birth of the Newspaper.* Folger Shakespeare Library, Washington, 2008.

Lamelas, David. Interview by Fay Nicholson. *Nottingham Visual Arts Magazine,* July 8, 2009. http://www.nottinghamvisualarts.net/articles/jul08/274/outside-frame-interview-david-lamelas (accessed September 2011).

Lavin, Maud. *Clean New World: Culture, Politics, and Graphic Design.* Cambridge, MA, 2001.

———. *Cut with the Kitchen Knife: The Weimar Photomontages of Hannah Höch.* New Haven, 1993.

Leighten, Patricia. "Cubist Anachronisms: Ahistoricity, Cryptoformalism, and Business-as-Usual in New York." *Oxford Art Journal* 17, no. 2 (1994): 91–102.

———. "Picasso's Collages and the Threat of War, 1912–1913." *Art Bulletin* 67, no. 4 (December 1985): 653–672.

———. *Re-Ordering the Universe: Picasso and Anarchism, 1897–1914.* Princeton, 1989.

Lenin, Vladimir I. "Where to Begin?" *Iskra,* no. 4 (May 1901). Reprinted in *May 1901–Feb. 1902.* Vol. 5 of *V. I. Lenin Collected Work,* edited

142

by Victor Jerome, translated by Joe Fineberg and George Hanna, 17–24. London, 1961.

Lista, Giovanni. *Futurisme: Manifestes, proclamations, documents.* Lausanne, 1973.

———. "Genesis and Analysis of Marinetti's 'Manifesto of Futurism,' 1908–1909." In *Futurism,* edited by Didier Ottinger, 78–83. Centre Pompidou, Paris, 2009.

Makela, Maria. "By Design: The Early Work of Hannah Höch in Context." In *The Photomontages of Hannah Höch,* edited by Maria Makela and Peter Boswell, 49–79. Walker Art Center, Minneapolis, 1996.

Mallarmé, Stéphane. "L'action restreinte." 1895. In *Oeuvres complètes*, edited by Henri Mondor and G. Jean-Aubry, 369–373. Paris, 1945.

———. "Action Restricted." 1895. Translated by Mary Ann Caws. In *Mallarme: Selected Poetry and Prose*, edited by Mary Ann Caws, 77–80. New York, 1982.

———. "The Book: A Spiritual Instrument." 1895. Translated by Bradford Cook. In *Mallarmé, Stéphane: Selected Poetry and Prose*, edited by Mary Ann Caws, 80–84. New York, 1982.

———. "The Book as Spiritual Instrument." 1895. In *Divagations*, translated by Barbara Johnson, 226–230. Cambridge, MA, 2007.

———. "Le livre: instrument spirituel." 1895. In *Oeuvres complètes*, edited by Henri Mondor and G. Jean-Aubry, 378–382. Paris, 1945.

———. "Le mystére dans les lettres." 1896. In *Oeuvres complètes*, edited by Henri Mondor and G. Jean-Aubry, 382–387. Paris, 1945.

———. "The Mystery in Letters." 1896. In *Divagations*, translated by Barbara Johnson, 231–236. Cambridge, MA, 2007.

Marinetti, F. T. "The Founding and Manifesto of Futurism." In *Futurism: An Anthology*, edited by Lawrence Rainey, Christine Poggi, and Laura Wittman, 49–53. New Haven, 2009.

Martin, Marianne W. *Futurist Art and Theory: 1909–1915.* Oxford, 1968.

McCabe, Cynthia Jaffee. *Hans Richter's* Stalingrad (Victory in the East). Hirshhorn Museum and Sculpture Garden, Washington, 1980.

McVity, Jonathan. "The Twist: *Dicta and Contradicta* in Context." In Karl Kraus, *Dicta and Contradicta,* translated by Jonathan McVity, 129–160. Champaign, IL, 2001.

Meyer, James. *Minimalism: Art and Polemics in the Sixties.* New Haven, 2001.

Micchelli, Thomas. "Life on Mars: 55th Carnegie International." *Brooklyn Rail* (September 2008), http://brooklynrail.org/2008/09/artseen/life-on-mars-55th-carnegie-international (accessed February 7, 2012).

Ministerio de Cultura, Museo Nacional Reina Sofía. *Marcel Broodthaers.* Museo Nacional Reina Sofía, Madrid, 1992.

Molesworth, Helen. "Before *Bed.*" *October* 63 (Winter 1993): 68–82.

Monod-Fontaine, Isabelle, and E. A. Carmean Jr. *Braque: The Papiers Collés.* National Gallery of Art, Washington, 1982.

Musée d'art moderne de Saint-Etienne. *Raoul Hausmann.* Musée d'art moderne de Saint-Etienne, 1994.

Naumann, Francis. "Cryptography and the Arensberg Circle." *Arts Magazine* 51, no. 9 (May 1977): 127–133.

———. "Man Ray and America: The New York and Ridgefield Years: 1907–1921." PhD diss., City University of New York, 1988.

Newman, Michael, and Jon Bird. *Rewriting Conceptual Art.* London, 1999.

Nieto, Margarita, and Louis Stern. *Alfredo Ramos Martinez and Modernismo.* West Hollywood, CA, 2009.

North, Percy. "Bringing Cubism to America: Max Weber and Pablo Picasso." *American Art* 14, no. 3 (Autumn 2000): 59–77.

———. *Max Weber: American Modern.* Jewish Museum, New York, 1982.

———. *Max Weber: The Cubist Decade, 1910–1920.* High Museum of Art, Atlanta, 1991.

Nzongola-Ntalaja, Georges. *The Congo from Leopold to Kabila: A People's History.* London, 2002.

O'Donnell, Edward T. *Ship Ablaze: The Tragedy of the Steamboat General Slocum.* New York, 2003.

Oldenburg, Claes. Recorded interview by Anne Reeve, October 27, 2009. Glenstone, Potomac, MD.

Ottinger, Didier. "Cubism + Futurism = Cubofuturism." In *Futurism,* edited by Didier Ottinger, 20–41. Centre Pompidou, Paris, 2009.

Phillips, Lisa. "Sarah Charlesworth: Rite of Passage." In *Sarah Charlesworth: A Retrospective,* edited by Louis Grachos and Susan Fisher Sterling, 38–47. SITE Santa Fe, 1998.

Piper, Adrian. *Out of Order, Out of Sight.* 2 vols. Cambridge, MA, 1996.

Poggi, Christine. *In Defiance of Painting: Cubism, Futurism, and the Invention of Collage.* New Haven, 1992.

———. *Inventing Futurism: The Art and Politics of Artificial Optimism.* Princeton, 2009.

———. "*Lacerba:* Interventionist Art and Politics in Pre-World War I Italy." In *Art and Journals on the Political Front, 1910–40,* edited by Virginia Hagelstein Marquardt, 17–62. Gainesville, FL, 1997.

———. "Mallarmé, Picasso, and the Newspaper as Commodity." *Yale Journal of Criticism* 1, no. 1 (Fall 1987): 133–151.

Powell, Kirsten Hoving. "Resurrecting Content in de Kooning's *Easter Monday.*" *American Art* 4, no. 3/4 (Summer–Autumn 1990): 86–101.

Prather, Marla. *Willem de Kooning: Paintings.* National Gallery of Art, Washington, 1994.

Rainey, Lawrence S., Christine Poggi, and Laura Wittman, eds. *Futurism: An Anthology.* New Haven, 2009.

Restany, Pierre. *Chryssa.* New York, 1978.

Retallack, Joan, ed. *Musicage: Cage Muses on Words, Art, Music.* Hanover, NH, 1996.

Richardson, Brenda. *Mel Bochner: Number and Shape.* Baltimore Museum of Art, 1976.

———. *A Robert Gober Lexicon.* 2 vols. Matthew Marks Gallery, New York, 2005.

Richardson, John, with the collaboration of Marilyn McCully. *A Life of Picasso.* Vol. 2: *1907–1917.* New York, 1996.

Robinson, Julia E. *Claes Oldenburg: Early Work.* Zwirner and Wirth, 2005.

Rondeau, James, and Douglas Druick. *Jasper Johns: Gray.* Art Institute of Chicago, 2007.

Rose, Bernice, Michelle White, and Gary Garrels. *Richard Serra Drawing: A Retrospective.* Menil Collection, Houston, 2011.

Rosenblum, Robert. *Cubism and Twentieth-Century Art.* New York, 1960.

———. "Picasso and the Coronation of Alexander III: A Note on the Dating of Some *Papiers Collés.*" *Burlington Magazine* 113, no. 823 (October 1971): 602, 604–607.

———. "Picasso and the Typography of Cubism." In *Picasso in Retrospect,* edited by Roland Penrose and John Golding, 49–75. London, 1973.

Roth, Nancy Ann. "The Politics of Collaboration: Brothers, Friends, the Party, and the Performance of John Heartfield, 1915–1938." PhD diss., City University of New York, 1996.

Rubin, William. *Picasso and Braque: Pioneering Cubism.* Museum of Modern Art, New York, 1989.

Rubin, William, Kirk Varnedoe, and Lynn Zelevansky, eds. *Picasso and Braque: A Symposium.* Museum of Modern Art, New York, 1992.

Sandarg, Robert. "Jean Genet and the Black Panther Party." *Journal of Black Studies* 16, no. 3 (March 1986): 269–282.

Schampers, Karel. *On Kawara: Date Paintings in 89 Cities.* Museum Boijmans Van Beuningen, Rotterdam, 1992.

Schnapp, Jeffrey T. "A Preface to Futurism (on the 100-year anniversary of the publication of the *Foundation and Manifesto of Futurism*)." *Modernism/Modernity* 16, no. 2 (April 2009): 203–209.

Schneemann, Carolee. *More than Meat Joy: Complete Performance Works and Selected Writings.* Edited by Bruce McPherson. New York, 1979.

Schultz, Deborah. *Marcel Broodthaers: Strategy and Dialogue.* Oxford, 2007.

Schwarz, Arturo. *Man Ray: The Rigour of Imagination.* New York, 1977.

Schwarz, Dieter. "'Look! Books in Plaster!': On the First Phase of the Works of Marcel Broodthaers." *October* 42 (Fall 1987): 57–66.

Shannon, Joshua. "Claes Oldenburg's *The Street* and Urban Renewal in Greenwich Village, 1960." *Art Bulletin* 86, no. 1 (March 2004): 136–161.

Simmons, Sherwin. "Picture as Weapon in the German Mass Media, 1914–1930." In *Art and Journals on the Political Front, 1910–1940,* edited by Virginia Hagelstein Marquardt, 142–182. Gainesville, FL, 1997.

Smith, Cherise. "Re-Member the Audience: Adrian Piper's Mythic Being Advertisements." *Art Journal* 66, no. 1 (2007): 46–58.

Starr, Paul. *The Creation of the Media: Political Origins of Modern Communications.* New York, 2004.

Stedelijk Van Abbemuseum. *Douglas Huebler.* Van Abbemuseum, Eindhoven, 1979.

Steinberg, Leo. Commentary in "Discussion." In *Picasso and Braque: A Symposium,* edited by William Rubin, Kirk Varnedoe, and Lynn Zelevansky, 77–78. Museum of Modern Art, New York, 1992.

Stevens, Mark, and Annalyn Swan. *De Kooning: An American Master.* New York, 2004.

Sussman, Elisabeth, and Lynn Zelevansky. *Paul Thek: Diver, a Retrospective.* Whitney Museum of Modern Art, New York, 2010.

Taylor, Brandon. *Collage: The Making of Modern Art.* New York, 2004.

Teicher, Hendel, ed. *Cut-Outs and Cut-Ups: Hans Christian Andersen and William Seward Burroughs.* Irish Museum of Modern Art, Dublin, 2008.

Temkin, Ann, and Bernice Rose. *Thinking Is Form: The Drawings of Joseph Beuys.* Philadelphia Museum of Art, 1993.

Terdiman, Richard. "Newspaper Culture: Institutions of Discourse; Discourse of Institutions." In *Discourse/Counter-Discourse: The Theory and Practice of Symbolic Resistance in Nineteenth-Century France,* edited by Richard Terdiman, 117–146. Ithaca, NY, 1985.

Thogmartin, Clyde. *The National Daily Press of France.* Birmingham, AL, 1998.

Tisdall, Caroline. *Joseph Beuys.* Solomon R. Guggenheim Museum, New York, 1979.

Tomkins, Calvin. *Off the Wall: Robert Rauschenberg and the Art of Our Time.* Garden City, NY, 1980.

Tramar, [Comtesse de]. *L'amour obligatoire, les étapes de la vie d'une femme, la carrier de l'homme.* Paris, 1909.

Tuma, Kathryn A. "The Color and Compass of Things: Paul Cézanne and the Early Work of Jasper Johns." In *Jasper Johns: An Alle-*

gory of Painting, 1955–1965, edited by Jeffrey Weiss, 170–187. National Gallery of Art, Washington, 2007.

Tzara, Tristan. "Le papier collé ou le proverbe en peinture." 1931. Reprinted as "The Pasted Paper or the Proverb in Painting." In *The Surrealists Look at Art: Eluard, Aragon, Soupault, Breton, Tzara,* edited by Pontus Hultén, 217–220. Venice, CA, 1990.

Umland, Anne. *Picasso Guitars, 1912–1914.* Museum of Modern Art, New York, 2011.

Upright, Diane. *Ellsworth Kelly: Works on Paper.* Fort Worth Art Museum, 1987.

Varnedoe, Kirk. *Jasper Johns: A Retrospective.* Museum of Modern Art, New York, 1996.

Varnedoe, Kirk, and Adam Gopnik. *High and Low: Modern Art and Popular Culture.* Museum of Modern Art, New York, 1990.

Vischer, Theodora, and Bernadette Walter. *Roth Time: A Dieter Roth Retrospective.* Museum of Modern Art, New York, 2004.

Wagner-Pacifici, Robin Erica. *The Moro Morality Play: Terrorism as Social Drama.* Chicago, 1986.

Waldman, Diane. *Collage, Assemblage, and the Found Object.* New York, 1992.

Warhol, Andy, and Pat Hackett. *POPism: The Warhol '60s.* New York, 1980.

Wayland-Smith, Ellen. "Passing Fashion: Mallarmé and the Future of Poetry in the Age of Mechanical Reproduction." *MLN* 117 (2002): 887–907.

Weber, Ronald. *News of Paris: American Journalists in the City of Light Between the Wars.* Chicago, 2006.

Weiss, Jeffrey. *Jasper Johns: An Allegory of Painting, 1955–1965.* National Gallery of Art, Washington, 2007.

———. *The Popular Culture of Modern Art: Picasso, Duchamp, and Avant-Gardism.* New Haven, 1994.

Witkovsky, Matthew S. "Avant-Garde and Center: Devětsil in Czech Culture, 1918–1938." PhD diss., University of Pennsylvania, 2002.

Wolf, Erika. "Selected New Acquisitions." *Zimmerli Journal* 2 (Fall 2004): 106–117.

———. "The Soviet Union: From Worker to Proletarian Photography." In *The Worker Photography Movement (1926–1939): Essay and Documents,* edited by Jorge Ribalta, 32–46. Madrid, 2011.

Wolfram, Eddie. *History of Collage: An Anthology of Collage, Assemblage and Event Structures.* London, 1975.

Young, Joseph E. "Jasper Johns: An Appraisal." *Art International* 13, no. 7 (September 1969): 50–56.

ACKNOWLEDGMENTS

Judith Brodie

The inception of this project dates back to the summer of 2007 and a conversation I had with my National Gallery of Art colleague Molly Donovan, curator of the exhibition *Warhol: Headlines*, which opened at the Gallery in 2011. Warhol's interest in the tabloids prompted me to think about organizing a small exhibition focused on the newspaper's impact on modern art. My thought was to draw from the Gallery's collection and supplement the selection with a few borrowed works. It was not long before I realized that the subject begged for deeper inquiry and that I would need to borrow important works from private and public collections. Five years hence, I have accrued many debts.

My profound thanks go to the lenders of artworks who graciously endured questions, visits, paperwork, scheduling, and more. I especially want to acknowledge Michael Baumgartner of the Zentrum Paul Klee, Merrill C. Berman, Mariano Boggia of Archivio Merz, Mary Beth and Walter Buck, Alvin Friedman-Kien, Tony Ganz, Alexander Groenert of the Museum Schloss Moyland, Christine Schuster Husser, Anette Kruszynski of the Kunstsammlung Nordrhein-Westfalen, Ursula Ohnesorge Martin-Malburet, Isabel Schulz of the Sprengel Museum Hannover, Barbara Wien, and Christian Wolsdorff of the Bauhaus-Archiv Berlin.

Curators rarely have uninterrupted time for research. Thus it was an enormous privilege to spend four glorious months in 2010 as a Clark Fellow at the Sterling and Francine Clark Art Institute. My thanks go especially to Michael Ann Holly, Starr Director of Research and Academic Program at the Clark, as well as Mark Ledbury, Melina Doerring, Karen Bucky, and Camran Mani.

Many generous people at artists' studios and foundations, commercial galleries, museums, and private collections went out of their way to be helpful: Dirk Armstrong of the Salvador Dalí Museum; Emily Braun; Ralf Burmeister and Annelie Lütgens of the Berlinische Galerie; Maureen Bray of the Sean Kelly Gallery; Jack Brown of the Art Institute of Chicago; Connie Butler, Kathy Curry, Lucy Gallun, Blair Hartzell, and Anne Umland of the Museum of Modern Art, New York; Jacquie Cartwright and Trevor Noble of Lefevre Fine Art; Barbara Bertozzi Castelli of the Leo Castelli Gallery; John Connelly of the Felix Gonzalez-Torres Foundation; Jacqueline Crist and Andrea Merrell of the James Castle Collection and Archive; Brenda Danilowitz of the Josef and Anni Albers Foundation; Stephanie Dorsey of the Matthew Marks Gallery; Michael Findlay of Acquavella Galleries; Moira Fitzgerald and Kevin Repp of the Beinecke Rare Book Library; Benoit Forgeot; Carter Foster of the Whitney Museum of American Art; Jeannie Freilich of the Gladstone Gallery; Jan Grosfeld; Brad Hampton and Cooper Holoweski at Laurie Anderson's studio; Jay Heuman of the Salt Lake Art Center; Sandi Knakal and Eva Huber Walters at Ellsworth Kelly's studio; Bob Monk of the Gagosian Gallery; Peter Nobel; Ann-Sofi Noring of the Moderna Museet; Laura Paulson; Marc Payot and Mirella Roma of Hauser & Wirth; Anne Reeve of Glenstone; Philip Rylands and Paul Schwartzbaum of the Peggy Guggenheim Collection; Louis Stern of Louis Stern Fine Arts; Solana Molina Viamonte of the Ruth Benzacar Galería de Arte; Catherine Whitney of the Gerald Peters Gallery; Lyle W. Williams of the McNay Art Museum; and Amy Worthen of the Des Moines Art Center.

One of the privileges of being a curator of modern art is the opportunity to work with artists. Those who kept me honest were Laurie Anderson, Mel Bochner, Sarah Charlesworth, Emory Douglas, Ellsworth Kelly, Jorge Macchi, and Kim Rugg.

Another privilege is partnering with authors who share one's passion. In that regard, I could not have had a more congenial or inspired team. My sincere appreciation goes to Sarah Boxer, Janine Mileaf, Christine Poggi, and Matthew Witkovsky for their groundbreaking essays.

Many scholars and knowledgeable individuals not only shared information but shed light on my thinking: Timothy O. Benson on Raoul Hausmann, Roberta Bernstein on Jasper Johns, Annie Bourneuf on Paul Klee, Dennis Brack and Hugh Price on newspaper design and production, Kathan Brown on John Cage, Jessica Helfand on the modernist grid, Jochen Hung on the history of newspapers, Lewis Kachur on Georges Braque, Sabine Kriebel and Mark Levitch on John Heartfield, Maria Makela on Hannah Höch, Francis Naumann on Man Ray, Percy North on Max Weber, Gabriel Pérez-Barreiro on Jorge Macchi, Julia Robinson on Fluxus, Deborah Roldán on *L'Opinió*, Margarita Tupitsyn on Soviet art, Jeffrey Weiss on Picasso, and Erika Wolf on Semen Fridliand. For foreign-language translations, I called upon Lindsay Harris, Marta Horgan, Liliana Milkova, Giselle Larroque Obermeier, Ismail Sentissi El Idrissi, and especially Linda Parshall.

At the National Gallery, my appreciation goes to director Earl A. Powell III and deputy director and chief curator Franklin Kelly for their support. I am likewise grateful to Andrew Robison, A.W. Mellon Senior Curator of Prints and Drawings, who showed enthusiasm for the project from the outset and granted me flexibility when deadlines loomed. To D. Dodge Thompson, chief of exhibitions, and Jennifer Cipriano, exhibition officer, I offer my sincere thanks, as well as to Susan Arensberg, Lynn Matheny, Allison Keilman, and Lauren Mecca. Mark Leithauser, chief of design, and Jamé Anderson, architect, are to be credited for the exhibition's sensitive design. Gordon Anson and Jon Frederick, also in the design department, could not have been more accommodating.

As always, registrar Michelle Fondas demonstrated the utmost professionalism. Chief of conservation, Mervin Richard, and paper conservator, Michelle Facini, not only facilitated loans of works but looked after their safety, as did preparator Virginia Ritchie. I am grateful for the resourcefulness of chief development officer Christine Myers and her colleagues Cathryn Scoville, Patricia Donovan, and Jeanette Crangle Beers, as well as for the tireless efforts of Deborah Ziska, chief press and publication officer, and her deputy, Anabeth Guthrie.

My colleagues in the department of modern prints and drawings were continually supportive. Warm thanks go to Amy Johnston, Carlotta Owens, Charles Ritchie, former curatorial assistant Josephine Rodgers, and former academic-year intern Olujimi Akili Tommasino. For their support, I also want to thank my colleagues in the department of modern and contemporary art: Harry Cooper, Molly Donovan, and James Meyer, as well as former curatorial assistant Sydney Skelton.

This catalogue, no less than the exhibition, was a collaborative effort. My deep appreciation goes to editor in chief Judy Metro and deputy publisher Chris Vogel. Laura Jones Dooley edited the catalogue with precision, and senior editor Tam Curry Bryfogle brought the project to completion with her usual thoughtfulness. Designer Wendy Schleicher created a catalogue that surpassed my expectations. Sara Sanders-Buell secured images and permissions for works in the exhibition, as Ira Bartfield, Kate Mayo, and Mariah Shay did for comparative illustrations.

Marek Ożyhar, an intern at the National Gallery in 2009–2010, played a critical role in getting *Shock of the News* off the ground and shaping its content. Adam Greenhalgh, Andrew W. Mellon Postdoctoral Curatorial Fellow, not only came to my rescue as this catalogue was nearing completion but treated it as if it were his own. For their critical input and encouragement, my heartfelt thanks go to Linda and Peter Parshall. And my deepest gratitude goes to Merv Richard, who cheered me on throughout and selflessly flew solo during countless weekends.

ARTISTS IN THE EXHIBITION

Laurie Anderson (American, born 1947), pl. 50
Jean (Hans) Arp (French, born Germany [Alsace], 1886–1966), pl. 35
Eugen Batz (German, 1905–1986), pl. 15
Herbert Bayer (American, born Austria, 1900–1985), pl. 36
Thomas Bayerle (German, born 1937), pl. 20
Joseph Beuys (German, 1921–1986), pl. 45
Mel Bochner (American, born 1940), pl. 56
Georges Braque (French, 1882–1963), pl. 3
Bazon Brock (German, born 1936), pl. 20
Marcel Broodthaers (Belgian, 1924–1976), pl. 46
Edward Burra (British, 1905–1976), pl. 41
John Cage (American, 1912–1992), pl. 17
Carlo Carrà (Italian, 1881–1966), pl. 5
James Castle (American, 1899–1977), pl. 40
Sarah Charlesworth (American, born 1947), pl. 26
Salvador Dalí (Spanish, 1904–1989), pl. 21
Stephen Dean (American, born France, 1968), pl. 57
Emory Douglas (American, born 1943), pl. 49
Arthur Dove (American, 1880–1946), pl. 10
Jean Dubuffet (French, 1901–1985), pl. 47
Fluxus (collective, founded 1962), pl. 23
Semen Fridliand (Russian, 1905–1964), pl. 32
Robert Gober (American, born 1954), pls. 28, 29
Felix Gonzalez-Torres (American, born Cuba, 1957–1996), pl. 54
Juan Gris (Spanish, 1887–1927), pl. 4
Guerrilla Girls (collective, founded 1985), pl. 58
Raoul Hausmann (Austrian, 1886–1971), pl. 9
John Heartfield (German, 1891–1968), pl. 8
Jim Hodges (American, born 1957), pl. 31
Gerhard Hoehme (German, 1920–1989), pl. 44
Douglas Huebler (American, 1924–1997), pl. 25
Marine Hugonnier (French, born 1969), pl. 60
Bernhard Jäger (German, born 1935), pl. 20
Jasper Johns (American, born 1930), pl. 18
On Kawara (Japanese, born 1933), pl. 55
Ellsworth Kelly (American, born 1923), pl. 14
Paul Klee (Swiss, 1879–1940), pl. 39
Willem de Kooning (American, born the Netherlands, 1904–1997), pl. 52
Yves Klein (French, 1928–1962), pl. 22
El Lissitzky (Russian, 1890–1941), pl. 37
Jorge Macchi (Argentine, born 1963), pl. 27
Filippo Tommaso Marinetti (Italian, 1876–1974), pl. 1
Alfredo Ramos Martinez (Mexican, 1871–1946), pl. 42
Mario Merz (Italian, 1925–2003), pl. 59
Robert Morris (American, born 1931), pl. 19
Claes Oldenburg (American, born Sweden, 1929), pl. 48
Pablo Picasso (Spanish, 1881–1973), pls. 2, 6, 13
Adrian Piper (American, born 1948), pl. 53
Robert Rauschenberg (American, 1925–2008), pl. 16
Man Ray (American, 1890–1976), pl. 7
Hans Richter (German, 1888–1976), pl. 11
Dieter Roth (Swiss, born Germany, 1930–1998), pl. 43
Kim Rugg (Canadian, born 1963), pl. 61
Kurt Schwitters (German, 1887–1948), pl. 12
Sergei Sen'kin (Russian, 1894–1963), pl. 37
Paul Sietsema (American, born 1968), pl. 30
Ardengo Soffici (Italian, 1879–1964), pl. 34
Spanish 20th Century, pl. 38
Paul Thek (American, 1933–1988), pl. 51
Andy Warhol (American, 1928–1987), pl. 24
Max Weber (American, 1881–1961), pl. 33

INDEX

Note: Page numbers in italic type indicate illustrations.

L

M

N

O

P

R

PHOTOGRAPHIC CREDITS

Every effort has been made to locate the copyright holders for the photographs used in this book. Any omissions will be corrected in subsequent editions.

Plates

pl. 2: © 2012 Estate of Pablo Picasso / Artists Rights Society (ARS), New York

pl. 3: © 2012 Artists Rights Society (ARS), New York / ADAGP, Paris

pl. 4: Photographer Walter Klein

pl. 5: Photograph © 2010 The Solomon R. Guggenheim Foundation; photographer David Heald

pls. 6, 13: © 2012 Estate of Pablo Picasso / Artists Rights Society (ARS), New York; Stinehour Photography

pl. 8: Copy photograph © The Metropolitan Museum of Art

pl. 10: Courtesy of and copyright The Estate of Arthur G. Dove; photographer Steven Sloman

pl. 11: Photographer John Tennant

pl. 12: © 2012 Artists Rights Society (ARS), New York / VG Bild-Kunst, Bonn; photograph courtesy Kurt Schwitters Archive at the Sprengel Museum Hannover, photographer Michael Herling,

pl. 14: © Ellsworth Kelly

pl. 15: Bauhaus-Archiv Berlin

pl. 16: Art © Estate of Robert Rauschenberg / Licensed by VAGA, New York, NY; Digital Image © The Museum of Modern Art / Licensed by SCALA / Art Resource, NY

pl. 18: Art © Jasper Johns / Licensed by VAGA, New York, NY

pl. 19: © 2012 Robert Morris / Artists Rights Society (ARS), New York; photograph courtesy the artist and Castelli Gallery

pls. 20, 57, 58, 60, 61: Image courtesy of the Board of Trustees, National Gallery of Art, Washington, photographer Ric Blanc

pl. 21: © Salvador Dalí. Fundación Gala-Salvador Dalí, 2012

pl. 22: Image courtesy of the Board of Trustees, National Gallery of Art, Washington, photographer Erica Abbey

pl. 24: © 2012 The Andy Warhol Foundation for the Visual Arts, Inc. / Artists Rights Society (ARS), New York; photograph courtesy Gagosian Gallery, photographer Robert McKeever

pl. 25: © 2012 Douglas Huebler, courtesy Darcy Huebler / Artists Rights Society (ARS), New York; Digital Image © The Museum of Modern Art / Licensed by SCALA / Art Resource, NY

pl. 26: Copyright Sarah Charlesworth

pls. 27, 29: Image courtesy of the Board of Trustees, National Gallery of Art, Washington

pl. 28: © Robert Gober; photograph courtesy Matthew Marks Gallery

pl. 30: © Paul Sietsma; photograph courtesy Regen Projects, Los Angeles

pl. 31: © Jim Hodges; photograph courtesy Gladstone Gallery, New York and Brussels

pl. 32: Image courtesy of the Board of Trustees, National Gallery of Art, Washington, photographer Lea Ingold

pl. 36: © 2012 Artists Rights Society (ARS), New York / VG Bild-Kunst, Bonn; photograph courtesy Bauhaus-Archiv Berlin

pl. 40: © James Castle Collection and Archive

pl. 42: © The Alfredo Ramos Martinez Research Project, reproduced by permission, Collection of Madeline and Bruce Ramer; photographer Gerard Vuilleumier

pl. 45: © 2012 Artists Rights Society (ARS), New York / VG Bild-Kunst, Bonn; Museum Schloss Moyland, photographer Maurice Dorren

pl. 47: © 2012 Artists Rights Society (ARS), New York / ADAGP, Paris; Digital Image © The Museum of Modern Art / Licensed by SCALA / Art Resource, NY

pl. 48: © Claes Oldenburg; photographer Tim Nighswander / Imaging4Art

pl. 49: © 2012 Emory Douglas / Artists Rights Society (ARS), New York

pl. 50: © Laurie Anderson; Digital Image © 2009 Museum Associates / LACMA / Art Resource, NY

pl. 52: © 2012 The Willem de Kooning Foundation / Artists Rights Society (ARS), New York; Image courtesy of the Board of Trustees, National Gallery of Art, Washington, photographer Greg Williams

pl. 53: © Adrian Piper Research Archive Foundation Berlin

pl. 54: © The Felix Gonzalez-Torres Foundation; photograph courtesy of Andrea Rosen Gallery, New York; photographer James Franklin

pl. 55: Photographer Lee Stalsworth

pl. 56: copyright the artist, 2012

pl. 59: © 2012 Artists Rights Society (ARS), New York / SIAE, Rome

Figures

Director's Foreword

© 2012 Artists Rights Society (ARS), New York / VG Bild-Kunst, Bonn; photographed from Barbara Haskell et al., *Lyonel Feininger: At the Edge of the World* (Whitney Museum of American Art, New York, 2011)

Brodie: Introduction

detail: © 2012 The Willem de Kooning Foundation / Artists Rights Society (ARS), New York; Image © The Metropolitan Museum of Art; image source: Art Resource, NY; photographer Malcolm Varon

fig. 1: © 2012 Artists Rights Society (ARS), New York / DACS, London; Digital Image © The Museum of Modern Art / Licensed by SCALA / Art Resource, NY

Brodie: Reading the Newspapers

fig. 2: Photograph courtesy of the National Gallery of Art, Washington

fig. 3: © 2012 Artists Rights Society (ARS), New York / ADAGP, Paris; Image © The Metropolitan Museum of Art. Image source: Art Resource, NY

fig. 4: © 2012 Man Ray Trust / Artists Rights Society (ARS), NY / ADAGP, Paris; Photo © Christie's Images / The Bridgeman Art Library

fig. 5: © 2012 Artists Rights Society (ARS), New York / VG Bild-Kunst, Bonn; photographer Kai-Annett Becker

fig. 6: © 2012 Artists Rights Society (ARS), New York / ADAGP, Paris; Image © Tate, London 2012

fig. 7: Book Rights Copyright © 1943 The Norman Rockwell Family Entities

fig. 9: Image courtesy of the Board of Trustees, National Gallery of Art, Washington

fig. 10: Photographed from Francis M. Naumann et al., *Making Mischief: Dada Invades New York* (Whitney Museum of American Art, New York, 1996)

fig. 14: Photographed from Enrique Rosito et al., *Abuelas de Plaza de Mayo. Fotografía de 30 años de lucha* (Buenos Aires, 2007)

Boxer: Ripped from the Headlines

fig. 1: © 2012 Richard Serra / Artists Rights Society (ARS), New York
fig. 2: © 2012 Estate of Pablo Picasso / Artists Rights Society (ARS), New York; photograph courtesy CNAC / MNAM / Dist. Réunion des Musées Nationaux / Art Resource, NY

fig. 3: Photographed from Stéphane Mallarmé, *Un coup de dés jamais n'abolira le hasard* (Paris, 2007)

fig. 4: Courtesy of the Library of Congress, *Chronicling America.* Image provided by: The New York Public Library, Astor, Lenox and Tilden Foundation

fig. 5: © 2012 Artists Rights Society (ARS), New York / SIAE, Rome; Photograph © 2010 The Solomon R. Guggenheim Foundation

fig. 6: Image courtesy of the Board of Trustees, National Gallery of Art, Washington

fig. 9: © 2012 Estate of Pablo Picasso / Artists Rights Society (ARS), New York; photograph courtesy Moderna Museet, Stockholm

Mileaf and Witkovsky: Newsprint and News Time

fig. 2: Photographed from Věra Ptáčková, *Česká scénografie XX. století* (Prague, 1982)

fig. 3: Image courtesy of the Board of Trustees, National Gallery of Art, Washington, photographer Adam Davies

fig. 5: © Adrian Piper Research Archive Foundation Berlin; photographer David Campos

fig. 6: Courtesy Sprueth Magers Berlin London

Poggi: Inflexions of the Times

fig. 1: © 2012 Estate of Pablo Picasso / Artists Rights Society (ARS), New York; photograph courtesy CNAC / MNAM / Dist. Réunion des Musées Nationaux / Art Resource, NY

fig. 2: © 2012 Estate of Pablo Picasso / Artists Rights Society (ARS), New York; photograph © Sucession Picasso; photographer Philip Bernard

fig. 3: © Ellsworth Kelly

fig. 4: Art © The Estate of Robert Rauschenberg, licensed by VAGA, New York; photographer Robert Rauschenberg

fig. 5: Art © Jasper Johns / Licensed by VAGA, New York, NY

fig. 6: Courtesy Allan Kaprow Estate and Hauser & Wirth; photograph © Peter Geoffrion

fig. 8: © 2012 Artists Rights Society (ARS), New York / ADAGP, Paris; Courtesy of Corice Arman; photographer Eeva-Inkeri

fig. 9: Photographed from Pierre Restany, *Chryssa* (New York, 1977)